Studies in Comparative World History

Africa and Africans in the making of the Atlantic world, 1400–1800

Studies in Comparative World History

Editors

Other books in the series

Michael Adas, *Prophets of Rebellion: Millenarian Protest Movements against the European Colonial Order* (1979)

Philip D. Curtin, *Cross-Cultural Trade in World History* (1984)

Leo Spitzer, *Lives in Between: Assimilation and Marginality in Austria, Brazil, and West Africa, 1780–1945* (1989)

John Thornton, *Africa and Africans in the Making of the Atlantic World, 1400–1680* (1992)

Marshall G. S. Hodgson and Edmund Burke III (eds.), *Rethinking World History* (1993)

David Northrup, *Indentured Labor in the Age of Imperialism, 1834–1922* (1995)

Africa and Africans in the making of the Atlantic world, 1400–1800

Second edition

JOHN THORNTON

PUBLISHED BY THE PRESS SYNDICATE OF THE UNIVERSITY OF CAMBRIDGE
The Pitt Building, Trumpington Street, Cambridge, United Kingdom

CAMBRIDGE UNIVERSITY PRESS
The Edinburgh Building, Cambridge CB2 2RU, UK http://www.cup.cam.ac.uk
40 West 20th Street, New York, NY 10011-4211, USA http://www.cup.org
10 Stamford Road, Oakleigh, Melbourne 3166, Australia

First edition published 1992
Second edition published 1998
Reprinted 1998, 1999

Printed in the United States of America

Typeset in Palatino 10/12

Library of Congress Cataloging-in-Publication Data

Thornton, John Kelly, 1949–
Africa and Africans in the making of the Atlantic world, 1400–1800
– 2nd [expanded] ed.
p. cm.
Rev. ed. of: Africa and Africans in the making of the Atlantic
world, 1400–1680. 1992.
Includes bibliographical references (p.) and index.
ISBN 0-521-62217-4. – ISBN 0-521-62724-9 (pbk.)
1. Africa – Relations – Europe. 2. Europe – Relations – Africa.
3. Africa – Relations – America. 4. America – Relations – Africa.
5. Slavery. 6. Europe – History – 1492–1648. I. Thornton, John
Kelly, 1949– Africa and Africans in the making of the Atlantic
world, 1400–1680. II. Title.
DT31.T516 1997
303.48′2604 – dc21 97-39728

*A catalog record for this book is available from
the British Library.*

ISBN 0-521-62217-4 hardback
ISBN 0-521-62724-9 paperback

Contents

Preface to the second edition

When I began writing this book in 1984, I imagined that I would be writing a fairly specialized work for scholars and a few interested laypeople, as a way of advancing Africa into the Braudelian scheme of Atlantic history that inspired me. In my vision, it was to be a reference book for the non-Africanist historian and would be based on a virtually complete reading of the primary sources. To that aim, it was originally to offer coverage up to about 1650 (the limit within which I felt I could handle the sources comprehensively) and would be mostly confined to Africa, my area of expertise. In fact, the first draft of the book had only one rather sketchy chapter on the American side of the exchange.

I was gradually persuaded that the book would be more useful if it were more ambitious, and as it grew into the volume published in 1992, I added a much larger and more carefully argued section on the Americas in place of the original chapter. I also expanded the time frame to 1680, mostly so that I could have a few meaningful things to say about early colonial North America.

As I expanded the territorial and temporal boundaries of the book, I also slowly and reluctantly recognized that I could never deal with the primary sources comprehensively, especially for the American side of the ocean. I still held on to the idea of mastering a large sample of the primary sources as a goal, even on the American side, however. It was for that reason that I put aside suggestions that the book would be better if it extended up to about 1800, particularly because this would allow me to cover much more about North America. Until I knew the primary documentation better, I did not feel confident that I could achieve the goals I originally set out.

I was surprised to see that the book was widely adopted as a textbook rather than simply becoming a reference book for scholars as I had expected. Many colleagues who used the book for teaching, however, objected that its limited chronological focus did not give it full value as a text, especially in U.S. history courses. While generally accepting my contention that I did not feel I could master the extensive primary source material for the eighteenth century, they encouraged me to consider trying a chronological extension to enhance the value of the book as a teaching text.

As I was considering these arguments, my research interests started to focus more on the eighteenth century, and as I felt more comfortable with this period, I decided that I could handle the demands of writing a new chapter that would cover that century. The result is this new edition. It adds a substantial new chapter on the eighteenth century to the otherwise unchanged 1992 edition, in hopes that it will make the book serve better as a general introduction to the role of Africans in the Atlantic world through the main years of the Atlantic slave trade. Just as the final version of the 1992 edition fell short of my original goal of comprehensive use of primary sources, so the final chapter in this edition falls short of even the 1992 standards and relies much more on secondary materials for important parts of the argument, while still making use of some primary material where I have done additional research. I hope this compromise will enhance the book's value as a reference work and teaching tool.

Abbreviations

ANTT	Arquivo Nacional do Torre de Tombo (Lisbon)
ARSI	Archivum Romanum Societatis Iesu (Rome)
BIFAN	*Bulletin, Institut fondamental de l'Afrique Noire* (Dakar)
BM Rouen	Bibliothèque Municipale de Rouen
BN Colombia	Biblioteca Nacional da Colombia
BSGL	Biblioteca da Sociedade de Geografia de Lisboa
MMA	António Brásio, ed., *Monumenta missionaria africana,* series 1, 15 vols. (Lisbon, 1952–88)
MMA^{2}	António Brásio, ed., *Monumenta missionaria africana,* series 2, 5 vols. (Lisbon, 1958–79)
PRO	Public Record Office, London
UBL: BPL	Universitets Bibliotek, Leiden: Biblioteca Publica Latina

WEST AFRICAN STATES
1625

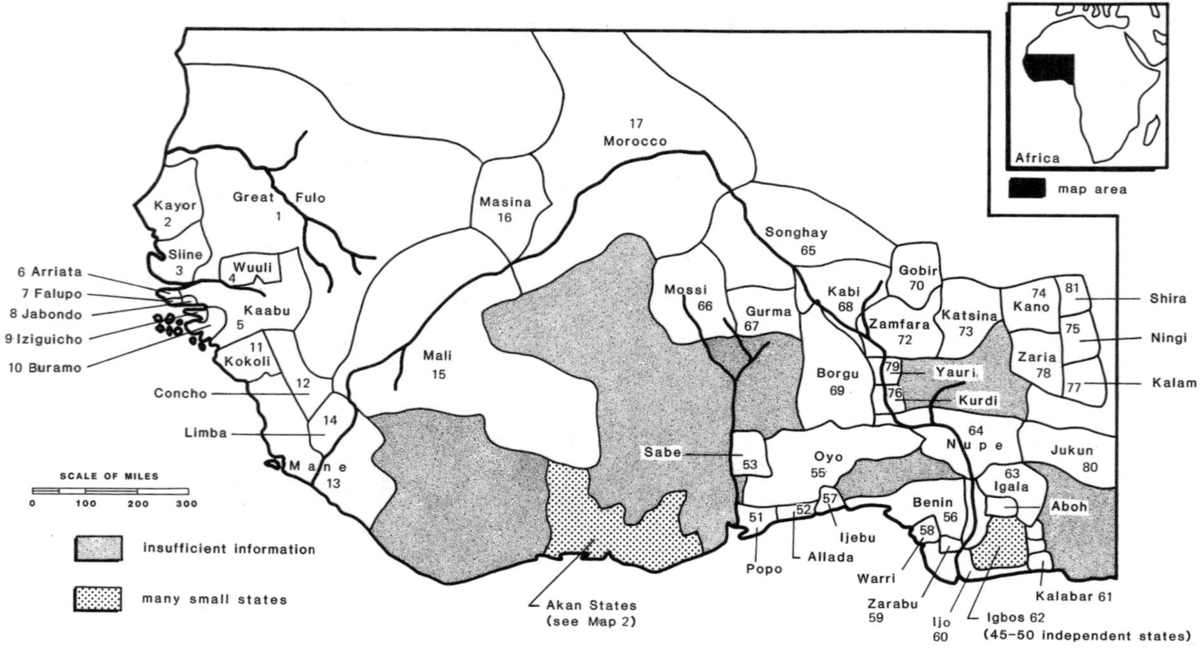

Map 1. See Source Notes for Maps 1–3.

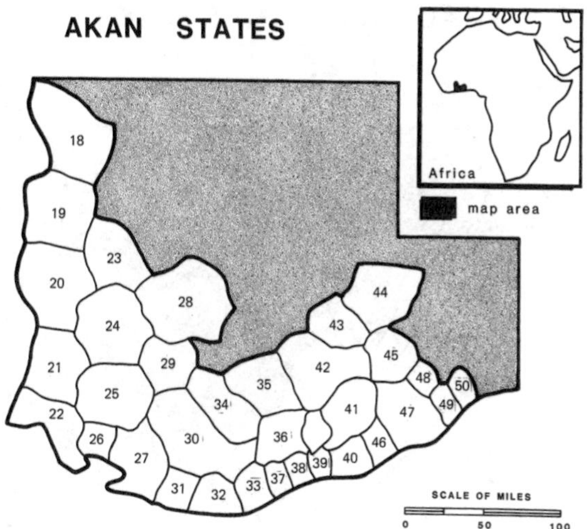

Map 2. See Source Notes for Maps 1–3.

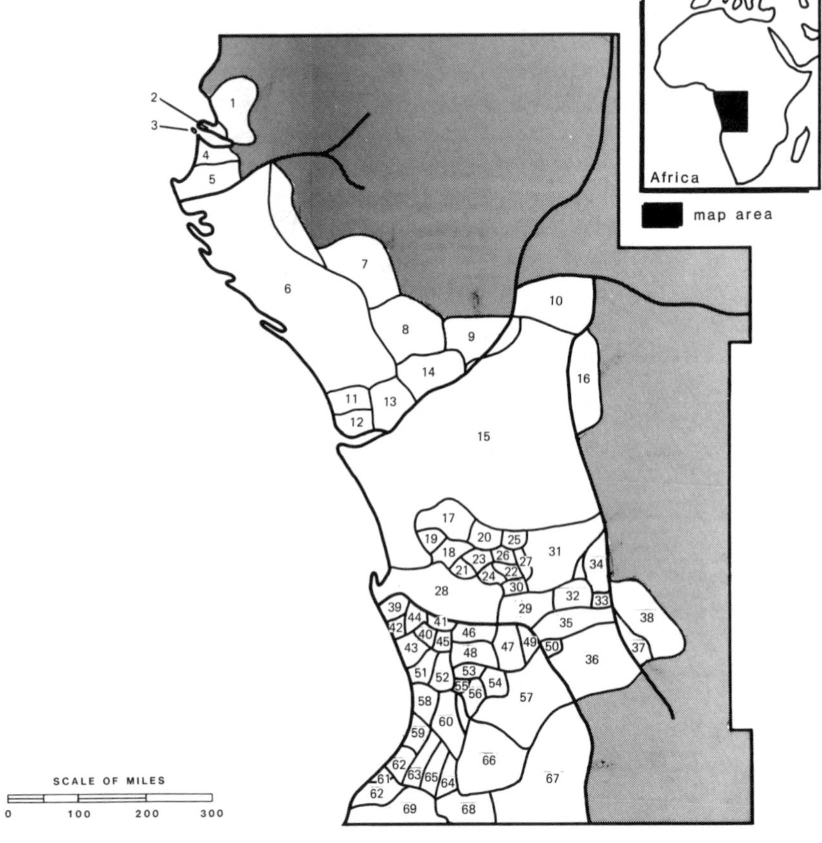

Map 3. See Source Notes for Maps 1–3.

Distribution of Population of African Origin in the Americas 1650

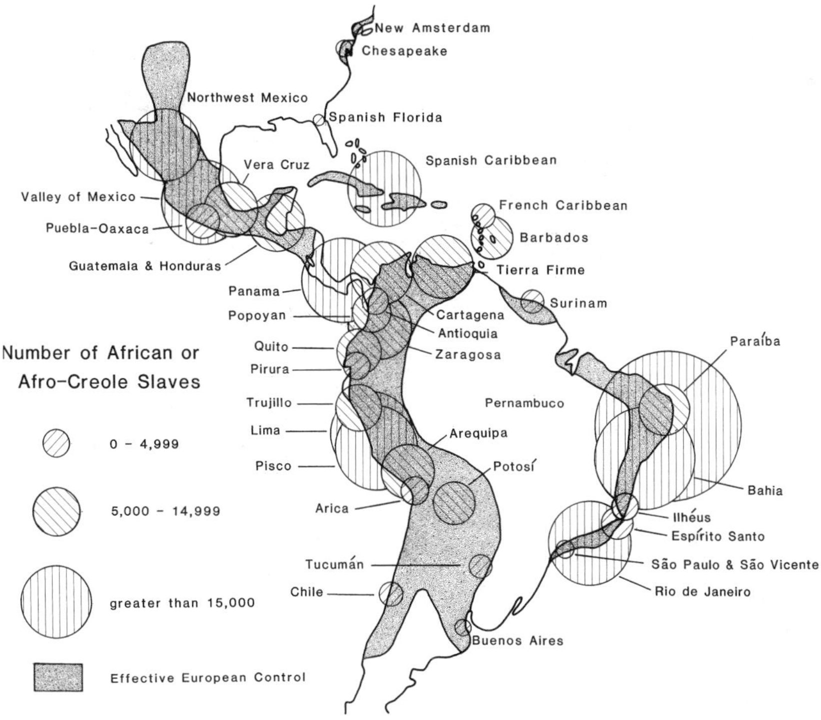

Map 4

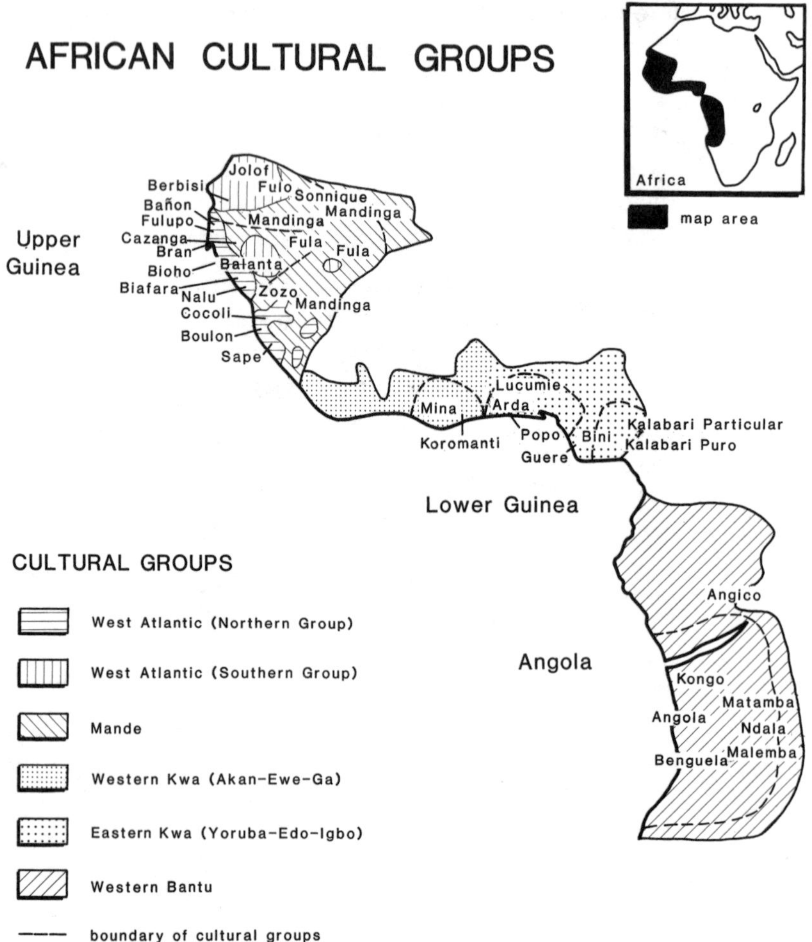
AFRICAN CULTURAL GROUPS
Africa
map area
Upper Guinea
Berbisi
Bañon
Fulupo
Cazanga
Bran
Bioho
Biafara
Nalu
Cocoli
Boulon
Sape
Jolof
Fulo
Sonnique
Mandinga
Mandinga
Fula
Fula
Balanta
Zozo
Mandinga
Lucumie
Mina
Arda
Koromanti
Popo
Guere
Bini
Kalabari Particular
Kalabari Puro
Lower Guinea
Angico
Angola
Kongo
Matamba
Angola
Ndala
Malemba
Benguela
CULTURAL GROUPS
West Atlantic (Northern Group)
West Atlantic (Southern Group)
Mande
Western Kwa (Akan-Ewe-Ga)
Eastern Kwa (Yoruba-Edo-Igbo)
Western Bantu
boundary of cultural groups

Map 5

Source notes for Maps 1–3

Unfortunately, many Africanists produce maps of precolonial geography without adequate references to establish precisely how the boundaries of units were documented. The maps presented here are the result of considerable research and hence require considerable documentation, which is provided.

The determination of state boundaries in precolonial Africa is a difficult task, largely because of the nature of the source material. For some regions, documentation specifies certain landmarks that separate one state from another, but in most cases, geographical information is fairly vague. This explains the widespread cartographic convention of placing names on maps without attempting to establish precise boundaries, a convention with some merit. Such a practice can produce an unnecessarily imprecise map; on the other hand, in most cases attempting to place boundaries gives an erroneous impression that precision is possible. However, establishing exact, even if arbitrary and perhaps inaccurate, boundaries does have its place, for example, in estimating the area or population of the polities in question. These maps have boundaries marked simply as a convenience to the reader and to show the precise areas used when making my estimates of population, given later in the book.

In order to justify my decisions, I have appended here a gazetteer of the state names on the maps, with documentary source entries for each one.

Maps 1–2: West Africa, ca. 1625 (proceeding roughly north to south and west to east)

Senegal region (nos. 1–17):

1. Great Fulo. This state is known principally through the anonymous "Relacion" of 1600, which gives a list of its provinces on p. 48. These

provinces are identified in the Teixeira da Mota edition of the text, but the identifications have been corrected by Jean Boulègue ("Un empire peul dans le Soudan occidental au début du XVIIe siècle," in *Le parole, le sol, l'écrit: 2000 ans d'historie africaine* [Paris, 1981]: 702), principally to include the headwaters of the Senegal and Futa Jallon mountains. Its borders on the Atlantic are more precisely defined by the boundaries of Kayor, Siine, and Wuuli. Saalum seems to have been absorbed into the Great Fulo Empire in the late sixteenth century (André Alvares de Almada, "Tratado breve dos Rios da Guiné," 1594, *MMA*[2] 3:239). Support for Boulègue's ideas about Great Fulo's southwestern border is found in de Almada's statement that the "Fulos" stood behind the Mandingas (Kaabu and Concho) "like a wall" and that they assisted the Souzos of Concho in wars against the Mane ("Tratado breve," *MMA*[2] 3:348, 370).

2. Kayor (Budumel, Encalhor). De Almada gives its borders ("Tratado breve," *MMA*[2] 3:239) as including the Wolof state of Bala (Bawol) and the coast from Cape Verde to Cavaceira, including the coastal ports and their European merchants, and inland as far as Saalum (Borçalo), which was then under Great Fulo.

3. Siine (Berbaciis). André Donelha lists Siine as the only independent Serer state (*Descrição da Serra Leoa e dos Rios de Guiné do Capo Verde* (*1625*) [modern ed. Avelino Teixeira da Mota, Leon Bourdon, and Paul Hair] [Lisbon, 1977], fol. 166v). Its borders are given in de Almada, "Tratado breve," *MMA*[2] 3:259.

4. Wuuli (Olimansa). De Almada lists it as ruling all the Mandingas north of the Gambia, while Kaabu ruled those to the south ("Tratado breve," *MMA*[2] 3:238).

5. Kaabu (Cabo). He was the most powerful king in the Upper Guinea West. Both de Almada (ibid., pp. 283, 298) and Donelha (*Descrição da Serra Leoa*) make him subordinate to Mali, but even if true this probably only applies to the period before 1585, before the final weakness of Mali's power and the final establishment of the power of the empire of Great Fulo over the Futa Jallon region and the upper reaches of the affluents of the Senegal, which would have cut them off from Mali. In any case, the "Farim Cabo" had two powerful subordinate units: Braso (cited by Donelha, *Descrição da Serra Leoa*, fol. 16), which ruled over the Rio Grande region, and Kasa (Casa, Casamansa), which dominated the Beafares and the upper Casamance River. They are not deemed to be sufficiently independent to warrant being delineated. Kaabu's jurisdiction seems to have reached the sea south of the Gambia except in the "wild" country of the Arriatas, Falupos, Jabondos, and Iziguichas, according to de Almada ("Tratado breve," *MMA*[2] 3:288–9). The Buramos (Papels), straddling the north and south banks of the Rio São Domingos,

were not under Kaabu's sovereignty (de Almada, "Tratado breve," *MMA*[2] 3:299). The Banhuns in the Rio Grande region were on Kaabu's southern border (de Almada, "Tratado breve," *MMA*[2] 3:298). Kaabu territory also bordered the Nalu country, which was under a ruler called Farim Cocoli (Kokoli) (Donelha, *Descrição da Serra Leoa,* fol. 16; de Almada, "Tratado breve," *MMA*[2] 3:341).

6. Arriata. De Almada gives their location as along the coast as far as the shoals of São Pedro from just south of the mouth of the Gambia ("Tratado breve," *MMA*[2] 3:288).

7. Falupo. De Almada has them stretch along the coast from the Arriatas to the Casamance River (ibid.).

8. Jabondo. De Almada places them just inside the bar of the Casamance River on the north bank (ibid.).

9. Iziguicho. Placed by de Almada on the south bank of the Casamance controlling the mouth, along with the Jabondos (ibid.).

10. Buramo. An independent kingdom north and south of the Rio São Domingos, with Mandingas (of Kaabu) as their inland neighbors (de Almada, pp. 299–300).

11. Kokoli (Cocoli). Listed by Donelha (*Descrição da Serra Leoa,* fol. 16) as ruling the Nalus and other nations. Their coastal borders are given by de Almada ("Tratado breve," *MMA*[2] 3:339, 341) as extending from the "island of slaves" as far as the Rio Nuno (Nunez), where they divide with the Baga, the farthest north group of the "kingdom of the Sapes" (Mane kingdom), whose southern border is Cape Vega (de Almada, "Tratado breve," *MMA*[2] 3:341; Baltasar Barreira to João Alvares, 1 August 1606, *MMA*[2] 4:168).

12. Concho (Souzos, Putazes, Farim Puta). This state bordered the Baga on the east, the border here being fixed at approximately the foothills of the Futa Jallon range (de Almada, "Tratado breve," *MMA*[2] 3:344–5). On the north, according to de Almada, they bordered the Fulas (3:348), presumably the Fulas's southern province of Futa Jallon. De Sandoval described the ruler Concho as an emperor (Alonso de Sandoval, *Naturaleza . . . de todos Etiopes* [Seville, 1627]; modern ed., Angel Valtierra, *Instauranda Etiopia salute: El mundo del esclavitude negra en America* [Bogotá, 1957], p. 62), and Barreira noted he had seven kings under him, including the ruler of Bena, who became a Christian (Barreira to Alvares, 1 August 1606, *MMA*[2] 4:169). The state of Concho seems to have included the Yalunkas of the southern Futa Jallon range (called Jalongas by de Almada (3:353), because de Sandoval calls them the "Zape Yalunka called Zozo" (*Instauranda,* p. 62) implying that the Concho (also called Soso) had hegemony over a group of Yalunka with some affinities to the people of the coast (Sapes).

13. Mane (Sapes, Sumbas). This was a large kingdom established in

Sierra Leone by the Mane invasions of ca. 1545. Contemporary sources describe it as having a hierarchical organization, de Almada specifying that all the kings had to pay royal dues (*marefa*) to a chief ruler situated somewhere to the south (p. 16.4), which Hair has suggested was the Cape Mount region, or the Kingdom of Kqoja (see annotation to Hair edition of Almada, notes 16.4, and Adam Jones, "Who Were the Vai?" *Journal of African History* 22 [1981]: 159–78). On this basis I have defined the Mane kingdom as a single unit. I have placed its western border west of the St. Paul River, as both Folgia and Manou, subunits mentioned by Olifert Dapper (*Naukeurige beschrijvinge der Afrikaensche gewesten* . . . , 2d ed. [Amsterdam, 1676], p. 42), seem to be located in that direction but east of the mountain ranges that reach almost to the coast in that region (see also the map in Jones, "Who Were the Vai?" pp. 160–1, 172). The Limba, mentioned by de Almada as successfully resisting Mane attacks in 1594 (3:353), are listed among the kingdoms subject to the Mane by Donelha in 1625 (*Descrição da Serra Leoa*, fols. 11–11v). Thus they are shown here as independent.

14. Limba. Mentioned most specifically as lying inland from the coast of Bullom (de Almada, "Tratada breve," *MMA*[2] 3:353). Hair identifies them with the modern Limba, and his map has guided my location (in edition of Donelha, *Descriçao da Serra Leoa*, fig. 13).

Interior countries in the western Sudan:

15. Mali. Despite its territorial losses in the late fifteenth and early sixteenth centuries to Songhay in the north, and to Great Fulo at the end of the sixteenth in the west, Mali still had considerable power in 1600, the year after Mahmud IV's unsuccessful bid to take control of Jenne ('Abd al-Rahman b. 'Abd Allah al-Sa'di, *Tarikh al-Sudan* [modern ed., Olivier Houdas and E. Benoist, French trans. by Olivier Houdas, 2 vols. (Paris, 1898–1900)], p. 279, all references are to the French translation in vol. 2), which remained under Moroccan control. Its western provinces – Kaabu, Wuuli, Concho, and Kokoli – are all shown here as having broken away, although Donelha still speaks of the empire as having at least symbolic significance (*Descriçao da Serra Leoa*, fol. 16), but this is perhaps based on earlier impressions from his visits in the late sixteenth century to the Gambia. Mali's southern border is a complete mystery; I have drawn a line at the headwaters of the upper Niger basin, enough to give it the cola-producing lands cited by the *Tarikh al-Fettash* (Muhammad b. al-Hadjdj al-Mutakawakkil al-Kati [completed by ibn al-Mukhtar], *Tarikh al-Fettash* [modern ed. and French trans., Olivier Houdas and Maurice Delafosse (Paris, 1913–14; reprinted in one vol., Paris, 1981)], p. 67) as being in its power in the mid- to late sixteenth century. I have extended its eastern border over as far as the town of Bighu, largely on the strength of the

reference on the map illustrating de Marees (said to be drawn in 1572; see Ray Kea, *Settlements, Trade and Politics on the Seventeenth Century Gold Coast* [Baltimore, 1982], p. 23–5, for discussion) showing Incassa or a country near that as being under a "cabessero" of the "Elephante Grande," the Akan name for the empire of Mali (according to de Almada, "Tratado breve," *MMA*[2] 3:278). If cabessero is taken to mean an appointed official, then Malian administrative control in the late sixteenth century must be considered likely. Wilks cites local chronicles of the early eighteenth century suggesting a resurgence of Malian control in the area at the end of the sixteenth century, although the exact nature of the evidence is unclear and may be oral data of varying significance and interpretation (Ivor Wilks, "Wangara, Akan and Portuguese in the Fifteenth and Sixteenth Centuries. I. The Matter of Bitu," *Journal of African History* 23 [1982]: 333–6). The remainder of Mali's eastern border is arbitrary, simply giving it control of the waters of the upper Niger basin.

16. Masina. This compact district represents the territory of Hamadi Amina, a Fula ruler who cooperated with, then betrayed, Mahmud IV in his attack of 1599 on Jenne (al-Sa'di, *Tarikh al-Sudan*, p. 279). Although a Fula he appears to have been independent of Great Fulo, although it is not impossible that he was simply an eastern governer of the empire, since Wagadu, which borders Masina and may well have controlled it, was listed in the anonymous 1600 document "Relacion y breue suma delas cosas del reyno del Gran Fulò" (in Avelino Teixeira da Mota, "Un document nouveau pour l'histoire des Peuls au Senegal pendant les XVème et XVIème siècles," *Boletim Cultural da Guiné Portuguesa* 24, no. 96 [1969], p. 48; reprint Agrupamento de Estudos de Cartografia Antiga, no. 56, Lisbon, 1969).

17. Moroccan Pashalik. The Battle of Tondibi, 1591, and occupation of Gao seem to have given the Moroccans undisputed power over the Niger bend, just as their later occupation of Jenne gave them the whole of the inner Niger delta. On the other hand, the resistance in Dendi put up by Askia Nuh clearly ended their sovereignty any farther down the Niger in that direction. I have assumed that they had administrative control of all the Songhay provinces not contesting their rule. al-Sa'di provides details on the wars of the time that seem to define this boundary well (*Tarikh al-Sudan*, pp. 224–80).

Gold Coast (modern Ghana) region (Map 2):

The location and identification of the multitude of tiny states on the Gold Coast rely on two cartographical sources for the most part, the first being the Luis Teixeira map that illustrated de Marees, drawn from information of the late sixteenth century and published in 1602, and the second being Hans Propheet's map of the states of the Gold Coast done at Mouree on 25 December 1629. These sources and contemporary documents have been carefully studied by Kea, who has in turn attempted to identify the states and place them on maps of his own – an invaluable starting point for the political geography of the seventeenth-century Gold Coast.

18. Shabanda (Xabanda). On the Teixeira map just below "Elephante Grande" (see entry on Mali) on an itinerary that leads up the Tano River (Rio Sueiro da Costa).

19. Ushu (Uxoo). Situated on same itinerary of map for Shabanda, at a bend in the river.

20. Inkasa Igwiya (Caceres Aguines). On a major branch of same river, on same itinerary as above. Probably same as Incassa Iggijna of the Propheet map (cf. Kea, *Settlements*, p. 74, who provides modern spelling).

21. Aowin (Famba). On same itinerary as above, cited as Famba in Dutch sources as well as Portuguese (ibid., 75, who provides a modern name).

22. Asoka (Bagno). Located at mouth and east side of Tano on the Teixeira map. Kea supplies this name from late seventeenth-century sources (ibid., p. 76).

23. Labore. East of river on Teixeira map's Tano itinerary, perhaps bordering on Famba (Aowin, no. 21).

24. Wassa. Located approximately midway between the Tana and Ankobra rivers on Propheet's map.

25. Egwira (Alderrada, Groot Inkasser). Located near Labore and Famba (Aowin) on Teixeira's Tano itinerary, east of the river. Kea identifies two locations on Teixeira's Ankobra River (Rio Mancu) itinerary, Parisom and Brum, as being subunits of this state (ibid., p. 81).

26. Axim. Placed by numerous documents on the coast at this location and by the Propheet map (cf. ibid., p. 26).

27. Ampira (Ampago). East of mouth of Ankobra on Teixeira's map. Legends on the map indicate that it warred with Alderrada (Egwira), suggesting the common border.

28. Boennoe. According to Propheet, these were a "simple people" whose land had no forest. Located here by reference to their neighbors.

29. Kwifero. Located according to position of its neighbors from Propheet map.

30. Adom (Semsee). Located according to its position on the Propheet map. Kea (ibid., p. 81) makes the town of Semsee on Teixeira's Ankobra itinerary the capital of this state.

31. Ahanta. On the coast near Cape Three Points on the Propheet map.

32. Cape Three Points. Listed as deserted on the Teixeira map; shown with no comment on the Propheet map.

33. Sabeu. Shown west of a river, probably the Pra, on the Propheet map, next to Komenda (Commendo).

34. Abrem (Abramboe). Located according to its neighbors, Komenda (Commendo) and Futu (Futo) on the coast and Etsi (Atij) on the east, from the Propheet map.

35. Assin (Acanes pequenos, Akanij). Kea has shown its location in the Pra basin from numerous sources, among them the Teixeira and Propheet maps (see discussion in ibid., pp. 85–6).

36. Etsi (Atins, Atij). Both Propheet and Teixeira place it in the interior behind Futu (see also ibid., pp. 67–9).

37. Komenda (Comane, Commendo). Location given by both Propheet and Teixeira.

38. Futu (Futo, Affuto). Location given by both Propheet and Teixeira.

39. Sabu. Location given by both Propheet and Teixeira.

40. Fante (Fantin). This location is given only on the Propheet map. (All these coastal districts from Komenda to Fante are described in a wealth of contemporary documents, see ibid., pp. 57–64).

41. Akwamu (Abramboe). These people, whom Propheet described as "thievish," bordered on Akyem, Eguafo, and Accra, according to his map.

42. Akyem (Acanes grandes, Akim). Its location is discussed in detail in ibid., pp. 86–8. It is found on both the Teixeira and Propheet maps.

43. Akan. This territory is given a location northeast of Akyem on the Propheet map. Kea identifies it with Sekyere, though without much evidence (ibid., p. 86).

44. Tafo (Tafoe). Mentioned in Portuguese sources but not on the Teixeira map. It appears, bordering "Akan," on the Propheet map (see ibid., pp. 15–17).

45. Abuna (Abaans, Bonoe). Mentioned in Portuguese sources as lying on the route to Tafo, and appears in such a location on the Propheet map (ibid., pp. 26–32).

46. Aguano (Biambi). Placed here on both Teixeira (as Biambi) and Propheet maps (as Agwano, with Biambi as one of its towns), bordering Accra.

47. Accra (Cracra). Shown here on both the Propheet and Teixeira maps and well described in contemporary sources (ibid., pp. 24–6, 36, 72).

48. Latebi (Latebij). Placed by its relative location on the Propheet map.

49. Labidi (Labidan). Shown between Accra and Ningo on the Propheet map.

50. Ningo. Borders the Volta on the Propheet map.

Gulf of Guinea region (nos. 51–64):

51. Popo. According to de Sandoval (*Instauranda*, p. 16) Popo bordered on the Volta and on Allada. In his time there was a small breakaway state called Fulao in between the two (p. 77). This map does not depict it, as de Sandoval's account gives the impression that the breakaway was quite recent. Popo's interior border is quite uncertain; de Sandoval comments only that it extended considerably inland, although this is not indicated by the position of its capital, just inland from the coast.

52. Allada (Ardra, Axaraes). De Sandoval places its borders between Popo and Benin (ibid., p. 16), which as we will see, extended as far as the Lagos Lagoon. Elsewhere he placed the "Ofoons" in Allada's domain (ibid., p. 94), probably the people of the western end of the Lagos Lagoon, perhaps those associated with what traditionalists have called the kingdom of Weme, along the lower course of the Weme River (Robin Law, *The Oyo Empire, c. 1600–c. 1836* [Oxford, 1977], p. 154, 156). He noted that Allada's ruler resided some seventy leagues inland, much farther than the town of Allada, well located just a few years later by Dapper (*Naukeurige beschrijvinge*, p. 115).

53. Sabe (Lucumies Chabas). According to de Sandoval, the land of the "Lucumies" bordered Allada on the inland side (*Instauranda*, p. 16), and we can say with confidence that in the seventeenth century Lucumies were speakers of Yoruba (cf. Law, *Oyo Empire*, p. 16) but not necessarily subjects of Oyo, the largest Yoruba state. Indeed, de Sandoval distinguishes several types of Lucumies, including "Lucumies Chabas," evidently those from Sabe, and "Lucumies Barbas," presumably from Bariba (Borgu), not a Yoruba-speaking region at the time but perhaps in control of some Yoruba-speaking areas from which slaves were exported to provide de Sandoval with his informants. The extent and borders of Sabe shown here are guesswork, extracted from the traditional borders of the country as reported in the twentieth century (see Law, *Oyo Empire*, p. 88)

54. Ede (Temnes) (not shown on maps). De Sandoval records "Temnes" among the peoples exported from this coast of Africa and found among those in São Tomé (*Instauranda*, p. 94). This may refer to the kingdom of Ede, whose ruler bore the title Timi. Tradition holds that Ede was independent in this period (cf. Law, *Oyo Empire*, pp. 35–8).

55. Oyo (kingdom of Lucumie). The territorial extent of the kingdom of Oyo is a matter of considerable difficulty. Traditional accounts that appear to date from this period suggest that Oyo had difficulty maintaining internal order and experienced external invasion from Nupe and Borgu, only to emerge in the early seventeenth century as well on its way to the substantial empire it would build toward the end of the seventeenth century (Law, *Oyo Empire*, pp. 39–44). The presence of vari-

ous divisions of Lucumies in de Sandoval's account suggests, though does not prove, a somewhat diminished unit with an independent southern province (Ede) and a Borgu presence remaining (i.e., the Lucumies Barbas; see no. 53). That there may at least have been a kingdom of some size but not much strength is suggested by the work of Ahmed Baba, writing in Timbuktu in the early seventeenth century, arguing that "Yoruba" were legitimate to enslave. The map attempts to represent this situation, albeit without much commitment to the boundaries thus drawn, following Law's map of "pre-imperial Oyo" (ibid., p. 35), but allowing for an independent Ede and giving the Borgu a presence in the northern towns which they have traditionally been credited with founding (cf. ibid., p. 42).

56. Benin. Its coastal boundaries are easy to fix – Ulsheimer specifically mentions the island of Lagos as a Benin post and shows us its army active in the surrounding region in 1601 (Andreas Ulsheimer, "Warhaffte Beschreibung ettlicher Raysen . . . in Europa, Africa, Ostindien und America" [1616] [modern ed. with English trans. in Adam Jones, *Brandenburg Sources for West African History, 1559–1669*], fols. 32–32b). De Sandoval suggests similar boundaries along the lagoon on the east (*Instauranda*, p. 78) while allowing that at least some of the north bank of the lagoon was under the control of Ijebu (no. 57). On the east, de Sandoval has it border Warri (*Instauranda*, p. 17), but its interior boundaries are not described at all except in relation to other kingdoms whose boundaries are equally uncertain. I have traced the interior boundaries in accordance with those fixed (albeit for a later period) by R. E. Bradbury (*Benin Studies* [Oxford, 1973], pp. 44–75).

57. Ijebu (Iabu, Gabu, Jabboe). De Sandoval locates it between Benin and Allada on the Lagos Lagoon (where it is a walled town circled by a moat [*Instauranda*, p. 78]), in accordance with other sixteenth-century placements and that of Dapper, as well as the modern city of the same name.

58. Warri (Oeri, Guere). De Sandoval locates it "east" of Benin (ibid., p. 17). It is shown here following more specific data from the mid-seventeenth century in Dapper (*Naukeurige beschrijvinge*, p. 133) and Bonaventura da Firenze ("Come entrò la Fede di Giesu Christo nel Regno d'Ouere per la Prima Volta," published in Vittorio Salvadorini, *Le missioni a Benin e Warri nel XVII secolo: La relazione inedita di Bonaventura da Firenze* [Milan, 1972], fols. 8v–10, 15–15v).

59. Zarabu. A state, said to be occupied by cannibals, that lay beyond Warri, according to de Sandoval (*Instauranda*, p. 17).

60. Ijo (Jos). No such state is mentioned by de Sandoval, otherwise a good informant on the area, but given its presence being cited in the sixteenth century and in the later seventeenth, it seems safe to continue

locating it here in this period. It is not impossible that it fell under Benin control at this time and hence disappeared as an independent entity.

61. Kalabar (Caravalies puros). A general idea of the location is from de Sandoval (*Instauranda*, p. 17), who lists them as "beyond Zarabu"; more specifics are found in Dapper (*Naukeurige beschrijvinge*, p. 133).

62. Igbos (Caravalies particulares). De Sandoval describes a group of people living near the Caravalies puros, "but who really are not," who lived in forty to fifty independent villages (*aldeas*) and recognized no king, but fought regularly, belonged to different "castas y naciones," traded with the Caravalies puros, often sold their women and children as slaves, and were all cannibals (*Instauranda*, p. 17). Elsewhere he provides the names of seventeen such groups, some of which are recognizably of the Igbo linguistic group: Abalomo, Bila, Cubai, Coco, Cola, Dembe, Done, Evo, Ibo, Ido, Mana, Moco, Oquema, Ormapri, Quereca, Tebo, Teguo (ibid., p. 94). I have not tried to locate individual places, even among these seventeen, but have simply grouped them all together on the map.

63. Igala (Agare). According to de Sandoval, one of the countries that surrounded Benin, and held by Nupe and Benin as their emperor (*Instauranda*, p. 17).

64. Nupe (Mosiaco, Lycosagou, Isago). Listed by de Sandoval (ibid.) under the name of Mosiaco, which appears to match Pacheco Pereira's "Lycosagou" and Dapper's "Isago," as one of the kingdoms that "surrounded" Benin on the north. Its borders suppose contact with Oyo (no. 55) and Benin (no. 56) but are still quite approximate. For further details see John Thornton, "Traditions, Documents, and the Ife-Benin Relationship," *History in Africa* 15 (1988): 351–62.

Central Nigerian region (nos. 65–83):

65. Songhay. Remainder of a once great empire, under the control of Askia Nuh, that held out against the Moroccans in the wake of the 1591 invasion (al-Sa'di, *Tarikh al-Sudan*, pp. 224–80).

66. Mossi. Izard's analysis suggests that the Mossi known throughout the sixteenth century in the Sudanese chronicles lay in the northern part of the Mossi zone, near Songhay, and had at least some presence along the Niger in earlier times (M. Izard, "The Peoples and Kingdoms of the Niger Bend and the Volta Basin from the 12th to the 16th Century," *General History of Africa* 4: 211–16, 225–9). However, his conclusion that the Songhay attack of about 1575 (al-Sa'di, *Tarikh al-Sudan*, pp. 168, 173, 179) destroyed it seems unwarranted, and the map shows a fairly substantial country reemerging after the fall of Songhay.

67. Gurma. Its location is inferred from passing references in the Chronicles (*Tarikh al-Fettash*, pp. 134–5), but its size cannot really be told,

the boundaries being simply a guess and fixed in reference to neighboring states.

68. Kabi (Cabi, Guangara). Kabi enjoyed a brief period of military superiority in the mid-sixteenth century, including attacks on most of the Hausa states and Aihr. Giovanni Lorenzo Anania listed it as both Guangara and Cabi and noted that its ruler was rich and powerful and styled as emperor (*La vniversal fabrica del mondo*, excerpt on Africa published in variorum edition from editions of 1573, 1576, and 1582 by Dierick Lange and Silvio Berthoud, "L'intérieur de l'Afrique occidentale d'après Giovanni Lorenzo Anania," *Journal of World History* 14 [1972]: 336 and 336b; see also Mervyn Hiskett, *The Development of Islam in West Africa* [London and New York, 1984], map, p. 90).

69. Borgu (Barba, Bariba). Apparently a militarily active state that must have been close to Songhay because it suffered in a Songhay invasion in 1576 (al-Sa'di, *Tarikh al-Sudan*, p. 179). On the south it was aggressive against Oyo (see no. 55) and occupied several northern districts in Yoruba country, where de Sandoval knew them as "Lucumies Barbas." These boundaries show it as a single administrative unit, whereas later geography suggests at best a loose federation, but the larger boundaries are justified by its military strength.

70. Gobir. The location of the Hausa states that follows depend, for this period, largely on the 1582 edition of Anania, which incorporates the detailed observations of Vincenzo Matteo (see *La vniversal fabrica del mondo*, p. 336).

71. Aihr (Agades) (not shown on map). Listed in Anania as a city (ibid., p. 336) in the desert, presumably the capital of the sultanate of Aihr, sometimes under the sovereignty of Songhay and Kabi, but at this time probably independent.

72. Zamfara. Anania locates this place beyond Zaria (ibid., p. 336; cf. Hiskett, *Islam in West Africa*, map, p. 90).

73. Katsina. Anania says it was continuously at war with Kano (*La vniversal fabrica del mondo*, p. 336), as confirmed in the *Kano Chronicle* (English trans. published in H. R. Palmer, *Sudanese Memoirs* [London, 1967], p. 116). Its borders have been adjusted to give it proximity with both Zamfara and Kano, with whom it fought (*Katsina Chronicle* in *Sudanese Memoirs*, p. 81).

74. Kano. Placed with reference to modern city of Kano, and described in some detail by Anania (*La vniversal fabrica del mondo*, pp. 336b–37). In this period it was free from attack or pressure by Kabi or Songhay, although still bothered by Bornu and the Jukun.

75. Ningi (Nin). Anania places it simply "beyond Kano" (ibid., p. 336b). His modern editors suggest Ningi, east of Kano, which Hiskett (*Islam in West Africa*, p. 109) suggests should be Nunkoro.

76. Kurdi (Cardi, Kanakuma). Anania places it south of Zaria (*La vniversal fabrica del mondo,* p. 336), but Hiskett reinterprets the itinerary of Matteo and suggests a location southwest of Zaria (*Islam in West Africa,* p. 90).

77. Kalam (Calon). Anania (*La vniversal fabrica del mondo,* p. 337) places it simply beyond Zaria in the general direction of Doma, but it appears as the place called Kalam in the *Kano Chronicle* (pp. 112, 117; see map and discussion in Hiskett, *Islam in West Africa,* p. 90.)

78. Zaria (Zegzeg). Placed with reference to the modern city, but noted in Anania as between Kano and "Cardi" (*La vniversal fabrica del mondo,* p. 336).

79. Yauri. Anania gives it a location apparently between Zaria and Jukun (ibid., p. 336).

80. Jukun (Doma). Anania has Doma as a state, although the region would only be a part of what was probably a larger unit (ibid., p. 337). Since the *Kano Chronicle* cites wars between the Kwararafa (Jukun) and Kano in this period (p. 116), we can assume a common border and Doma as being a part of that. Of course, this assumes a fairly strong administrative centralization, or Doma as an important subregion, which may not be the case, but I have drawn the boundaries of Jukun to include the traditional capital and both banks of the Benue in Jukun territory today.

81. Shira (Scira). Anania places this simply beyond Zamfara (*La vniversal fabrica del mondo,* p. 336), and Hiskett sees it as the small Hausa state of Shira, buffer between Kano and Bornu (*Islam in West Africa,* p. 73).

82. Bornu (not shown on map). Located according to Anania (*La vniversal fabrica del mondo,* pp. 349–50) but allowing for the existence of Shira and a common border with Jukun.

83. Aboh (Gaboe). Located according to Dapper (*Naukeurige beschrijvinge,* p. 132) eight days upriver from Benin.

Map 3: Central Africa, ca. 1625 (proceeding roughly north to south and west to east)

North coast from Gabon to Kongo (nos. 1–16):

1. Rio d'Angra. This state is not given an African name in the sources but is described in Pieter de Marees, *Beschryvinge ende historische verhael vant Gout koninckvijck van Guinei . . .* (Amsterdam, 1602), p. 102a, as having a weak king and being at war with the states of the Gabon estuary (and hence sharing a common boundary somewhere between the two). However, de Marees believed they spoke separate languages, though sharing a common culture.

2. Kayombo (Caiombo). Named as king of the "northern hook" of the Gabon area in ibid., p. 120b.

3. Mpongwe (Pongo). Kingdom on an island in the Gabon estuary (in ibid., p. 121a) with a mountain of "prodigious height"; often fights with the rulers of Gabon.

4. Gabon. A state of the "southern hook" of the Gabon estuary in ibid., p. 120b. Said to be friends of the inhabitants of Olibata (no. 5) in this source, but Pieter van den Broecke (modern ed. K. Ratelband, *Reizen near West-Afrika van Pieter van den Broecke, 1604–14* [The Hague, 1950], p. 23) says the two were at war, both statements implying a common boundary.

5. Olibata. Dominated Cape of Lopo Gonsalves according to de Marees (*Beschryvinge*, p. 120a, 120b, 121a) and van den Broecke (*Reizen*, p. 23).

6. Loango. Unlike the northern states, Loango was a large and complex unit. The boundaries shown here represent the maximum extent of Loango's effective control but include a number of tributary states who exercised considerable internal control and who were bound to Loango by tribute payments more than administrative fiat. These relationships and subordinate states are described in Dapper, *Naukeurige beschrijvinge*, based on data collected by Dutch traders from 1620 to 1650. It is not clear when Loango gained control of all the regions, and only Dapper gives the kind of detail that allows subunits to be identified. The following are some of these semi-independent units (used to establish Loango's borders on the map). On the north are Komma (ibid., p. 147), in marshy country just south of Cape Lopo Gonsalves; Gobby (p. 147), south of Komma along the coast north of Cape St. Catherine; Sette (p. 147), said to be 15 miles up from Mayumba, near modern Sette Cama, which still carries its name; and Mayumba (Majumba) (pp. 145–6). On the east is Dingy (p. 148), said to border on nuclear Loango, Kakongo, and Vungu. Nuclear Loango (described in detail in ibid. on pp. 143, 159–60) can be placed between the Chiloango River and Mayumba.

7. Bukameale. A kingdom rich in elephants and ivory in a mountainous area, described vaguely in ibid., p. 158, as bordering on Loango and the Yaka country. This placement follows Phyllis Martin's logic, defended in "The Trade of Loango in the Seventeenth and Eighteenth Centuries" (in Richard Gray and David Birmingham, eds., *PreColonial African Trade: Essays on Trade in Central and Eastern Africa before 1800* [London, 1970], pp. 144–5).

8. Yaka (Jaga). The term "Jaga" in sixteenth- and seventeenth-century sources describes, in general terms, a rootless, usually cannibal group of raiders. At least three such groups can be identified in central Africa: the

inhabitants of the Niari valley, cited here; the people living between the Kwango and the Wamba rivers, presently called the Yaka; and the Imbangala (in many bands) operating in the Angolan central highlands and Ndongo regions (see John Thornton, "A Resurrection for the Jagas," *Cahiers d'études africaines* 18, nos. 69–70 [1978]: 224–5). The Niari valley group probably did not call themselves Yakas or Jagas, these being terms used in Kongo sources. They are first mentioned in 1624 as having destroyed Vungu with the consent of the king of Loango (Manuel Cardoso to Manuel Rodrigues, 1624, *MMA* 7:294). Dapper gives more information on them, as bordering Loango and the Nziko kingdom, in land that had to be crossed to go from Loango to the copper-producing region of the Niari valley (*Naukeurige beschrijvinge,* p. 158). He believed they were organized in three separate armies under distinct captains, named Singe, Kobak, and Kabango (though this may be secondhand information concerning the Imbangala of the Ndongo region).

9. Nziko kingdom. Its early boundaries were well described in Filippo Pigafetta, *Relatione del reame di Congo* (edited by Georgio Cardona [Milan, 1978] [with pagination of 1591 edition]; French translation, Willy Bal, ed. and trans., *Description du royaume de Congo et des contrées environnantes* [Louvain, 1965], also with original pagination). Pigafetta's work was the source for many later descriptions. Also called the Kingdom of Great Makoko (see Jesuit sources cited in Guerreiro, *Relaçam annual,* extract in *MMA* 5:241–2, and the account of Garcia Mendes Castelobranco, 16 January 1620, *MMA* 6:438 [as source of cloth, along with the neighboring kingdom of Ybare, which is mentioned nowhere else]). Dapper (*Naukeurige beschrijvinge,* pp. 143, 182) gives information that extends that of Pigafetta, is based probably on notes of the traveler Herder in 1641–2 and on Loango sources, and helps to define its western borders north of the Zaire River.

10. Fungeno (Fungenas). Located north at Okango, a district of Kongo located between the Nkisi and Kwango rivers near Mpumbu, the large widening of the Zaire formerly called Stanley Pool (now Malebo Pool). Mateus Cardoso says it was separated from Okango by the Enselle River and stretched as far as the Kwango River (ARSI, Assistencia Lusitania, 55, "Relação do alevamento," fol. 116; also see Dapper, *Naukeurige beschrijvinge,* p. 182).

11. Kakongo. Jesuit sources located this kingdom north of the Zaire River in 1606–7 and gave as its neighbors Nziko, Bungo (Vungu), Angoi (Ngoyo), and Biangá (unknown state) (*MMA* 5:241–2; also see Dapper, *Naukeurige beschrijvinge*, p. 183).

12. Ngoyo. Located at the mouth of the Zaire and neighbor of Kakongo in Jesuit sources (*MMA* 5:242–2).

13. Nzari (Zarry, Zerry). Its location is fixed by notes in Dapper,

Naukeurige beschrijvinge, p. 184, and the account of F. Capelle, 1642 (in Louis Jadin, "Rivaltés luso-néerlandaise au Soyo, Congo, 1600–1675," *Bulletin de l'Institut Historique Belge de Rome* 37 [1966]:137–359).

14. Vungu (Bungo). Noted as a neighbor of Kakongo in Guerreiro (see *MMA* 5:242–1) in 1606–7. Mateus Cardoso noted that it was destroyed by Yaka armies in 1627 and gave it a location north of the Zaire in 1624 (see Cardoso to Rodrigues, 1624, *MMA* 7:294, and "História do Reino de Congo," fol. 14). Dapper also notes its proximity to the coastal states and the Yaka (*Naukeurige beschrijvinge*, p. 158).

15. Kingdom of Kongo. Kongo's eastern borders are carefully delineated by Cardoso (ARSI, Assistencia Lusitania, 55, "Relação do alevamento," fols. 116–116v for 1622). They include in this area the subject kingdoms of Ocanga, between the Enselle and Wamba rivers south of Fungunas, then south of Ocanga the states of Congo Riamulaça (Kongo dia Mulaza) and Sonço (Nsonso), all along the Kwango, finally including the smaller subject states of Ncusu (Nkusu) and Damba (Ndamba) in the mountains that give rise to the Kwilu River and the Mbrize River. Its north boundary seems to have followed the Zaire, except for Masinga, a trans-Zaire province located about where the Kwilu enters the Zaire, according to Cardoso. This trans-Zaire province was subject to Kongo's Nsundi province and thus was a market for Loango-based merchants to buy copper in the 1630s and 1640s (Dapper, *Naukeurige beschrijvinge*, p. 158, which speaks of Sondi). On the south its border with Angola was fixed after the battle of Mbumbi (1622) on the Dande River ("Regimento do Governador de Angola, 20 March 1624, in Heintze, *Fontes* 1: 149). East of this, however, Kongo's precise sovereignty is cloudy. The "Dembos" (Ndembu) region (not marked on map), which began in the mountains, was sometimes under Kongo control, but never certainly; it is shown here as independent. These Ndembu states mark Kongo's south boundary, and the Wandu (Kongo's southeastern province)–Matamba border, the last remaining piece, is fixed somewhat arbritrarily by the mountains.

16. Kingdom of Soa (Yaka of Kwango). Identified by Mateus Cardoso as lying south of the mouth of the Wamba River in the valley of the Kwango in 1622 (ARSI, Assistencia Lusitania 55, "Relação do alevamento," fol. 116). The extent of this kingdom to the south is unknown; in 1657, however, Matamba was at war with Yaka (Giagha), which bordered Matamba across the Kwango; this may be the same kingdom (Giovanni Antonio Cavazzi de Montecuccolo, *Istorica descrizione de' tre regni Congo Matamba ed Angola* [Bologna, 1687], bk. 5, no. 33).

The Dembos (Ndembu) region (nos. 17–27):

The politics of this area was quite unstable, with many small states lying in the upper valleys of the Bengo, Dande Loze, Mbrize, Lukala, and Nkisi rivers in this mountainous region. Larger states, like Kongo, Portuguese Angola, Ndongo, and Matamba, made claims and campaigns in the area, and most of the region was nominally a part of one or another (or several simultaneously) of these states. Moreover, the larger Ndembu states built up confederations with the smaller ones, but these were often no more stable than the claims of the larger states. The boundaries drawn on the map simply make a guess at the political configuration at any given time.

17. Nambu a Ngongo (Nambuangongo). Cited as victim of Portuguese attacks in 1615–16 (Cadornega, *História* 1:78), hence an independent state. Joined a large confederation that fought Portugal in 1642; geographical notes from that encounter help to fix its location near but north of the Dande River and also near the Mutemo and Kavango rivers (Pedro Cesar de Meneses to João IV, 9 March 1643, *MMA* 9:32–3; Cadornega, *História* 1:291–2).

18. Mutemo (Motemo). Nominally a vassal to Portuguese Angola in 1629 and contained a large Portuguese community, with a captain and church (Fernão de Sousa to sons, in Beatrix Heintze, *Fontes para a historía de Angola do século XVII*, 2 vols. [Wiesbaden, 1985–8], 1:327). Mutemo was head of a powerful coalition that fought against the Portuguese during the Dutch period (1641–8) in Angola. Accounts of this war (1642) in Portuguese sources (Pedro Cesar de Meneses to João IV, 9 March 1643, *MMA* 9:32; and António de Oliveira de Cadornega, *História geral das guerras angolanas (1680–81)* [Lisbon, 1972], 1:289) give details on subordinate units of this coalition/state, including smaller states of Motemo Aquigongo, Motemo Quingengo. Dapper, using Dutch sources, gives the geography of the region in detail with reference to the hydrography and its neighbors (*Naukeurige beschrijvinge*, p. 185).

19. Ngombe a Mukiama (Engombe a Muquiama). A state whose lands lay west of Mutemo according to Dapper (*Naukeurige beschrijvinge*, p. 185), whose geography of this region probably results from the war of 1642, because Portuguese sources list it as a participant (Pedro Cesar de Meneses to João IV, 9 March 1643, *MMA* 9:30–1). Probably independent in 1625, though not mentioned in contemporary sources.

20. Mbwila (Ambuila, Boila). A powerful state that was building a coalition including the neighboring states of Cabonda and Cheque around 1626, which concerned both the Portuguese in Angola and the king of Kongo (Fernão de Sousa to his sons [n.d.] in Heintze, *Fontes* 1:258–9). Its location is given in Dapper, *Naukeurige beschrijvinge*, p. 158, with references to the Loze River and neighboring states; de Sousa notes Mbwila's lands lay across the Dande from Angola ("Relação da costa de Angola e Congo," 21 February 1632, *MMA* 8:212).

21. Kahenda (Caenda). Located southeast of Mutemo and south of

Mbwila in Dapper's geography (*Naukeurige beschrijvinge,* p. 185). Involved in the 1642 war and probably independent earlier (see Pedro Cesar de Meneses to João IV, 9 March 1643, *MMA* 9:32; and Cadornega, *História* 1:288, where it is called Caculo ca Caenda).

22. Kavanga (Cavanga, Caoanga, Caoganga). A state that was nominally subordinate to the Portuguese in 1629 and was under attack by Mbwila from north of the Dande. It formed a coalition of neighboring states (Cavanga Pequena, Capele, Caculo Canquy, Angola Candala Cabaça) to resist the attack (Fernão de Sousa to sons, in Heintze, *Fontes* 1:327). In 1632, de Sousa described Kavanga along with other Ndembu rulers as being hostile to Portugal and in a coalition headed by Mbwila ("Relação," *MMA* 8:121).

23. Kiluanje Ka Nkangu (Quiloange Camcango). One of the trans-Lukala states listed by de Sousa in a report of 1630–1 (Heintze, *Fontes* 1:213). In 1629, it was considered a friend of Njinga when Njinga was readying the army of Ndongo to fight Portugal, along with Mbwila (de Sousa to his sons, ibid 1:252) and then under Mbwila (in "Relação," *MMA* 8:212).

24. Kitexi (Quitexi). Listed as a hostile power across the Lukala River by de Sousa in a report of 1630–1 (Heintze, *Fontes* 1:213) and as lying on the upper Dande and under Mbwila's control in 1632 (in "Relação," *MMA* 8:121). A participant in the 1642 war, it is there noted as being in the Dande–Lumanha watershed (Cadornega, *História* 1:286–7).

25. Kampangala (Cambangala). Mentioned as hostile ruler across the Lukala by de Sousa in a report of 1630–1 (Heintze, *Fontes* 1:213) and as lying on the upper Dande and under Mbwila's control in 1632 (in "Relação" *MMA* 8:121). Its exact location and that of its neighbor Nsamba a Ngombe are unknown.

26. Nsamba a Ngombe (Sambamgombe). Documented in the same way as no. 25, Kampangala.

27. Ndambi. A Dambi Angonga is shown on the map in Dapper, *Naukeurige beschrijvinge,* as neighboring Kavanga, and it is mentioned as one of the participants in the 1642 war in the Dande–Lumanha watershed by Cadornega (*História* 1:286). He also notes it was a neighbor of Kitexi (ibid. 1:294).

28. Angola. The Portuguese colony, whose north boundary with Kongo was fixed at the Dande River (see no. 15) and by the independent Ndembu states. Its eastern boundary is quite uncertain; it bordered on Ndongo at the fortress of Embaca. To the south its border was more or less fixed by the Kwanza River. Its effective borders are well described in de Sousa's account of 1630–1 (Heintze, *Fontes* 1:212–13).

29. Ndongo. In 1624 Ndongo faced a major succession crisis that split

the kingdom into partisans of Ngola Aire and Queen Njinga. This crisis resulted in a civil war that gave Ngola Aire power as king of Ndongo but made him formally a vassal of Portugal. Njinga was driven out of the country. She retained only the islands of Kindonga on the Kwanza River, but by 1631, she had conquered Matamba. The final resolution of these events did not really come until 1655, when a treaty divided her lands from those of Ngola Aire and his successors at the Lukala River. The boundaries shown here acknowledge that Ngola Aire's vassalage to Portugal did not correspond to annexation (which would only occur in 1672). See de Sousa's report of 1630–1 in Heintze, *Fontes* 1:212–13.

30. Kituxela (Quituchila, Quituquela). State lying across the Lukala from Portuguese possessions, once subject to Ndongo (Cadornega, *História* 1:219). When Portuguese armies crossed it on their way to Matamba in 1629, it was an independent region including Puto Ahango (de Sousa to sons, in Heintze, *Fontes* 1:324).

31. Matamba. This kingdom was conquered by Njinga about 1631 and became her principal seat. Dapper's map places it between the Kwanza River and, to the north, Kongo's eastern provinces about 1640. See also Cavazzi, *Istorica descrizione*, bk. 1, nos. 1–10 (boundaries by tradition of ca. 1660).

32. Ndala Kisuba (Andalla Quesuua). Ruler of a province called Mbondo, which is given as an eastern neighbor of the lands of Kasanje by Cavazzi in about 1660 (*Istorica descrizione*, bk. 7, no. 31). In 1625, it bordered on Ndongo, whose easternmost subordinates were Dambe Angola, Dungo Amoiza, Kina, and Matamba according to de Sousa (de Sousa to sons, in Heintze, *Fontes* 1:334). It was split in three parts by the ruler's three sons when he died in 1629. It was linked to a province called Bondo at that time (Heintze, *Fontes* 1:328).

33. Akikimbo kia Nginje (Aquicumbo Quianginge). Ruler whose lands bordered on the Kwango River east of Ndala Kisuba and bordering on Kina (Quisumo, a ruler of the Ganguelas) (de Sousa to sons, in Heintze, *Fontes* 1:345).

34. Kina (Quina Grande and Quina Pequeno, or Greater and Lesser Ganguelas). Neighbor of Matamba according to de Sousa (de Sousa to sons, ibid., 334). Some location geography given in Cavazzi, *Istorica descrizione*, bk. 7, no. 31. Dapper (*Naukeurige beschrijvinge*, p. 185) places it east of Kongo's province of Wandu (though probably not correctly) at the end of a long itinerary. A "Ganguellas" listed along with Malemba, Songo, and Ndala Kisuba by de Sousa in 21 February 1632 (*MMA* 8:122) may be Kina, though de Sousa uses the name "Quina" frequently as well.

35. Malemba. According to Baltasar Rebello de Aragão, this was one of the five great kings whose territories surrounded Kongo and Ndongo in 1618 (*MMA* 6:340–1). He is listed as a major enemy to the east in de

Sousa's report of 1630–1 (ibid. 8:122). Pigafetta located the Kwari River in its middle region (*Relazione*, pp. 17 and 24). It lay west of Kina according to Cavazzi (*Istorica descrizione*, bk. 7, no. 31). Heintze, citing numerous documents in the Fernão de Sousa collection, places it south of Ndala Kisuba and east of the curve of the Kwanza (*Fontes* 1:212, n. 79).

36. Songo (Massongos). One of the five great kingdoms listed by Rebello de Aragão, and one of the enemies cited by de Sousa in 1630–1 (see no. 33).

37. Ndonji (Dongi). Cited only by Cavazzi in the 1660s (*Istorica descrizione*, bk. 7, no. 31). No document of 1625 places it on the map or as an independent state, but it may have been in existence earlier. I have calculated its location from Cavazzi's references.

38. Xinje (Massingas, Cachinga). A powerful kingdom listed among Kongo and Ndongo's neighbors in 1618 (*MMA* 6:340–1). No other references illuminate it, but Cadornega mentions "Cachinga" across the Kwango River from Kasanje in the third quarter of the seventeenth century (*História* 3:218). Its placement on the map accepts the identity of the two places in the area of the modern Xinjes.

South of the Kwanza River to Benguela (nos. 39–56):

The southern highlands of Angola were traditionally divided into fairly large "provinces." Each province was composed of numerous smaller states, and usually one state was dominant. In this way it resembled the Ndembu region, though the Ndembu area did not have a tradition of provinces. Where the references up until 1625 support it, the provinces are represented here as sovereign units and the smaller states as sub-units. This may not be correct; detailed political information is lacking for this period. For the late 1650s Cavazzi's detailed description and the notes of Cadornega provide considerable geographic detail.

39. Nsonga (Songa). De Sousa refers to Nsonga as an independent ruler of the province of Kisama (Quissama), which was located south of the mouth of the Kwanza River on the coast (de Sousa to sons, in Heintze, *Fontes* 1:290; located more precisely in Cadornega, *História* 3:248).

40. Langere a Mbumba (Langere Ambumba). According to de Sousa, this was a ruler hostile to the Portuguese whose territory was located near Kafuxi ("Relação," 21 February 1632, *MMA* 8:121; see also de Sousa to sons, in Heintze, *Fontes* 1:335, 344).

41. Kapakasa ka Kixindo (Capacaça Caquixindo). This was a territory located across the Kwanza from the fort at Cambambe (de Sousa to sons, in Heintze, *Fontes* 1:244, 285, 323). It was the last province of Kisama to the east according to Cadornega (*História* 3:249).

42. Kikulo kia Kimone (Quiculo Quiaquimone). This ruler of Kisama

is said by de Sousa to be lord of the salt mines of Demba. Cadornega says his lands lay across the Kwanza River from the Portuguese fort at Muxima (*História* 3:248).

43. Kafuxe ka Mbare (Cafuche Cambare). De Sousa lists him among several rulers hostile to the Portuguese in Kisama and closely associated with his neighbor Langere ("Relação," 21 February 1632, *MMA* 8:121). Cadornega says his lands lay in the south of the region of Kisama and included the seacoast (*História* 3:248–9).

44. Katala ka Sala (Catala Casala). The former Portuguese presidio at Demba was located on his lands, south of the Kwanza and halfway to the Longa (Cadornega, *História* 3:248).

45. Malundu a Kambolo (Malundo Acambolo). This was an independent, powerful ruler of Kisama hostile to Portugal whose lands bordered on Lubolo (no. 48) (de Sousa to sons, in Heintze, *Fontes* 1:285). He was the next most powerful ruler after Catala Casala, according to Cadornega, who located his territory along the Kwanza River (*História* 3:248).

46. Tunda. This was a province across the Kwanza from Dumbo a Pebo in the eastern regions of Portuguese-occupied Angola (de Sousa to sons, in Heintze, *Fontes* 1:328–9).

47. Haku (Aco, Haco). This was a province south of the Kwanza before reaching the bend. It was fairly centralized under the ruler Ngunza a Mbande (Gunza Ambande) (de Sousa to sons, in Heintze, *Fontes* 1:288, 289).

48. Lubolo (Libolo). This was a land inland of Tunda past the Kwanza (de Sousa to sons, in Heintze, *Fontes* 1:328–9). According to Heintze, Lubolo absorbed Tunda during the following half century, and its core was located along the Longa River.

49. Mbolo Kasaxi (Ambolo Casague). This ruler was located just south of the Kwanza bend, upstream from the province of Tunda. Njinga and her army fled to this ruler after her defeat in 1626 (de Sousa to sons, in Heintze, *Fontes* 1:255–6).

50. Zungi a Moke (Zungui Amoque). This ruler was probably located east of Mbolo Kasaxi along the Kwanza. He was attacked by Njinga in 1626 after she passed through Mbolo Kasaxi's lands and before she reached Malemba (de Sousa to sons, in Heintze, *Fontes* 1:255–6).

51. Kilembe (Quilembe). This state included the port of Sumbe a Mbale (Sumbe Ambale), just north of the Kuvo River, in 1645 ("Relação da viagem do Sottomaior em socorro de Angola, 1645, *MMA* 9:374). Its lands stretched inland to the edge of the plateau, where it controlled some copper mines ("Relação da viagem que fizerão o Captão Mor Antonio Texieria de Mendonça," 11 June 1645, *MMA* 9:334).

52. Lulembe (Lubembe). This ruler of the interior east of Kilembe was described as a "great Jaga who ruled from Quilembe to Mozambique" in

1645 ("Relação da viagem de Sottomaior," *MMA* 9:373–4). He was contacted and gave nominal submission to Lopo Soares Lasso during the latter's northern campaign of 1629 to take over the mines of Sumbi (Auto of Manuel Pereira, 23 July 1629, in Heintze, *Fontes* 2:304).

53. Kabeso (Cabesso). This state in the central highlands was first described by Cavazzi, probably as a result of knowledge gained in 1658–9. It was located south of Lubolo, west of Tamba, and northwest of Nsele along the mid-reaches of the Longa River (*Istorica descrizione,* bk. 1, no. 27). Its location here in 1625 is speculative because it is referred to in no earlier sources.

54. Tamba. Like Kabeso, this state is known first from Cavazzi, who locates it on the upper Ngango River in hills and plains (ibid., no. 24).

55. Rimba. Like Kabeso and Tamba, this state is known first from Cavazzi, who located it east of Nsele and in the mountains behind Sumbi (ibid., no. 21).

56. Nsele (Selles, Chela). This state was first described by Cavazzi, who says its people lived on the tops of the mountains inland from Sumbi (ibid., no. 22).

57. Upper Bembe. This state was described by Cavazzi in the late 1650s as lying south of Tamba and Haku and bordering the Kwanza River (ibid., no. 23). Lopo Soares Lasso placed a state he called Bambe in this area, probably Bembe, in 1629.

58. Kikombo (Mani Quicombo). This coastal state was located nine leagues from Sumbe a Mbale (Sumbe Amballa), where Lopo Soares Lasso first disembarked in 1627 (Fernão de Sousa to Governo, 1 June 1627, in Heintze, *Fontes* 2:181). It bordered on Lubolo and was north of the Kuvo River, according to Cadornega, in the first part of the seventeenth century (*História* 3:181).

59. Sumbi. This was probably not the unified region this map shows. It was regarded as a province, though other states, shown here as independent, were included in it. The area was crossed by and made submissions to Lopo Soares Lasso in his northern expedition to the mines, north of the Kuvo, in 1628–9. Some of the rulers of the area were listed in Manuel Pereira's account of the campaign, including Nhanga, Quitemo, Cabmombo, Conzamba, Monadundo, Caungueca, Cabambe, Gumbe, and Canguanda as well as the rulers of Lubembe (Lulembe), Catumbela, and Songo (Auto of Manuel Pereira, 29 July 1629, in Heintze, *Fontes* 2:304).

60. Lukeko (Luqueco). In 1629, Cabambe ruled this Ovimbundu (ethnic group) state. Lukeko sent traders to Benguela in about 1626. It was attacked by the forces of Lopo Soares Lasso from 3 September to 1 October 1628 (Auto of Manuel Pereira, 23 July 1629, in Heintze, *Fontes* 2:302, 304).

61. Katumbela (Catumbela). This ruler's jurisdiction began nine leagues north of Benguela. He gave submission to Manuel Cerveira Pereira in 1618 (Representation of Manuel Cerveira Pereira, 6 March 1618, *MMA* 6:299). He was not sufficiently loyal to be considered part of the colony of Benguela (see Auto of Manuel Pereira, 23 July 1629, in Heintze, *Fontes* 2:304).

62. Portuguese Benguela. Portuguese positions around the fort at Benguela. Its borders have been defined by neighboring African states.

63. Songo. This land lay just inland of the Portuguese positions at Benguela; in 1627, it was recorded as friendly but not obedient (Auto of Manuel Pereira, 23 July 1629, in Heintze, *Fontes* 2:303).

64. Biasisongo. This land lying roughly forty leagues east of Benguela was reached by the forces of Lopo Soares Lasso in his campaign (May–September 1627) against the Imbangala forces of Nguri (ibid., 303–4).

65. Kisango (Quissange). Territory lying approximately forty leagues east of Benguela, reached by forces of Lopo Soares Lasso in campaign against Nguri (ibid., pp. 303–4).

66. Lower Bembe (Bambe). This area was inland of Biasisango and Kisango over forty leagues from the coast (ibid.). Its location was given by Cavazzi relative to northern regions based on information about 1658 (*Istorica descrizione*, bk. 1, nos. 1–10).

67. Muzumbu a Kalunga. This area was east of the Kunene River and was reached by Lopo Soares Lasso sometime before his death in 1639. Cadornega says its ruler was very powerful (*História* 3:176–7, 218). Its location in 1625 is speculative.

68. Wila (Huila, Hila). This state was located east of the Kunene River and bordered on Muzumbu a Kalunga south of Ovimbundu territory. It was probably first contacted in the 1640s. Cadornega is the only one who mentions it (*História* 3:159, 172), and its placement here is speculative.

69. Kulimata. This state was on the middle Koporolo River and was attacked by the forces of Lopo Soares Lasso from 21 February to 22 March 1628. It was twenty leagues southeast of Benguela (Auto of Manuel Pereira, 23 July 1629, in Heintze, *Fontes* 2:303).

Africa and Africans in the making of the Atlantic world, 1400–1800

Introduction

Atlantic history has become fashionable in the last few years. Where once historians were content to study continents and countries in isolation, they have increasingly sought to study interactions on an intercontinental scale. This is particularly true of the early Atlantic, where the dramatic European navigations of the fifteenth century suddenly brought four continents into interaction where there had been little or no communication before. As a result of these navigations, the Atlantic became the scene of major intercontinental migrations. Thousands of European settlers moved from their homes to the Americas, and joining them was a still larger group of Africans.

On the whole, the European migration and its effects have received much more attention from historians than the African migration. This is true even though the African migration was larger, at least before the nineteenth century. This book is an attempt to assess this less well known migration of Africans to the Americas and to place this assessment in the growing field of Atlantic history.

When Fernand Braudel published *The Mediterranean and the Mediterranean World* in 1949,[1] he pioneered, especially in France, a new way of looking at regional history. Braudel's approach changed the way regions were defined, introducing the concept of a history integrated by the sea. His approach was also noteworthy for placing economic and social factors at the center of things rather than in the background. It was hardly surprising, then, that French scholars and scholars trained in France should apply his method and approach to other great maritime regions. In this regard, it was not long before the Atlantic became an object of study along Braudelian lines.

[1] Fernand Braudel, *La Méditerranée et le monde méditerranéen dans les temps de Phillippe II* (Paris, 1949; 2d rev. ed., 1966); trans. Siân Reynolds under the title *The Mediterranean and the Mediterranean World in the Age of Philip II*, 2 vols. (New York, 1972–3).

Pierre and Hugette Chaunu devoted a massive study to the Atlantic, published in 1955–60, from the archives of Seville.[2] Their work was followed by Frédéric Mauro's study of the Portuguese Atlantic published in 1960.[3] Vitorino Magalhães-Godinho published his study of the Portuguese world economy in 1962–68, in which the Atlantic economy played a substantial role.[4] Although none of these works had quite the depth or the ambition of Braudel's *Mediterranean,* they frankly acknowledged their debt to him, both in methods and in approach. They did, moreover, "cover" the Atlantic quite thoroughly, at least for the period before the late seventeenth century.

One reason why these studies lacked the depth of Braudel's was their very strong concentration on European efforts, almost to the exclusion of the role of other Atlantic societies. Although none completely forgot that the indigenous inhabitants of the Americas and Africa also participated in the Atlantic economy, none gave them the kind of social and economic examination that Braudel gave to all the societies and civilizations of the Mediterranean basin. Braudel eventually attempted to redress some of the imbalance by devoting a section in the final edition of his survey of the world, *Civilization and Capitalism* (1979), to various Atlantic societies, capping three decades of interest on his part and vast quantities of research inspired by his original example.[5]

For all these efforts, however, the Atlantic still appeared largely from a European perspective. This was not simply chauvinistic Eurocentrism, however, but a crucial point of analysis. The Atlantic, it seems, unlike the Mediterranean, was regarded by all these researchers as being particularly dominated by Europeans. Braudel believed that the societies of the Mediterranean basin were all roughly in the same stage of economic development and were thus roughly equal contributors, and when he appeared to waver on this point with regard to the Moslem world, Turkish historians strove to correct him.[6] But the Atlantic seemed to be different, for most of the historians who approached it seemed to believe

[2] Pierre Chaunu and Hugette Chaunu, *Séville et l'Atlantique, 1504–1650,* 9 vols. (Paris, 1955–60).

[3] Frédéric Mauro, *Portugal et l'Atlantique, 1570–1670* (Paris, 1960).

[4] Vitorino Magalhães-Godinho, *Os descobrimentos e a economia mundial,* 2 vols. (Lisbon, 1963–5). See also his shorter work, *L'économie de l'empire portugais aux XVe et XVIe siècles* (Paris, 1969).

[5] Fernand Braudel, *Civilization and Capitalism, Fifteenth to Eighteenth Centuries,* 3 vols., trans. Siân Reynolds (New York, 1982–4; original French edition, 1979). See vol. 3:387–440.

[6] Omer Lufti Barkan, "La Méditerranée de F. Braudel," *Annales: Economies, sociétés, civilisations* 9 (1954). For an overview of historiography and a development of themes concerning the role of the Ottoman Empire in the wider world economy, see Huri Islamoglu-inan, ed., *The Ottoman Empire and the World-Economy* (Cambridge, 1987), especially the introductory essay by Islamoglu-inan, "Introduction: 'Oriental Despotism' in a World System Perspective," pp. 1–26.

that Africa (and the indigenous societies of the Americas) were on a significantly lower level of development. Therefore, an unusually prominent role for Europeans in the formation of the Atlantic world seemed especially appropriate for "scientific" reasons, and not simply because the authors were committed to Eurocentrism.

Pierre Chaunu has been most forceful in his defense of the "Eurocentrism" of French scholarship. Europe possessed a lead over the rest of the world, he argued, a lead originating in the complex changes of late medieval society, which gave Europeans an extraordinarily dominant position in the world – so dominant, in fact, that for better or worse, they became the sole significant actors. Chaunu reproduced a map that Braudel and the anthropologist Gordon Hewes drew for the first edition of *Capitalism and Material Life* in 1967 in which world societies were divided into levels on the basis of technology and population density.[7] African and Native American societies were at a lower level, and thus the imbalance of the Atlantic interaction was explained.

Of course, the French writers began their studies of the Atlantic world at a time when Eurocentrism was the order of the day, in the last years of European colonial domination of Africa and when the European modes of nation building and development were the expected norms for newly independent African states. African and Latin American nationalist movements and their historians and apologists changed this emphasis in the late 1960s and 1970s. Eurocentrism met numerous challenges from the historians of the newly emerging non-Western world.

The nationalist school of history sought to demonstrate that European world supremacy in recent times had worked strongly to the detriment of the various non-European peoples in the Atlantic basin and elsewhere. Much of their work focused on European exploitation, largely in seeking to explode the colonialist myth that European domination had brought backward societies into the modern world.[8] In response to such criticism, Chaunu reiterated his position in 1969 by asserting that these arguments did not invalidate French Eurocentrism, and that its relevance had been confirmed by many other historians of the time period. European domination was founded on European superiority, and whether this was good or bad for the people being dominated was not necessarily a relevant point. The history of the Atlantic still ought to be the history of

7 Pierre Chaunu, *L'expansion européen du XIIIe à XVe siècles* (Paris, 1969), pp. 56–7. The original map was drawn for the 1967 edition of Braudel, *Civilization and Capitalism*, trans. Siân Reynolds (New York, 1973), and can be found in the 1982–4 English version at 1:56–7.

8 The work of an early pioneer is Celso Furtado, *The Economic Growth of Brazil: A Survey from Colonial to Modern Times* (Berkeley and Los Angeles, 1963). See also Stanley Stein and Barbara Stein, *The Colonial Heritage of Latin America* (Oxford, 1970). For Africa, see the work of Basil Davidson, especially *Black Mother: The Atlantic Slave Trade* (London, 1961).

Europeans, and the rest was still only background.[9] According to Chaunu, if history is the story of movement and initiative, then European history is the only history that is really important.

On the whole, Chaunu's analysis does not contradict much of the work of the nationalist historians and their more recent manifestations – dependency theory and world systems analysis, as characterized by the work of such scholars as André Gunder Frank, Walter Rodney, Immanuel Wallerstein, and Eric Wolf.[10] These writers infused the work of the Annalistes[11] with a neo-Marxist focus and reinforced and reiterated the essence of Chaunu's conclusions. However much they were committed to the study of the non-Western world, or however sympathetic they were to its people, they still agreed that the non-Western world, including Africa, had played a passive role in the development of the Atlantic. Although their radical perspective and their advocacy of Third World causes tended to make them sympathetic to Africa, the effect was simply to reinforce the tentative conclusions of the French pioneers that Africa was a victim, and a passive victim at that, for it lacked the economic strength to put up an effective resistance.

Coupled with these various lines of research that suggested African passivity in its relations with the Atlantic economy was an equally strong emphasis on the passivity of the Africans who were brought out of Africa in the slave trade. Slaves left very little documentation reflecting their point of view. Much of the research on slavery thus echoed the work of the dependency theorists. Just as the rise of partisans of the emerging Third World had sought to refute the rosy colonialist image of a progressive Europe rescuing the colonial world from backwardness, so historians of American slavery in the era of the civil rights struggle and black power movements in the United States sought to demolish the earlier portrait of the slave as contented. Pointing to the harshness of American slavery, they argued that the institution stripped the slave of culture, initiative, and even personality.[12] Thus, in spite of their general sympathy to the plight of the slaves and their descendants in the New World, they nevertheless reinforced the image of the slave as helpless

9 Pierre Chaunu, *Expansion européen*, pp. 53–54.

10 André Gunder Frank, *Capitalism and Underdevelopment in Latin America* (New York, 1969); Walter Rodney, *How Europe Underdeveloped Africa* (London, 1972; reprint, Washington, D.C., 1974); Immanuel Wallerstein, *The Modern World System*, 2 vols. to date (New York, 1974–80); Eric Wolf, *Europe and the People without History* (Berkeley, 1982).

11 The Annaliste school, named after its principal journal, *Annales: Economies, Sociétés, Civilisations*, was founded on the initiative of Fernand Braudel and Lucien Febure after the Second World War. It sought to integrate social and economic history as the focal point for historians and deemphasized traditional themes of political, military, and diplomatic history.

12 See the very influential work of Stanley Elkins, *Slavery: A Problem in American Institutional and Intellectual Life* (New York, 1959).

and necessarily passive. Radical historians sought to explain slave culture and slave religion in terms of the institution of slavery and thus reduced the African identity of the slave.[13]

It is ironic that the development of nationalist historiography of Africa and Afro-America should have produced these results. Some of the earliest nationalist historians of Africa, such as Basil Davidson, from whom so much of the fervor of early Africanist historiography derived, sought to refute the notion in colonialist ideology that Africans had never had a "real history" of their own; rather, they demonstrated the impressive achievements of African cultures and showed that before the colonial occupation, Africans had been firmly in control of the destiny of their continent.[14] But even as African initiative, skill, and progress were being researched, the dependency theorists clung to and developed the ideas of ultimate African weakness, while making concessions to the research on the reinterpretation of the African past.

Some historians of Afro-America sought to assess the Afro-Americans as purveyors of a unique variant of African culture to the New World. Indeed, Afro-America has not lacked its nationalist historians who, like their colleagues in African history, have seen the Afro-American as exercising initiative and preserving and creating in spite of slavery and racism. Some of these historians have come to appreciate the slave as an African and increasingly have sought the African background as a means of understanding the unique contributions of Afro-Americans to the culture of the United States. Their work, though often focusing on the nineteenth-century United States, has been to try to restore what they see as a positive dimension to the Afro-American experience, a program emphasized by the nationalist historian Sterling Stuckey.[15] Thus, for example, Sydney Mintz and Richard Price sought to connect the African background of Afro-Americans with the development of Afro-American culture, while Albert Raboteau and Mechal Sobel and more recently Margaret Washington Creel have focused on religion.[16] Sobel has extended her research to a wider world view and has tried to show the African influence not only on Afro-American culture but on

[13] Here the work of Eugene Genovese is significant; see *Roll Jordan Roll: The World the Slaves Made* (New York, 1974) and compare it with his earlier *The World the Slaveholders Made* (New York, 1969).

[14] Basil Davidson, *Lost Cities of Africa* (Boston, 1959).

[15] Sterling Stuckey, "Through the Prism of Folklore: The Black Ethos in Slavery," *Massachusetts Review* 9 (1968): 417–37, and more recently, his summation of this and other work, *Slave Culture: Nationalist Theory and the Foundations of Black America* (Oxford, 1987).

[16] Sydney Mintz and Richard Price, *An Anthropological Approach to the Afro-American Past: A Caribbean Perspective* (Philadelphia, 1976); Albert Raboteau, *Slave Religion: The "Invisible Institution" in the Antebellum South* (New York, 1978); Mechal Sobel, *Trabelin' On: The Slave Journey to an Afro-Baptist Faith* (Westport, Conn., 1979); Margaret Washington Creel, *"A Peculiar People": Community Life and Religion among the Gullah* (New York, 1988).

that of Euro-Americans as well.[17] They have relied on the revived Africanist historiography to give them a dynamic and creative background for the African people in America, while emphasizing the role of the African in American culture and life.

This interest in the African background of American culture has led many historians of the Americas back to Africa. Unfortunately, all too often, these specialists in the history of the Americas have not fully grasped the dynamic of precolonial African societies. Frequently, they have studied African culture through the medium of modern anthropology rather than the careful study of contemporary documents. Because anthropologists' knowledge is based on fieldwork in contemporary (usually mid–twentieth-century) Africa, until quite recently their statements about earlier times were based on theoretical supposition or an assumption that African society and culture did not change. Reading contemporary documents helps to offset this modern bias. The latter approach is just beginning to bear fruit in African studies, especially in the field of cultural and social history.

Even among these historians, with their acceptance of the importance of African history to American history, there is still strong debate concerning the exact way in which Africans have affected New World societies as cultural actors (as opposed to their undoubted role as workers). Mintz and Price, for example, argue that the conditions of slavery in the Americas and the cultural diversity of imported Africans made the direct transmission of African culture to America difficult, whereas Sobel has gone quite far in arguing that these factors were much less significant and an African world view prevailed among Afro-Americans. In part, the debate continues to hinge on the issue of the degree to which the exploitation of slavery and the denigration of racism crippled the slaves' ability to maintain and transmit an African culture in the New World.

This book seeks to resolve a number of these contradictory positions. Is it correct to see Africa as being on a lower level of development than Europe and this imbalance as being the cause for the slave trade? Did Africans participate in the Atlantic trade as equal partners, or were they the victims of European power and greed? Were the African slaves in the Americas too brutalized to express themselves culturally and socially, and thus, to what degree was their specifically African background important in shaping Afro-American culture? On the whole, the conclusions of the research on which this book is based support the idea that Africans were active participants in the Atlantic world, both in African

[17] Mechal Sobel, *The World They Made Together: Black and White Values in Eighteenth Century Virginia* (Princeton, 1987).

trade with Europe (including the slave trade) and as slaves in the New World.

The present book is divided into two parts. The first part examines in detail the nature of the interaction between Africa and Europe. The second part of the book deals with the role that those Africans who went to live in the non-African parts of the Atlantic played in their new societies. It examines some of the institutional background that shaped their participation from the point of view of the dominant powers of the non-African Atlantic, but focuses more particularly on the economic, political, and cultural life of the newly transplanted Africans.

Thus, after a chapter sketching the geographical and historical origins of the Atlantic world, the book moves on to an analysis of Euro-African trade and the African productive economy. I conclude that the Atlantic trade was not economically essential to African well-being or development, being as it was largely luxury goods that did not even displace the African luxury goods industry (for example, in the case of textiles) or a relatively minor supplement to existing African industries (for example, the mining and metallurgical industries). Finally, the examination of the economy emphasizes what has increasingly been noted by recent research into African production – that Africa possessed a much more varied and productive economy than has been believed previously.

Moreover, my examination of the military and political relations between Africans and Europeans concludes that Africans controlled the nature of their interactions with Europe. Europeans did not possess the military power to force Africans to participate in any type of trade in which their leaders did not wish to engage. Therefore all African trade with the Atlantic, including the slave trade, had to be voluntary. Finally, a careful look at the slave trade and the process of acquisition of slaves argues that slaves had long been used in African societies, that African political systems placed great importance on the legal relationship of slavery for political purposes, and that relatively large numbers of people were likely to be slaves at any one time. Because so much of the process of acquisition, transfer, and sale of slaves was under the control of African states and elites, they were able to protect themselves from the demographic impact and transfer the considerable social dislocations to poorer members of their own societies.

In the second part of the book, the emphasis shifts to the New World and the contributions of African slaves to the Americas. After considering the conditions that made African slaves so attractive to European colonists in the New World and also ironically placed them in a good position to be central actors in the new cultural milieu of the Atlantic world, the analysis then focuses on the nature of slavery with an eye to assessing the likelihood of enslaved Africans playing a larger role than is usually assigned to them in the cultural and social world of their enslavers. On the whole, the evidence supports the idea that at least some, and probably a significant number, in all parts of the Atlantic world possessed sufficient freedom of movement and social interaction to participate actively in the cultural life of the region. The focus then shifts to the issue of culture and examines the cultural zones of Africa, their interactions with each other and with Europeans, and the development of an Afro-Atlantic culture. It then examines the role that Africans, African culture, and African institutions have played in such diverse matters as slave rebellions, communities of runaways, and the cultural and religious life of the New World.

The second part of the book has been buttressed by research that demonstrates that European influences on African life, such as Christianity, creole languages, and fashion, were often encountered first in Africa and only later transferred to the Americas. Thus, where Africans have borrowed from Europeans they often did so willingly and on their own terms in their home territories, and not always under the stultifying influence of slavery. How African culture changed on its own and how it incorporated foreign influences are examined to reveal a deep dynamic functioning in Africa that would be unleashed in the Americas.

The research that supports these conclusions, both for Africa and for the New World, has necessarily had to involve a reassessment that goes counter to the analysis of much of the secondary literature. In large measure this is because the primary concern of most researchers has been local rather than international. Thus, Africanists have not always addressed themselves to those issues in African society and history that would clarify African interactions with the Atlantic world, especially how the African background of Afro-American slaves affected their response to their new environment. As a result, Americanists, whose principal concern is the fate of Africans once they have arrived in the Americas, have not had a secondary literature about Africa written with their concerns in mind. Of those whose interest is in trade and economic interactions, few indeed have known enough about the areas outside their specialty to attempt independent analysis and synthesis.

Consequently, I have consulted primary sources as much as possible. Obviously, such a strategy is essential if one wishes to make any substantial revision in the existing historiography, and it is particularly necessary when the specialists in Atlantic history, African history, and the history of Africans in the New World have not attempted to ask questions that include the whole Atlantic world. This task is almost impossible to accomplish as completely as one would wish, even though the eventual success of the analysis depends on thorough examination of all the primary material. The research results must be able to convince the Africanist that no violence has been done to the primary evidence on African history and society, the Europeanist that the essence of European economic and political background is respected, and the Americanist that the full range of slave societies is considered.

No scholar can single-handedly tackle the primary literature in its entirety, even with the help of the existing secondary literature, and readers should be aware of this. The documentation consulted is most complete with regard to African societies and the societies of the Atlantic islands, and I have examined an extremely large sample of the published and unpublished material. In the Americas the material on slaves is much more scattered, and each item of documentation less complete than for Africa, and moreover, I have consulted only a small, but I trust representative, sample.

In any case, the documentation is incomplete, and the analysis thus must be considered more suggestive than conclusive. I can only hope that my reanalysis points in directions that others will find fruitful and that they will take up more detailed examination and case studies to refute or support the results reached here.

Part I
Africans in Africa

1

The birth of an Atlantic world

The shape of the Atlantic zone

The European navigations of the fifteenth century in the Atlantic opened up a new and virtually unprecedented chapter in human history. Not only did European sailors provide direct ocean routes to areas that had been in contact with Europe through more expensive and difficult overland routes (such as West Africa and East Asia), but the ships reached areas that had had no previous sustained and reciprocal contact with the outside world. Of course, this was obviously true of the American continents, and historians have rightly focused their attention on this immense new world in their discussions of the period. But it was not just the Americans who came into outside contact, for virtually the entire region of west central Africa, south of modern Cameroon, was also without outside contacts, in spite of the fact that it was geographically a part of the landmass whose eastern and western parts had long-standing connections to the Mediterranean and Indian Ocean.[1] Thus, in addition to easing and intensifying relations between various parts of the Old World (which in this case also included West Africa), the European navigations opened up connections between the Old World and two new worlds – the two sections of the American continent and the western part of central Africa.

The French historian Pierre Chaunu has argued that perhaps the most

[1] The paradox of west central Africa is that its isolation in commercial and intersocietal relations was not matched by a uniquely different culture. Indeed, west central Africa was in many ways culturally similar to parts of West Africa and even more so to East Africa, especially in language and basic world outlook. The most common explanation for the linguistic situation is the "Bantu migration" hypothesis, which connects all African languages north of South Africa and south of the equator into a single family. But the separation between the western Bantu and eastern Bantu sections is ancient, reflecting, perhaps, an ancient isolation. See the general discussion F. van Noten with Pierre de Maret and D. Cohen, "L'Afrique centrale," in *UNESCO histoire générale de l'Afrique* (Paris, 1980–), 2:673–93.

significant consequence of European navigation was what he calls "disenclavement" – the ending of isolation for some areas and the increase in intersocietal contacts in most areas. This allowed an increased flow of ideas as well as trade throughout the world, ultimately leading to a unified world economy and potentially, at least, to higher levels of economic development.[2] As such then, the opening of the Atlantic was crucial in this process, all the more so because it was only here that true isolation was broken.

More than this, however, the birth of an Atlantic world also involved a gigantic international migration of people, certainly without precedent in the Old World and undertaken nowhere else in the field of European expansion. Not only did thousands of Europeans move to the Atlantic islands and the Americas, but literally millions of Africans crossed to the Atlantic and Caribbean islands and the Americas, becoming the dominant population in some areas. This demographic fact was not lost on early residents and visitors: Gonzalo Fernández Oviedo y Valdez described Hispaniola as a "New Guinea"[3] in the mid-sixteenth century when slave imports for its burgeoning sugar industry had changed its demography; Ambrósio Fernandes Brandão used exactly the same term to describe Brazil's sugar-rich northeast in 1618.[4] In the Atlantic, disenclavement meant much more than it did elsewhere in the world; it was not just increased communication but a reshaping of whole societies and the literal creation of a "New World." Moreover, it was a reshaping that involved Africa quite directly, for by 1650 in any case, Africans were the majority of new settlers in the new Atlantic world.

Understanding the origin and direction of this gigantic episode in intersocial relations requires a knowledge of the basic geography of the areas involved – areas in which transport by water defined for most purposes the entire region. One must always remember that in the age before rail and air travel, waterborne travel was immensely cheaper and more practical – despite the risks of storm and shipwreck – than overland travel. Not only could boats and ships average fairly good time, but they were energy efficient in an era that had few energy resources, and they could, moreover, carry heavy and bulky goods easily. Thus, creating a geography of the Atlantic area must take areas accessible by water transport as its first dimension, for use of the water would greatly alter other considerations of space and distance, linking regions that were

[2] Pierre Chaunu, *Expansion européen*, pp. 54–8.

[3] Gonzalo Fernández Oviedo y Valdez, *Historia general y natural de las Indias*, ed. Juan Pérez de Tudela Bueso, 5 vols. (Madrid, 1959), bk. 4, chap. 8.

[4] Ambrósio Fernandes Brandão, *Diálogos das Grandezas do Brasil*, 2d integral ed., edited by José Antonio Gonçalves de Mello (Recife, 1968), dialogue 2, p. 44.

apparently distant more easily than regions that apparently lay close to each other.

The first of these great water routes was the Atlantic itself, opened for practical use in the fifteenth and early sixteenth centuries. But the Atlantic was also linked to riverine routes in both Africa and the Americas, which formed a vital supplement to the ocean, bringing societies and states that often lay hundreds of kilometers from the coast into contact with the ocean and, thus, with other societies and states. Even the rivers that did not allow ocean-going vessels to pass into interior regions (because of falls, narrows, or sandbanks) served as connections to extensive travel and commercial networks in the interior. The combination of ocean and river routes defined the shape of the Atlantic zone.

But one must not simply look at a map of the Atlantic and imagine that it was equally penetrable and that those who sailed it had equal access to all parts of the zone. In many ways, in the days of wooden sailing ships, the ocean was as much channeled as were rivers, whose direction of flow is clearly defined. No sailor could ignore the patterns of prevailing winds and currents on the ocean. This was crucial for the development of Atlantic navigation, for the winds and currents created barriers to traffic for thousands of years. They limited contact between the Mediterranean and Africa for a very long time and thwarted whatever potential Africans might have had for effective navigation into the Atlantic beyond their coastal waters, just as it would act as a brake on American ventures to Africa and Europe.

Raymond Mauny has shown that the constant north-to-south flow of the Canary Current along the Saharan coast made it possible for ships from the Mediterranean to sail southward as far as West Africa but prevented a return voyage.[5] For Mediterranean sailors, Cape Bojador, just south of the Canary Islands, represented a point of no return, and even if voyages, intentional and unintentional, went beyond it, they did not pioneer any route with practical significance. Arabic accounts cite several voyages made by accident beyond this point. al-Idrisi (1154) cites one that left from Lisbon,[6] ibn Sa'id heard from a Moroccan traveler named Ibn Fatima of a similar voyage sometime before 1270,[7] and al-'Umari heard of another one from Almeira in Spain made by Muhammad b. Raghanuh in the early fourteenth century – all were forced to return to the Mediterra-

5 Raymond Mauny, *Les navigations médiévales sur les côtes sahariennes antérieures à la découverte portugaise (1434)* (Lisbon, 1960).

6 Abu 'Abd Allah Muhammad b. Muhammad al-Sharif al-Idrisi, "Nuzhat al-mushtaq fi iktiraq al-afaq" (1154), in Nehemia Levtzion and J. F. P. Hopkins, eds., *Corpus of Early Arabic Sources for West African History* (Cambridge, 1981), pp. 130–1.

7 'Ali b. Musa ibn Sa'id al-Maghribi, "Kitab Bast al-ard fi 'l-tul wa-'l-'ard" (ca. 1270), in ibid., pp. 190–1.

nean area by overland routes.[8] It was only in the fifteenth century, and then using routes leading back through the Canaries, Madeira, and the Azores and risking a high-seas voyage, that Europeans were able to finally conquer the difficulties of the Bojador on a regular basis.

If the problems with the winds and currents off the Saharan coast checked Mediterraneans from entering the African portion of the Atlantic, a similar problem hampered African navigators. Of course, Africans would have been just as interested in going to North Africa and Iberia by sea as the Mediterranean people were interested in reaching Africa, given the knowledge that each area had of the other through the overland trade,[9] but the constant current that prevented return trips to the Mediterranean also frustrated African efforts to go to the Mediterranean from the very start. The extent of northward sailing by African vessels seems to have been the saltworks of Ijil on the Mauretanian coast, at least according to al-Idrisi's twelfth-century account.[10]

On the other hand, Africans faced the strongly prevailing westward-flowing Equatorial Current from the Senegambian region into the Caribbean basin. Although this current may have made African voyages to the Americas possible, it required fairly well developed techniques for high-seas navigation to even begin, and Africans could not develop such technology on short voyages in calm seas. Thus, Ivan van Sertima, who has championed the idea that Africans made frequent voyages to the Americas since around 800 B.C., has had to acknowledge that these voyages, if they occurred at all, were accidental and initiated no transatlantic commerce. However well such African navigators may have fared in long crossings in craft not designed to sail in the high seas, they faced insuperable barriers to making return trips to any familiar point on the African coast.[11]

Of course, some of the Caribbean peoples developed sufficiently large craft to sail regularly in the Caribbean, and such ships might well have traveled to the Old World. Historian Aurelio Tió has shown how important the native people of the Caribbean were in guiding early European voyages from Florida to the Orinoco, and how they knew the regime of wind and current throughout the basin well. He suggests that they also knew a good deal of the oceanic geography of the western Atlantic.[12] But

8 ibn Fadl Allah al-'Umari, "Masalik al-absar fi mamalik al-amsar," in ibid., pp. 272–3.

9 See Jean Devisse with S. Labib, "Africa in Intercontinental Relations," in *UNESCO General History of Africa* 4:635–6.

10 al-Idrisi, "Nuzhat," pp. 106–7.

11 Ivan van Sertima, *They Came before Columbus: The African Presence in Ancient America* (New York, 1976), pp. 37–109.

12 Aurelio Tió, "Relaciones iniciales Hispano-Araguacas," *Boletin de la Academia Puertoriqueña de la Historia* 9 (1985): 33–61; van Sertima, *Before Columbus*, pp. 253–6, cites some classical references to suggest that a lost canoe of Arawaks may have visited Gaul during Roman times.

for them, as well, the problem of a return voyage was similar to that the Europeans faced in their own early Atlantic navigations. Indeed, not until the late fifteenth century, when the entire system of Atlantic winds and currents was understood and European sailors knew all the potential landfalls on either side of the Atlantic, was a truly practical round-trip navigation achieved.

But even when the system was understood and European ships could travel (at least in theory) to every point in the Atlantic, they were nevertheless forced to respect the wind and currents. Pierre and Hugette Chaunu, examining the usual voyages of Spanish ships from Seville into the Atlantic, and Frédéric Mauro, considering Portuguese navigation in the same area, have shown that the habitual routes of commerce, stopping points, and even commercial developments were strongly conditioned by these winds.[13]

The regime of wind and current explains a number of developments not immediately apparent to modern travelers. One of the strongest motives for the establishment of an English colony in Barbados in 1624 was that its upwind position relative to Caribbean navigation made it difficult of access for Spanish fleets – fleets that had defeated earlier English attempts in the area. At the same time, British colonies in North America were bound more strongly to their Caribbean counterparts by the fact that return navigation from the Caribbean on the Gulf Stream naturally brought Caribbean settlers and traders to the North American coast. Thus navigational considerations joined economic ones to link the two regions.[14]

If water routes were the earliest form of travel, then the streams of the ocean must be joined to land streams if we are to see the full dimensions of the Atlantic world. This is abundantly demonstrated by the connections of the western Sudan to the Atlantic. Riverine routes going deep into West Africa connected points quite distant from the coast to the Atlantic. Although narrows and sandbars blocking the mouths often obstructed the travel of large, sea-going vessels on African rivers, smaller craft designed for river travel navigated them easily, and portages reduced the obstructions caused by falls.

Michal Tymowski has shown convincingly how important the Niger River was to the economic life of the central portions of the western Sudan, where very large craft were constructed and carried bulky cargoes along the river. Although there were falls from time to time that interrupted the navigations, each segment of the Niger divided by the

[13] Chaunu and Chaunu, *Séville et l'Atlantique*, vol. 7 and atlas attached; Mauro, *Portugal et l'Atlantique*, pp. 71–3.

[14] Richard S. Dunn, *Sugar and Slaves: The Rise of the Planter Class in the English West Indies, 1624–1713* (Chapel Hill, N.C., 1972), pp. 8–15.

falls was a veritable highway, and fairly short overland routes around the falls did not form an insurmountable barrier to long-range navigation.[15]

One could make an equally good case for the Senegal River, even if the falls at Felu made inland voyages from the ocean difficult. Certainly there was substantial traffic on the Senegal above and below the falls from medieval times onward, for it was probably on this river that the "strongly made boats" of the people of Ghana traveled in al-Idrisi's account of the Sudan of the twelfth century.[16] Moreover, items were transshipped through overland routes from the Senegal to the Niger or from these two rivers to the Gambia River, which formed the third member in a triad of much-used West African rivers. An overland route that took approximately twenty-five days to complete connected the Niger and the Senegal, and a portage of about 250 kilometers connected the Senegal and the Gambia rivers.[17]

The empire of Mali remained the heart of political power in the western part of the Sudan from the thirteenth century until well into the seventeenth century largely because of its central position at the headwaters of these three river systems. Philip Curtin has demonstrated how merchants based on the upper courses of these rivers could switch exports to the Atlantic from one of the systems to another to make the best of market opportunities in the seventeenth and eighteenth centuries.[18] Some of the earliest accounts of Senegambia speak of "Jaga" (probably the town of Diakha on the Senegal or Dia on the Niger, both near the headwaters of the river systems) as both the capital of Mali (which it may never have been) and a source for all the gold in Senegambia and the Gold Coast, indicating the crucial position that such a central location could play in the shifting gold trade.[19] Even in the early sixteenth century, merchants based that far away were capable of diverting the trade from the Gambia to the Gold Coast or back should it suit their interests.[20]

15 Michal Tymowski, "Le Niger, voie de communication des grands états du Soudan Occidental jusqu'à la fin du XVIe siècle," *Africana Bulletin* 6 (1967): 73–98.

16 al-Idrisi, "Nuzhat," p. 110.

17 Philip Curtin, *Economic Change in Precolonial Africa: Senegambia in the Era of the Slave Trade*, 2 vols. (Madison, 1975), 1:278–86.

18 Ibid., 1:83–91.

19 E.g., Jean Fonteneau dit Alfonse de Saintogne [João Afonso], *La cosmographie* (1544), fols. 122v, 124 (the edition of Georges Musset [Paris, 1904] marks the original foliation); Martin Fernandez de Enciso, *Suma de geographia q̃ trata de todas las partidas & provincias del mundo . . .* (Seville, 1519), p. 107 (original has no pagination, pagination given here written in pencil on the edition I consulted, Biblioteca Nacional de Lisboa, Reservados, 717 V). These two accounts were probably based on the same material; see Paul E. H. Hair, "Some Minor Sources for Guinea, 1519–1559; Enciso and Alfonse/Fonteneau," *History in Africa* 3 (1976): 19–46, which gives a partial English translation and comparison.

20 See documents and analysis in Avelino Teixeira da Mota, "The Mande Trade in Coast da Mina according to Portuguese Documents until the Mid-sixteenth Century," paper presented at the Conference on Manding Studies, School of Oriental and African Studies, London, 1972.

An indication of the significance of the river system to the geography of the western Sudan is revealed by the fact that many Moslem writers regarded the rivers as forming a single complex system – the "Nile of the Sudan" – a view that was shared not just by amateurs living in North Africa but by West African merchants themselves.[21] Not only did the Niger-Senegal-Gambia complex unite a considerable portion of West Africa, but the Niger provided a corridor that ultimately added the Hausa kingdoms, the Yoruba states, and the Nupe, Igala, and Benin kingdoms to a hydrographic system that was ultimately connected to the Atlantic. When one considers the Benue River as an extension, then one can get an idea of how deeply the riverine system penetrated into West Africa. Geographical ideas held by Africans and outsiders alike in the sixteenth century conflated all these rivers – the Senegal, Gambia, Niger, and Benue – into a single "Nile of the Blacks" ultimately connected to the Nile of Egypt.[22] Although it is mistaken geography, it is a real reflection of the transport possibilities of river routes.

West central Africa was also oriented by its rivers, especially the Zaire and the Kwanza. Likewise, António de Oliveira de Cadornega used rivers to orient his geography of central Africa (and his knowledge extended far into the interior) and combined it with a lengthy paean to the Kwanza River.[23] These rivers bore substantial commerce. Not only was the Kwanza used by the Portuguese in their conquest of Angola, but it was a major artery of commerce for Africans as well, as Paulo Dias de Novais, the first Portuguese to describe the region, made clear in the mid-sixteenth century. Riverine commerce was connected with coastal commerce and African craft plied the coastal waters between the Zaire and the Kwanza.[24]

For many Africans elsewhere as well, the coast was like a river system that connected distant points; it nourished a trade that predated and

[21] E.g., ibn Sa'id, "Kitab Bast," pp. 184–5; al-'Umari, "Masalik al-absar," pp. 156–7. For the same ideas presented to early European travelers by West Africans themselves, see Diogo Gomes, "De prima inuentione Gujnee" (composed ca. 1490), in Valentim Fernandes, "Desçricã da çepta e sua costa" (1507), in António Baião, ed., *O manuscrito "Valentim Fernandes"* (Lisbon, 1940), fols. 276v–7; André Donelha, *Descrição da Serra Leoa e dos Rios de Guiné do Capo Verde (1625)* (modern ed. Avelino Teixeira da Mota, Leon Bourdon, and Paul Hair [Lisbon, 1977]), fols. 29v–30. Europeans often knew of the deep interior of West Africa from sources on the Niger, or near Benin, and sometimes oriented their geography by the river; see Alan F. C. Ryder, *Benin and the Europeans, 1485–1897* (London, 1969), pp. 32–3, 126–34; for political units on the river, see John Thornton, "Traditions, Documents, and the Ife-Benin Relationship," *History in Africa* 15 (1988); 351–62.

[22] Thornton, "Ife-Benin Relationship."

[23] António de Oliveira de Cadornega, *História geral das guerras angolanas (1680–81)* (modern ed. José Delgado and Matias da Cunha, 3 vols. [Lisbon, 1972]), 3:58–61 (on the Kwanza), 219 (with notices of the Kasai River and the first mention of the Lunda of central Africa).

[24] António Mendes to Jesuit Father General, 9 May 1563, *MMA* 2:499, 503.

often complemented that of the Europeans operating on the high seas. Jean-Pierre Chauveau has examined the role of coastal societies and navigation in West Africa and shows that maritime navigation provided coastwise communication between substantial regions, which has often been overlooked in earlier assessments. In Loango, Senegambia, Sierra Leone, and Liberia, coastal estuaries, creeks, and lagoons form an interconnected, protected system of waterways facilitating the large-scale movement of goods. Such coastal waterways also allow easy communication between the mouths of the Senegal and the Gambia. Likewise, the coast of modern Ivory Coast possessed a system of lagoons and coastal lakes; however, it was less active in Atlantic commerce and thus less well known to modern scholarship.[25] Finally, of course, was the network of waterways that stretched from the mouth of the Volta River across the Niger delta to modern Cameroon, which is beginning to be understood as both a political and an economic axis.[26] Here, as in the Senegambian case, the coastal stretch linked up with rivers flowing into the interior. The Niger, of course, was one such river, but there were others as well. Capuchin priests who visited Allada in West Africa in 1660–62 observed that the several rivers that flowed into the coastal lagoon were navigated by large locally built canoes that permitted the people to travel far into the interior.[27]

American rivers also extended the Atlantic zone. Thus, geographers of North American settlement have noted that major rivers such as the Saint Lawrence, the watershed of the Chesapeake Bay, the Connecticut, and the Hudson formed major roads deep into the interior largely because these rivers were easily navigable for small sea-going vessels and were used heavily by Europeans as an axis for settlement. The Amazon, which is navigable from the Atlantic to the Andes, and the Orinoco, which also is navigable far into the interior, were also connected to Atlantic commerce. Control of both river systems lay in the hands of Native American societies, whose cultural sophistication has only recently been appreciated. From the earliest days of European contact, visitors on the Amazon and Orinoco noted extensive local traffic, and traders at the mouths of the rivers were the end points of riverine trade routes equivalent to the Senegal–Niger corridor of West Africa, where European metal goods were traded for gold, slaves, and cotton ham-

[25] Jean-Pierre Chauveau, "Une histoire maritime africaine est-elle possible? Historiographie et histoire de la navigation et de la pêche africaines à la côte occidentale depuis le XVe siècle," *Cahiers d'études africaines* 36 (1986): 173–235.

[26] Robin Law, "Trade and Politics behind the Slave Coast: The Lagoon Traffic and the Rise of Lagos, 1500–1800," *Journal of African History* 24 (1983): 321–48.

[27] Biblioteca Provincial de Toledo, Colecíon de MSS Bourbón-Lorenzana, MS. 244, Basilio de Zamora, "Cosmografia o descripcion del mundo" (1675), fol. 53.

mocks, which were exported by the thousands.[28] Because the natives of these regions (like the inhabitants of the Mississippi valley in North America)[29] controlled commerce and held the Europeans at bay, we know much less about these areas than we do of those that formed arteries of communication for Old World settlers.

Thus, water routes defined the Atlantic zone, and rivers extended the zone far beyond the shores of the ocean itself. The mastery of the sea, however, made it possible for all these continental routes to be in communication. There were considerable problems to be overcome before the connections could be made, in spite of the occasional transatlantic voyages that may have preceded Columbus's voyages and the Portuguese voyages along the African coast. Such problems had proved practically insurmountable to Africans, Americans, and Mediterranean people before 1400. It is therefore worth exploring the circumstances that enabled the Europeans to make transatlantic voyages practicable.

Origins of Atlantic navigation

Europeans' experience with waterborne travel was probably the most significant factor in allowing them to be the ones who finally conquered the Atlantic. The difficulties of tackling South Atlantic navigation may explain why Africans, for their part, seem to have focused their boatbuilding talents on craft designed for coastal and riverine navigation[30] and as a result had engaged in little deliberate oceanic navigation, leaving even fairly close islands, such as the Cape Verdes and São Tomé, uncolonized and uninhabited. Indeed, they had even eschewed long-range navigation in the Gulf of Guinea (beyond the colonization of Bioko Island, visible from the mainland), which might have proved economically feasible, though hampered by the same problems of currents that prevented transatlantic navigation.

[28] For an early account of the Orinoco, see "Memoria y relacion que hizo Martin Lopez de su viaje desde la Margarita hasta el Rio Coretin" (1550), in Antonio Arellano Moreno, *Relaciones geográficas de Venezuela* (Caracas, 1964), pp. 45–7. The significance of Amazonian and Orinoco societies is highlighted by the work of Anna Curtenius Roosevelt; see, among others, "Chiefdoms in the Amazon and Orinoco," in Robert Drennan and Carlos Uribe, eds., *Chiefdoms in the Americas* (Washington, D.C., 1987), pp. 153–84.

[29] The strength and commerce of the Mississippian societies is well documented archeologically. For an attempt to link this with the Atlantic and European activities, see the paper presented by William Swaggerty at the American Historical Association, 102d Annual Meeting, Washington, D.C., 28 December 1987.

[30] Van Sertima, *Before Columbus*, pp. 52–3, though here emphasizing the possibility of standing up to long-distance travel as well. See also Stewart C. Malloy, "Traditional African Watercraft: A New Look," in Ivan van Sertima, ed., *Blacks in Science: Ancient and Modern* (New Brunswick and London, 1983), pp. 163–76, which makes the same point but still shows clearly the focus on riverine and coastal navigation.

The people of the Americas had a slightly better chance than the Africans, for the Caribbean was fully navigable by them long before the Europeans arrived. Thus, the boats of the Caribs and Arawaks were often seen at sea and, unlike African craft, could undertake long sea voyages.[31] But just as the predictability of the monsoons in Asia may have inhibited certain breakthroughs in shipbuilding technology by presenting few challenges, perhaps also navigation of the Caribbean, with its long chain of islands, was too easy.

Europeans had two large inland seas, however: the Mediterranean in the south and the North and Baltic seas in the north, along with a difficult, but passable, stretch of coast between them. Thus, separate navigation traditions could develop to solve the specific problems in each area and then merge through intercommunication to present solutions to further problems. By the fourteenth or fifteenth century, these major seas were regularly navigated, and seagoing vessels were a standard part of every European inventory. Thus, as Pierre Chaunu has argued, it was the opening (or reopening, for such connections were frequent in Classical times) of regular commerce between the Mediterranean Sea and the northern seas in the late thirteenth century that ultimately would lead to European navigation in the Atlantic as well. This trade, signaled by the first recorded voyage of a Genoese ship to northern Europe in 1277, was largely connected with the grain trade and movement of other bulk commodities that could not stand the cost of overland trade.[32]

These early voyages not only helped to start, as we shall see, the Europeans on their conquest of the Atlantic, they linked the various European seas and ultimately helped shape the European boundaries of the Atlantic world. Fernand Braudel has argued strongly in favor of the significance of the connection between the northern seas and the Mediterranean, and it was sailors familiar with each of these two great bodies of water and with the attached riverine areas (such as Germany along the Rhine and even Poland along the Vistula) who came to participate in the larger oceanic economy of the Atlantic.[33]

Although the northern Europeans were late in entering the South Atlantic commerce that linked Africa to the Americas, the Vikings had long pioneered the northern routes westward, colonizing Greenland at

[31] Desmond Nicholson, "Precolumbian Seafaring Capabilities in the Lesser Antilles," *Proceedings of the International Congress for Study of Pre-Columbian Culture of the Lesser Antilles* 6 (Pointe à Pitre, 1976), pp. 98–105.

[32] Pierre Chaunu, *Expansion européen*, pp. 92–3.

[33] For an illuminating discussion of the boundaries of the Mediterranean, see Braudel, *Mediterranean*, 1:168–230. For the significance of the Mediterranean connections to the northern seas, see idem, *Civilization and Capitalism, Fifteenth to Eighteenth Centuries*, 3 vols., trans. Siân Reynolds (New York, 1982–4), 3:92–173.

the least and providing the first strong links between the northern seas and the Mediterranean. The English and the Dutch were fairly early and frequent in the Atlantic; the Swedes settled in North America early in the seventeenth century and had posts on the African coast as well, and in Africa they were joined by the Danes and by Baltic countries like Kurland and Brandenburg.

Not only did the needs of this seaborne trade between the Mediterranean and northern Europe serve as a stimulus to Iberian shipbuilding and interest in the interregional trade, but the fairly large number of ships involved increased the potential for accidental voyages of discovery. The career of Lanzaroto Malocello is a case in point. Malocello was a Genoese merchant who had commercial connections with Cherbourg in northern France and Ceuta in Morocco and thus had frequent recourse to travel in the Atlantic both north and south of Gibraltar. On one of these voyages he discovered (or rediscovered, for they were known in Classical times), probably by accident, the Canaries in about 1312. The Canaries were the first Atlantic islands rediscovered by Europeans, and their colonization, by Malocello around 1335, represented an early and important step into the Atlantic.[34]

In addition to multiplying the opportunities for accidental voyages of discovery, maritime travel between the Mediterranean and North Atlantic, especially because it involved bulk shipping, allowed the diffusion of shipbuilding techniques. Thus, the sturdy round ships of the North Sea and Baltic were blended with the long and maneuverable galleys of the Mediterranean. This eventually resulted in the creation of ships capable of carrying more cargo and sailing under a wider variety of conditions than could be found in either the Mediterranean or the North Atlantic. To these discoveries were added techniques in sailing and navigation borrowed from the Moslem world, with which the Genoese and Iberians had constant commerce.[35]

Possessing the means to make oceanic voyages and to discover new lands did not necessarily mean that extensive oceanic travel or exploration would be undertaken, however. There also had to be a reasonable

34 See the discussion in Charles de la Roncière, *La découverte de l'Afrique au moyen âge: Cartographes et explorateurs*, 3 vols. (Cairo, 1925–6), 2:3–4. Much of the material on Malocello's activity comes from a now lost genealogy of 1453 cited in a polemical work of 1632 to counter claims made by the eventual conquerors, the family of Jean de Bethencourt, and must be viewed with suspicion. On the other hand, the map of Angelino Dulcert, drawn in 1339, clearly shows the Genoese in possession of the island that still bears Malocello's name. According to the genealogy, Malocello ruled the island for twenty years before being expelled by the local inhabitants (ibid., p. 3, n. 2, and documents quoted).

35 See the summary of an extensive literature in Pierre Chaunu, *Expansion européen*, pp. 273–308.

set of motives, and financial backers had to have some confidence that such voyages would be worth the considerable risks that their undertaking entailed.

European motives: long-range geopolitical and economic goals

A number of technical and geographical factors combined to make Europeans the most likely people to explore the Atlantic and develop its commerce. But the task also required strong political or economic motives before it would be undertaken. An older, romantic school of historians maintained that Europeans undertook this exploration for the pure joy of discovery or to break the Moslem stranglehold on the eastern trade. These motives were enough, in this interpretation, to allow visionaries like Infante Henrique (Prince Henry the Navigator) of Portugal or Queen Isabella of Spain to finance the voyages.[36]

This romantic vision has been reduced to more mundane dimensions by the work of Portuguese historians, especially Duarte Leite and Vitorino Magalhães-Godinho. They have stressed that exploration and voyages proceeded step-by-step, over a long period of time, and were fueled by the prospect of immediate profits that were readily attainable using existing (or only slightly modified) technology.[37] Under such conditions the capital costs were small, profits and returns were all but certain, and the potential for dramatic discoveries was limited. Even the greatest leaps – Columbus's transatlantic voyage of 1492 and da Gama's circumnavigation of Africa in 1498 – were built on many years of profitable exploitation of the Atlantic and excellent intelligence of the prospects (in da Gama's case) or potentially profitable fallbacks such as the hope of finding new Atlantic islands (in Columbus's case).

In this scenario, it is possible to see the technological breakthroughs in sailing methods as following rather than leading the discoveries. People developed the technology once they knew for sure that they could profit by improving their techniques.

There is evidence, however, to support both cases, and it is dangerous to accept more quickly the research of the recent scholars with their less romantic interpretations. After all, many of those who described voyages wrote of the romantic vision themselves. For example, the fifteenth-century chronicler Gomes Eannes de Zurara stresses principally geopolitical motives when he gives a list of reasons that compelled Infante Henrique to send out the ships that pioneered direct sea travel between West Africa and Europe. These motives derived from the centuries-long

36 Summarized in ibid., pp. 233–40.
37 Summarized in ibid., pp. 243–5.

struggle between Christians and Moslems for control of the Mediterranean world. Henrique's principal desire, according to Zurara, was his wish to defeat the North African Moslems, and economic considerations were secondary. He hoped that his mariners would contact a Christian power south of Morocco with whom to form an anti-Moslem alliance or establish trade with non-Moslem southern neighbors who might be converted to Christianity and agree to such an alliance or who at least might be persuaded to cease trade with Morocco.[38]

Zurara was expressing a long-held hope of Christians in Iberia. Writers and visionaries living in the period before the voyages sponsored by Infante Henrique had proposed several schemes to outflank the Moslems in one way or another. In 1285, for example, a Mallorcan theologian named Ramon Llull dreamed of converting the king of Ghana to Christianity, thus creating a Christian state in the hinterland of Moslem North Africa.[39] Since 1306, when an Ethiopian delegation had arrived in Europe seeking a Christian alliance with the "King of the Spains," to "offer him aid against the infidels,"[40] the idea of an Iberian–Ethiopian connection had been considered. Indeed, King Anfós IV of Aragon came close to arranging a double marriage with the negus of Ethiopia in 1428,[41] and the Portuguese Crown sent Pedro de Corvilhão to Ethiopia in 1487 to prepare similar alliances.[42]

Modern scholars have been less convinced by grand geopolitical schemes of a religious and military nature than they have been by eco-

[38] Gomes Eannes de Zurara, *Crónica dos feitos de Guiné,* chap. 8. There are many editions, the best being that of Torquado de Sousa Soares (2 vols.; Lisbon, 1978). The French translation (Leon Bourdon, *Chronique de Guinée* [Dakar, 1960]) contains a valuable introduction to the history and discussion of textual problems. An English translation, from a less thorough edition and with dated notes, is by C. R. Beazley and E. Prestage (2 vols.; London, 1896–9).

[39] Ramon Llull, "Libre d'Evast e d'Aloma e de Blanquerna" (ca. 1283–5), chap. 84 (ed. Joan Pons i Marquès), in Ramon Llull, *Obres essencials,* 2 vols. (Barcelona, 1957), 1:241–2. On Llull's geopolitical philosophy, see Armand Llinares, *Raymond Lulle, philosophe de l'action* (Paris, 1963).

[40] Recorded in Jacopo Filippo Foresti da Bergamo, "Supplementum Chronicarum" (1483), from notes taken by Giovanni da Carignano at the time the mission passed through Genoa. Published (from the 1492 edition) in Youssouf Kamal, *Monumenta Cartographica Africae et Egypti* (Leiden, 1926–53), vol. 4, fol. 1139. A translation (from the 1483 edition) and discussion by R. A. Skelton appears in O. G. S. Crawford, *Ethiopian Itineraries, circa 1400–1524* (Cambridge, 1958), pp. 212–15. As a result of this visit, the geographer Giovanni da Carignano concluded that Ethiopia was the home of the legendary "Prester John," more or less permanently displacing an Asian location. See Enrico Cerulli, "Giovanni da Carignano e la cartografia dei paesi a Sud dell'Egitto agli inizi del secolo XIV," *Atti del XIV Congresso geografico italiano* (Bologna, 1949), p. 507.

[41] See a discussion in the light of Catalan activity and plans in the eastern Mediterranean in Lluís Nicolau d'Olwer, *L'expansió de Catalunya en la Mediterrània oriental,* 3d ed. (Barcelona, 1974), pp. 171–5.

[42] Mordechai Abir, *Ethiopia and the Red Sea: The Rise and Decline of the Solomonic Dynasty and Muslim–European Rivalry in the Region* (London, 1980), pp. 19–40.

nomic motives, and consequently some emphasize the fabulous wealth to be had through oceanic trade, with the spice-rich islands of India and Southeast Asia or with West Africa, mainly for its gold. Such an interpretation is supported by the correlation between Atlantic exploration and the fall of Acre, the last outpost of direct European commercial relations with the eastern Mediterranean, which passed into Moslem hands in 1291. Thus, in the same year that Acre fell, the Vivaldi brothers set sail from Venice to find an Atlantic route to the Indies; they never returned.[43] The cartography of the age, admittedly very speculative, encouraged such attempts by representing Africa in a form that suggested an easy circumnavigation.[44] A Franciscan friar from Castille reported his own circumnavigation of Africa in 1360, but his book was fictional, being based on speculation and the kind of knowledge that well-connected Franciscans might glean from contemporary maps, cosmographies, and commercial gossip in the western Mediterranean.[45]

Of all the economic possibilities that might provide motives for Atlantic navigation, however, the prospect of a short route to the West African goldfields seems the most likely. The Indies, after all, were far away in anyone's conception of world geography, whereas West Africa, known to be wealthy in gold, was much closer and clearly accessible by a sea route. West Africa had been a source of gold for Mediterranean countries for centuries, perhaps since Byzantine times.[46] Moslem writers since the ninth century at least were aware of the gold-producing areas, and a steady stream of Arabic-language descriptions of West Africa resulted, including one made by the famed North African al-Idrisi for the Christian king Roger II of Sicily in 1154.[47] These were joined by Christian accounts, especially those generated by the Catalan and Italian merchant communities of North Africa, who had been dealing in the gold (called the "gold of Palolus" in these sources) since the twelfth century.[48]

43 De la Roncière, *Découverte* 1:50–1.

44 See Jaime Cortesão, *Os descobrimentos portugueses*, 2 vols. (Lisbon, 1960), 1:304–5.

45 "Libro del consçimiento de todas las tierras y señorios que son por el mundo y de las señales y armas que han cada tierra y señorio," in Kamal, *Monumenta* 4: fol. 1259–9v (note that folios are numbered consecutively from volume to volume). This includes an English translation.

46 Timothy Garrad, "Myth and Metrology: Trans Saharan Gold Trade," *Journal of African History* 23 (1982): 443–61.

47 For example, the early descriptions of Abu al-'Qasim ibn Hawqal, "Kitab Surat al-ard," in Levtzion and Hopkins, *Corpus*, p. 49; Abu 'Ubayd 'Abd Allah b. 'Abd al-'Aziz al-Bakri, "Kitab al-masalik wa-'l-mamalik," in ibid., pp. 77–85; and al-Idrisi, "Nuzhat," in ibid., pp. 110–11.

48 These sources are often reflected in the maps of the era; see the discussion in de la Roncière, *Découverte* 1:121–41. Most of these maps are reproduced in Kamal, *Monumenta*. For a detailed discussion of the sources of the Mallorcan group, see Yoro K. Fall, *L'Afrique à la naissance de la cartographie moderne: Les cartes majorquines, XIVe–XVe siècles* (Paris, 1982), pp. 55–120. The problem of "Palolus" has been discussed in detail in Susan

A sea route to the goldfields seemed relatively practical, because it did not involve the circumnavigation of Africa. Many maps of the period showed the "River of Gold" (probably the Senegal) and, according to the legend on the map of Mecia de Villadestes (1413), where one could "obtain the gold of Palolus." Although the actual field lay upstream, the "mouth of the river is large and deep enough for the biggest ship in the river."[49] Christians believed that Moslems regularly sailed to the river – the anonymous Franciscan friar even claimed (falsely) to have sailed there himself around 1360 on a Moslem ship,[50] and as early as 1346 Jacme Ferrer, a Catalan merchant, actually attempted to reach it.[51]

European motives: the prevalence of short-range goals

Whatever their dreams or fantasies, whether it was encircling and isolating the Moslems or reaching the spices of Asia or the gold of West Africa, these long-range plans were largely restricted to kings and intellectuals, and neither group proved particularly willing to actually finance the voyages they considered, and private or small-scale ventures (such as those of the Vivaldis and Ferrer) failed. Thus, whatever contemporary writers may have said about motives, or how much rulers may have desired the results of such schemes, the progress of Atlantic exploration ultimately depended on financial considerations. Financial considerations must ultimately force us to agree with the Portuguese historians on the prevalence of short-range, unromantic, step-by-step exploration as the principal method of European expansion.

It is also important to note that another romantic fantasy – that the Iberians were the sole leaders of the exploration – is untrue. The exploration of the Atlantic was a truly international exercise, even if many of the dramatic discoveries were made under the sponsorship of the Iberian monarchs. The people who undertook the voyages gathered the human and material resources from wherever they were available. English, French, Polish, Italian people, ships, and capital joined Iberians in this effort. If the Iberians were pioneers in anything, it was that monarchs of these countries were quick to claim sovereignty (or to offer their protection to the earliest colonists) and to make the effort necessary to enforce

K. MacIntosh, "A Reconstruction of Wangara (Palōlus, Island of Gold)," *Journal of African History* 22 (1981): 145–58. This gold was sufficiently common in Barcelona that a public ordinance of that city in 1271 simply refers to gold as "gold of Palolus" (de la Roncière, *Découverte* 1:114).

49 Kamal, *Monumenta* 4: fol. 1370.

50 "Libro del consçimiento" in ibid., fol. 1258v.

51 *Monumenta* 4: fol. 1235.

these claims, usually after the economic benefits were clearly revealed by an international group of pioneers.

We can conveniently divide the expansion into two "wings," or two directions. The first of these was an African wing, which sought mainland products such as slaves and then gold as the means to finance short voyages along the coast, and whose leaders expected to find people to raid or to trade with all along the route. The second was an Atlantic wing, which sought exploitable but not necessarily inhabited land in which to collect valuable wild products or to begin agricultural production of cultivated products in high demand in Europe. The colonization of these lands began with cutting timber or gathering wild honey, but its real profitability was ultimately realized by producing wheat, sugar, or wine in rich tropical and volcanic soils.

In many respects, the Canary Islands, rediscovered by Malocello in the early fourteenth century, provided the common starting point for both wings and combined in itself both sources of profit. The islands were inhabited and could thus be raided or support commerce, they possessed wild products of interest, and ultimately they became a center for the production of both wine and sugar. Moreover, because traveling to them was fairly easy and profitable, they provided financial security to those who sought more profits on the adjacent Saharan coast or the uninhabited Atlantic islands farther out.

Malocello and those who followed him in the early to mid-fourteenth century rapidly discovered that the Canaries produced a number of useful products. Perhaps the most useful were orchil (a dyestuff derived from lichens that grew on the rocks of the islands) and "dragon's blood," a resin also used as a dyestuff. The islands could also be profitably raided for cattle and people; slaves were always in demand in the Mediterranean world.[52]

An early voyage to the Canaries (under Portuguese auspices, but with a mixed crew and an Italian captain) in 1341 went both to trade and to raid, buying hides, dyestuffs and wood products, but also carrying weapons for raiding, and King Afonso IV of Portugal reported that slave raiding was under way at least as early as 1346.[53] Catalan merchants joined the Portuguese at an early date in both raiding and trading with

52 An excellent recent survey of Mediterranean slavery at this time is Jacques Heers, *Esclaves et domestiques dans le monde méditerranéen* (Paris, 1981), esp. pp. 23–64, on the long Mediterranean background of slave raiding and its Atlantic extensions.

53 Chronicle attributed to Giovanni Boccaccio, "De Canaria et insulla reliquis, ultra Ispaniam, in occeano nouiter repertis," *Monumenta Henricina*, 14 vols. (Lisbon, 1960–74), 1:202–6, on the 1341 expedition; Afonso IV to Clement VI, 12 February 1345, *Monumenta Henricina* 1: 230.

the Canarians.[54] Attempts to colonize grew out of these ventures. The earliest colonization in various parts of the islands, by Malocello around 1339, an Aragonese group in 1342, and a group under French auspices in 1344, were all probably simply attempts to set up a trading factory and slave-raiding fort, and none brought any long-term and productive settlement. Castillians always seemed to have favored simply raiding and trading from Spain itself.[55]

Castille, however, sponsored the first permanent colonization, though it was Norman nobles Gadifer de la Salle and Jean de Bethencourt who actually organized and carried it out, in 1402–5. Like their predecessors, they seem to have been most interested in dyestuffs (they both came from textile-producing areas), organizing the Canarians to gather it. They also brought in Norman colonists and made a land division, although the export of profitable crops seems to have required a century.[56] Later Castillian-Spanish colonization continued agricultural expansion, and by 1520 the islands were producing sugar, wines, and sheep and cattle products.[57]

But whether visited for conquest and raiding or trade, the islands were seen as a source of profit, and much attention was paid to navigation to them throughout the fourteenth century. This activity brought more shipping into the area south of the Straits of Gibraltar, extending Christian raiding and commercial activity farther south and acquainting them with the area and the nearby regions of the African coast. In this way the Canaries, whether as colonies or simply as convenient landfalls, served as bases for further operations along the African coast or to the uninhabited islands farther out in the Atlantic, such as Madeira and the Azores, which were probably known to Europeans since the voyages of da Recco in 1341.

The African wing of expansion

The raiding and commerce of the Canaries provided the base and the motives for European activities farther down the Atlantic coast of Africa.

54 Charles Verlinden, *L'esclavage dans l'Europe médiéval: I. Péninsule iberique-france* (Bruges, 1955), pp. 628.

55 On Malocello and the Aragonese, see Charles Verlinden, "Lanzarotto Malocello et la découverte portugaise des Canaries," *Revue belge de philologie et d'histoire* (1958): 1173–90; on the French attempt, Clement VI, "Tue deuotionis sinceritas," 15 November 1344, *Monumenta Henricina* 1:207–14; and on Castillian tactics, B. Bonnet Reverón, "Las expediciones a las Canarias en el siglo XIV," *Revista de Indias* 6 (1945): 215–18.

56 Pierre Boutier and Jean le Verrier, *Le Canarien* (modern ed. Elias Serra Rafuls and A. Cloranescu, 2 vols. [Teneriffe, 1959]), vol. 1, chap. 87.

57 Described in detail in Fernández-Armesto, *The Canaries after the Conquest* (London, 1982).

Thus, Jacme Ferrer began his ill-fated voyage to the River of Gold in 1346 with a stop at the Canaries.[58] Likewise, Jean de Bethencourt, conqueror of the eastern group of islands, took some time off from his efforts to raid the Atlantic coast of Africa, although he attempted no voyages beyond the customary limits of navigation.[59]

When Bethencourt did homage to the king of Castille in 1405, Portugal found its claim to the islands, vigorously pressed since at least 1341, and its commercial connections there weakened. In this context, Infante Henrique of Portugal pressed hard for conquering the remaining islands and launched an expedition against them in 1415. In 1424 he sent a much larger expedition, involving some 2,500 infantry and 120 cavalry.[60] This increase in Portuguese activity in the Canaries resulted in the papal bull *Romanus Pontifex* of 1436 renewing Portuguese claims on the still-unconquered islands[61] and a corresponding increase in activity along the Saharan coast.

These renewed attacks on the remaining Canaries and the Saharan shore resulted in the doubling of Cape Bojador (though he proceeded little farther) by the Portuguese sailor Gil Eannes in 1434.[62] The year before this feat Eannes had led a slave-raiding expedition against Gran Canaria Island, and the Bojador expedition was a natural excursion in the same vein. Indeed, the sailing craft of the time could avoid some of the difficulties of the currents by sailing out to the Canaries, thus alleviating the age-long problem of return navigation from beyond Bojador.

In spite of the potential for this breakthrough, however, the Portuguese did not immediately reach the Senegal; although expeditions to the "River of Gold" were sent out almost immediately, they did not actually sail so far. Some of these expeditions brought back commodities such as oils and skins (as did one in 1436),[63] but most were simply slave raids, in the tradition of the attacks on the Canaries or southern Morocco, and rarely ventured farther along the coast than was necessary to secure a profitable cargo. It was only in 1444 that the Portuguese actually reached the Senegal, although they had attacked and intercepted caravans bound from there northward in previous years.[64]

58 See the legends to various maps in Kamal, *Monumenta* 4: fol. 1235.

59 Boutier, *Le Canarien*, vol. 1, chap. 00.

60 Recounted in Zurara, *Crónica*, chap. 79; see additional details in de Barros, *Decadas de Asia* I, bk. 1, chap. 12; de Barros was a sixteenth-century writer who saw documents on this expedition in the archives of Portugal. On the general situation, see Florentino Perez Embid, *Los descubrimientos en el Atlantico y la rivalidad castellano-portuguesa hasta el Tratado de Tordesillas* (Seville, 1948).

61 See Luiz Suárez Fernández, *Relaciones entre Portugal y Castilla en la epoca del Infante D. Henrique* (Valladolid, 1960), pp. 244–72.

62 Zurara, *Crónica*, chap. 8.

63 Ibid., chap. 11.

64 Ibid., chaps. 8–16.

Thus, the actual motivation for European expansion and for navigational breakthroughs was little more than to exploit the opportunity for immediate profits made by raiding and the seizure or purchase of trade commodities. It was these more limited objectives that ultimately made possible the voyage to the Senegal that geographers and thinkers contemplating longer-range commercial or geopolitical schemes had dreamed of since at least the fourteenth century. It was more or less an extension of these same sorts of motives that eventually allowed the Portuguese to attain that even more distant long-range goal – so important both to commercial and to geopolitical thinking – the rounding of Africa and the discovery of a sea route to India and Ethiopia.[65] The predominance of limited aims in the voyages of reconnaisance and expansion explains why the necessary exploration took so long – from 1434, when the major navigational obstacle was overcome, until 1488, when Dias showed that the Cape of Good Hope was the end of the African continent.

In the Senegal region the profits were made from gold and slaves (first captured in raids, later purchased). Gold was available from many points along the coast, and sailors expanded rapidly southward until they reached the coast of modern Sierra Leone around 1460. Much of the energy of traveling even during those years, however, was spent on commercial or military voyages intended to consolidate and explore the possibilities of the areas already known[66] or to establish bases. The uninhabited archipelago of Cape Verde Islands was crucial to further expansion and was colonized in the 1460s.[67]

But there were other commercial possibilities to be found further on, and perhaps the prospects of the next stretch of coast to produce the pepper known as malaguetta pepper[68] were known to Fernão Gomes when he petitioned the Crown for exclusive rights to the trade of West Africa exclusive of the areas earlier granted to the settlers of Cape

[65] Several Portuguese historians, such as Duarte Leite and Vitorino Magalhães-Godinho, have stressed the short-range plans and immediate profits of expansion, although their specific arguments differ from the one presented here; see the historiographical discussion in Chaunu, *Expansion européen*, pp. 243–51.

[66] The exact timing of these trips is difficult to ascertain; a good survey and new argumentation are found in Joaquim Veríssimo Serrão, *História de Portugal*, (Lisbon, 1977), 2:164–70.

[67] Cf. Orlando Ribeiro, "Primórdios da ocupação das ilhas de Cabo Verde," in *Aspectos e problemas da expansão portuguesa* (Lisbon, 1962), pp. 130–8. See also, on the general use of the Cape Verdes as a base, T. Bentley Duncan, *Atlantic Islands: Madeira, the Azores and the Cape Verdes in Seventeenth-Century Commerce and Navigation* (Chicago and London, 1972), pp. 166–9.

[68] An early description of the pepper trade can be found in Eustace de la Fosse, "Voyage à la côte occidentale d'Afrique," 1479–80, *MMA*[2] 1:473–4. Pepper was being exported from the Gambia region and northern Sierra Leone by the mid-1450s (Magalhães-Godinho, *Descobrimentos* 1:476–8.

Verde in 1469.[69] In any case, his grant included a provision that he explore further sections of the coast, and his expeditions rapidly began exporting the pepper. Shortly afterward (perhaps about 1471), to his infinite good luck, Gomes's sailors reached the gold-producing region of the Gold Coast (modern Ghana), an unexpected find that paid off handsomely for both Gomes and eventually for the Crown.[70] His sailors located another pepper-producing region at Benin the next year, although it was only in 1485–6 that regular trade began there.[71] They also discovered, on the island of São Tomé, another potential base for operations in the region.

Thus, for a long stretch of time, between about 1340 and 1470, European expansion proceeded slowly along the African coast. It paid off handsomely for the private parties who had sponsored most of it, and in 1482, for the first time, the Portuguese Crown decided to sponsor its own expedition into the Atlantic rather than to charter other people, who raised their own capital.[72] Unlike the earlier voyages, the royal voyages of Diogo Cão had a clearly geopolitical goal. According to João de Barros, intelligence received from Benin suggested to the court that Portuguese sailors were near the lands of Prester John and a circumnavigation of Africa was now possible.[73] Thus, Cão made the first attempt at expansion cast in the romantic mold, but he discovered only that the African continent turned south and ran thousands more kilometers before eventually turning. But fortunately for the Crown, Cão did come to the kingdom of Kongo, whose export products helped recoup the cost of the voyages and contributed to the success of the colony on São Tomé.[74] Undeterred by the length of Africa, the Portuguese Crown continued sponsoring exploration, first by Bartolomeu Dias and finally by Vasco da Gama, whose voyages have generally replaced the more prosaic earlier travels in textbook and romantic history as the search for the Indies.

69 The terms are known only from their citation in de Barros, *Decadas de Asia* I, bk. 2, chap. 2.

70 See the discussion in Cortesão, *Os descobrimentos portugueses*, 2:416.

71 If one accepts Rui de Siqueira, in 1472, as the first European visitor; see Ryder, *Benin and the Europeans*, pp. 30–2.

72 Martin Behaim, *Liber Cronicarum cum figuris et ymaginibus ab inicio mũndi usq̃ nũnc temporis*, 1497, fol. 326v, *MMA* 1:30.

73 De Barros, *Decadas de Asia* I, bk. 3, chap. 3.

74 Rui de Pina, "Chronica del Rei Dom João II," chap. 57, *MMA* 1:32–5; de Barros, *Decadas de Asia* I, bk. 3, chap. 3. On Kongo's export trade see Duarte Pacheco Pereira, *Esmeraldo de Situ Orbis* (ca. 1506), bk. 2, chap. 2 (modern variorum ed., Augusto Epiphânio da Silva Dias [Lisbon, 1905; reprint, 1975]), p. 134; and legend on the Cantino Atlas (1502), reproduced in Armando Cortesão and Avelino Teixeira da Mota, eds., *Portvgalliae monumenta cartographica*, 6 vols. (Lisbon, 1960), 1:12.

The Atlantic wing and the discovery of America

Like the African wing, the Atlantic wing of exploration began from the Canaries, but it was fueled by the potential for collecting wild products and colonizing otherwise uninhabited areas. Because its results were less impressive, it was slower. Madeira, for example, was probably known (as a result of exploration of the Canary Islands, no doubt) as early as 1339,[75] but its colonization was not undertaken until about 1425.[76] However, its colonization set a strong precedent, because the Azores, reached by Diogo de Silves only in 1427,[77] were already being colonized in 1440.[78]

Because they were uninhabited, islands such as Madeira and the Azores offered no commercial prospects for trading, but they could still be exploited for wild products. In all probability, its early settlers (João Gonçalves Zarco, Tristão Vaz Teixeira, and Bartolomeu Perestrello) relied heavily on the export of available wild products such as wax, honey,[79] wood,[80] and dyestuffs or they raised cattle, which could be easily maintained on the unwooded islands of Porto Santo and Ilha Deserta.[81] Early colonization of the Azores was similar. The order for colonization, given in 1439, already mentioned such products,[82] and Zurara, referring to 1446, indicates that some were already being exported.[83] On the other hand, the Azores were never particularly rich and served more as a base for operations in the Atlantic than as a major center of production.

The process was repeated on all the other uninhabited Atlantic islands. The royal charter giving the Cape Verde Islands to Infante D. Fernando in 1462 clearly indicates that he expected early earnings to be from wild products or those that required little investment to obtain.[84]

75 It appears on Dulcert's map of 1339, as well as the Atlas Mediceo of 1351 (Kamal, *Monumenta* 4: fols. 1222 and 1248).

76 A date favored, with good reason, by Duncan, *Atlantic Islands*, pp. 7–8.

77 See Damião Peres, *História dos descobrimentos*, 2d ed. (Coimbra, 1960), pp. 78–87, citing a map of Gabriel Valseca dated 1439.

78 Duncan, *Atlantic Islands*, p. 12. Colonization of the "seven newly discovered islands" was begun in 1439 (Authorization of Infante Henrique, 2 July 1439, *Monumenta Henricina* 6:334).

79 Alvise da Mosto, "Mondo Novo" (title from one of four recensions) (modern ed. Tullia Gasparrini-Leporace, *Le navigazione atlantiche de Alvise da Mosto* [Milan, 1966]), p. 17.

80 Zurara, *Crónica*, chap. 5, lists wood, wax, honey, dyestuffs, and other products. Several documents of the fifteenth century also refer to water-powered saws, evidently for cutting the wood.

81 Ibid., chap. 83, from circa 1446; similar observations can be found in da Mosto, "Mondo Novo," pp. 14–15.

82 Order of Infante Henrique, 6 July 1439, *Monumenta Henricina*, vol. 6.

83 Zurara, *Crónica*, chap. 83.

84 Donation to D. Fernando, 29 October 1462, *MMA*[2] 1:423–4.

Likewise, the earliest settlers of São Tomé in 1485 had a charter that also specified duties for export of wild products expected for that tropical island.[85] In each case, the king, in granting the charter, specified easy terms for the export of a variety of products, both wild and cultivated, that were expected to thrive in the tropics.

The gathering of wild products, the first incentive to visit these islands, gave way to cultivation of readily exportable agricultural products once soil and climate conditions were reasonably well known. In Madeira, clearing land and planting wheat, the first cultivated export, required extra labor; some workers were brought as dependent workers from Europe,[86] and others were probably obtained in attacks on the Canaries.[87] Indeed, the Madeira settlers assisted in the 1424 attack on the Canaries on the very eve of the colonization, so that the two operations went hand in hand.[88]

Madeira and the Canaries rapidly began to export wheat in large quantities, and the virgin soil produced, according to the enthusiastic testimony of Zurara in 1446, 50 for 1;[89] a more sober da Mosto said initial yields of 60–70 for 1 had declined to 30–40 for 1 in 1455,[90] still a boon by the standards of the time. The wheat was exported to Portugal and to Portuguese forces in Morocco, on the Saharan coast, and in West Africa, much of it already baked into bread.[91] But the real earnings came from wine, already described as an excellent product in 1455 by da Mosto,[92] and especially from sugar, which flourished and for which slaves, especially Canarians, provided the labor.[93] Exports of sugar were substantial by 1455 and grew rapidly until Madeira was one of the leading producers of sugar in the European economy.[94]

The success of the Madeira venture encouraged others and showed that even uninhabited islands, especially if they lay in tropical or subtropical zones, could be of economic value and could fairly quickly repay the efforts of populating them.

Not all the islands were as successfully exploited as Madeira was, although some, such as São Tomé, became very profitable indeed. But

85 Letter of Privilege to São Tomé settlers, 24 September 1485, *MMA* 1:50–1.
86 Alberto Iria, *O Algarve e a Ilha da Madeira no século XV* (Lisbon, 1974).
87 An argument cogently made by Sidney Greenfield, "Madeira and the Beginnings of New World Sugar Cane Civilization and Plantation Slavery: A Study in Institution Building," *Annals of the New York Academy of Sciences*, 292 (1977): 541–3.
88 See document cited in ibid., p. 550, n. 34, thanking them for their participation in the attack, dated 1425.
89 Zurara, *Crónica*, chap. 83.
90 Da Mosto, "Mondo Novo" (ed. Gasparrini-Leporace), p. 16.
91 Magalhães-Godinho, *Descobrimentos* 1:282–6.
92 Da Mosto, "Mondo Novo" (ed. Gasparrini-Leporace), p. 17.
93 Ibid., p. 22; Greenfield, "Madeira."
94 Magalhães-Godinho, *Descobrimentos* 1:426–50.

they did serve as bases for ventures along the African coast (such as the Cape Verdes and São Tomé) or for further Atlantic navigation (as the Azores would for the Brazil and India fleets). More than that, however, the prospect of finding uncharted and uninhabited islands in an Atlantic seemingly full of them encouraged sailors to look west into the Atlantic as well as south to Africa for their fortune. Indeed, just a few years before Columbus's journey, in 1486, the Crown granted Fernão Dulmo, the captain of the island of Terceira (in the Azores group), title to all lands he might discover in the Atlantic, including "a great island or islands, or coastal parts of a mainland."[95]

It was the combination of the prospect of finding new islands and the dream of reaching India that inspired Christopher Columbus's voyage of 1492 – for though he may well have thought his trip would take him to the lands of the Great Khan, his charter specified islands as well.[96] Columbus, of course, discovered many islands and, shortly afterward, a great continent, which (even though Columbus died believing he was in Asia) was soon recognized as being an entirely new and completely unexpected landmass.

In short, then, European navigation in the South Atlantic was not the product of long-range visionary schemes, an explosion of pent-up commercial energy, or even the response to new technology. Instead it was the cautious advance of a new frontier, using or slightly modifying existing technology and relying on relatively small amounts of private capital. Only in the last, dramatic voyages to round Africa or cross the Atlantic did royal patronage, substantial capital, and geopolitical thinking come to dominate the activity. For example, only when Portuguese sailors visiting Benin reported the possibility of contacts with Prester John (in Ethiopia) did the Portuguese Crown decide to fund its own voyage, Diogo Cão's attempt to circumnavigate Africa.[97] All the previous century of expansion had been privately funded though royally sponsored. Likewise, only the conquest of the last of the Canaries and Columbus's voyages received Spanish funding.[98]

It was a pattern that would continue to dominate European activity. The wealthier merchants, government officials, and grand schemes would be saved until politically weaker people had demonstrated the certainty of success, and then the wealthy and powerful would follow

95 Donation to Fernão Dulmo, 3 March 1486, in José Ramos Coelho, ed., *Alguns documentos do Archivo Nacional da Torre do Tombo àcerca das navagações e conquistas portuguezas* (Lisbon, 1892), pp. 58–9.

96 See the remarks of Samuel Elliot Morrison, *Journals and Other Documents on the Life of Admiral Christopher Columbus* (New York, 1963), pp. 26–30; idem, *Admiral of the Ocean Sea: A Life of Christopher Columbus* (Boston, 1942), pp. 138–45.

97 De Barros, *Decadas de Asia* I, bk. 3, chap. 4.

98 Rumeu de Armas, *España en el Africa Atlántida* (Madrid, 1956).

up, absorb the activities and profits of the pioneers, and turn the exploitation of the new discoveries over to those who dominated all society.

Thus, by the late fifteenth century the pioneers had fully tested the regime of wind and currents that dominated Atlantic navigation.[99] By discovering this key, Europeans were able to unlock the commerce of the Atlantic, and because they had single-handedly developed the routes, their domination of the high seas in the Atlantic was ensured in a way that was not possible in any other extra-European area of navigation. In neither techniques nor experience did they dominate the Indian Ocean and South China Sea with the completeness that they dominated the Atlantic.[100]

Oceanic navigation and political domination

Scholars have argued that this domination of the seas gave Europeans insuperable political and commercial advantages over local people in Africa and the Americas.[101] This claim, although possessing some merit, overlooks the complexity of the situation, especially on the coasts of the continents, and when studied in detail is not as persuasive as it first appears. Although Europeans did make some conquests in both Africa and the Americas, it was not naval power that secured the conquests. Their failure to dominate local coastal commerce or overwhelm coastal societies, most pronounced in Africa but also the case in some parts of the Americas, means that we must amplify our estimation of the role played by these societies in the shaping of the Atlantic world. Domination of high-seas commerce is significant, to be sure, but perhaps not as significant as domination of the mainlands.

Naval encounters and Afro-European commerce. Europeans clearly hoped that their maritime abilities would give them military advantages that would result in large profits and perhaps conquests. They were prepared to take over territory and enslave people, and their actions in the Canary Islands bore witness to that desire. However much some visitors to the Canaries might have wanted to engage in peaceful trade, it was ultimately the slave raiders and conquerors who won out. Control of the seas allowed Europeans to land freely on the islands, resupply their forces when necessary, and concentrate large forces for their final

99 Avelino Teixeira da Mota, "As rotas maritímas portuguesas no Atlântico de meados do século XV ao penúltimo quartal do século XVI," *Do Tempo e da História* 3 (1970): 13–33.

100 See the important work of K. N. Chaudhuri, *Trade and Civilization in the Indian Ocean: An Economic History from the Rise of Islam to 1750* (London, 1985), pp. 138–59.

101 This discussion has been summarized and examined in Chauveau, "Histoire maritime africaine," pp. 176–90.

battles – and thus maritime superiority could arguably have been the cause of their success.

The earliest sailors who reached the African coast in the fifteenth century naturally hoped to continue this tradition, as apparently did the Spanish sailors who began the conquest of the larger Caribbean islands in the late fifteenth and early sixteenth centuries. But in Africa at least, their confident approach was rebuffed. Unlike the Canarians, who possessed no boats at all, the West Africans had a well-developed specialized maritime culture that was fully capable of protecting its own waters.

One of the first expeditions to the Senegal River, led by Lançarote de Lagos in 1444, brutally seized the residents of several off-shore islands. The inhabitants, although they managed to inflict some casualties, had little other recourse than to try to flee to areas of difficult access. Other expeditions that followed did more or less the same, but it was not long before African naval forces were alerted to the new dangers, and the Portuguese ships began to meet strong and effective resistance. For example, in 1446 a ship under Nuno Tristão attempting to land an armed force in the Senegambian region was attacked by African vessels, and the Africans succeeded in killing nearly all the raiders. Likewise, in 1447 Valarte, a Danish sailor in Portuguese service, was killed along with most of his crew when local craft attacked him near the island of Gorée.[102]

Although African vessels were not designed for high-seas navigation, they were capable of repelling attacks on the coast. They were specialized craft, designed specifically for the navigational problems of the West African coast and the associated river systems. From the Angolan coast up to Senegal, African military and commercial craft tended to be built similarly. Generally, they were carved from single logs of tropical trees and only occasionally had their sides built up. Consequently, they tended to be long and very low in the water. They were almost always powered by oars or paddles and thus were maneuverable independent of the wind. They drew little water and could operate on the coast and in rivers, creeks, and inland estuaries and lagoons. Craft that were designed to carry soldiers could, according to contemporary witnesses, carry from fifty to one hundred men.[103]

These specialized craft presented a small, fast, and difficult target for European weapons, and they carried substantial firepower in their archers and javelinmen. However, they could not go far out to sea, and the larger, high-sided Portuguese vessels were difficult for them to storm.

[102] Zurara, *Crónica*, chaps. 24–5, 30–6, 86, and 94.

[103] On West African boats and especially their military characteristics, see Chauveau, "Histoire maritime africaine," pp. 191–7.

Alvise da Mosto, a Venetian trading in Africa with a Portuguese license, records an encounter he had with an African flotilla in the Gambia in 1456. Da Mosto was mistaken, with justice, for being another raiding party from Portugal and was immediately attacked by seventeen large craft carrying about 150 armed men. They showered his ships with arrows as they approached, and da Mosto fired his artillery (bombards) at them, without, however, hitting anything. Although the attackers were temporarily stunned by this unexpected weapon, they nevertheless pressed the attack, at which point crossbowmen in the upper rigging of the Venetian ship opened fire, inflicting some casualties. Again, although impressed by the weaponry, the Africans continued fighting until da Mosto eventually made it known he did not mean to attack them, and a cease-fire ensued.[104]

The Africans were unable, in most circumstances, to take a European ship by storm, and the Europeans had little success in their seaborne attacks on the mainland. As a result, the Europeans had to abandon the time-honored tradition of trading and raiding and substitute a relationship based more or less completely on peaceful regulated trade. Da Mosto attempted this in his voyage, and the Portuguese Crown eventually dispatched Diogo Gomes in 1456 to negotiate treaties of peace and commerce with the African rulers of the coast.[105] As a result, Portugal established and maintained diplomatic relations with a host of African states. Already in 1494, Hieronymous Münzer, a German visitor to Lisbon, noted that the king sent frequent presents to the rulers of African states to win their favor, and as a result Portuguese could travel freely in Africa under the protection of these rulers.[106] These diplomatic and commercial relations easily replaced the raid-and-trade or raid-and-conquer patterns of other parts of the Atlantic, especially because the Portuguese soon discovered to their pleasure that there was also a well-developed commercial economy in Africa that maritime commerce could tap into without engaging in hostilities.

The presence of African naval craft along most of the coast seems to have deterred a recurrence of a raid-and-trade pattern by most subsequent Portuguese voyages to Africa, although, of course, the policy of refraining from attacks on Africans was not always followed. Newcomers or less established powers might still go for the short-term advantages of raiding, as did a Castillian expedition that was sent in 1475 to

104 Da Mosto, "Mondo Novo" (ed. Gasparrini-Leporace), pp. 82–4.

105 Gomes related his mission in "De prima inuentione Gujnee," in Fernandes, "Descriçã," fols. 272–83 (this is the foliation of the original text).

106 Hieronymous Münzer, "Itinerarium," 23 November 1494, *MMA*[2] 1:247–8. Some of these diplomats are known: Records exist for missions from Kongo, Benin, Labida, and Jolof, all to Lisbon.

trade for gold on the Gold Coast but that also raided fairly extensively.[107] Likewise, early English voyages, in the late sixteenth century, especially those to volatile areas like Sierra Leone with its many states, also raided or at least let violence and seizure of people predominate over peaceful trade.[108] But such violence "spoiled" trade in an area, and most countries that had a long-term stake in trade took steps to prevent hostilities. Indeed, one of the earliest North American voyages, made from Boston in 1645, was involved in raiding, and the city officials actually returned the slaves seized by the ship with an apologetic note, probably to retain or regain good relations with their potential trade partners.[109]

Even the Portuguese Crown sometimes had to relearn these lessons. In 1535 the Portuguese attempted to conquer the Bissagos Islands, home of some of the most renowned sailors and raiders on the Guinea coast, but with disastrous results.[110] For the most part, however, such exceptions were sporadic, and peaceful trade became the rule all along the African coast, and given the large number of participants and the somewhat uncertain nature of virtually all long-distance trade in the preindustrial period, it is not surprising that some breaches occurred.

Not only did African naval power make raiding difficult, it also allowed Africans to conduct trade with the Europeans on their own terms, collecting customs and other duties as they liked. For example, Afonso I, king of Kongo, seized a French ship and its crew in 1525 because it was trading illegally on his coast.[111] It was perhaps because of incidents such as this that João Afonso, a Portuguese sailor in French service, writing at about the same time, advised potential travelers from France to Kongo to take care to conduct trade properly, explaining that when a ship enters the Zaire, it should wait until the officials on shore send one of their boats and do nothing without royal permission from the king of Kongo.[112]

107 Alonso Fernández de Palencia, *Cronica de Enrique IV,* 5 vols. (Madrid, 1904–9), 4:127.

108 For example, Cavendish's attack in August 1586 and Cumberland's in October 1586, of which various accounts have been gathered and edited in P. E. H. Hair, "Early European Sources for Sierra Leone," *Africana Research Bulletin* 13 (1974): 71–2, 76–7.

109 Richard Saltonstall to Massachusetts General Court, 7 October 1645, in Robert Moody, ed., *The Saltonstall Papers, 1607–1815,* 2 vols. (Boston, 1972–4), 1:138–9; Boston Council meeting minutes, sessions of 1 and 14 October 1645, 4 September, 1 October, and 4 November 1646, in Nathaniel B. Shurtleff, ed., *Records of the Governor and Company of the Massachusetts Bay in New England,* 5 vols. (Boston, 1853–4; reprint, New York, 1968), 2:84, 129, 136, and 168.

110 See the retrospective account of André Alvares de Almada, "Tratado breve dos Rios da Guiné," 1594, *MMA*[2] 3:319; and contemporary documentation, Donation to Infante Luis, 27 March 1532 and 5 September 1534, *MMA*[2] 2:226–9 and 263–5.

111 Alvará of Afonso I to Officials of São Tomé, 27 December 1525, *MMA* 1:455–6.

112 Jean Alfonse de Saintogne, *Les voyages advantureux* (Paris, 1559), fol. 55. Although published in 1559, this text was probably written around 1530 – Afonso died, in any case, around 1544.

Portugal's one sustained military excursion into Atlantic Africa, the conquest of Angola, was the result of economic controversy rather than territorial aspirations. The colony was originally intended to be a commercial factory to regulate the trade from Ndongo and for four years functioned as such.[113] When a trade dispute led to war in 1579, the Portuguese position was saved only by the intervention of a Kongo army, and even though Kongo itself joined an anti-Portuguese coalition in 1591, Portugal had acquired a foothold and local allies sufficient to maintain itself.[114]

Naval conflict and conquest in the Americas. Although our purpose is principally to reveal the African role in shaping the Atlantic world, it is worth noting, at least briefly, that in some parts of the Americas European naval superiority was not particularly decisive. Most of the spectacular conquests by Europeans in America involved inland empires, in which naval power was relatively unimportant (with the possible well-known exception of the role played by Spanish brigantines in the siege of Tenochtitlán by Cortés).[115]

It was the Spanish failure in the Caribbean that is most dramatic, however. The Spanish did, of course, conquer (with considerable local help) the larger islands. But in some ways they simply forestalled their conquest by the militaristic inhabitants of the southern and eastern Caribbean. The Kulinago of the Lesser Antilles and the Carib and Arawak people of the mainland of Venezuela and the Guianas (often, though not always accurately, designated "Caribs" in Spanish documents)[116] not only proved capable of resisting Spanish attempts to attack their homes but managed to raid the Spanish possessions of the Caribbean throughout the sixteenth and seventeenth centuries. The people of the eastern Caribbean basin possessed sufficient naval technology (on African lines, composed of fairly small, maneuverable craft)[117] to defeat Spanish ships,

113 See the 1571 contract between Paulo Dias de Novais and the Crown, which stipulated commercial relations, although it did allow Dias de Novais to conquer a section of the barren southern coast, then outside of Ndongo's jurisdiction (Carta de Doação a Paulo Dias de Novais, 19 September 1571, *MMA* 3:36–51).

114 Detailed in Beatrix Heintze, "Die portugiesische Besiedlungs- und Wirtschaftpolitik in Angola, 1570–1607," *Aufsätze zur portugiesischen Kulturgeschichte* 17 (1981–2): 200–19.

115 There are several surveys of the period, the best, perhaps being Carl Sauer, *The Early Spanish Main* (Berkeley and Los Angeles, 1966); and Troy Floyd, *The Columbus Dynasty in the Caribbean, 1492–1526* (Albuquerque, 1973).

116 On the complexities of the ethnological, historical, and archeological situation in the southern Caribbean basin (including the Guianas and the Orinoco basin), see Marc de Civrieux, "Los Caribes y la conquista de la Guyana española," *Montalbán* 5 (1976): 875–1021.

117 For an account of naval war between Carib canoes and European vessels that is equivalent in some ways to da Mosto's account for Africa, see the eyewitness account of Jean Baptiste du Terte, *Histoire generale des Antilles habitées par les François,* 4 vols. (Paris, 1667), 1:508–12.

for they did actually take ships on the high seas.[118] The French, English, and Dutch who eventually settled in the West Indies and the mainland were forced into first a co-dominion and then a long-lasting military struggle, which was really only decided by the superior numeric strength of the settlers.

Even in the mainland areas, the European conquest of the Americas was far from complete. Outside the central areas of Mexico and Peru there were many Native American peoples who resisted European incursions or yielded to them only slowly after long-standing military pressure. Among these one might mention the indigenous inhabitants of Florida, who not only defeated Ponce de Leon's celebrated attack on them but pursued his men out to sea in canoes, capturing several of his ships.[119] Even on land, Europeans were unable to easily defeat either the Araucanians of Chile[120] or the "Chichimecas" of Mexico,[121] each of whom resisted European settlers and conquerors with such success that settlement was slowed and undertaken either with their concurrence and assistance or only after long struggle. The Tupinambá and Tapuya of Brazil gave ground to Portuguese settlement very slowly, and by 1680 many regions in South America were either entirely in the hands of natives or were jointly ruled by Native Americans with European settlers in an uneasy co-dominion.[122]

One should not therefore imagine the Americas as simply lying securely under European sovereignty. In many places a long struggle for control ensued; in other places frontier conditions without secure European sovereignty continued for a long time. When Africans were brought to the Americas as slaves, they found this situation often worked to their advantage, and for them, the unsettled nature of the Americas provided the opportunity to escape, to play off the contending parties, or to use the potential for defection or escape to improve their situation.

By the middle of the sixteenth century, then, the Atlantic world had begun to take shape. European sailors, who had come to understand the

118 For a good survey of Spanish relations with the inhabitants of Dominica and for Carib military prowess in general, see Joseph Baromé, "Spain and Dominica, 1493–1647," *Caribbean Quarterly* 12 (1966): 30–47.

119 Antonio Herrera y Tordesillas, *Historia general de los hechos de los castellanos . . .* (1724) (several modern eds.), decade 7, bk. 7, chaps. 5, 8–10.

120 Louis de Armond, "Frontier Warfare in Colonial Chile," *Pacific Historical Review* 23 (1954): 125–32; Robert C. Padden, "Cultural Change and Military Resistance in Araucanian Chile, 1550–1730," *Southwestern Journal of Anthropology* (1957): 103–21.

121 See the admirable discussion in Phillip Powell, *Soldiers, Indians and Silver: The Northward Advance of New Spain, 1550–1600* (Berkeley, 1952).

122 John Hemming, *Red Gold: The Conquest of the Brazilian Indians, 1500–1760* (Cambridge, Mass., 1978), is the best survey; for other regions, such as Paraguay, see James Lockhart and Stuart Schwartz, *Early Latin America: A History of Colonial Spanish America and Brazil* (Cambridge, 1983), pp. 253–304.

winds and currents of the Atlantic, had established a system of navigation that bound Europe, Africa, and the Americas into a single system of commerce. European rulers and the more powerful of their subjects had come to see the system as being of great significance and holding potential for wealth and were well on their way to wresting political and economic control away from the pioneers who had created it. But if the powerful of Europe controlled the commerce of the seas, in Africa they were unable to dominate either the coast or coastal navigation, and in the Americas the subdued regions were surrounded by hostile and sometimes aggressive unconquered people. Thus the African role in the development of the Atlantic would not simply be a secondary one, on either side of the Atlantic. In Africa, it was they who would determine their commercial role, and in America they were often the most important group among the early colonists. Even when they played no particular political role, they often could capitalize on the incompleteness of European domination.

2

The development of commerce between Europeans and Africans

The success of Africans in resisting the early European attempts at raiding their coasts meant that the interactions that would follow would be largely peaceful and commercial – for it would not be until 1579 that a major war would develop, in Angola, and even there it rapidly became an indecisive standstill. There would be no dramatic European conquests in Africa, and even the slaves who would flood the South Atlantic and sustain colonization in America would be purchased more often than captured. This state of affairs was already being put in place by Diogo Gomes's expeditions in 1456–62 and would characterize relations between Europeans and Africans for centuries to come.

African naval victories might not necessarily guarantee that the commerce that grew up in place of raiding was truly under African control or necessarily served their interests (or the interests of the wealthy and powerful in African society). Indeed, many scholars in recent years have most often seen the commerce of Atlantic Africa with Europeans as destructive and unequal, with Europeans reaping most of the long-range profits and Africans unable to benefit or being forced, through commercial weakness, into accepting trade that ultimately placed Africa in its current situation of dependency and underdevelopment.

Perhaps the most influential scholar to advocate such a position was Walter Rodney, whose work on Africa's Atlantic trade concluded that the commerce with Europe was a first, decisive step in the underdevelopment of Africa. As Rodney saw it, this was because Africa was at a lower level of economic development than Europe and was thus forced into a sort of "colonial" trade in which Africans gave up raw materials and human resources (in the form of slaves) in exchange for manufactured goods – a form of dependency that certainly characterizes modern African trade.[1]

[1] Rodney, *How Europe Underdeveloped Africa*, pp. 95–113; idem, *A History of the Upper Guinea Coast, 1545–1800* (London, 1970), pp. 171–99.

Although not all scholars have shared Rodney's radical views on many aspects of the relationship, recent interpretations have continued to stress that African backwardness necessarily led it into a type of trade that diverted its potential to develop. Thus, Ralph Austen, whose views are much more conservative than Rodney's, still agreed that the commerce begun in the fifteenth century led Africa to greater marginality in the world economy and tended to stifle technological development and some lines of economic growth.[2]

An examination of African economic development by 1500 and the exact nature of the Atlantic trade, however, does not support this pessimistic position. Africans played a more active role in developing the commerce, and they did so on their own initiative. On the one hand, the Atlantic trade was not nearly as critical to the African economy as these scholars believed, and on the other hand, African manufacturing was more than capable of handling competition from preindustrial Europe.

In order to understand the role of the African economy in the Atlantic trade we need to examine two related issues, both of which are raised in the works of scholars who see Africans as junior and dependent trading partners. First is the assumption of African backwardness in manufacturing, based largely on the analogy with Africa's present lack of manufacturing capacity and its impact on modern African economies. Second is the assumption of commercial domination, in which Europeans somehow were able to control the market for African goods, either through monopoly or through commercial manipulation of some other sort.

Industry and terms of trade

Comparisons between the trade of the sixteenth and seventeenth centuries and that of the present day linking industrialized with less developed countries are invalid. Although many of the goods that Africa imported before 1650 were manufactured goods (such as iron or cloth) and many of their exports were at most semimanufactured (hides, copper and gold, gum, ivory, and slaves), a closer examination reveals that early African manufacturing was in many ways quite capable of providing for the continent's needs.

Perhaps one of the most interesting facts of the early Atlantic trade was that Europe offered nothing to Africa that Africa did not already produce – a fact often overlooked in analyses of the trade. This immediately differentiates the early period from the present day, for today domestic African industry produces none of the manufactured goods that they import from the developed world.

[2] Ralph Austen, *African Economic History* (London, 1987), pp. 81–108.

Europe exported a wide range of goods to Africa before 1650, of which we can recognize several categories. First and surely foremost in terms of volume was cloth – a whole world of textiles of dozens of types by the seventeenth century. Then there were metal goods, principally iron and copper, in raw (iron bars and copper manillas)[3] and worked form (knives, swords, copper basins and bowls, etc.). Next there was currency, consisting of tons of cowry shells. This trade was especially important in Benin and the Slave Coast though shells were also imported into central Africa. Finally there is what we might describe as nonutilitarian items, such as jewelry (beads for the most part), mechanical toys and curiosities, and alcoholic beverages.

What is significant about all of these items is that none were "essential commodities." Africa had well-developed industries producing every single item on the list, and although not all of them were produced in every district, a substantial number of these items were imported into regions where there was clearly no pressing need, in a strictly functional sense, to import them.

It was, in short, not to meet African needs that the trade developed or even to make up for shortfalls in production or failures in quality of the African manufactures. Rather, Africa's trade with Europe was largely moved by prestige, fancy, changing taste, and a desire for variety – and such whimsical motivations were backed up by a relatively well developed productive economy and substantial purchasing power. The Atlantic trade of Africa was not simply motivated by the filling of basic needs, and the propensity to import on the part of Africans was not simply a measure of their need or inefficiency, but instead, it was a measure of the extent of their domestic market.

We can begin to see the complexities of the trade if we look at the trade in metals, and particularly iron, for iron was surely the best example of a commodity that was imported and could be used in tools and one where technique is essential to producing quality. The Portuguese exported little iron to Africa, perhaps because they felt obliged to honor papal injunctions against selling materials with potential military value to infidels. However, Christian Kongo received little Portuguese iron either, so the more likely reason was that they produced little themselves and could not make a good profit exporting it. The Dutch, with access to good German and Scandinavian sources, and the English, with iron of their own, pioneered the sale of iron into Africa, iron bars already being prominent in the gifts that van den Broecke gave out in 1605.[4] Iron

3 A manilla was a horseshoe-shaped copper ingot, the most common form in which copper was transported and sold.

4 Pieter van den Broecke, *Reizen naar West-Afrika van Pieter van de Broecke, 1604–14*, edited by K. Ratelband (The Hague, 1950), p. 5.

appears in Dutch trade lists of the seventeenth century as useful in every part of Africa, and they were sure to bring considerable quantities each year. Based on French and English trading company statistics, Curtin has estimated that Senegambia imported something on the order of 150 tons of European iron every year by the last half of the seventeenth century, although this figure is probably higher than earlier quantities.[5]

But Africa was an iron-producing part of the world, and Senegambia was already being served by producers in Futa Jallon (and perhaps also by some poor-quality local iron) at the time the Portuguese arrived.[6] Indeed, the Portuguese bought iron in Sierra Leone to sell in Senegambia and other points, as the books of the ship *Santiago,* sailing this route in 1526, clearly show.[7] But European trade with Senegambia in iron later on was not simply an attempt to compete with other West African producers in fulfilling the needs of an iron-poor region. Instead, the iron trade was more complicated.

The peculiarities of African iron production that made European iron attractive come, perhaps, from its earliest years. According to recent work on ancient African ironworking, the technology was developed by 600 B.C. or even earlier on the Sudanese fringe of the emerging Sahara desert, perhaps as a result of discoveries made in the copper-producing areas of the desert north of modern Nigeria. Because this was a fuel-poor environment, African ironworkers developed methods to conserve fuel, of which the most important was devising a system to preheat the air blast that entered the furnace, which prefigured techniques used in Europe only in the nineteenth century. This not only saved fuel, but it allowed Africans to produce an amazingly good-quality steel – perhaps the best steel in the world of the time, and certainly equal to or even better than the steel produced in early modern Europe.[8]

Certainly research into the quality of metal produced by African foundries in West Africa in modern times and recent archeology suggest that African steel was equal to that made anywhere in the fifteenth century.[9] But African steel still required considerable quantities of wood, and this was not always available, which meant that increasingly the best ironwork was done on the northern edge of the rain forest where there was a conjunction of wood supplies and iron ore (as well as abundant waterborne transportation). This sometimes made iron expensive in regions

5 Curtin, *Economic Change,* p. 210.

6 Pacheco Pereira, *Esmeraldo,* bk. 1, chap. 33 (ed. Silva Dias), p. 96.

7 Avelino Teixeira da Mota, "A viagem do navio Santiago à Serra Leoa e Rio S. Domingus em 1526," *Boletim Cultural da Guiné Portuguesa* 24 (1969): 567, 572.

8 See Peter Schmidt and S. Terry Childs, "Innovation and Industry during the Early Iron Age in East Africa: The KM2 and KM5 Sites of Northwest Tanzania," *African Archaeological Review* 3 (1985): 53–94.

9 Curtin, *Economic Change,* pp. 207–11.

like Senegambia that were located some distance from the centers of production. As a result, European iron, even though of poorer quality, might be competitive in price and could be employed for those uses that did not require the qualities of steel.[10]

But even if its price were competitive, one should not imagine that imported iron came particularly close to fulfilling even the Senegambian needs for iron before 1680. According to Curtin's estimates, annual Senegambian imports of iron in 1680 amounted to 150 tons and was probably less in the half-century earlier. This iron would go to serve the needs of what might be a rather restricted iron-using population, along the coast north of the Gambia and inland along the Senegal to approximately Futa Tooro, where a local industry reduced the need for imported stocks. Curtin notes, in fact, that traders found little market for imported iron on the upper reaches of both rivers before the middle of the eighteenth century.[11]

If we assume that each household had a minimum tool kit composed of a hoe, axe, large knife (machete or cutlass for clearing fields), smaller knives for cutting, and some arrowheads and spears for hunting (excluding for the moment military uses), then we can estimate that each household owned approximately two kilograms of iron at a time, which required replacement every two years (for the locally produced iron; lower-quality, imported iron needed biannual or even triannual replacement), and thus each household had an annual consumption of one kilogram of iron per annum.[12] If we accept that this restricted coastal region had a total population in 1650 of about 1.5 million,[13] organized into perhaps 300,000 households,[14] then these households required 300 tons of local iron per year. But if they used imported iron (at the higher replacement rate) they would need at least 1,200 tons to meet their needs. Thus, imports could probably only have met about 10–15 percent of their needs.

These estimates of consumption are low, assuming minimum household consumption, and completely exclude military uses, one of the most important additional uses of iron. For example, the average Sene-

10 See Candice Goucher, "Iron Is Iron 'Til It Rust: Trade and Ecology in the Decline of West African Iron-Smelting," *Journal of African History* 22 (1981): 179–89; L. M. Poole, "Decline or Survival? Iron Production in West Africa from the Seventeenth to the Twentieth Centuries," ibid. 23 (1982): 503–13.

11 Curtin, *Economic Change*, pp. 210–11.

12 On the replacement rate, see Poole, "Decline or Survival?" p. 507.

13 I have arrived at this figure by recalculating the densities for the region given in Thornton, "Demographic Effect," pp. 710–14 by an approximate area for this part of the region.

14 At five people per household. For these purposes, the total number of households roughly equals the number of males in the age-group 16–50, or about 20 percent of total.

gambian horseman, according to descriptions of the late sixteenth century, carried a sword, a broad-bladed spear, and seven or eight smaller throwing spears, and his horse and saddle also required a small amount of iron[15] – in all perhaps two kilograms. Thus a unit of 500 horse by itself used as much as a ton of iron, with a higher annual replacement because some supplies were expended before wearing out (such as throwing spears, which might, for this reason, be made of inferior iron from the imports), and even according to conservative estimates of cavalry forces, the perhaps 15,000 horsemen of the coastal and lower rivers region required thirty tons of iron – not to mention the numerous infantry, some of whose weapons must be considered in the earlier estimates of household consumption, but who probably demanded ten or twenty more tons total.

But if European iron was not simply to fill the needs of an iron-poor region, and surely not to replace poor-quality iron with better-quality metal (if anything, as we have seen, the relationship was the reverse), then European iron clearly played a more complex role. Thus, Africans in Senegambia and elsewhere bought cheap European iron in bars (perhaps the most common form of purchase) but they also bought high-quality steel swords, which were certainly used in their finished form. Africans could, of course, have made their own swords, for they possessed both the skills and the quality metal, but no doubt the imported sword was also an item of prestige whose value was not simply counted by its utility as a weapon. This might well explain why archeologists found a European sword in a burial site at Rao that must have been purchased (through the trans-Saharan trade) in the twelfth or thirteenth century.[16] The distance this sword must have traveled was far from simply being a measure of its utility.

This same point can be even more abundantly detailed in the issue of cloth imports, for unlike iron, whose distribution and working conditions predispose it to long-distance trade, cloth can be made almost anywhere. Certainly there were no Africans who bought European cloth simply because they lacked cloth themselves, nor should we believe that European cloth was necessarily better (in a functional sense of providing protection from the elements) or even cheaper than its African counterpart. Early European travelers praised West African cloth; for example, both Fernandes and Pacheco Pereira had much to say on the Mandinga

[15] De Almada, "Tratado breve," *MMA*[2] 3:241; Donelha, *Descrição da Serra Leoa*, fols. 18v–19.
[16] J. Joire, "Découvertes archéologiques dans la région de Rao (Bas-Sénégal)," *BIFAN* 17 (1955): 262.

cloth they and their informants encountered.[17] This cloth was widely traded in West Africa, and the Portuguese even carried Mandinga weavers to the Cape Verde Islands, where they created the distinctive trade cloth that was a staple of West African commerce for the next several centuries.[18]

Some measure of the vitality of African textile industries can be seen in the central African case, where unlike European or Asian cloth (and even much of West African cloth), the local textile industry used tree bark to make a wide variety of cloth types. This cloth could be of very high quality, for Pacheco Pereira wrote in the early sixteenth century, "In this kingdom of Congo they make some cloths of palms, with a surface like velvet, and those with fancy work like velvetized satin, so beautiful that there is no better work done in Italy."[19]

This cloth was also plentiful, for African cloth makers appear to have been efficient producers as well as skilled ones. The Portuguese purchased considerable cloth from eastern Kongo for export to the lands to the east of Angola, and a memorandum on this trade in 1611 indicates that the eastern Kongo region was exporting over 100,000 meters of cloth to Angola alone per year.[20] Such a level of exports might indicate, when domestic consumption and exports to other parts of Africa are considered, total production perhaps twice as high. This level of exports, from a region whose total population probably did not exceed 150,000, places eastern Kongo on a par with the great Dutch textile-manufacturing centers of the same time (such as Leiden) – whose total annual production ran to the 100,000-meter range and whose total population (urban and rural) was also perhaps in the same range.[21]

That European imports did not simply go to clothe the naked is demonstrated by considering the consumption of the Gold Coast, a big importer of European cloth that absorbed something on the order of 20,000 meters of European and Asian cloth per year by the early to mid-seventeenth century.[22] This trade provided cloth to a population that we can tenta-

17 Fernandes, "Descriçã," fol. 110v, 115; Pacheco Pereira, *Esmeraldo*, bk. 1, chap. 29 (ed. Silva Dias), pp. 86–8.

18 António Carreira, *Panaria cabo-verdiano-guineense: Aspectos históricos e sócio-economicos* (Lisbon, 1960). On Senegambian cloth in general, see Curtin, *Economic Change*, pp. 211–13.

19 Pacheco Pereira, *Esmeraldo*, bk. 3, chap. 2 (ed. Silva Dias), p. 134.

20 Alvitre de Pero Sardinha, ca. 1611, *MMA* 6:52–3.

21 See statistics in Braudel, *Wheels of Commerce*, p. 347.

22 My estimate is based largely on ships' records of the 1640s as cited in Ray Kea, *Settlements, Trade and Politics on the Seventeenth Century Gold Coast* (Baltimore, 1982), pp. 208–10 and 405, nn. 10–16. Kea has estimated that *each* of 200 ships that visited the Gold Coast between 1593 and 1607 carried 150,000 yards of cloth for a total of 30–40 million yards of cloth imports, or upward of 2,500,000 yards (2,300,000 meters) per year (p. 208, sources cited on p. 405, n. 10). But neither the documents he cites nor those in the note

tively estimate as being composed of 1,500,000 people, of which approximately 750,000 would be adults, roughly equal numbers of males and females.[23] It is possible to estimate, based on descriptions of clothing of ordinary Akan people presented in travelers' accounts, such as those of de Marees (1601) and Müller (1688), that each adult male wore about 3–4 meters of cloth, and each female perhaps 4–5 meters (including cloth for carrying infants), most of which was a single piece of cloth used to wrap the body.[24] If one makes some very minimal assumptions (to allow for the poorest slaves) and posits a two-year life for this supply of cloth, then the average adult required at least 1 meter of cloth per year, and thus the annual consumption on the Gold Coast ran to something on the order of 750,000 meters of cloth. Cloth arriving from Europe and Asia thus accounted for about 2 percent of total consumption, and even then this assumes no elite consumption (often many times higher than average), no child consumption, and no nonclothing use for textiles.

In fact, the consumption of cloth, much more than the consumption of iron, is a means of demonstrating prestige, because its principal use is as much bodily decoration as protection from the elements. Accumulations of large quantities of cloth and displays of this accumulation form a major part of conspicuous consumption, which, given the fairly low cost of some cloth, was available not just to the rich or powerful but also to ambitious and successful peasants, artisans, or petty traders. Acquiring luxury cloth, foreign cloth, and cloth with unusual colors, designs, textures, and shapes could also play a role in conspicuous consumption.

following (p. 405, n. 11) come close to supporting the very high per-ship totals. Instead, they appear to suggest that the 150,000 yards is for the *total*, giving annual imports at a level of 10–12,000 meters, rising throughout the century.

23 My estimate is based on the average density method used for Senegal, from data in Thornton, "Demographic Effect," pp. 710–14, for the southern half of the Gold Coast region. Kea (*Settlements*, p. 139) estimates the total population of this area at 656,000 (thus an adult population of 325,000) based on a projection from army sizes reported in the literature. In a note, however, he suggests that his multiplier (4) to convert armies to population is quite low (indeed, it would assume every adult male served) and cites an opinion of Marion Johnson that for the nineteenth century a number closer to 8 (which would give a population of 1,312,000, almost the same as my estimate) might be closer (p. 380, n. 64). Johnson's opinion is strengthened by the fact that unlike nineteenth-century armies, Kea has shown (pp. 149–67) that seventeenth-century armies were small elite forces and not mass armies, implying that an even higher multiplier should be applied.

24 Pieter de Marees, *Beschryvinge ende historische verhael vant Govt koninckvijck van Guinea . . .* (Amsterdam, 1602; modern ed. with original pagination marked, S. P. L'Honoré Naber, The Hague, 1912); English trans. with original pagination marked, Albert van Dantzig and Adam Jones, *Description and Historical Account of the Gold Kingdom of Guinea (1602)* (London, 1987), pp. 17a, 19b, 26a–b. Wilhelm Johann Müller, *Die Afrikansche auf der guineischen Gold Cost gelegene Landschaft Fetu* (Hamburg, 1673; facsimile reprint, Graz, 1968; English translation with original pagination marked in Adam Jones, ed. and trans., *German Sources for West African History, 1599–1669* (Wiesbaden, 1983), pp. 150–9.

Thus, Müller, in describing Gold Coast cloth consumption, chided the people for their vanity in hoarding and displaying cloth and for the great public show that wealthier members (and even commoners) of society made when going out.[25] With this in mind, we can understand better the dynamics of the demand for European cloth. The Akan "are so vain about what they wear . . . and whatever appeals to them at a particular time they must have, even if they have to pay twice as much for it."[26] Hence he observed that the price paid for cloth often was determined more by its prestige value than any measure of its utility. It is noteworthy that the most expensive and sought-after cloth was not a European import but Mandinga cloth imported from the regions north of the Gold Coast.[27]

We can make similar observations about the cloth horde displayed upon the death of the king of Loango in 1624. Although Loango was a region that produced an excellent cloth of its own and exported somewhere around 20,000 meters to Angola in 1611,[28] the ruler's heirs proudly displayed a horde that included a wide variety of European and Asian cloth and nearly 700 meters of cloth from eastern Kongo.[29] In the context of a display, intended to demonstrate the wealth and prestige of the ruler, foreign and luxury cloth held pride of place.

This feature of textile production can explain why so many African regions both exported their own cloth to Europeans and imported cloth from Europe, at times in the same transactions. Thus, João Afonso's guide for French traders of the 1530s lists cloth among items to be bought and items to be sold along the Kongo coast.[30] Even Benin, which exported as many as 5–10,000 meters of cloth annually from its ports to other parts of Africa (principally the Gold Coast),[31] also imported Dutch linen and Indian cloth.[32] In all probability, the reason that the very areas that produced large quantities of cloth were the same as the regions that imported it is that the market for cloth in those areas was well developed by the extensive local production. European cloth was imported into these areas to tap the ever-changing demands of a discriminating consumer who had already become accustomed to using large quantities of

[25] Müller, *Afrikansche*, pp. 151–5.
[26] Ibid., p. 152.
[27] Ibid., p. 158 (Mandinga cloth sold for 1.5 pounds of gold, while expensive cloth brought by Europeans ran up to 2 guilders, p. 156).
[28] Pero Sardinha, ca. 1611, *MMA* 6:53–4.
[29] Nicholas van Wassenaer, *Historisch verhael aller gedenckwaerdiger geschiedenissen die en Europa . . .*, eighth part, October 1624 to April 1625 (Amsterdam, 20 May 1625), fol. 28v.
[30] Alphonse de Saintogne, *Voyages advantureux*, fol. 55.
[31] Kea, *Settlements*, p. 210.
[32] Ryder, *Benin and the Europeans*, pp. 86, 93–8.

cloth and could be counted on to purchase more, especially if it was different and new.

Thus, some of the imports into cloth-producing regions, as in Loango, were intended for conspicuous consumption and a sign of prestige, but others, such as the cloth sold in Allada, were to undergo yet another transformation. According to the English captain John Phillips, who visited Allada in 1694, most of the "says and perpetuans" that they sold were unraveled and then rewoven into their own cloth and resold in other parts of Africa. Some of these Allada cloths even crossed the Atlantic, for Phillips noted that they fetched a crown each in Barbados.[33] Such complex remanufacturing of European cloth surely predated Phillips's visit, and perhaps a good number of the thousands of cloths from Allada being sold by the Dutch on the Gold Coast in the 1640s were of similar composition.[34]

All of this demonstrates that Euro-African trade cannot be seen simply as an exchange of essential commodities, fulfilling the needs of a deficient economy. In this context, it is easier to understand why Africans also demanded a wide range of trinkets and beads, such as the ubiquitous *alaquequas*, a yellow North African bead that Pacheco Pereira noted sold all along the Senegambian coast.[35] Various beads were long manufactured in Africa – akori beads, for example, have a respectable antiquity in the region of modern Nigeria.[36] But even more than in the case of cloth, beads were valued for their prestige and foreignness, and even perhaps their outrageous price! In the case of such commodities the idea of function must yield to consumer preferences.

Consumer preferences no doubt explain why Africans demanded such a wide variety of commodities from Europe. After studying the lists of Dutch imports to the Gold Coast, Kea estimates that as many as 150 different commodities were in demand, including 40 different types of cloth.[37] Furthermore, demand for this or that item shifted dramatically, often to the consternation of merchants who brought thousands of items only to find no demand for them. Such shifts are clear indications that the purchasers were responding far more to the changing fashions of nonessential commodities than a real need to trade to satisfy basic wants. As Müller noted about the consumer on the Gold Coast: "at one

33 John Phillips, "A Journal of the Voyage in the Hannibal of London, Ann. 1693, 1694," in Awnsham Churchill and John Churchill, eds., *A Collection of Voyages and Travels*, 5 vols. (London, 1732), 5:236.

34 Kea, *Settlements*, p. 210.

35 Pacheco Pereira, *Esmeraldo*, bk. 1, chaps. 26, 27, 29, 31 (ed. Silva Dias), pp. 79–91 passim.

36 J. D. Fage, "Some Remarks on Beads and Trade in Lower Guinea in the Sixteenth and Seventeenth Centuries," *Journal of African History* 3 (1962): 343–7.

37 Kea, *Settlements*, pp. 207–12.

moment they like this new fashion, at another moment that; and whatever appeals to them at a particular time they must have. . . . This is why so many goods remain unsold and are sent back to Europe at great loss."[38]

Finally, most scholars who examine Afro-European trade often forget that Africa exported manufactured goods to Europe as well, including textiles. We have already mentioned the famous rewoven Allada cloths that Captain Phillips noted fetched a high price in Barbados, clearly showing that someone (could it have been African slaves?) was willing to pay dearly for it. Senegambian mats clearly went to the European market, and in large quantities. The trade is mentioned in the earliest sources, and such mats were often used in Europe as bedcovers. Not only that, but they must have been manufactured and exported in considerable quantities, for in the early eighteenth century an English factor at Sierra Leone was instructed to acquire no less than one million of them, "if they could be got." Africans also manufactured other items for European customers. Most famous of these were the "Afro-Portuguese ivories," including mostly spoons but also horns and saltcellars. These goods were artistically wrought in a hybrid art style and were definitely for elite consumption, but they were sufficiently numerous to go beyond simply curiosity production.[39]

In the end, then, the European trade with Africa can scarcely be seen as disruptive in itself, for it did not oust any line of African production, nor did it thwart development by providing items through trade that might have otherwise been manufactured in Africa, even if one differentiates, say, high-quality cloth from low or high-grade steel from low. There was no reason, therefore, that Africans should have wanted to stop the trade, or that their desire to continue it was based on necessity.

The market and the state in Atlantic commerce

Europeans did not pillage Africa, either as raiders or indirectly as traders from a more advanced economy. However, scholars (such as Rodney) have also proposed that whatever the level of economic development, Europeans may still have possessed some organizational advantages, either that they had more of a profit orientation than the Africans, possessed superior commercial organization, or were able to restrict imports to Africa in such a way as to exercise a partial monopoly. Any of these factors might have given the Europeans commercial advantages and

38 Müller, *Afrikansche*, p. 152.
39 The mat trade is discussed in Kathy Curnow, "The Afro-Portuguese Ivories: Classification and Stylistic Analysis of a Hybrid Art Form," 2 vols. (Ph.D. diss., Indiana University, 1983), pp. 61–2.

perhaps allowed them to extract high profits or force Africans into unwelcome lines of commerce.[40]

Before proceeding to an analysis of this aspect of the problem, we must note immediately that the interregional trade of the period was not a matter of groups of merchants from Europe traveling to Africa and buying whatever they wanted in African markets or from African producers, and in the exchange following the laws of supply and demand. Although village markets may have functioned in this way in both areas, and although merchants may have preferred the undisturbed flow of commerce, the long-distance trade was almost never so simple a transaction. This is because most governments, the world over, regarded long-distance trade as falling under their jurisdiction, to be ruled and controlled by them and ultimately to serve their needs ahead of those of the buyers or sellers.

Rulers in both Africa and Europe undoubtedly realized that they could not really control long-distance trade, for the distances, risks, and other market imperfections implicit in this type of commerce were too great. Indeed, the states would surely have lost money had they literally taken control of the trade, which bore very little resemblance to modern international trade with its currency regulations, international banking, security of lanes, and rapid communication. Instead, the states probably hoped that by claiming control over trade they could "bend" market forces enough to generate revenue and limit risks marginally, just enough in fact to make trade pay them. If we say their policies failed to attain their stated goals, we must add that such claims were more to establish the right in the international community to play the game of distorting the market than to actually accomplish it.

When examined from its organizational dimension, then, African trade with Europe was very much the mirror image of European trade with Africa. Both partners sought an "administered" trade, under state control, that attempted to eliminate or control the effects of market mechanisms like competition in the hope of securing maximum revenue from commerce. This was true even though the state usually preferred to allow private merchants to pioneer new trades (as in the case of early European exploration) or if possible to take the risks and absorb the costs. From the very start – Gomes's negotiations with a series of West African rulers – the commerce was controlled by the respective states of African and European countries, and although the mundane economics of supply and demand and the need to reward private initiative could not be wholly forgotten, they were always seen as secondary to the

[40] See Rodney, *Upper Guinea Coast*, pp. 83–94, 122–51, 171–99; Austen, *African Economic History*, pp. 90–5.

principal goal of all the controlling participants, which was to use the trade as a means of expanding state revenues. The expansion of revenues would take priority over other economic considerations, even those that might have increased volume or global revenues. If private merchants made profits, well and good, but it was not an essential part of state thinking, although most governments realized that only by ensuring some level of private profit could they expect trade to continue.

Often, this concern for revenue meant that states preferred to engage in trade themselves using salaried or commissioned agents and selling goods they obtained through their control of taxation and production. In other cases, they were content to simply tax a product, which then came under the control of the bourgeoisie, a group of merchants who lived principally on the proceeds of commerce. When possible they might enhance that bourgeoisie profit by ensuring favored members a monopoly or at least by distorting markets in their favor, and presumably increasing both the amount of profit (and hence tax revenues) and their ability to tax a single, visible source.

In the case of the northern Europeans after 1600, the state's role was vested in the hands of parastatal chartered companies, such as the Dutch West India Company, the English Royal Africa Company, or the French Senegal Company, which made their own arrangements with private traders. Often, the two types of trade, which we might crudely call private versus state-sponsored, coexisted or alternated uneasily as rulers sought to find a formula that maximized revenues and minimized efforts and costs.

Thus, we see that European merchants intending to deal in African markets often had to undergo a complex series of negotiations before actually exchanging commodities. Da Mosto, arriving on the Senegal River in 1455 and among the first to record such transactions, provides us with an interesting example. We can designate the Venetian merchant as a "private" trader, and his first action was to negotiate with the Portuguese state to obtain a license to sail in Guinea.[41] This requirement arose because the Portuguese king had claimed sovereignty over the trading lanes of the Atlantic Ocean, and through this claim of sovereignty, which popes[42] (but not all other European powers) recognized, also claimed the right to limit access, fix itineraries, or tax those trading in the area.[43]

[41] Da Mosto, "Novo Mondo" (ed. Gasparrini-Leporace), pp. 11–13.

[42] After the publication of the crucial bull, *Romanus Pontifex*, 8 January 1455, in *MMA*² 1: 277–86.

[43] The legal complexities of the Portuguese claims are discussed in detail in Martina Elbl, "Portuguese Trade with West Africa, 1440–1520" (Ph.D. diss., University of Toronto, 1986), pp. 243–55.

Having obtained his license from the state controlling the European end of the trade, da Mosto then sailed to where he had to undergo another series of negotiations with the ruler of Kayor, head of the state that controlled the African end. Although he does not reveal all the complexities in a setting that was in any case just beginning to be fixed, it is fairly clear that his discussions with the ruler and his extended lodging with a local noble were part of the transaction, by which he was eventually able to obtain a cargo.[44] The private African merchants with whom da Mosto had to deal no doubt had to make their own arrangements in Kayor, although he does not reveal these.

Later visitors reveal the changing nature of the relationships. When Pieter van den Broecke, a Dutch merchant operating without much European state interference, undertook a voyage to the same area in 1605, he sought no permission from Portugal, although he was aware that Portuguese ships could attack him for violating their claims to sovereignty – which in any case was being violated with impunity by English and French ships as well.[45] But Dutch merchants, like those of the other European countries that visited Africa in his time, soon found that they met restrictions at home, for in 1621 the Dutch West India Company was chartered and exercised similar claims to those of Portugal over Dutch merchants wishing to deal with Africa. This company provided the model for numerous other chartered companies operating out of France, England, and a host of other northern European countries, such as Denmark, Brandenburg, Sweden, and Kurland.

But for van den Broecke, and all those who followed, the African states still exerted a variety of state control mechanisms. Although he had no lengthy visits with the rulers of Kayor, he did have to make a courtesy visit to an "alcaide" of the ruler, to whom he paid a tax, presumably in exchange for the right to trade privately. On the other hand, when van den Broecke visited other parts of Africa, his experience resembled that of da Mosto. In Loango, which he visited three times between 1606 and 1612, he regularly had to visit the ruler and pay taxes and negotiate trading terms, as he did in Ngoyo and Nsoyo, other African states in the general central African region.[46] In spite of the fact that these states had been engaging in the Atlantic trade for well over a century when van den Broecke visited them, the necessity for state control still required negotiations, taxes in the form of presents, and courtesy calls on rulers.

These two visitors to Africa reveal some of the complexities that gov-

44 Da Mosto, "Novo Mondo" (ed. Gasparrini-Leporace), pp. 49–50.
45 Van den Broecke, *Reizen* (ed. Ratelband), pp. 5–8.
46 Ibid., pp. 6, 22, 30–1, 59.

erned the African trade. On the one hand, there was a series of claims made on navigation by European powers or, as later Dutch, French, and English traders would reveal, by chartered companies from their home countries, which included taxation, control over routes and itineraries, or specifications concerning commodities to be bought and sold. On the other hand, there was another series of procedures required by the Africans concerning commodities to be bought, taxes or customs, prices for people of varying status, and the like, originating from the needs and requirements of the various African states.

Monopoly and competition in Atlantic trade

Although the strict control over the trading activities of Europeans was largely a matter of ensuring that trade be conducted according to state rules and for the benefit of the ruler and the exchequer, there was also at least to some degree an attempt to obtain a monopoly vis-à-vis African trading partners. Thus, at least part of the revenue-ensuring system of control also aimed to boost revenues by obtaining better prices through control over the supply of the goods. In short, Europeans trading in Africa did try to distort the market in their favor and against their African partners. The degree to which such a policy was successful might well indicate whether the Europeans were the senior, or dynamic, partners in the trading relationship.

It was in this regard that Pacheco Pereira, in his survey of Portuguese trade at the start of the sixteenth century, often complained that because the trade was not "well managed," the terms of trade in the sale of horses for slaves were slipping in favor of the Africans.[47] Clearly the implication was that as long as the Crown carefully controlled stocks and offering prices to Africans, the Africans would have to take that price, whose top would be fixed only by the much higher price set in the trans-Saharan horse trade or by other sources of supply.

As Pacheco Pereira and no doubt the Portuguese Crown as well saw it, creating a monopoly on the supply of European goods in the hands of the Crown or its designates would ensure a higher revenue position and an increase in the Crown's income. But, in fact, the Portuguese Crown and all other agents who attempted it failed. With that failure also came the failure to exploit the African commercial community.

There were two factors working against this policy on the European side (and we should definitely assume African hostility to it). First of all, there was the chance that foreign powers, cognizant of the rewards to be gained by African trade, would seek to trade on the African coast and

47 Pacheco Pereira, *Esmeraldo*, bk. 1, chaps. 26, 28 (ed. Silva Dias), pp. 79, 82.

undercut Portuguese prices through competition. Second, there was the danger that Portuguese agents, either state officials or private traders operating with or without a license, would reduce the state's control or go into competition with each other.

To meet the first eventuality, the Portuguese Crown sought to obtain the recognition by other European powers of their claims to the Guinea trade. They obtained papal support for it and sought to win acceptance of their sovereignty from other European powers. Even though the popes recognized Portuguese claims to sovereignty, the recognition was never completely secure or widely respected. From the very start of the Portuguese navigations, there were Castillian competitors. Not until 1479 as a part of the general settlement of affairs between Portugal and Castille, did the Castillian Crown reluctantly accept Portuguese sovereignty over the sea lanes outside the Canaries, though its own records reveal that it did little to stop private sailings and even collected tax on their proceeds.[48] The Castillians were not alone, for in that same year Eustace de la Fosse undertook his voyage from Flanders to the Gold Coast, although it ended in his capture by Portuguese ships.[49] Plans for English voyages followed soon afterward, and by the early sixteenth century French ships were regularly sailing into the South Atlantic in violation of Portuguese claims and papal dictates.[50]

As was typical of the nature of the Portuguese claims, the Portuguese government sought to end the voyages on the one hand by seizing the vessels and their cargoes (a fate made more fearful by the fact that the Portuguese announced a policy of putting the crews into the sea) and on the other hand by making formal diplomatic petition to the home countries of the various rival European traders. Portuguese ambassadors in Spain, France, and England regularly sought to get the rulers of these states to order their subjects to desist in their plans to sail in the Atlantic; they met with various degrees of success.[51] The appeal to state powers to exercise this control over trade reveals the general European attitude concerning the role of the state in promoting trade, granting licenses to trade, and the like, even though all parties recognized that there would be some illegal voyages made privately in spite of royal displeasure.

At the same time that they were seeking to end foreign participation,

48 See Elbl, "Portuguese Trade," pp. 246–51, for a useful discussion of this issue. Spanish archival records that Elbl studied reveal numerous Castillian vessels traded in the area and paid the "fifth" upon their return (pp. 340–1).

49 See his account published in *MMA*[2] 1:464–79.

50 John Blake, *Europeans in West Africa (1450–1560)*, 2 vols. (London, 1942), 2:107; Teixeira da Mota, "As rotas maritimos," pp. 27–33.

51 Much of this diplomatic activity can be followed in the various early sixteenth-century letters in ANTT, Colleção São Vicente, vol. 2, fols. 258–60; vol. 5, fols. 156–62, 457–62, 463, 471, 519. See also M. E. Gomes de Carvalho, *D João III e os Franceses* (Lisbon, 1909).

the Crown was also trying to control participation by its own citizens. Here the costs of supervising the trade had to be weighed against the benefits of monopoly, and the dynamic of these two factors shaped Portuguese policy in the earliest years. In general, the Crown sometimes sought to participate in commerce directly and at other times to avoid direct participation, for long-distance trade is always risky.

Therefore, during the earliest commercial voyages, the Portuguese ruler decided to allow private traders (whether of Portuguese nationality or foreigners, such as da Mosto) to obtain licenses in exchange for a fee.[52] In this way the Crown obtained some revenue from the trade but engaged in no risks, for unsuccessful voyages paid the fee along with successful ones. However, as the utility and value of some products were demonstrated, rulers were less content with a simple fee from merchants and began to insist on a royal monopoly to deal in an ever-lengthening list of products, beginning with gold and slaves but soon extended to various types of cloth, shells, and other trade goods that were used in Atlantic exchange.[53] Soon royal ships were being fitted to sail in the Atlantic; indeed, by 1504 there were fourteen ships employed in the African trade by the Crown.[54]

On the other hand, royal monopolies and direct participation in trading did not mean that the Crown simply took over commerce. For the most part the Crown still preferred to rent out commerce, exchanging the sure income of a rent (paid in advance) for the uncertainties that always accompanied a commerce that involved lengthy sea travel, faced a variety of pirates and privateers, and carried commodities that might perish or spoil before they reached the market. Thus, the Crown decided to rent out its monopoly power to private persons, giving them each a section of the royal monopoly in exchange for a fixed rent. The monopoly ensured the grant holder a greater certainty of profit and a larger volume, other (noneconomic) factors permitting, although in practice the Crown did little to assist in the enforcement and often violated the holder's monopoly itself.[55] Ultimately, the Crown rented out virtually all its rights save that to the trade in gold.[56]

One big problem that the Portuguese Crown faced in making good its claims to monopoly over European trade was the cost of enforcement. In

[52] For details on this period see Elbl, "Portuguese Trade," pp. 253–9, 312–18.

[53] Ibid., pp. 159–66.

[54] ANTT, nucleo Antigo, vol. 799, fols. 115–58, as analyzed in Elbl, "Portuguese Trade," p. 619.

[55] Elbl's careful examination of the documents reveals that realities were less clear-cut ("Portuguese Trade," chaps. 6 and 7).

[56] John Vogt, *Portuguese Rule on the Gold Coast, 1469–1682* (Athens, Georgia, 1979), pp. 58–92. This trade seems to have remained profitable for the Crown until the mid-sixteenth century, (Elbl, "Portuguese Trade," pp. 618–19).

order to ensure that the system worked according to its interests, the Crown began to send factors out to Africa – to Arguim in 1469 to supervise the gold and slave trade of the desert coast, to the Cape Verdes to oversee royal interests in Guinea, to Mina to supervise the royal gold trade, to São Tomé, and then to points along the African coast: to Cacheu in the "Rivers of Guinea," briefly at Ughoton to supervise trade in the Benin area, to Mpinda and Mbanza Kongo in Kongo, and eventually to the colony of Angola.[57] Such factors and officials associated with them had the responsibility of seeing that the royal trade in monopolized commodities was handled according to a set of rules, including a series of elaborate safeguards against official chicanery, and that private traders, foreign nationals, and the like were following Portuguese rules concerning licensing and commodity control.[58]

In the end, however, the fact that both private citizens and government officials (who typically were themselves rich merchants who had purchased their positions) participated in the trade helped to undermine the effectiveness of any monopoly on the terms of trade. In order to work properly, trade needed to take place completely under government supervision, and yet this was impossible on the African coast – particularly because private European traders and some officials rapidly discovered that African rulers were quite willing to permit them private concessions of their own that allowed them to profit from the trade instead of being simply agents. Private traders and low-ranking officials in Portuguese service, who chafed under regulation and who moreover realized that their place in the Portuguese system of rewards under controlled trade would remain permanently low, thus defected to the Africans, or at least offered their services to Africans in exchange for a higher place in the system than they might be offered by Portugal.

By the 1520s there were a number of unofficial settlers, often called *lançados*, who were widely distributed in Africa and who operated in league with the African authorities. The royal ship *Santiago* purchased goods from them in Sierra Leone in 1526, and travelers all along the coast noted their presence. By the late sixteenth century some held important positions in Senegambian states, and most of them in the Rivers of Guinea region were married to local women and were allowed to form their own settlements. Many of these settlers were from the Cape Verde Islands and had their connections to private trade from that area; not surprisingly a number were New Christians (converted

57 Avelino Teixeira da Mota, "Alguns aspectos da colonização e do comércio marítimo dos portugueses na Africa ocidental nos séculos XV e XVI," *Anais do Clube Militar Naval* 101 (1976): 687–92.

58 Ibid., pp. 690–2, for an analysis of the surviving *regimentos*, or instructions to factors.

Portuguese Jews), whose chances for advancement in Portuguese service were limited.[59]

Although the presence of a royal factory and close supervision limited the growth of this type of community on the Gold Coast,[60] groups of Portuguese from São Tomé and Príncipe found their way to most of the states of the Gulf of Guinea. Portuguese from São Tomé were certainly well in evidence at such places as Allada in the mid-seventeeth century and had an honored place in the government system: The Dutch trading guide of 1655 even noted the presents that should be given to "Portuguese."[61] Likewise, Villault, sailing down the coast in 1667, noted that Portuguese mulatto settlers living along the coast from Sierra Leone to Cape Mount completely dominated trade, allegedly having withdrawn to the interior from the coast under royal pressure in 1604.[62] Although the date is questionable, it is clear that these defectors also had local political connections – otherwise, they could not have dominated trade.

In central Africa where no gold trade attracted direct Crown interests, the same trend was even clearer. Portuguese settlers from São Tomé rapidly became a favored community in Kongo, and then in Ndongo as well, whose rulers were willing to support them against claims made by the Portuguese government against them.[63] Portuguese ships visiting Kongo in the period between 1525 and 1535 record making their purchases of slaves from locally settled Portuguese settlers – some, like Manuel Varela, who were established as officials in Kongo and enjoyed royal favor.[64] Like their counterparts in West Africa, many of the central African defectors were New Christians. An investigation conducted in Luanda in 1596–7 by the Inquisition of Lisbon revealed a whole chain of

59 Ibid., p. 687.

60 Ibid., pp. 689–91.

61 UBL: BPL, MS. 927, "Aenwijsingse van diversche Beschrijvingen van de Noort-Cust van Africa," fol. 12v.

62 Nicholas Villault, Sieur de Bellefond, *Relation des costes d'Afrique apellée Guinée* (Paris, 1669); the English translation, *A Relation of the Coasts of Africa called Guinea* (London, 1670), p. 84, is cited.

63 John Thornton, "Early Kongo-Portuguese Relations: A New Interpretation," *History in Africa* 8 (1981): 193–4.

64 The books of four ships that visited Kongo in this period have survived in ANTT CC, sec. II. All record the purchase of slaves from residents in Kongo; see 128/3, Book of *Conceição*, 28 August 1535 (misdated to 1525 on the archive cover sheet); 197/27, Book of *Santo Espirito*, 30 January 1535 (*MMA* 15:98–102); 203/16, Book of *Urbano*, 11 August 1535 (*MMA* 15:115–18); and 204/39, Book of *Conceição*, 6 October 1535 (*MMA* 15:124–30). Manuel Varela is listed as selling slaves on both the *Conceição* runs in 1535 (ANTT CC II/128/3, II/204/39) (*MMA* 15: 125). Other sources noted him as carrying a letter for Afonso I to Portugal (Afonso to João III, 25 July 1526, *MMA* 1:480). He also testified to losing over 70 cruzados worth of *nzimbu* money because ships did not come to pick up his slaves at the port of Mpinda (inquest conducted by Diogo I, 12 October 1548, *MMA* 2:200–1).

settlements established by New Christians throughout the area with posts in Kongo (and often positions in the church and administration of Kongo) and its eastern neighbors as well as in states in the Ndembu region and Ndongo.[65]

To counter the potential for these defectors to gain ground at the expense of the Portuguese state, the Crown attempted to group all Portuguese in supervised settlements under control of a royally appointed factor, though most such attempts yielded less, even to the Crown, than anticipated. The fact that they were not continued reveals that the Crown decided that the project was a failure. This seems to have been the result when the Crown tried to base all its Upper Guinea coast operations at a single point – maintaining that they could better protect their citizens against abuse by local people and fend off foreign "pirates." A fort was completed in 1591 and was attacked by the local people shortly thereafter, and although de Almada, who reported the whole episode, was clearly in favor of the move, it is also clear that it was bad for government trade and perhaps for those *lançados* who were resettled there.[66] Similarly, plans undertaken in 1606 for a "conquest" of Sierra Leone not unlike the one achieved earlier in Angola also included grouping merchants and resident Portuguese in one place under the control of a captain.[67]

Such ideas also lay behind numerous attempts on the part of Portuguese rulers to appoint a captain over the Portuguese community in Kongo, which the Kongo rulers sometimes supported, as long as it did not interfere with their own clients among the Portuguese community.[68] For example, in 1574 King Sebastião of Portugal sought to regroup the Portuguese community in Kongo again after having helped the king of Kongo drive the "Jagas" from his country.[69]

Ultimately, though, the Crown hoped that the establishment of the colony of Angola would accomplish what diplomacy in Kongo failed to accomplish. Although the colony certainly did help in maintaining control around the mouth of the Kwanza River, the Portuguese communities further afield continued local alliances and were thus unsupervised. To counter this, the policy of seventeenth-century governors was a variant of earlier ones. They forced trade to take place at *feiras,* markets under the direction of a Portuguese official, in the capitals of major

65 ANTT, Inquisição de Lisboa, 159/7/877, Visita a Angola, 1596–7, fols. 23–23v, 54v–55v, 58, 63, 64–88v.

66 De Almada, "Tratado breve," *MMA*[2] 3:285–6, 300–4.

67 Donation of the Captaincy of Serra Leoa to Pedro Alvares Pereira, 4 March 1606, *MMA*[2] 4:129–39.

68 Thornton, "Early Kongo-Portuguese Relations," pp. 195–7.

69 Sebastião I to Francisco de Gouveia, 19 March 1574, *MMA* 3:120–1.

trading partners of Angola. Similar official markets seem to have been organized by the late sixteenth century,[70] but the system was formalized only in the early seventeenth.[71] This system probably still failed to control the *sertanejos* – those Portuguese who continued to make their own arrangements with African authorities.

Thus policies to ensure the Crown's control and participation on its terms in the trade in Africa resulted in the conquest of Angola in the 1570s and lay behind plans for other conquests, especially those in the Rivers of Guinea and Sierra Leone. Indeed, all these attempts were ultimately outgrowths of the plan by the Portuguese Crown to centralize and monopolize trade, probably to obtain a monopoly price against the Africans, certainly to ensure its own revenue or the revenue of its licensees. But in the end, as long as African states preserved their sovereignty, the Portuguese Crown could never succeed in completely dominating the trade.

Throughout the sixteenth century the Portuguese made serious and often temporarily successful attempts to keep other foreign powers out of the African trade, although in the long run they failed even in the Gold Coast, where their strongest position lay. In part their failure was due to the impossibility of maintaining the sea power to keep foreign ships out, but mostly it was because the Africans were not under Portuguese rule and could not be made to refrain from dealing with foreigners any more than with agents and subofficers of the Portuguese Crown.[72]

These foreign traders of the sixteenth century were normally private traders, and their home governments did not necessarily support them against Portuguese claims (though they rarely actually accepted Portuguese demands that they stop their activity). But in the seventeenth century, the Dutch made a serious attack on the Portuguese monopoly claims. The Dutch argued that this was an extension of the Spanish war in the Low Countries, and because Spain absorbed the Portuguese crown in 1580, the Dutch were also at war with Portugal. The Dutch did not undertake this attack simply by sending out private traders, though Dutch merchants had been frequenting the African coast since the 1590s, but instead they chartered a company, the first Dutch West India Company, in 1621. This company, a reflection of the disparate and uncoordinated polity of the Dutch Republic itself, combined capital from each of

70 As implied in the statements concerning *resgates* and *feiras* in ANTT, Inquisição de Lisboa, 159/7/877, Visita a Angola, e.g., fol. 23 ("Cabonda, terra de Angola em q̃ os portugueses residẽ"), and passim.

71 Beatrix Heintze, "Das Ende des Unabhängigen Staates Ndongo (Angola): Neue Chronologie und Reinterpretation (1617–30)," *Paideuma* 27 (1981): 200–1.

72 For a reasoned and up-to-date discussion of the Portuguese policy on the Gold Coast, and English success in thwarting it, see Avelino Teixeira da Mota and P. E. H. Hair, *East of Mina: Afro-European Relations on the Gold Coast in the 1550s and 1560s* (Madison, 1988).

the towns that made up the state, and in exchange for paying dividends to the participating town councils from the proceeds of its trade (i.e., a sort of tax) it was granted the powers of a state. In short, it was a sort of state itself, and quickly began to operate in the trade as if it were a state.[73]

At the beginning of its career, the Dutch West India Company attempted to wrest control of the South Atlantic away from Portugal, conquering parts of Brazil and then moving systematically against Portuguese possessions in Africa – the post at Mina fell in 1637, those on Príncipe and in Angola fell in 1641, and that on São Tomé in 1647.[74] Although the Dutch had justified their attack on Portuguese monopoly claims by asserting the rights of freedom of the seas, they were quick to claim sovereignty in much the same way. Thus, when English, Danish, Swedish, French, and German companies organized on the same lines as the Dutch West India Company attempted to trade on the Gold Coast, the Dutch maintained that they had hegemony and sought to seize ships and cargoes.[75] Thus, in the 1660s the English and Dutch waged war over supremacy on the Gold Coast.[76]

But these claims, of course, did not extend to the actual African inhabitants of the coast. At best, like the Portuguese claims that they had now appropriated, the Dutch company hoped that they could dominate seaborne imports into Africa in such a way as to achieve a monopoly position in commerce. Like their Portuguese predecessors, the directors of the Dutch West India Company hoped that they could capitalize on their military capacity to limit competition in order to increase their profit.

In actual fact, however, the Dutch were even less successful than the Portuguese, as is clearly revealed in a retrospective report written by Heerman Abramsz to the directors of the Dutch West India Company upon his return to the Netherlands after long service as director of company operations in western Africa in 1679. The report shows how much the Dutch had been incapable of maintaining the monopoly they had wrested from the Portuguese, and how English, Swedish, and Danish companies had encroached on the trade, established lodges and posts, and made their own arrangements with African rulers, while

73 Charles Ralph Boxer, *The Dutch Seaborne Empire, 1600–1800* (New York, 1965), pp. 21–9.

74 Ibid., pp. 26–7.

75 "Statement by Joost van Colster on the Attitude of the Dutch West India Company toward Interlopers and Foreign Ships," 1/11 August 1682, in Adam Jones, ed. and trans., *Brandenburg Sources for West African History, 1680–1700* (Wiesbaden, 1985), pp. 22–3.

76 See "Captain Holmes, his Journalls of two voyages into Guynea in his Majesty's Ship the Henrietta and the Jersey in the year 1660/1 and 1663/4," Cambridge University, Magdalen College, Pepysian Library, MS. 2698.

steadily denying Dutch claims even in areas where the Dutch had posts.[77]

Even when they had given up their grandiose plans for control over the whole sea trade, such companies still hoped to form an exclusive relationship, usually by treaty, with a single African state in hopes that they could stabilize prices and eliminate competition. The constant complaints in companies' reports about undercutting prices paid by European rivals and the "inconstancy" of Africans who refused to be bound by trade treaties clearly reveal both the attempt and its results.[78]

The price-fixing aspects of such treaties were not successful, but the treaties did guarantee that the goods supplied would find a market. Thus, even if they could not impose a monopoly price on their African buyers, Europeans would at least be assured that their ships would be allowed to sell their cargoes ahead of those of other nations or companies in exchange for African goods. This took some of the risk out of trade – for no trader wants to undertake a long and hazardous journey only to find that there is nothing to buy. The hope that commercial risk would be reduced led Europeans to continue seeking treaty relationships with Africans – and the same reason perhaps motivated Africans to continue to agree to them. But these arrangements clearly did not amount to monopolistic distortions of trade.

If the problems of maintaining their probably rhetorical claims of primacy were not enough, the chartered companies, like the Portuguese before, could not necessarily control their "servants," the factors on the coast, from entering into service with the Africans or at least conniving with them. Instructions regularly emphasized the need to prevent company factors from dealing directly with or defecting to the Africans. Likewise, although the Dutch and other European powers found it convenient to deal with the previous group of defectors – the now well established communities of Portuguese (or their largely Africanized descendants) – they clearly hoped to get away from relying on them as well; these communities exemplified the potential for failure in their own attempts to control trade.

Company servants could easily be assimilated into trading communities under African sovereignty. Renegade servants of the companies sometimes went into business for themselves, perhaps through the re-

[77] Heerman Abramsz to Assembly of Ten, 23 November 1679, in Albert van Danzig, ed. and trans., *The Dutch and the Guinea Coast, 1674–1742: A Collection of Documents from the General State Archive at the Hague* (Accra, 1978), pp. 13–20.

[78] See ibid., pp. 13–20, and Short Memoir on Trade within the Present Limits of the Charter of the WIC, 1670, ibid., pp. 10–12 (for Dutch reports); Public Record Office, London (hereafter PRO), T/70, vol. 1134, Henry Greenhill letter, 7 December 1680 and 6 April 1681, and John Sowe, 10 June 1683; Oxford University, Bodleian Library, MSS Rawlinson C 745, fols. 209–10, 212, John Winder, 24 June 1683; fol. 215, Mark Whiting, 26 June 1683; fol. 217, 30 June 1683.

sults of a fortunate marriage with a local woman. Thus, when the Prussian officer Otto Friedrich von der Gröben visited the English post at Bence Island (Sierra Leone) in 1682, he noted that most officers, including the governor, had "concubines," who had borne them children.[79] These concubines provided local connections. A report on the situation to the Royal African Company (to which all the officers had to report) noted that "every man hath his whore ffor whom they steal, &c."[80] From such communities there arose an English-oriented, racially mixed group of country traders all over Sierra Leone, with connections to both the companies and the African rulers.[81] By the eighteenth century these groups would be of special benefit to English trade.

African states and commerce

It is fairly clear, then, that European merchants, whether acting under the direction of states or companies, were unable to monopolize the trade of Africa. It is just as clear that African states, although attempting the same sort of thing, were ultimately no more successful. No African state ever really dominated the trade of any part of the African coast. African sovereignty was just as fragmented as the theoretical sovereignty that Europeans tried to maintain over the trade.

However, the African states did help to balance whatever economies of scale individual European merchants or companies may have had. Thus, it might be argued that a well-capitalized European merchant could have taken economic advantage, at least in the short run, of intense competition between hundreds of African traders. The African states' role in commerce limited this effect, however, thus offsetting whatever advantages a shipper's scale of operations might have afforded.

State requirements put a great number of legal and technical obstacles between European merchants and African buyers, as well as making the state itself a regular participant in the trade. A Dutch commercial guide of about 1655, for example, records the gifts and taxes that had to be paid in a variety of countries along the "Slave Coast" area from the Volta to Cameroon. Those at Allada were perhaps the most complicated, although perhaps only because the writer of the guide (apparently resident in São Tomé) understood them best. There, the prospective buyer

79 Otto Friedrich von der Gröben, *Guineische Reisebeschreibung nebst einem Anhang der Expedition in Morea* (Marienwerder, 1694; modern facsimile ed., 1913), pp. 28–9. Adam Jones has produced a new (English) edition from manuscript sources (with original pagination) in *Brandenburg Sources*.

80 Clarke to Company, 1 March 1684/4, PRO, T70/11, p. 134; quoted in Jones, *Brandenburg Sources*, p. 27, n. 10.

81 Rodney, *Upper Guinea Coast*, pp. 216–22.

of slaves and cloth from Allada had to present a complex series of presents to dancers, food sellers, linguists, brokers, Allada nobles, and the king himself, both upon arrival and upon departure.[82] That such a system was not unique to Allada is clearly shown in the variety of customs the guide describes at Benin, Calabar, the Niger delta, and the Gabon region. Although few were as complicated as those at Allada, all involved gifts to rulers or councillors, with the amount varying by status or position.[83]

On the Gold Coast, where a Portuguese post and fort had existed since 1482, the lengthy personal visits of the traders were replaced by regular presents given by the Portuguese state to all the local potentates. Documents of the early sixteenth century are filled with notices of these presents, which are only indirectly tied to trade.[84] When conducting trade, the Portuguese still had to deal with, and pay, the *xarife*[85] (so-called by analogy to their own system), an official in charge of commercial affairs, who was sufficiently important in Efuto at least that he stood a chance of eventually becoming king.[86]

Sometimes the arrangements varied over time. In Benin, for example, the earliest Portuguese ships' books from the 1520s stress a lengthy series of gifts to officials and a visit to the ruler, who then "opened the market" for each of the commodities to be traded (including separate markets for male and female slaves). English visitors a half century later, on the other hand, negotiated only with the ruler himself, perhaps because their interest was largely in pepper and the king was the only producer, or perhaps because the political system in Benin had changed. Subsequent visitors in the seventeenth century found officials once again in charge of trade, and moreover, traders were no longer taken to the capital to negotiate but conducted their business at the port of Ughoton.[87]

Likewise, on the Gold Coast, the gifts paid by the Portuguese to local rulers gradually became an annual tax of rent, although always bearing the guise of a gift.[88] On the other hand, anyone trading in the region still had to deal with officials, even though these officials occasionally used the complexities of local politics to set themselves up as rulers of what seemed to be independent states. Even what seemed like private trade

[82] UBL: BPL, MS. 927, "Aenwijsingse," fols. 12–13v. The author of this guide seems to have resided in São Tomé and to have detailed information about the period 1647–54.
[83] Ibid., fols. 9v, 10v–11, 13v.
[84] Vogt, *Portuguese Rule,* pp. 82–7, 231, nn. 63–79.
[85] Ibid., p. 87; such transactions are numerous in the surviving records; cf. Elbl, "Portuguese Trade," p. 640, n. 48, for a list of relevant documents.
[86] ANTT CC, sec. I, 3/119, Nuno Vas de Castello Branco to King, 2 October 1502.
[87] Traced in Ryder, *Benin and the Europeans,* pp. 43–79.
[88] Kwame Daaku, *Trade and Politics on the Gold Coast, 1600–1720* (London, 1970).

with merchant caravans, such as the Akani traders, was in fact state-sanctioned – hence carefully controlled.[89]

These negotiations, which were often time-consuming and which many European visitors thought to complain of, were essentially a manifestation of the insistence on the part of authorities in African states that they benefit first and certainly from trade. They were often willing to provide return gifts, sometimes of substantial value, after customs were paid (as van den Broecke noted in Loango),[90] as a way of making a special connection between themselves and the European with whom they were trading. But typically their desire was to ensure that they received first choice of the best goods and the best price, which perhaps constituted a second tax that went along with the gifts that made up the customs charges.

Thus, rulers generally insisted on getting a special price for their own goods and for the purchase of the European goods. Da Mosto noted that the ruler of Kayor with whom he dealt insisted on taking his pick of the goods, and their understanding that the trade was an extension of their friendship probably meant he also got a special price.[91] More specifically, the Dutch guide to trade at Allada emphasized that the king and his officials must get a better price on what they sold and on what they bought than the rest of the people when discussing maximum and minimum prices to fix for goods.[92]

Similarly, André Donelha noted that Gaspar Vaz, a Mandinga linguist and tailor who had once been a slave of one of Donelha's friends and was closely related to the "Duke" of Cassanga in the Gambia, could get him the "current" price for his goods, rather than the one usually charged to foreign purveyors of European goods.[93] Richard Jobson, an English merchant who was on the Gambia at the same time, shows how this special price was arranged. When dealing with the king iron bars twelve inches long were used, whereas with commoners the bars were only eight inches.[94] Thus, only by using a state connection could a foreign merchant avoid the general custom of paying special prices to high-status Africans.

Related to this was the concept that African rulers, should they deem it expedient, could start and stop trade at will. The ruler of Benin, as we have already seen, had the power to open and close the market – and

89 Cf. Kea, *Settlements*, pp. 226–36, 248–87.
90 Van den Broecke, *Reizen* (ed. Ratelband), p. 28.
91 Da Mosto, "Novo Mondo" (ed. Gasparrini-Leporace), pp. 49–50.
92 UBL: BPL, MS. 927, "Aenwijsingse," fol. 12v.
93 Donelha, *Descrição da Serra Leoa*, fol. 25v.
94 Richard Jobson, *The Golden Trade; or, A Discovery of the R. Gambia and the Golden Trade of the Aethiopians . . .* (London, 1623; facsimile reprint, London, 1968), p. 120.

there were separate markets for a wide range of commodities. It was surely for reasons of state, though these are unknown for certain, that the king of Benin decided to shut down the male slave market in the early sixteenth century, and then eventually to eliminate trading in slaves altogether.[95] Likewise, the king of Kongo occasionally instituted strict regulation or even prohibited commerce altogether. Both Afonso I and his successor Diogo regulated commerce in this way.[96]

But after African rulers had insisted on involving their sovereign rights to control trade or guarantee their profits, they were usually content to allow trade to take place freely once they had received their share. But very often even this trade was far from being the commercial free-for-all of a real market. This was because although African states allowed private trade, they played a major role in determining which Africans would be able to trade. The African bourgeoisie, like their counterparts in Europe, thrived largely because the state supported their position, and in many ways they used this patronage to their advantage.

Consider the case of the trade between Julas and various European traders along the Senegambian coast. Jobson's description of the commercial life of the Gambia in 1620 reveals that most of the commerce with visiting ships was handled by local Portuguese settlers (often from the Cape Verde Islands) near the mouth of the river (on whom, more later), while upstream it was in the hands of the "Marybuckes" (marabouts – traveling Moslem scholars who also traded). Jobson noted that the Marybuckes, whom he reveals in other contexts to be *jula*s (a Mandinka term for merchants), possessed their own towns (worked by their own slaves) in a great network that stretched deep into the country, by which they were in touch with the commercial life of the interior.[97] André Donelha, for his part, also noted that as Moslem scholars these merchants were important counselors of the rulers and enjoyed a special relationship with and privileges from the state. Whether directly or indirectly, one of these privileges seems to have been the right to control trade and certainly to control the negotiations between the state and visiting traders.[98]

That these or other African merchant groups should have this favored position in the state is not surprising. Just as the European states found that it was better to leave commercial risks in private hands and charge a steady and sure tax and only monopolize lines of business that were of interest to state security, so African rulers adopted the same policies with

95 Ryder, *Benin and the Europeans*, pp. 45, 167–9.

96 Afonso to João III, 18 October 1526, *MMA* 1:489–90; Francisco Barros da Paiva to King, 18 February 1549, *MMA* 2:231–7.

97 Jobson, *Golden Trade*, pp. 3–7, 62, 75–6.

98 Donelha, *Descrição da Serra Leoa*, fols. 29–29v; Jobson, *Golden Trade*, p. 98.

merchants from their own region (or with Europeans and mulattos who defected to them). That such a concession would also be useful to the commercial group was, of course, part of the enticement rulers offered to attract settlers.

Of course, the close control of trade by African states had its origins in their legal systems and represented a type of market interference that their European counterparts followed as well. What happened in those areas where there was little state control demonstrates the value of state oversight and reveals how potentially dangerous and unpredictable trade in the early modern world was. For example, in the southern part of Sierra Leone, along the Gabon coast, and along what was variously called the Grain Coast, the Malaguetta Coast, or the Ivory Coast, European vessels often paid no taxes and engaged in no special negotiations in order to trade. Instead, Africans in groups of two or three would sail small canoes out to the ships for small-scale, impromptu bargaining over ivory, malaguetta pepper, foodstuffs, and occasionally gold.[99] But the commerce was always risky. Without the protection of a state, the Africans were sometimes carried away by the Europeans as slaves, or African traders would jump ship with European commodities in their possession before payment had been completed. Trading was always conducted with great caution and much bad faith on both sides – and perhaps in the end, without much profit.[100]

In Africa, as in Europe, of course, state attempts to monitor and control access to the market were defeated by some of the private merchants themselves. The Jula merchants involved in the Gold Coast gold trade did not hesitate to send their products to Senegambian or even North African markets if the proper quantity and quality of trade goods were not found on the Gold Coast. Francisco de Goes, the Portuguese factor on the Gold Coast in 1506, spoke of this tendency as the "Mandinga leak" in one of his reports complaining of the lack of suitable trade goods at his post.[101] Later, in the seventeenth century, Curtin has carefully documented the degree to which the Julas switched their trade from one port to another on the Senegambian coast to receive the best price and to thwart occasional attempts on the part of European companies to monopolize one region.[102]

99 Dierick Ruiters, *Toortse der zee-vaart*, p. 303 (Vlissingen, 1623; reprint, Hague, 1913), p. 71 (original pagination is marked, and followed hereafter).

100 Ibid., pp. 303, 316. See the remarks in Arent Roggeveen and Jacob Robjin, *The Burning Fen* (Amsterdam, 1687; facsimile ed., Amsterdam, 1971), pp. 19, 30. The book, though late in publication, probably reflects a view of the whole previous century of Dutch experience.

101 Francisco de Goes to King, 19 August 1506, ANTT, CC I/13/48, Manuel Góis to King, 18 April 1510, *MMA* 1:210–11.

102 Curtin, *Economic Change*, pp. 83–91.

In central Africa, one finds the same situation with regard to the Vili merchants of Loango, who regularly sent slaves from as far away as Matamba to Loango to circumvent Portuguese attempts to restrict the trade to the Luanda market. This rivalry was behind Portuguese complaints of Vili behavior in 1655[103] and a similar attempt to get Queen Njinga to put them out of Matamba in the treaty of 1683.[104]

Thus, although the states of the Atlantic persistently sought to direct and control trade, their purpose was really more to enhance their revenue by marginally distorting the market and not to achieve the kind of real monopoly that would seriously change the overall terms of trade between African sellers and European buyers. For even though states wanted control, and even though they were fairly successful in gaining control at the point of any given transaction, the presence of private traders, their interconnections, and the military and political rivalries of both African and European state systems went a long way to reduce the potential impact of state control. Although the state might be a silent beneficiary, employ the trade as a tool for taxing traders, and insist that its own interests and those of its favored clients take precedence, trade remained competitive, probably favoring no particular national or regional actors – and certainly not Europeans at the expense of Africans.[105]

103 John Thornton, *The Kingdom of Kongo: Civil War and Transition, 1641–1718* (Madison, 1983), p. 26.

104 David Birmingham, *Trade and Conflict in Angola: The Mbundu and Their Neighbours under the Influence of the Portuguese, 1483–1790* (Oxford, 1966), pp. 131–3.

105 For an excellent discussion and critique of contrary views, see Curtin, *Economic Change*, pp. 299–302; and Elbl, "Portuguese Trade," pp. 614–17, 653–69.

3

Slavery and African social structure

If Africans were experienced traders and were not somehow dominated by European merchants due to European market control or some superiority in manufacturing or trading techniques, then we can say confidently that Africa's commercial relationship with Europe was not unlike international trade anywhere in the world of the period. But historians have balked at this conclusion because they believe that the slave trade, which was an important branch of Afro-European commerce from the beginning, should not be viewed as a simple commodity exchange. After all, slaves are also a source of labor, and at least to some extent, their removal from Africa represented a major loss to Africa. The sale of slaves must therefore have been harmful to Africa, and African decisions to sell must have been forced or involuntary for one or more reasons.

The idea of the slave trade as a harmful commerce is especially supported by the work of historical demographers. Most who have studied the question of the demographic consequences of the trade have reached broad agreement that the trade was demographically damaging from a fairly early period, especially when examined from a local or regional (as opposed to a continental) perspective. In addition to the net demographic drain, which began early in some areas (like Angola), the loss of adult males had potentially damaging impacts on sex ratios, dependency rates, and perhaps the sexual division of labor.[1]

[1] John Thornton, "Demographic Effect of the Slave Trade"; also see idem, "Sexual Demography: The Impact of the Slave Trade on Family Structure," in Martin Klein and Claire Robertson, eds., *Women and Slavery in Africa* (Madison, 1983): 39–48; and (for a later period) idem, "The Slave Trade in Eighteenth Century Angola: Effects on Demographic Structures," *Canadian Journal of African Studies* 14 (1980): 417–27; Patrick Manning, numerous articles, e.g., "Local versus Regional Impact of the Export Slave Trade," in Dennis Cordell and Joel Gregory, eds., *African Population and Capitalism: Historical Perspectives* (Boulder and London, 1987): 35–49. More recent work dealing with the constantly evolving statistical study of exports (but mostly concerned with the eighteenth century) is

In addition to these demographic effects, historians interested in social and political history have followed Walter Rodney in arguing that the slave trade caused social disruption (such as increasing warfare and related military damage), adversely altered judicial systems, or increased inequality. Moreover, Rodney argued that the slave trade increased the numbers of slaves being held in Africa and intensified their exploitation, a position that Paul Lovejoy, its most recent advocate, calls the "transformation thesis."[2] Because of this perception of a widespread negative impact, many scholars have argued that the slave trade, if not other forms of commerce, must have been forced on unwilling African participants, perhaps through the type of commercial inequities that we have already discussed or perhaps through some sort of military pressure (to be discussed in a subsequent chapter).

When Rodney presented his conclusions on the negative impact and hence special status of the slave trade as a branch of trade, it was quickly contested by J. D. Fage, and more recently, the transformation thesis has been attacked by David Eltis. As these scholars see it, slavery was widespread and indigenous in African society, as was, naturally enough, a commerce in slaves. Europeans simply tapped this existing market, and Africans responded to the increased demand over the centuries by providing more slaves. The demographic impact, although important, was local and difficult to disentangle from losses due to internal wars and slave trading on the domestic African market. In any case, the decision makers who allowed the trade to continue, whether merchants or political leaders, did not personally suffer the larger-scale losses and were able to maintain their operations. Consequently, one need not accept that they were forced into participation against their will or made decisions irrationally.[3]

The evidence for the period before 1680 generally supports this second

reviewed in Paul Lovejoy, "The Impact of the Atlantic Slave Trade on Africa: A Review of the Literature," *Journal of African History* 30 (1989): 365–94.

[2] For example, Walter Rodney, "African Slavery and Other Forms of Social Oppression on the Upper Guinea Coast in the Context of the Atlantic Slave Trade," *Journal of African History* 7 (1966): 431–43. Rodney modified his views in this article in response to criticism; see idem, "The Guinea Coast," in *Cambridge History of Africa*, 8 vols. (London, 1975–85), 4:223–324. For a recent modified restatement, see Paul Lovejoy, *Transformations in Slavery: A History of Slavery in Africa* (Cambridge, 1983), pp. 108–34, 269–82.

[3] The original Rodney–Fage debate, in the *Journal of African History* (1966–9), is reprinted in J. E. Inikori, ed., *Forced Migration: The Impact of the Export Slave Trade on African Societies* (New York, 1982). Fage returned to the theme in "Slaves and Society in Western Africa, 1440–c. 1700," *Journal of African History* 21 (1980): 289–310. More recently, the issue has been argued by David Eltis, *Economic Growth and the Ending of the Transatlantic Slave Trade* (Cambridge, 1987), pp. 72–8 (largely for the eighteenth and nineteenth centuries), and in a more general way by Eltis and Lawrence C. Jennings, "Trade between Western Africa and the Atlantic World in the Pre-Colonial Era," *American Historical Review* 93 (1988): 936–59.

position. Slavery was widespread in Africa, and its growth and development were largely independent of the Atlantic trade, except that insofar as the Atlantic commerce stimulated internal commerce and development it also led to more widespread holding of slaves. The Atlantic slave trade was the outgrowth of this internal slavery. Its demographic impact, however, even in the early stages was significant, but the people adversely affected by this impact were not the ones making the decisions about participation.

In order to understand this position it is critical to correctly comprehend the place of the institution of slavery in Africa and furthermore to understand why the structure of African societies gave slavery a different meaning than it had in Europe or the colonial Americas. The same analysis explains the reasons for slavery's extension (if indeed it was extended) during the period of the Atlantic trade and its correlation with commercial and economic growth.

Thus, as we will see in this chapter and the next, the slave trade (and the Atlantic trade in general) should not be seen as an "impact" brought in from outside and functioning as some sort of autonomous factor in African history. Instead, it grew out of and was rationalized by the African societies who participated in it and had complete control over it until the slaves were loaded onto European ships for transfer to Atlantic societies.

The reason that slavery was widespread in Africa was not, as some have asserted, because Africa was an economically underdeveloped region in which forced labor had not yet been replaced by free labor.[4] Instead, slavery was rooted in deep-seated legal and institutional structures of African societies, and it functioned quite differently from the way it functioned in European societies.

Slavery was widespread in Atlantic Africa because slaves were the only form of private, revenue-producing property recognized in African law. By contrast, in European legal systems, land was the primary form of private, revenue-producing property, and slavery was relatively minor. Indeed, ownership of land was usually a precondition in Europe to making productive use of slaves, at least in agriculture. Because of this legal feature, slavery was in many ways the functional equivalent of the landlord–tenant relationship in Europe and was perhaps as widespread.

Thus, it was the absence of landed private property – or, to be more precise, it was the corporate ownership of land – that made slavery so pervasive an aspect of African society. Anthropologists have noted this

4 This argument is found in a number of analyses of African political economy, e.g., Jack Goody, *Tradition, Technology and the State in Africa* (London, 1971), and more recently in Ralph Austen, *African Economic History*.

feature among modern Africans, or those living in the so-called ethnographic present or traditional societies.[5] Anthropologists have regarded the absence of private or personal ownership of landed property as unusual, because it departs from the European pattern and from the home cultural experience of most anthropological observers, and has therefore seemed to require an explanation.

For example, Jack Goody argued that technological backwardness and low population densities made land plentiful, and hence personal property in land had to await technological change. Likewise, he and others, perhaps influenced by European socialist thinking or the liberal economic notion of opportunity for all, argued that the absence of private property in land also meant an absence or at least a mitigation of exploitation and inequality.[6]

The evidence, however, does not necessarily support such explanations. For example, African population densities in many areas were surely large enough to warrant division of land, if landed property is somehow the result of competition for land. The average density in seventeenth-century Lower Guinea (roughly the southern half of Ghana, Benin, Togo, and Nigeria) was probably well over thirty people per square kilometer, or well over the average European density of the time.[7] Indeed, the Capuchins who visited the area in 1662 regarded it as so populated it resembled "a continuous and black anthill" and noted that "this kingdom of Arda [Allada] and most of this region [Lower Guinea] exceed in number and density [the population] of all other parts of the world."[8] Moreover, African societies surely did possess inequalities and exploitation, as we shall see.

One must remember that landownership is ultimately simply a legal fiction. Owning land in the end never amounts to more than owning dirt, and it is ownership of the product of the land that really matters. European landowning actually established the right of the owner to claim the product or a rent on the product. Landownership was therefore really ownership of one of the factors of production, with a concomitant right to claim the product of the factor. The division of land was

5 A general description, based on extensive anthropological investigation, can be found in Paul Bohannan and Philip Curtin, *Africa and Africans*, 3d ed. (Prospect Heights, Ill., 1988), pp. 129–46.

6 This is the core argument of *Tradition, Technology and the State*, and is adopted in a variety of ways in other work, such as Austen, *African Economic History*, John Iliffe, *The Development of Capitalism in Africa* (London, 1983), and more recently idem, *The African Poor: A History* (Cambridge, 1987). For a position rooted in liberal economics, see A. G. Hopkins, *An Economic History of West Africa* (London, 1973), pp. 22–7.

7 For this estimation, built on the possible "carrying capacity" of the area for the slave trade, see the argument in Thornton, "Demographic Effect."

8 Biblioteca Provincial de Toledo, Colección de MSS Borbón-Lorenzano, MS. 244, Basilio de Zamora, "Cosmographia," fol. 50.

more the result of legal claims than simply a reaction to population pressure. In any case, population pressure itself has historically often been more the result of unequal landownership claims than a product of demography.

But there are other ways to establish a claim of social product, such as taxation (through the rights of the state or other corporate group) or slavery and other personal relations of dependency. Thus, just as ownership of land as a factor of production establishes a right to the product of that factor, so, too, ownership or control of labor (people or slaves) can provide the same right. African law established claims on product through taxation and slavery rather than through the fiction of landownership.

The African social system was thus not backward or egalitarian, but only legally divergent. Although the origins and ultimate significance of this divergence are a matter for further research, one important result was that it allowed African political and economic elites to sell large numbers of slaves to whoever would pay and thus fueled the Atlantic slave trade. This legal feature made slavery and slave trading widespread, and its role in producing secure wealth linked it to economic development.

Exploring this legal divergence can help to elucidate this important factor in African participation in the Atlantic economy. Sixteenth- and seventeenth-century European observers were fully aware that African societies were both politically and economically inegalitarian and that these inequalities were represented in social and legal structures. But their understanding of those social and legal structures was usually shaped by European terms and the institutions they represented. Thus, although some recognized the absence of landed private property, many made Africans into landholders in spite of themselves.

European witnesses, after all, came from an area where the concept of landownership and income based on its lease to tenants was the fundamental starting point of law. Church law on landed property placed its origin in ancient times and made it a universal principle of "Natural Law."[9] The *Siete partidas*, the Castillian law code that formed the basis for most Iberian law and had a major impact even on modern law codes, argued that all land should have an owner and that if land was not owned by private persons, it ought to be owned by the state. Thus, productive resources would be divided up (the purpose of law being to

9 E.g., Innocent IV, *Commentaria doctissima in Quinque Libros Decretalium* (Turin, 1581), 3.34.8, fol. 176v, quoted and discussed in James Muldoon, *Popes, Lawyers and Infidels* (Liverpool, 1979), p. 8.

allow everyone to "know his own") so that people could derive their support and income from the production of their own part of these resources.[10] Considerable space was devoted to specifying how ownership of land was established, to preventing tenants from claiming ownership of their landlord's land, and the like.[11]

Coming from this background, the idea that land was not private property was inconceivable. One common way to reconcile African law and the concept that landed property was a natural and essential part of civilization was to describe land in Africa as being owned by the king (as a substitute for corporate ownership by the state). Hence, in 1602, the Dutch trader and traveler Pieter de Marees described the rulers of the Gold Coast as owners of the land, their income being a form of ground rent,[12] and the Italian Capuchin missionary Giacinto Brugiotti da Vetralla spoke of royal ownership of all land in Kongo in 1659.[13]

Perhaps conscious that royal ownership might not be the best explanation of African revenue systems, others sought to explain royal incomes through the idiom of taxes. In European law, the state had the right to tax land without owning it, and hence when states took income that did not derive from rent, this might be seen as a tax. In Europe, of course, the tax was assessed on land, and thus owners paid tax based on how much land they owned and its assessed value. But in Africa people rather than land were taxed, another indication of the absence of landed property. Thus, a text of about 1628 referring to Kongo noted that a source of royal income was a universal tax charged by "the head" rather than on land.[14] The idea that people were charged rather than land was also applied by some observers to Benin, where the entire population

10 *Las siete partidas del Rey D. Alfonso el Sabio* (ed. Gregorio Lopez, Madrid, 1555; indexed edition of Joseph Berní y Cefalá, Valencia, 1767), pt. 1, title 1, law 2.

11 Ibid., pt. 3, title 30, laws 1–5; pt. 4, title 30, law 5; pt. 4, title 28, laws 34–8.

12 De Marees, *Beschryvinge*, pp. 47a–49a, 56a. For a full discussion of this and other sources, see Kea, *Settlements*, pp. 16–20, 112–22.

13 Giacinto Brugiotti da Vetralla, "Infelicità felice o vero mondo alla rovversa" (lost MS of ca. 1659), summarized and quoted in Giuseppe Simonetti, "Il P. Giacinto da Vetralla e la sua missione nel regno di Congo," *Bolletino della Società Geografica Italiana* 10 (1907): 374.

14 Biblioteca Apostolica Vaticana, MS Vaticana Latina, 12156 (anonymous text of ca. 1628), partial French translation in Jean Cuvelier, *L'ancien Congo d'après les archives romaines* (Brussels, 1954), pp. 133–4. For a commentary on this text and its possible authors, see John Thornton, "The Correspondence of the Kongo Kings, 1614–35: Problems of Internal Written Evidence on a Central African Kingdom," *Paideuma* 33 (1987): 408–14. For a fuller discussion of Kongo's tax system, see Thornton, *Kingdom of Kongo*, pp. 23–7. Note that in this discussion, these taxes are described as "rent" (in large measure because Kongo economic texts used the term *renda*, meaning "rent-bearing land or estate" in Portuguese), but this should be taken as economic rent rather than rent in the legal sense; see Barry Hindress and Paul Hirst, *Pre-Capitalist Modes of Production* (London, 1975), pp. 221–55.

was regarded as being "slaves of the king" (although other types of slaves were recognized as well).[15]

One might also note that African systems of taxes, or state dues, included more than simple money charges: They might also include rights to labor and service. Hence, in describing the rights of kings in Sierra Leone, the early Portuguese resident Alvaro Velho (who lived there from 1499 to 1506) noted that "none of the kings . . . draw any income from their subjects, except when they wish to cultivate or sow or gather the harvest, then everyone in their jurisdiction must provide them free labor, or to build houses and town walls or go to help him in war."[16]

Since taxes, in the European concept, were charges assessed with the specific purpose of paying for a particular government service, some writers, noting the more general-purpose nature of African assessments, thought of them as "tribute" – payments owed a sovereign by virtue of his authority. It was in this regard that Alvaro Velho noted of the ruler of Falop (a state in modern Guinea-Bissau) that "no king in Ethiopia is so well paid his tribute as this king."[17]

These points converge to imply corporate ownership of land by the state, a convenient half-way house that modern research supports. But even in this case the state's real control was exercised more over people (as in Benin) than over land. The same claims might also be made by a family unit (as a corporation); that is, a kinship group can also be seen as owning both people and land. Modern anthropologists who have examined African kinship systems have found that most African societies have (or had in the recent past) kinship systems that define fairly large units of people. Each group is descended from a (usually mythical) common ancestor, and descent is often defined in such a way that an inegalitarian unit is created.[18] These units often control access to specified tracts of land. Restated in religious terms, land is often said to have been claimed by some ancient ancestor, typically the first to settle on unoccupied territory, on behalf of his descendants. Alternatively, a tutelary deity might be seen as owning the land and giving it to a descent

[15] Willem Bosman, *A New and Accurate Description of the Coast of Guinea* (Utrecht, 1704; first English trans., London 1705; facsimile, with annotations, by John D. Fage and Ray Bradbury, London, 1967), p. 430. This passage states directly that all were free men but treated as slaves, though it was judged to be an honor to bear the title of "king's slave."

[16] Fernandes, "Descriçã," fol. 129.

[17] Ibid., fol. 118.

[18] On the ideology of lineage in a modern context, see Pierre Phillipe Rey, *Colonialisme, néo-colonialisme et transition au capitalisme* (Paris, 1972), for a full development of the idea of a "lineage mode of production."

group. In some societies, the issue of land is secondary, and the lineage actually "owns" its people.[19]

The sixteenth- and seventeenth-century sources rarely give the kind of detailed information that will allow a description of the ideology of landownership or revenue claims or how kinship groups or lineages were constructed, but the traditions of states, especially their origin traditions, that survive from the period do provide some ideas. These traditions typically related to the foundation of the state and define others by kinship or other relationships with the founder. Such traditions were recorded for the central African states, such as Kongo and Ndongo.[20]

The Italian Capuchin Girolamo da Montesarchio, who spent twenty years in Kongo, observed that before any Kongo authority could collect income or exercise authority, he first had to pay homage to the *kitomi,* a priest of the tutelary deities (or ancestors) of the region.[21] In a similar vein, the rulers and officials of the states of Sierra Leone often governed their states and held their authority as members of "congregations" devoted to tutelary deities called *corofims* in Portuguese sources[22] (probably the modern Temne term *krifi*). The close connection between ancestral and territorial deities in much of Africa represents a merger of the corporate claims of lineages and different sorts of claims made on behalf of states. Furthermore, in the Ndongo traditions at least, the complex genealogy of the founding lineage that is included in the story of foundation certainly points to the idea of a particular lineage "owning" a state.[23] But we cannot go farther except to say that the basic idiom of these traditions

19 For a particularly clear explanation, see Philip Curtin, Stephen Feierman, Leonard Thompson, and Jan Vansina, *African History* (Boston, 1978), pp. 156–71 (a contribution by Stephen Feierman, based on East African data but applicable in general).

20 Kongo traditions are discussed in Thornton, "The Kingdom of Kongo, ca. 1390–1678: The Development of an African Social Formation," *Cahiers d'études africaines* 22 (1983): 325–42. For an overview of the Ndongo traditions (though not with this exercise in mind) see Beatrix Heintze, "Written Sources, Oral Traditions and Oral Traditions as Written Sources: The Steep and Thorny Way to Early Angolan History," *Paideuma* 33 (1987): 263–88.

21 Girolamo da Montesarchio, "Viaggio al Gongho," fols. 26, 32v–33. A modern edition, Calogero Piazza, *La Prefettura Apostolica del Congo alla Meta del XVII secolo: La relazione inedita di Girolamo da Montesarchio* (Milan, 1976), reproduces this with the original pagination, which I follow here. In my examination of the original in the Archivio Provinciale dei Cappuccini da Provincia di Toscana, Montughi Convent, Florence, I found the pages numbered consecutively on alternate pages, rather than only on the recto (and the text is so cited in Thornton, *Kingdom of Kongo*).

22 Fernandes, "Descriçã," fols. 1321v, 139; de Almada, "Tratado breve," *MMA*[2] 3:351–2; Biblioteca da Sociedade de Geografia de Lisboa (henceforward BSGL), Manuel Alvares, "Etiopia Menor e Descripção da Provincia de Serra Leoa" (ca. 1617), fols. 67–68v.

23 For a full elaboration of the various versions of these traditions, collected mostly in the mid-seventeenth century, see Heintze, "Written Sources."

conforms to modern patterns, and thus the ideology may have been the same.[24]

Finally, in other ideological statements, kings might claim the right to tax from the right of conquest. The Kongo traditions, for example, stress that the founder of the state had conquered the people of the country, and his rights to govern and tax them derived from this, rights he partitioned out to "captains" who were appointed by him, not for life but for the performance of service.[25] Likewise, the traditions of the Mane, who dominated Sierra Leone from the later sixteenth century onward, stressed their conquest of the region.[26] Seventeenth-century travelers also recorded traditions of subjugation and tribute exaction as the basis for income in Allada, as well as noting revolts that broke this control.[27]

If state ownership or at least corporate control by the state and its officials can be defined in this way, then obviously lesser property would not exist. But the travelers' accounts often speak of "nobles," occasionally as "owners" of land or at least as those who exercise rights over it. Yet these people ultimately derived their rights from their position in the state and not as landowners in the European sense. Thus, they can be regarded as noble because they held titles but not because they owned land.

For example, John Hawkins, describing Sierra Leone in 1562–8, contended that the nobles "owned" the land, and everyone else had to pay a rent (the payment appropriate for private land) for the right to use it.[28] But in Sierra Leone, as elsewhere, the real owner was the state, and these estates with their rents were really delegated state charges, or revenue assignments. André Donelha and André Alvares de Almada, two Cape Verdians who knew Sierra Leone well at about the same time as Hawkins, and Portuguese Jesuit Manuel Alvares, who resided there for a long time in the early seventeenth century, provide better observations of land and revenue.

As they understood it, the *solatiguis* (the "nobles" of the other descrip-

[24] For a full discussion of political ideology, see Wyatt MacGaffey, *Religion and Society in Central Africa: The Bakongo of Lower Zaire* (Chicago, 1986).

[25] See the discussion in Thornton, *Kingdom of Kongo*, pp. 15–17.

[26] A good synthesis of these traditions, which, however, probably takes them too literally, is found in Rodney, *Upper Guinea Coast*, pp. 38–70. Rodney does identify the continuity between Mane ideology and economic exploitation.

[27] For a summary of these traditions, see Robin Law, "Problems of Plagiarism, Harmonization and Misunderstanding in Contemporary European Sources: Early (Pre-1680s) Sources for the 'Slave Coast' of West Africa," *Paideuma* 33 (1987): 348–9. Echoes can also be found in Biblioteca Provincial de Toledo, MSS Bourbón Lorenzana 244, de Zamora, "Cosmographia," fols. 47–8.

[28] See the account of his voyage in Richard Hakluyt, *Principal Navigations of the English Nation . . .* (1598–1600), in C. R. Markham, ed., *The Hawkins voyages* (London, 1878), p. 20.

tions) did not obtain their territorial jurisdictions by heredity, could not sell or alienate it, and could not pass it on to their progeny (so it was clearly not "theirs"). Instead, it was given to them by the kings as a source of income while they served him as officials. These officials were dismissible at will and could not take their income when they lost office, though they could seek employment (and further income) from a neighboring king.[29]

Hence, rather than being private estates where tenants were charged rents, the nobles' "lands" in Sierra Leone were revenue assignments, as we have already seen. It was thus from charges levied by state authorites that the wealthy nobles lived. On the Gold Coast, for example, de Marees noted that the peasants had to work one day per week on land assigned to officials as a part of the tax system (though he still saw the ultimate owner as the king).[30] A similar system obtained in the central African kingdom of Loango, where peasants were required to work a special field set aside for them to support the nobility or state officials.[31]

In the state of Allada on the Lower Guinea coast, Capuchin travelers of 1660–2 noted that when a *fidalgo* ("noble") died, his office could be reassigned by the king, who also took half of his movable goods and divided the other half among the other nobility, indicating that property rights in income were very limited.[32] In Warri, a small state in the Niger delta, the king could replace members of the two governing councils at will when they died,[33] while in nearby Benin, with a similar system of government, the king's will was even more important for noble success and fortune.[34]

Finally, in Kongo, state officials, like those of Sierra Leone, had no right to income other than that assigned by the state, for if they were

29 De Almada, "Tratado breve," *MMA*[2] 3:334–6; Donelha, *Descrição da Serra Leoa*, fol. 35; BSGL, Manuel Alvares, "Etiopia Menor," fols. 58–58v, 60.

30 De Marees, *Beschryvinge*, pp. 56a–7a; see also Kea, *Settlements*, pp. 123–36, for an extended discussion of revenue systems.

31 Olifert Dapper, *Naukeurige beschrijvinge der Afrikaensche gewesten . . .* (1st ed., Amsterdam, 1668; 2d ed., cited here, Amsterdam, 1676), p. 167.

32 Biblioteca Provincial de Toledo, Coleción de MSS Borbón-Lorenzana, MS 244, Basilio de Zamora, "Cosmografía o descripcion del mvndo" (1675), fols. 64–5.

33 Bonaventura da Firenze, "Come entrò la Fede di Giesu Christo nel Regno d'Ouere per la Prima Volta," fols. 16–16v, published in Vittorio Salvadorini, *Le missioni a Benin e Warri nel XVII secolo: La relazione inedita di Bonaventura da Firenze* (Milan, 1972).

34 Ibid., fol. 29; Alonso de Sandoval, *Naturaleza . . . de todos Etiopes* (Seville, 1627); composed 1624; modern ed., Angel Valtierra, *Instauranda Etiopia salute: El mundo del esclavitude negra en America* (Bogotá, 1957), p. 80; Dapper, *Naukeurige beschrivinge*, p. 127. Alan Ryder has proposed, on the basis of careful reading of some of this literature (and other documents not cited here), that the councils in Benin gradually usurped power from the king during the course of the seventeenth century; a major civil war was necessary to return control to the king (*Benin and the Europeans*, pp. 12–20).

dismissed they possessed no income at all.[35] Our understanding of this might be confused because the Kongo themselves chose the Portuguese term *renda* (meaning "rent," or "rent-bearing property") in their own administrative and judicial texts to describe the revenue assignments they received. But if these lands bore "rent," it did not derive from the holders' claims, for Kongo texts clearly show that a *renda* could be taken away and reassigned freely by the king.[36]

In all this it is clear that what at first appears as private property, or what historians of early modern Europe sometimes call "great property," was not property at all. In each case the holders of titles and owners of income derived from property were beholden to larger corporate groups, sometimes lineages but typically the state, for their income. This was certainly not a source of freely disposable, personal income, even for the head of the corporation or state.

Although many European observers thought that the king or ruler of the state was the ultimate owner of all land, it is more accurate to see land as being owned by the state as a corporation and the ruler as collecting income or acting as an official (perhaps a senior executive officer) of the state. We can see this clearly in a well-documented state like Kongo, where, as we have already noted, many observers thought of the king as owner of the land, and where succession to office was apparently hereditary (though, it might be added, through a complex familial unit).[37] But though a king's son or brother was often the successor in Kongo, the ultimate choice of king lay in a group of electors who were stakeholders for the state. Some kings laid claim to the throne through hereditary rights, and some did not bother too much with the election, but the legal fiction that an election was necessary confirmed

35 Biblioteca Apostolica Vaticana, MSS Vaticana Latins, 12516, in Cuvelier, *L'ancien Congo*, pp. 133–4. For a fuller discussion of these aspects of Kongo's fiscal system, see Thornton, *Kingdom of Kongo*, pp. 38–55. For a different interpretation that stresses trading and control over resources as the source of Kongo's fiscal system (but also corporate property and taxation), see Ann Hilton, *The Kingdom of Kongo* (Oxford, 1985), pp. 19–49.

36 See the early and significant usage by Afonso I in his letter to King Manuel I of Portugal, 5 October 1514, *MMA* 1:295. See also the use in the legal inquest conducted by King Diogo I in the 1550 plot by Pedro Nkanga a Mvika to overthrow him, ANTT II/242/121, passim and esp. fol. 7v (my pagination of an unpaginated text) (this text, with significant omissions and errors of transcription, can also be found in *MMA* 2:248–62). I must confess to contributing to the confusion in my own discussion, for I consistently used the term "rent" in its economic form (as an exploitative charge) rather than its legal form, borrowing from Marxist concepts of rent as well (*Kingdom of Kongo*, pp. 17–20, and "The Development of an African Catholic Church in the Kingdom of Kongo, 1491–1750," *Journal of African History* 25 [1984]: 159–61).

37 I have dubbed this unit the "house" as it included both descent and clientage in its composition, though seventeenth-century traditions clearly show that houses defined themselves by descent from common ancestors; see Thornton, *Kingdom of Kongo*, pp. 47–55.

the idea that the state was not the property of the king or even of his family.[38] The concept of ultimate election by a group of officials was commonplace in central Africa. The same principles were found in neighboring Ndongo as well, where election of one sort or another ratified succession within a family, but here, the genealogical nature of traditions does suggest a stronger, though still checked, tradition of lineage ownership than in Kongo.[39]

Other regions had similar systems, and indeed, although sixteenth- and seventeenth-century sources routinely refer to African rulers as "kings," the term must always be qualified by noting that in many cases they were elected by officials, even if family or hereditary claims were honored and the rulers were overwhelmingly powerful relative to the electors. In Biguba, a state on the coast of modern Guinea-Bissau, Alvares de Almada observed that the executive ("king") was elected from among a group of related families, called *jagras,* and sometimes long civil wars were fought over the position.[40] In Sierra Leone, officials elected the ruler, but he in turn had the right to dismiss them at will upon his accession.[41] A similar process of election by officials of a powerful ruler who could dismiss them was noted by the sources of Dapper's account of the region around Accra on the Gold Coast about 1650.[42]

In Benin, though succession was deemed hereditary by seventeeth-century witnesses, the ruler's accession to the throne had to be confirmed and accepted by two senior officials.[43] He could then appoint or dismiss these officials at will, and he often chose his officials from foreigners (typically from the neighboring Yoruba areas) so as to ignore the claims of the officials' families.[44] A similar system also operated in Warri, south of Benin, where members of the two councils of nobility selected a king, but they could be replaced by the king only when they died, not at his will.[45]

In some cases, these elections did not result in a strong executive, nor were they necessarily limited to particular families. In many of the Gold Coast states, elections enthroned weak rulers or rulers who were checked by the officials. De Marees and early Portuguese sources both noted that

38 See the discussion in ibid., pp. 44–7. For a detailed discussion of Kongo legal views and conflicting claims by various Kongo kings in their own correspondence on the issue of rule of succession, see Thornton, "Correspondence of the Kongo Kings," pp. 414–18.

39 On the complicated situation in Ndongo, see John Thornton, "Legitimacy and Political Power: Queen Njinga, 1624–63," *Journal of African History* 32 (1991): 25–40.

40 De Almada, "Tratado breve," *MMA*² 3:323.

41 BSGL, Alvares, "Etiopia Menor," fol. 58; de Almada, "Tratado breve," *MMA*² 3:334.

42 Dapper, *Naukeurige beschrijvinge,* pp. 82–3, 120.

43 Ibid., pp. 128, 130.

44 De Sandoval, *Instauranda,* p. 80.

45 Bonaventura da Firenze, "Come entrò," fol. 16–16v.

rulers were elected "by the people" (leading families) or "by captains" (officials).[46] The executive power of such an official might be limited; Andreas Ulsheimer, visiting the Gold Coast in 1601, thought that "a village mayor in our country has more authority than such a king."[47] Similarly, at Guinala, a state on the coast of modern Guinea-Bissau, Alvares de Almada described elections by two groups of people, one of which he called "nobles" and the other "commons" (perhaps on the analogy of Republican Rome), that often chose someone who was old and weak and would not challenge them.[48]

Thus, in states where kings were powerful and could make some sort of hereditary claim on succession, describing the state and its revenue as the king's property might be reasonably correct. Likewise, cases where the officials laid hereditary claim on their offices and revenue assignments also might be seen as a form of private property not unlike the great landed estates of the European nobility. Michal Tymowski, for example, has argued that in the Songhay Empire of the Niger valley, certain sixteenth-century revenue assignments of rice-producing estates and hereditary grants of income from villages constituted the birth of "great landed property."[49] But even here, great property was limited by ultimate corporate control, at least in legal terms.

We have good reason to believe that Africa did not have small property, that is, plots of land owned by cultivators or let out to rent by petty landlords, just as it did not have great property. Of course, this must be conditioned by saying that African legal systems did ensure security of tenure for petty cultivators. What little we know about peasant land tenure in sixteenth- and seventeenth-century Africa suggests that those who cultivated land had fairly secure rights to farm but probably not to sell, alienate, or rent this land. However, we have every reason to believe that Africans owned *products* of the land (but not the land itself), for they clearly could alienate any agricultural or manufactured product by sale, and therefore it is clear that African law recognized a law of property in general. Presumably this right also protected crops under cultivation and perhaps even fallow land, thus

46 De Marees, *Beschryvinge*, p. 47a ("*ghemeen volk*" probably does not mean all the common people, but rather common in the sense of not being "noble"); Agustin Manuel y Vasconcellos, *Vida y acciones del Rey D. Juan el Segundo* (Madrid, 1639, translation based on a Portuguese original of 1624, which is not longer extant), pp. 81, 84.

47 Andreas Ulsheimer, "Warhaffte Beschreibung ettlicher Raysen . . . in Europa, Africa, Ostindien und America" (1616), fol. 47a, modern edition (with English translation) in Adam Jones, *Brandenburg Sources*, pp. 97–129.

48 De Almada, "Tratado breve," *MMA*[2] 3:334–6.

49 Michal Tymowski, "Les domains des princes du Songai: Comparaison avec la grande propriété foncière en Europe au début de l'époque féodale," *Annales: Economies, sociétiés, civilisations* 25 (1970): 1637–58.

providing secure land tenure that protected cultivated crops and the immediate agronomic rights of producers but did not extend to land as income-producing property.

Dapper, in describing land tenure in Loango, wrote that land was held in common (hence, no private property), and to secure the right to cultivate land, one had to do no more than begin farming in vacant land, although the rights would be surrendered once the peasant ceased cultivation.[50] Peasants in the Gold Coast, according to de Marees, had to seek royal permission to cultivate uncultivated land and agree to pay tax as a condition (hence very close to rent), but they were not bound to the land so cleared or vulnerable to expulsion.[51] The peasants might have individual tenure of the land, or they might work it in common. Dionigio Carli da Piacenza, an Italian Capuchin who lived in Kongo in 1667–8, gave a good description of communal tenure in which the whole village worked land together and divided the product by household "according to the number of people in each."[52]

At first glance, this corporatist social structure seems to allow no one to acquire sources of income beyond what they could produce by their own labor or trade if they were not granted a revenue assignment by the state. Modern commentators on Africa have occasionally noted this, and precolonial African societies have sometimes been characterized as unprogressive because the overdeveloped role of the state inhibited private initiative by limiting secure wealth. In particular, these commentators believed that the absence of any form of private wealth other than through the state greatly inhibited the growth of capitalism and, ultimately, progress in Africa.[53]

It is precisely here, however, that slavery is so important in Africa, and why it played such a large role there. If Africans did not have private ownership of one factor of production (land), they could still own another, labor (the third factor, capital, was relatively unimportant before the Industrial Revolution). Private ownership of labor therefore provided the African entrepreneur with secure and reproducing wealth. This ownership or control over labor might be developed through the

[50] Dapper, *Naukeurige beschrijvinge*, p. 167.

[51] De Marees, *Beschryvinge*, pp. 56a, 57b; Kea, *Settlements*, pp. 16–21.

[52] Dionigio Carli da Piacenza, "Relation nouvelle et curieuse d'un voyage au Congo, fait ès années 1666 et 1667," in Jean-Baptiste Labat, *Relation historique de l'Ethiopia occidentale*, 5 vols. (Paris, 1732), 5:131–3; see another version in idem, *Il moro trasportado nell'inclita citrà di Venezia* (Bassano, 1687), pp. 43–5.

[53] These conceptions are notable in Marxist writing. For instance, Maurice Godelier proposed applying the concept of the "Asiatic Mode of Production" to African societies; his views were followed up and modified in Catherine Coquery-Vidrovitch's classic article, "Towards an African Mode of Production," in David Seddon, ed., *Relations of Production: Marxist Approaches to Economic Anthropology* (London, 1978).

lineage, where junior members were subordinate to the senior members, though this is less visible in older documentation.[54]

Another important institution of dependency was marriage, where wives were generally subordinate to their husbands. Sometimes women might be used on a large scale as a labor force. For example, in Warri, Bonaventura da Firenze noted in 1656 that the ruler had a substantial harem of wives who produced cloth for sale.[55] Similarly, the king of Whydah's wives, reputed to number over a thousand, were employed constantly in making a special cloth that was exported.[56] Such examples give weight to the often-repeated assertion that African wealth was measured in wives, in the sense both that polygamy was indicative of prestige and that such wives were often labor forces.

Of course, the concept of ownership of labor also constituted slavery, and slavery was possibly the most important avenue for private, reproducing wealth available to Africans. Therefore, it is hardly surprising that it should be so widespread and, moreover, be a good indicator of the most dynamic segments of African society, where private initiative was operating most freely.

The significance of African slavery can be understood by comparing it briefly with slavery in Europe. Both societies possessed the institution, and both tended to define slaves in the same way – as subordinate family members, in some ways equivalent to permanent children. This is precisely how slaves are dealt with in *Siete partidas*, following a precedent that goes all the way back to Aristotle, if not before.[57] Modern research clearly reveals that this is also how Africans defined slavery in the late precolonial and early colonial period.[58]

Seventeenth-century African data do not deal with the legal technicalities, though we have little reason to believe that they differed from those uncovered by modern anthropological research. For Kongo, where the

54 However, it is much discussed in modern anthropological literature, for example, in Pierre Phillipe Rey, *Colonialisme, néo-colonialisme et transition au capitalisme* (Paris, 1974). In many cases, however, the idiom of kinship was simply the ideological expression of dependency or inferior status, and not necessarily the cause of it.

55 Da Firenze, "Come entrò," fols. 16, 19.

56 Thomas Phillips, "Journal of a Voyage Made in the *Hannibal* . . . to Africa . . . [1693–4]," in Awnsham Churchill and John Churchill, eds., *A Collection of Voyages and Travels*, 6 vols. (London, 1732), p. 236.

57 E.g., *Siete partidas*, pt. 1, title 1, law 3; pt. 3, title 30, law 3; pt. 4, title 25, law 2. For deeper Greek and Roman roots, see Aristotle *Politics* 1.2 and Justinian *Digest* 41 1.10.

58 For a lengthy discussion of data and debate, see Suzanne Meiers and Igor Kopytoff, "African 'Slavery' as an Institution of Marginality," in idem, eds., *Slavery in Africa: Historical and Anthropological Perspectives* (Madison, 1977), pp. 1–84. Although I accept many of their observations about differences between African and European or Euro-American slavery with regard to role and treatment, legally the institutions were indistinguishable, and I see no need for the use of quotation marks when using the term "slavery" in Africanist texts.

remarkable documentation allows glimpses of the underlying ideology, the term for a slave, *nleke*, was the same as for a child, suggesting the family idiom prevailed there.[59]

Where the differences can be found is not in the legal technicalities but in the way slaves were used. In theory, there might have been no differences in this respect either, but in practice, African slaves served in a much wider variety of ways than did European or Euro-American slaves. In Europe, if people acquired some wealth that they wished to invest in secure, reproducing form, they were likely to buy land. Of course, land did not produce wealth by itself, but usually the land was let out to tenants in exchange for rents or was worked under the owner's supervision by hired workers. In neither case would such people have to have recourse to slaves to acquire a work force.

From what we know of slave labor in Europe in this period, it would appear that they were employed in work for which no hired worker or tenant could be found or at least was willing to undertake the work under the conditions that the landowner wished.[60] As we shall see, this lay behind most of the employment of slaves in the New World as well. Consequently, slaves typically had difficult, demanding, and degrading work, and they were often mistreated by exploitative masters who were anxious to maximize profits. Even in the case of slaves with apparently good jobs, such as domestic servants, often the institution allowed highly talented or unusual persons to be retained at a lower cost than free people of similar qualifications.

This was not necessarily the case in Africa, however. People wishing to invest wealth in reproducing form could not buy land, for there was no landed property. Hence, their only recourse was to purchase slaves, which as their personal property could be inherited and could generate wealth for them. They would have no trouble in obtaining land to put these slaves into agricultural production, for African law made land available to whoever would cultivate it, free or slave, as long as no previous cultivator was actively using it.

Consequently, African slaves were often treated no differently from peasant cultivators, as indeed they were the functional equivalent of free tenants and hired workers in Europe. This situation, the result of the institutional differences between Europe and Africa, has given rise to the idea that African slaves were well treated, or at least better treated than European slaves. Giacinto Brugiotti da Vetralla described slaves in central Africa as "slaves in name only" by virtue of their relative freedom

[59] Thornton, *Kingdom of Kongo*, pp. 21–2.

[60] For a survey of slave employment in early modern Europe, see Heers, *Esclaves et domestiques*.

and the wide variety of employments to which they were put.[61] Likewise, as we shall see, slaves were often employed as administrators, soldiers, and even royal advisors, thus enjoying great freedom of movement and elite life-styles.

This did not mean, of course, that slaves never received the same sort of difficult, dangerous, or degrading work that slaves in Europe might have done, although in Africa often such work might just as easily have been done by free people doing labor service for the state. In any case, Valentim Fernandes's description of slave labor in Senegambia around 1500, one of the few explicit texts on the nature of slave labor, shows that slaves working in agricultural production worked one day a week for their own account and the rest for their master, a work regime that was identical for slaves serving in Portuguese sugar mills on the island colony of São Tomé in the same period.[62] Slaves employed in mining in Africa may have suffered under conditions similar to those of slaves in European mining operations, though the evidence is less certain.[63]

On the whole, however, African slavery need not have been degrading or the labor performed by slaves done under any more coercion (or involving any more resistance) than that of free laborers or tenants in Europe. Therefore, the idea that African dependence on slave labor led to the development of a reluctant work force or inhibited innovation is probably overdone.[64]

61 Giacinto Brugiotti da Vetralla, "Nelle schiavi che si cõprano e vendero nel regno di Congo" (ca. 1659), Archivo "De Propaganda Fide," Scritture originali referite nel congregazione generale, vol. 250, fol. 28.

62 On Senegambian slaves, see Fernandes, "Descriçã," fol. 92v (the page is placed backward in the manuscript in Bayerische Staatsbibliotek, Munich, Codex Hispanicus 102). The text at this point in the manuscript is independent in many places of da Mosto's (1455–6) description of Senegambia. Da Mosto describes slavery in general, but the passage on work days is only found in the Fernandes MS. (cf. fols. 344–47v and note the terms of trade in horses given on fol. 91, marginal note per 1455). For slavery on São Tomé around 1540, see "Navigazione da Lisbona all'isola di San Tomé, posta sotto la linea dell'equinoziale, scritta per un piloto portroghese e mandata al magnifico conte Rimondo della Torre . . . ," Giovanni Battista Ramusio, *Delle navigationi et unggi*, 3 vols. (Venice, 1550–9; facsimile ed., Amsterdam, 1980; modern reedition with new pagination, ed. M. Milanesi, 6 vols., Milan, 1978), 1:579.

63 See Kea, *Settlements*, pp. 201–2. Kea bases this assessment on two sources: a passage in Fernandes (mentioning slaves in mines and the establishment of slave households fed from royal stocks) and a second one in a memorial of 1572 proposing a Portuguese-sponsored project to seize and work the gold mines. Kea argues that the proposals reflected local use patterns and supplies some archeological evidence in support of enclosed work camps. One should note, however, that it also resembles European mining using slaves in Colombia (New Granada) in the same period (see Chapter 6).

64 My position differs from that of Lovejoy (*Transformations in Slavery*), who sees slavery moving from a marginal institution to a central one and focuses on changes in the "mode of production" (i.e., a labor regime) rather than the institution. Unfortunately, Lovejoy's analysis is marred by his inability to quantify the number of slaves in Africa in 1500 (and hence to judge the real growth) and his decision not to distinguish between

For Europe and the European colonies in America, the distinction between the productivity of slave and free labor may have validity (though even there it is a matter of intense debate);[65] in Africa the distinction is probably less applicable. The exact nature of the labor regime, rather than the legal status of the workers, is more relevant to a description of African economic history, and in this instance, different legal structures led Africans and Europeans to develop the institution of slavery in substantially different ways. Consequently, the conventional wisdom concerning slavery developed from the study of European or colonial American societies with landed private property simply cannot apply in Africa.

African slaves were typically used in two different ways. First of all, slaves became the preeminent form of private investment and the manifestation of private wealth – a secure form of reproducing wealth equivalent to landowning in Europe. Second, slaves were used by state officials as a dependent and loyal group, both for the production of revenue and for performing administrative and military service in the struggle between kings or executives who wished to centralize their states and other elite parties who sought to control royal absolutism.

The private employment of slaves as heritable, wealth-producing dependents was perhaps the most striking African use. Dapper, in describing private wealth in Kongo, noted that although the households of the nobility were not wealthy in ready cash, nor did they possess much in the way of luxury goods, they were wealthy in slaves. This, he believed, was the main form of wealth in central Africa.[66]

Likewise, slaves represented the way to achieve wealth for ambitious commoners in the Gold Coast states, and the state did attempt to regulate their acquisition. According to de Marees, a commoner who had become wealthy through trade might be able to attain noble status by sponsoring an expensive ceremony in which nobility was conferred upon him. Although the ceremony was ruinously expensive, the noble-to-be was willing to undertake it because it allowed him to acquire slaves,[67] which, as Dapper noted a few years later, would make it possible for him to recover the expenses of the ceremony, for "as soon as he

slavery as a legal institution and slavery as a "mode of production," in that he assumes people called "slaves" in documents all had a similar labor regime. For a blanket assessment of slavery as an essentially nonprogressive form of labor control (and a source of African backwardness), see Iliffe, *Development of Capitalism in Africa,* chap. 1.

[65] E.g., Robert Fogel and Stanley Engerman, *Time on the Cross: The Economics of American Negro Slavery,* 2 vols. (Boston, 1974), and the stormy critique led by Herbert Gutman (*Slavery and the Numbers Games: A Critique of* Time on the Cross [Urbana, 1975]) and Herbert Gutman and Richard Sutch (eds., *Reckoning with Slavery: A Critical Study in the Quantitative History of American Negro Slavery* [New York, 1976]).

[66] Dapper, *Naukeurige beschrijvinge,* p. 202.

[67] De Marees, *Beschryvinge,* pp. 85b–87a.

gets some goods he bestows them on slaves, for that is what their wealth consists of."[68]

Recently, several historians have followed the careers of some prominent Gold Coast merchants who rose from relative obscurity to become great economic and political actors on the coast, using documentation from the records of the Dutch, English, and Danish commercial houses. In all these accounts, the acquisition of slaves to carry goods, cultivate lands, protect the household, and assist in trading figures prominently as an essential step.[69] Indeed, the careers can in some ways be seen as parallel to that of the European commoners who invested first in land and then in titles of nobility, though in Africa, of course, the investment was in slaves and then in nobility.

Slaves as reproducing wealth figured prominently among the Julas and other Moslem commercial groups of the western Sudan and Senegambia. Richard Jobson, the English gold trader who spent considerable time traveling up the Gambia deep into the Sudan in the 1620s, noted that the Julas ("Juliettos") had constructed a chain of villages worked by their slaves, who provided them with provisions and served as carriers on their commercial expeditions.[70] The heads of these villages acquired special rights (in some ways equivalent to those of nobility) from the rulers of the states in which they settled. Philip Curtin's detailed study of the Julas and other Moslem commercial groups in the late seventeenth and early eighteenth centuries emphasizes their extent and organization.[71] Yves Person, focusing on a later period, compared them to the French bourgeoisie rising from common to noble status or seizing power if thwarted: hence he compared a series of "Dyula Revolutions" from the late eighteenth century onward to the French Revolution.[72]

Thus, in Africa the development of commerce and of social mobility based on commerce was intimately linked to the growth of slavery, for slaves in villages performing agricultural work or carrying goods in caravans or working in mines under private supervision were essential to private commercial development.

This last point is significant to consider in the transformation thesis.

68 Dapper, *Naukeurige beschrijvinge*, p. 114. This passage occurs in a section of Dapper that was clearly drawn from de Marees's account and can be taken to be a commentary upon it.

69 Daaku, *Trade and Politics;* David Henige, "John Kabes of Komenda: An Early African Entrepreneur and State Builder," *Journal of African History* 18 (1977): 1–19; Kea, *Settlements*, esp. pp. 288–320;

70 Jobson, *Golden Trade*, pp. 62–70 and passim. Jobson typically calls the Julas "Marybuckes" (marabouts), emphasizing their religious profession, but on occasion he mentions them as "Juliettos" (Julas).

71 Curtin, *Economic Change*, pp. 59–91. Curtin pays relatively little attention, however, to domestic uses of slaves; see pp. 153–6.

72 Yves Person, *Samori: Une révolution dyula*, 3 vols. (Paris, 1968–75).

Both Rodney and Lovejoy, advocates of the idea that the development of the Atlantic slave trade extended slavery and resulted in larger numbers of people being enslaved and being worse treated, see this as a direct external input, foreign to African political economy. Yet, the development and extension of slavery, if it did take place (and this point is never proved by either author),[73] might just as well be seen as the result of economic growth in Africa, perhaps stimulated by commercial opportunities from overseas, perhaps by a growing domestic economy. Even the increased incidence of maltreatment (another point that is completely without proof) may indicate only more aggressive use of the labor force by entrepreneurs, just as the European work force faced increased exploitation during the early stages of the Industrial Revolution.

The use of slaves by private people to increase and maintain their wealth was just one of the ways in which slaves were utilized in African societies. Another one, almost of equal importance, was their use by the political elite to increase their power. Slaves employed by the political elite might be used as a form of wealth-generating property, just as they were in private hands, or they might be used to create dependent administrations or armies. In this latter capacity, Africa created many wealthy and powerful slaves.

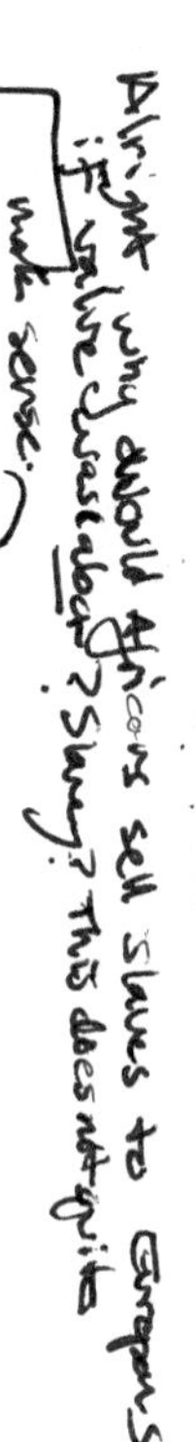

Most large African states were collections of smaller ones that had been joined through alliance and conquest, and typically the rulers of these smaller constituent states continued to exercise local authority, and the ruler of the large state found his power checked by them. Developing private resources that would answer only to themselves was an important way in which African rulers could overcome such checks and create hierarchical authority centered on their own thrones. Slaves, who could be the private property of a king or his family or might also be the property of the state, were an ideal form of loyal workers, soldiers, and retainers.

The powerful Sudanese empires relied heavily on slave armies and slave administrators to keep a fractious and locally ascendent nobility in check. These nobles were often descendants of the rulers of the constituent smaller states; this was probably the status of the territorial rulers of Mali in al-'Umari's fourteenth-century description.[74] These constituent states were called *civitas* by Antonio Malafante, a Genoese traveler who

[73] In order to prove the point, one would need statistical information on the numbers of people enslaved before and during the slave trade era relative to the overall level of population. The study of African demography is still in its infancy, and there are no data except manipulated assumptions (as, e.g., in Lovejoy, "Impact of Atlantic Slave Trade," pp. 390–2) on the numbers of slaves in any African society before colonial statistical inquiries of the late nineteenth century.

[74] al-'Umari, "Masalik al-absar," in Hopkins and Levtzion, *Corpus,* p. 260.

left a description of the empire of Songhay and its neighbors in 1477, a term that implies both subordination and self-government in Latin.[75] An anonymous description of the "Empire of Great Fulo" written about 1600 states that it dominated the whole Senegal valley and was composed of some twenty smaller units.[76] In accounts of the western provinces of Mali during the late fifteenth and early sixteenth centuries, Portuguese travelers describe local "kings" (heads of constituent states) as virtually sovereign in their local rights and government, yet simultaneously describe Mali as a powerful overlord.[77] These descriptions and later ones of Mali and Kaabu, a state that based its authority on being a province of Mali, all reveal apparent local sovereignty coexisting with the apparently strong rights of the overlord, who at least extracted tribute and obedience and might even intervene in local affairs.[78]

One can observe the same with regard to a somewhat shadowy kingdom of "Kquoja" that dominated Sierra Leone from a capital near Cape Mount in the late sixteenth and early seventeenth centuries. Although Alvares de Almada noted that the Kquoja kings collected regular tribute and taxes[79] from local rulers, historians have generally not seen it as a unitary state.[80]

In some cases, perhaps including both Kaabu and sixteenth-century Mali, the strength of local states did cut in on revenue and authority exercised by their overlords, but slaves often offered a way around this. Alvise da Mosto's description of Jolof in the mid-fifteenth century provides a good example. Here, according to da Mosto, the king was beholden to three or four other powerful nobles, each of whom controlled a region (clearly the constituent states), gave him revenue when they chose, and moreover exercised the right to elect him. But the king was

75 "Copia cujusdam littere per Antonium Malafante a Tueto Scripe Juane Johanni Mariono, 1447," edited with French translation in de la Roncière, *Découverte*, 1:153–5.

76 Anon., "Relacion y breue suma delas cosas del reyno del Gran Fulò," in Avelino Teixeira da Mota, "Un document nouveau pour l'histoire des Peuls au Senegal pendant les XVème et XVIème siècles," *Boletim Cultural da Guiné Portuguesa* 24, no. 96 (1969), p. 48 (reprint Agrupamento de Estudos de Cartografia Antiga, no. 56, Lisbon, 1969). Teixeira da Mota has attempted an identification of the units mentioned in this document on pp. 16–25.

77 Fernandes, "Descriçã," fols. 106–7v (clearly describing the prerogatives of local kings within "Mandinga") and 108–108v (a separate sheet, not genuinely connected to this first one, describing the powers of the emperor of Mali); see also Pacheco Pereira, *Esmeraldo*, bk. 1, chap. 29 (ed. Silva Dias).

78 de Almada, "Tratado breve," *MMA*[2] 3:271, 283, 298; Donelha, *Descrição da Serra Leoa*, fols. 15v–16v; BSGL, Alvares, "Etiopia Menor," fols. 8v, 10, 13, 133, and passim. Historical debates concerning when the empire of Mali declined arise because of the various interpretations of these texts; cf. Nehemia Levtzion, *Ancient Ghana and Mali* (London, 1973), pp. 94–102, with Madina Ly, "L'empire du Mali a-t-il survécu jusqu'à la fin du XVIe siècle? *Bulletin, Institut Fondamental de l'Afrique noire* 38 (1967): 234–56.

79 De Almada, "Tratato breve," *MMA*[2] 3:359–60.

80 See Adam Jones, "The Kquoja Kingdom: A Forest State in Seventeenth Century West Africa," *Paideuma* 29 (1983): 23–43.

able to obtain revenue of his own by distributing slaves in villages to each of his several wives; this income belonged to him. Not only did this give him independent support, but it allowed him to develop a large retinue of dependents who carried out his administrative tasks, numbering some 200 people in all. Unfortunately, the fact that at least one of his subordinates, "Budomel" (title of the ruler of Kajoor [Kayor]), was doing the same thing at the local level may well have ultimately limited his capacity to develop more central power.[81]

Sixteenth- and seventeenth-century evidence from the *Tarikh al-Fettash*, a locally composed source on Songhay, shows quite clearly how the development of an army and administration of slaves helped that empire to become centralized. Tymowski has analyzed this text and showed that rice plantations worked by slaves, as well as villages of slaves settled throughout the country, supported an army of slaves and a bureaucracy of slaves through which the emperors conducted their business,[82] neglecting whatever obligations they may have had to the local nobles.

Slavery probably also aided centralizing monarchs in central Africa as well as West Africa. Kongo seems to have originally been a federation of states, at least as sixteenth- and seventeenth-century tradition and law described it. The original kings of the federation owed their election to the votes of several electors, who were the heads of the member states.[83] But collecting slaves into a central place gave the Kongo kings great power – the capital city of Mbanza Kongo and its surrounding area formed a great agricultural center already in 1491,[84] and probably had ten times the population density of rural areas a century later.[85] The slaves, many of whom occupied estates around the capital, provided Kongo with both the wealth and the demographic resources to centralize. As early as 1526, documents from Kongo show that the provinces

81 Da Mosto, "Mondo Novo" (ed. Gasparrini-Leporace), pp. 42–3, 54.

82 Michal Tymowski, *Le développement et régression chez les peuples de la boucle du Niger à l'époque précoloniale* (Warsaw, 1974), pp. 86–97. Tymowski occasionally depends upon corrupt versions of the texts of these *Tarikhs* relating to slave groups, which were clearly inserted in the nineteenth century to justify local conditions. On these groups and the textual history of the *Tarikh al-Fettash*, see Nehemia Levtzion, "A Seventeenth Century Chronicle by Ibn al-Mukhtar: A Critical Study of the *Ta'rikh al-Fettash*," *Bulletin, School of Oriental and African Studies* 34 (1971): 571–93. I have checked Tymowski's references against the apparatus of the Arabic text (published by Oliver Houdas and Maurice Delafosse [Paris, 1913; reprint, 1964]) and found that most of the crucial ones (to slave villages given as gifts to *sharufa* or the rice plantations, as well as administrative and military positions) occur in the uncorrupted MS. A as well as in MS. C.

83 This interpretation is found in Thornton, "Kingdom of Kongo,"

84 It is described in a text of 1491 as equaling the Portuguese city of Evora in size (letter of the Milanese ambassador to Portugal, 7 November 1491, in Adriano Capelli, "A Proposito di conquiste africane," *Archivo Storico Lombardo*, ser. 3, 10 [1896]: 416).

85 John Thornton, "Demography and History in the Kingdom of Kongo, 1550–1750," *Journal of African History* 18 (1977): 524–7.

(constituent states) were in the hands of royally appointed people (mostly kinsmen),[86] and by the mid-seventeenth century local power and election were regarded more as a curse than a blessing.[87]

Slavery played a role in the centralization of nearby Ndongo as well. Like Kongo, Ndongo rulers may have benefited from the concentration of slaves in their capital – for Kabasa, Ndongo's capital, was also described as a large town in a densely populated area.[88] In addition, the ruler had villages of slaves who paid revenue to him scattered around in his domain. These villages were called *kijiko* (which actually means "slave" in Kimbundu), which a document of 1612 rendered as "populated places whose residents are slaves of the said king."[89] Perhaps more significant in Ndongo, however, was the use that the kings made of slaves as administrators, for the ruler had officials, the *tendala* and the *ngolambole* (judicial and military officials, respectively), who supervised subordinates and collected tax and tribute from his slaves.[90]

We have already seen that African rulers were sometimes limited in the amount of absolute power they could exercise. Some societies had rules of election that allowed officials to choose a weak ruler. In some of the smaller states, the use of slaves may have helped rulers develop more autocratic systems of government. In dealing with the states of the eastern Gold Coast, for example, Dapper noted that they were all quite strongly centralized and, moreover, had an abundance of slaves.[91] Similarly, Alvaro Velho noted that among the smaller states of Sierra Leone, the income that rulers obtained from their slaves was their only steady source of income.[92]

Thus slaves could be found in all parts of Atlantic Africa, performing all sorts of duties. When Europeans came to Africa and offered to buy slaves, it is hardly surprising that they were almost immediately accepted. Not only were slaves found widely in Africa, but the area had a well-developed slave trade, as evidenced by the numbers of slaves in private hands. Anyone who had the wherewithal could obtain slaves from the domestic market, though sometimes it required royal or state

86 See Afonso I to João III, 18 March 1526, *MMA* 1:460–2. Afonso revealed that such practices were already in force as early as 1506 in Nsundi province at least (and probably earlier still) (Afonso to Manuel I, 5 October 1514, *MMA* 1:294–5; and more explicitly in his no longer extant letter of ca. 1508, summarized in de Barros, *Decadas de Asia*, I, bk. 3, chap. 10).

87 Thornton, *Kingdom of Kongo*, pp. 38–43.

88 Francisco de Gouveia to Diogo Mirão, 1 November 1564, *MMA* 2:528.

89 Arquivo Histórico Ultramarino, Papeis avúlsos, Caixa 1, 4 March 1612, quoted in Beatrix Heintze, " Unbekanntes Angola: Der Staat Ndongo im 16. Jahrhundert," *Anthropos* 72 (1977): 776, n. 131.

90 Heintze, "Unbekanntes Angola," pp. 788–91.

91 Dapper, *Naukeurige beschrijvinge*, pp. 86–7.

92 Fernandes, "Descriçã," fol. 92v.

permission, as in the Gold Coast. Europeans could tap this market just as any African could.

Moreover, the most likely owners of slaves – wealthy merchants and state officials or rulers – were exactly the people with whom European traders came into contact. Because merchants selling gold, ivory products, mats, copper bracelets, pepper, or any other trade commodity in Africa would also be interested in the buying and selling of slaves, European merchants could readily find sources. This was not so much because Africans were inveterate slave dealers, as it was because the legal basis for wealth in Africa lay in the idea of transferring ownership of people. This legal structure made slavery and slave marketing widespread and created secondary legal machanisms for securing and regulating the sale of slaves, which Europeans could use as well as Africans.

The significance of African slavery in the development of the slave trade can be clearly seen in the remarkable speed with which the continent began exporting slaves. As soon as the Portuguese had reached the Senegal region and abandoned their early strategy of raiding for commerce, 700–1,000 slaves were exported per year, first with caravans bound for the Sahara (after 1448). After Diogo Gomes's diplomatic mission to the West African rulers in 1456, which opened markets north of the Gambia, exports took a dramatic turn upward, reaching as many as 1,200–2,500 slaves per year by the end of the century.[93]

Thus, from 1450 onward, even before their ships actually reached the Senegal River, Portuguese merchants were buying slaves from northward-bound caravans from the post at Arguim, tapping a longstanding trans-Saharan trade.[94] It is not surprising that Avelino Teixeira da Mota has been able to document the diversion of the Saharan slave trade from North Africa to the Atlantic coast in the same period.[95] The reason that such dramatic numbers were reached immediately may indicate nothing more, therefore, than that a preexisting engagement with foreign markets was transferred to Atlantic ones. Most of the early European slave trading with West Africa, even that with such relatively remote regions as Benin and the Niger delta, known in the sixteenth

93 Magalhães-Godinho, *Descobrimentos,* 2:520–30 (especially for the period 1400–50). Magalhães-Godinho's figures for century's end are what Curtin calls a "capacity estimate" (actually based on observations of Pacheco Pereira), and such figures were probably not reached every year. For a more conservative estimate (though not much different) based on actual statistics collected from quantitative fiscal sources not consulted by Magalhães-Godinho, see Elbl, "Portuguese Trade." One should note, however, that if capacity estimates tend to overestimate the long-term volume of trade, fiscal records probably underestimate it, both due to the erratic survival of relevant records and to the illegal and unrecorded exports.

94 See the comments of Diogo Gomes, "De prima inuentione Gujnee," in Fernandes, "Descriçã," fols. 275–8v.

95 "Aspectos da colonização," pp. 680–1.

century as the "River of Slaves," was simply an internal trade diverted to the Atlantic. Pacheco Pereira mentioned that the country of "Opuu," probably the Jukun kingdom on the Benue River, was a major source of slaves for the region.[96]

The slave trade of the Benin coast shows another interesting aspect of African slavery and the export slave trade. The Saharan trade was mainly an export trade, but it also involved some internal trade. This is demonstrated by the fact that the Portuguese resold a large number of the Benin coast slaves to the Gold Coast. We know that such slaves were not simply used in the coastal mines (though we can be sure that many were) because the king of Portugal ordered this trade to cease (unsuccessfully, as it turns out) to prevent them from being sold to Moslems.[97] These Moslems had to be northern Jula merchants who also visited the coastal goldfields, and thus these slaves may well have been employed in goldfields located quite far in the interior.

That existing internal use and commerce in slaves lay behind the export trade is even more strongly suggested by the trade of central Africa. Unlike the West African trade, which drew on an ancient slave trade with North Africa and might thus have already been affected by external contacts, the central African region had no such external links. Nevertheless, the king of Portugal regarded Kongo as sufficiently important a potential exporter of slaves that he granted settlers in São Tomé privileges to engage in the slave trade in 1493, just a few years after the development of official trade there.[98] Kongo indeed became an important source of slaves for the Tomistas by 1502.[99] Unfortunately we possess no early statistics for the volume of this trade, but Valentim Fernandes noted that around 1507, in addition to some 2,000 slaves working on sugar plantations, the island held 5,000–6,000 slaves awaiting reexport.[100] Presumably these slaves were recent imports who had probably arrived within the last year, and certainly half, but probably the majority, originated in central Africa. When the books of the royal factor on the island were inspected by Bernardo da Segura in 1516, they showed annual imports, mostly from Kongo, of nearly 4,500 slaves.[101]

96 Pacheco Pereira, *Esmeraldo*, bk. 2, chap. 7 (ed. Silva Dias), p. 119. This identification is based on the identification of Opuu as *apu*, the Jukun word for "man." Other identifications have been proposed. Raymond Mauny suggests that it was the kingdom of Nupe in his notes to the French translation of Pacheco Pereira (*Esmeraldo De Situ Orbis* [Bissau, 1956], p. 119), which would not change the tenor of this argument. Ryder's suggestion (*Benin and the Europeans*, p. 35) that Opuu was a name for the Igbo, would weaken it, but on the whole seems unlikely.

97 De Barros, *Decadas de Asia* I, bk. 3, chap. 3.

98 License to settlers in São Tomé, 11 December 1493, *MMA* 15:15.

99 See the legend for Kongo on the Cantino Atlas, drawn about 1502 and reproduced in Cortesão and Teixeira da Mota, *Portvgalliae monumenta Cartographica*, p. 149.

100 Fernandes, "Descriçã," fol. 198.

101 Bernardo da Segura to Crown, 15 March 1517, *MMA* 1:378–80.

Slaves from central Africa were so numerous that they soon exceeded the capacity of São Tomé and the Mina trade to absorb them, and so they began the long journey to European markets. Although most of the slaves available in the port towns of Lisbon, Valencia, and Seville in the 1470s and 1480s came from western West Africa, Jolof in particular,[102] by 1512 "Manicongos" were arriving in Seville,[103] and Portuguese reports of 1513 mention a whole ship from Kongo making delivery in Europe.[104]

Thus, at some point, probably within twenty years of first contact, central Africa was able to supply exports of slaves equal to the entire exports of West Africa. Clearly this sort of volume could not simply have been the occasional export of odd misfits. Nor have we any reason to believe that the Portuguese were able to either acquire the slaves themselves (except as clients of the Kongo kings) or force the Kongo to obtain the export slaves against their will. Instead, the growth of Kongo's trade had to draw on a well-developed system of slavery, slave marketing, and slave delivery that preexisted any European contact.

We must therefore conclude that the Atlantic slave trade and African participation in it had solid origins in African societies and legal systems. The institution of slavery was widespread in Africa and accepted in all the exporting regions, and the capture, purchase, transport, and sale of slaves was a regular feature of African society. This preexisting social arrangement was thus as much responsible as any external force for the development of the Atlantic slave trade.

102 Da Mota, "Aspectos da colonização," p. 681.

103 P. E. H. Hair, "Black African Slaves at Valencia, 1482–1516," *History in Africa* 7 (1980): 132; Alfonso Franco Silva, *Registro Documental sobre la esclavitud sevillano (1453–1513)* (Seville, 1979), no pagination, showing first Kongo slave in 1512.

104 Alvará to Gonçlo Lopes, 19 September 1513, *MMA* 1:278–80; and Alvará to Almoxarife of Ponte do Lima, 13 March 1514, *MMA* 1:285 (on "our ship from Manicongo," implying an annual shipment, perhaps of 300–500 slaves, bound for Spain).

4
The process of enslavement and the slave trade

Warfare and slavery

We have established so far that Africans were not under any direct commercial or economic pressure to deal in slaves. Furthermore, we have seen not only that Africans accepted the institution of slavery in their own societies, but that the special place of slaves as private productive property made slavery widespread. At the beginning, at least, Europeans were only tapping existing slave markets. Nevertheless, one need not accept that these factors alone can explain the slave trade. There are scholars who contend that although Europeans did not invade the continent and take slaves themselves, they did nevertheless promote the slave trade through indirect military pressure created by European control of important military technology, such as horses and guns. In this scenario – the "gun–slave cycle" or "horse–slave cycle" – Africans were compelled to trade in slaves, because without this commerce they could not obtain the necessary military technology (guns or horses) to defend themselves from any enemy. Furthermore, possession of the technology made them more capable of obtaining slaves, because successful war guaranteed large supplies of slaves.[1]

Hence, through the operation of their control over the "means of destruction," to use Jack Goody's descriptive term,[2] Europeans were able to influence Africans indirectly. They could direct commerce in ways that helped them and also compel Africans to wage wars that might otherwise not have been waged. This would cause Africans to seek more slaves than they needed for their own political and economic

[1] For an extreme statement, but carefully argued, see J. E. Inikori, "Introduction," in idem, *Forced Migration*, pp. 45–51, and his introduction to his article "The Import of Firearms into West Africa, 1750 to 1830: A Quantitative Analysis," ibid., pp. 126–53 (as well as the article itself). For a more cautions analysis that tends to the same conclusions, see Lovejoy, *Transformations in Slavery*, pp. 66–8, 78–87, 103–7.

[2] Goody, *Tradition, Technology and the State*.

ends and depopulate the country against their wishes. The quantitative increase would exceed Africans' own judgment of a proper level of exports. In the end, this not only might increase economic dependence but could result in large-scale destruction of goods, tools, and ultimately development potential. Hence, in the end, Africans would be helpless, exploited junior partners in a commerce directed by Europe.

However, this argument will ultimately not be any more sustainable than the earlier commercial and economic ones. Certainly in the period before 1680, European technology was not essential for warfare, even if Africans did accept some of it. Likewise, it is much easier to assert than to demonstrate that Africans went to war against their will or solely to service the slave trade. Indeed the more we know about African warfare and resulting enslavement, the less clear and direct the connections between war and the export slave trade become.

The contemporary evidence strongly supports the idea that there was a direct connection between wars and slavery, both for domestic work and for export. This did not mean that there was no nonmilitary enslavement, of course. Judicial enslavement was one common way of obtaining slaves, and judges, moreover, were not above distorting the law to provide more captives or enslaving distant relatives of guilty parties. Jesuit observers believed that this was common in Ndongo as early as 1600,[3] and missionary travelers often commented on it in the seventeenth-century Upper Guinea region.[4] But however scandalous this may have been, it is unlikely that judicial enslavement accounted for more than a few percent of the total exports from Africa.

Thus the fact that military enslavement was by far the most significant method is important, for it means that rulers were not, for the most part, selling their own subjects but people whom they, at least, regarded as aliens. The fact that many exported slaves were recent captives means that they were drawn from those captured in the course of warfare who had not yet been given an alternative employment within Africa. In these cases, rulers were deciding to forgo the potential future use of these slaves. Some of the exports were slaves whom local masters wished to dispose of for one reason or another and those who had been captured locally by brigands or judicially enslaved.

This is exactly the situation described by da Mosto in his account of Jolof in 1455. After a description of the use of the slaves in the domestic economy, da Mosto noted that most slaves were captured in wars with neighboring countries and the civil wars. Many of these captives were

3 Pierre du Jarric, *Histoire des choses les plus mémorables . . .* , 3 vols. (Bordeaux, 1608–14), 2:80–1.

4 See the documents cited and analyzed in Rodney, *Upper Guinea Coast*, pp. 106–9.

integrated into the domestic economy, but the rest were sold to the "Moors" for horses (i.e., they entered the Saharan trade), although "Christians" had recently entered the trade on the coast.[5] This account focuses on two aspects of African societies that predisposed them to participate in the slave trade. The first is the regular use of slaves in the domestic economy and particularly as revenue for centralizing states, and the second is the role of warfare.

The causes and motivations behind these wars are crucial for understanding the slave trade. Philip Curtin has examined the Senegambian slave trade of the eighteenth century and has proposed a schema for viewing African warfare that resulted in slave captures that can be fruitfully applied to the earlier period as well. He proposes that wars be classified as tending toward either an economic or a political model. In the economic model the wars were fought for the express purpose of acquiring slaves and perhaps to meet demands from European merchants; in the political model wars were fought for mostly political reasons, and slaves were simply a by-product that might yield a profit. Both models are seen as "ideal types," and individual wars might contain a mixture of motives, of course. On the whole, however, Curtin believes that the eighteenth-century Senegambian data support a political, rather than the economic, model.[6]

Actually, discerning between an economic and a political model is not easy in practice. Consider the case of Portuguese Angola, a state seemingly founded on the premise of exporting slaves. Angola's wars ought to fit the economic model if any state's would. Yet many of Angola's wars, and the majority of the most lucrative ones in terms of acquiring slaves, had more or less clear-cut political motives. Portugal's early wars in Angola, for example, were as much for establishing a foothold in the area as for capturing slaves. In 1579, after all, the Portuguese were nearly driven out by the forces of Ndongo, and the wars between then and about 1595 were defensive as much as offensive.[7]

When the Portuguese at last went on the offensive against Ndongo, their series of wars in the early seventeenth century also resulted in gains in territory, and after 1624 they became embroiled in a long series of wars that might be called the War of the Ndongo Succession, in which Portuguese officials hoped to place a pliant king on Ndongo's throne and met with the resistance of Queen Njinga (1624–63).[8] This war, al-

5 Da Mosto, "Mondo Novo" (ed. Gasparrini-Leporace), p. 42.

6 Curtin, *Economic Change*, pp. 153–68.

7 See the summary in Pero Rodrigues, "Relação," 1594, *MMA* 4:565–77, and other documentation in *MMA* 3, passim.

8 Heintze, "Ende," pp. 224–66, on the first ten years of the War of the Ndongo Succession. Later stages are chronicled in Cadornega, *História*, vols. 1 and 2. A concise summary can be found in Birmingham, *Trade and Conflict in Angola*.

most continuous from 1624 until 1655, can account for most of the activities of the Portuguese army in the period, and the expansion of the war to the east can account for the appearance of many eastern Angolan slaves in the New World during this time.[9] Of course, this does not mean that all of Angola's wars fit the political model, but only that we should keep in mind that in Africa, as elsewhere, wars could always be multivalent, even defensive or strategic ones. It was precisely in this context that Cadornega, the chronicler of the seventeenth-century Angolan wars, rejected charges made in Portugal that the Angolan wars were simply "guerras de negros" intended solely to capture slaves.[10]

The Jolof and Angolan models we have just examined suggest that the solution to the problem of the nature of African wars will not be easy to assess. In theory, wars with objectives that Europeans might see as political, such as annexing territory (or defending territory) or acquiring and strengthening political rights, should be classed as political, whereas raids conducted solely to acquire loot or trade goods should be classed as economic. In practice, however, as we have already seen from our previous examination of Jolof politics, capturing slaves made political sense to Jolof rulers as well as economic sense. Slaves were sources of wealth, and even in a hit-and-run operation that did not envision political conquest (although Jolof certainly did make conquests as well), the slaves could be made to produce wealth in the same way that a conquest would. Likewise, Jolof's rulers might employ the slaves to generate private revenue for them or to act as personal servants, soldiers, and administrators and thus raise them up against their rivals for power within Jolof. Hence, even a war that simply resembles a raid with no political objectives would have major political consequences if slaves were taken – and the fact that some were sold to outside parties should not lead us to the conclusion that the war had no political motives.

These considerations thus make it difficult to evaluate testimony about the motivations of warfare by European observers, who thought of wars that netted simply booty, even if this meant slaves, as being economic ventures (i.e., ventures aimed at securing slaves for export). Surely some of the ventures conducted by African rulers seem to have had no other purpose. Edward Fenton believed that his request for slaves in 1580 in Sierra Leone led the ruler to conduct a war merely to fill his requests – a war he thought would net 3,000–4,000 slaves.[11] De Almada, likewise, recalled that once the ruler of Kayor waged a war in 1576 solely to obtain

9 Bowser, *African Slave*, pp. 41–3. See also the amazing variety of central African ethnonyms in Venezuelan "Empadrono" documents in Ermila Trochis de Veracoechea, *Documentos para el estudio de los esclavos negros en Venezuela* (Caracas, 1969), pp. 194–200.

10 Hilton, *Kingdom of Kongo*, pp. 104–6.

11 Fenton, *Troublesome Voyage*, p. 109.

slaves to pay a debt he owed the Cape Verdian merchant.[12] Similarly, several contemporary observers believed that many of the wars waged by the Angolan governor Mendes de Vasconcellos in the early seventeenth century had the acquisition of slaves as their only motive.[13]

Such wars, however, may well have been waged solely in order to acquire slaves even without the demands of Atlantic traders. One example of this comes from Fernandes's late fifteenth-century informants. According to them, the Sanhaja of the desert made war against the people south of them "more for pillage than for power."[14] Likewise, Jannequin de Rochefort argued on the experience of his observations in 1639 that the wars were not for conquest but to raid for people and cattle.[15]

This issue goes to the heart of the unusual nature of African politics and one of the matters that makes it different from Eurasian politics. Just as slavery took the place of landed property in Africa, so slave raids were equivalent to wars of conquest. For this reason, one must apply a different logic to African wars than the equations of political motives equals war of conquest and economic motives equals slave raid. This analysis changes our understanding of the objectives of war and must ultimately change our assessment of African warfare.

Lovejoy, for example, has proposed that warfare was endemic in Africa as a result of political fragmentation. In other words, the very fact that Africa had few large-scale political units meant that wars would be more frequent, and thus enslavement increased. As fragmentation increased (a situation that he believes took place during the period of the slave trade), war naturally increased. Underlying this is the assumption that a political situation of small states would naturally lead to a movement to consolidate them into larger, Eurasian-style polities. Thus, although African politics actually determined the course of warfare, the intrinsic structure of those politics created more wars.[16] Furthermore, one need not consider most wars as being explained by the economic model but by the political model, in which wars were an attempt to remedy the fragmentation by consolidating power. The failure to consolidate was thus the fuel that fired the slave trade.

Lovejoy's solution would be more helpful if it were true that there is a correlation between political centralization and peace, but unfortunately this does not seem to have been the case. This emerges clearly from an

[12] De Almada, "Tratado breve," *MMA*[2] 3:243.

[13] Heintze, "Ende," pp. 231–9; see also documentation in *MMA* 6, passim, which regularly refers to "guerras de negros."

[14] Fernandes, "Descriçã", fol. 69v.

[15] Jannequin de Rochefort, *Voyage*, pp. 86–7.

[16] Lovejoy, *Transformations in Slavery*, pp. 66–87.

examination of the policies of the empire of Songhay, which controlled a huge area in the sixteenth century – larger than any other state at the time and on a scale that rivals most European states. Songhay was an expanding empire and thus waged wars of territorial conquest, capturing slaves along the way. According to the *Tarikh*s, local chronicle sources, for example, Sonni Ali, who ruled from 1468 to 1492 (about the same time as the Atlantic trade developed), conducted some sort of war or campaign in every year of his reign.[17] The campaigns varied in length, size, and complexity, and not all were conducted by the king himself. The chroniclers who described these wars commented often on the motivations of their ruler (which were usually to extend territory, punish insults, retaliate for attacks on his territory, and the like) but never specifically mentioned the capture of slaves as one of the goals, nor did they take the trouble to enumerate or boast of the slaves captured, clearly implying that the Songhay expansion was politically rather than economically motivated.[18]

The exploits of his successor, Askia Muhammed, are less clear, because a different chronicler discussed them, but he too conducted many large expeditions, although perhaps somewhat less frequently than his predecessor. As in the case of Sonni Ali, the acquisition of slaves was never mentioned or the number of captives discussed, and moreover, Askia Muhammed's motivations were similar to those of his predecessor.[19]

But the warfare of an expanding Songhay was perhaps the exception in Africa. This is because most of Africa was, as Lovejoy argues, fragmented. However, this fragmentation was not simply the result of a failure of politics, nor did it increase appreciably during the time in question. Instead, it appears as a constant feature of African society, characteristic of the entire precolonial period.

As a measure of African fragmentation, consider the normal size of African states, based on the boundaries of these states as drawn in Maps 1–3. There was no African state as large as the larger Asian or Euro-American empires of the period. Late imperial China occupied between 3 and 4 million square kilometers of land, the Ottoman Empire some 4 million square kilometers at its height, and the Russian Empire in the

[17] Adam Koraré Ba, *Sonni Ali Ber*, pp. 65–75, worked out from the complicated and not unambiguous notes in the *Tarikh*s.

[18] Cf. *Tarikh al-Fettash*, p. 91.

[19] According to the notes in the *Tarikh al-Fettash*, pp. 133–45, he had annual campaigns in the periods 1498–1502 and 1505–6 and two campaigns between 1507–10 and 1511–14, after which the chronicle becomes vague and ceases an annual account of events. During the period 1492–7, Askia Muhammed was away on a pilgrimage to Mecca and the chronicle covers his life there, though campaigns probably were waged in the Sudan in his absence. Likewise, there were probably campaigns conducted by Askia Muhammed or his generals in the 1514–29 period not recorded in the *Tarikh*.

seventeenth century covered some 2.5 million square kilometers and was expanding rapidly. Mogul India controlled as much as 2 million square kilometers of land. In its American possessions, Spain had effective control over as much as 4.5 million square kilometers.

In Africa, by contrast, the largest states (what historians call empires, like Songhay) controlled areas in the range of 500,000–1 million square kilometers. This was on the scale of Safavid Iran (1.5 million square kilometers) and the larger European states, such as France (with 550,000 square kilometers) and Spain (with its Italian and Burgundian but not Austrian or American possessions – at just under 1 million square kilometers). But states on the scale of Songhay occupied only one part of Africa, principally the rich river valleys of the western and central Sudan, and outside that area there were no states as large (the Lunda Empire, the next-largest state outside the western Sudan region, controlled some 300,000 square kilometers at its height in the nineteenth century, but it was only about half that size in 1680).

Medium-sized states, that is, states with a surface area in the range of 50,000–150,000 square kilometers, or the size of European states like England (150,000 square kilometers) and Portugal (90,000 square kilometers) or the larger of the Italian city-states and German principalities (in the 50,000-square-kilometer range), were found in more areas. By 1680, the Oyo Empire (in Nigeria) may have exceeded 150,000 square kilometers, though not by much. The states of the lower Niger valley, such as Nupe, Igala, and Benin, would have reached close to the middle of this range, and the Hausa states of northern Nigeria (Kano and Katsina at about 60,000 square kilometers, the rest smaller) were in the smaller range. In central Africa, Kongo was by far the largest of the states, with as much as 130,000 square kilometers; other states, like Ndongo, were somewhat smaller but still in this range.

In all, only perhaps 30 percent of Atlantic Africa's area was occupied by states with surface areas larger than 50,000 square kilometers, and at least half of that area was occupied by states in the medium-sized (50,000–150,000 square kilometers) range. The rest of Atlantic Africa was occupied by small, even tiny, states. Of this group, a few states in the southeastern part of modern Ghana and Benin-Togo – including Allada, the core of the later kingdom of Dahomey, and the larger Akan states (Akim, Denkyira, Akwamu, and the core of the later Asante kingdom) – each controlled perhaps 5,000 square kilometers in the late seventeenth century.[20] But they too occupied a relatively small part of the total, and

[20] The Asante kingdom, which would eventually form a medium-sized state with perhaps 100,000 square kilometers, and Dahomey, which eventually controlled a somewhat smaller area, were only beginning to form in 1680.

certainly more than half the area of Atlantic Africa was ruled by ministates whose surface area ranged from 500 to 1,000 square kilometers. If this were not dramatic enough, one should consider that if these statistics were broken down by population, a portion considerably greater than half of all of the people in Atlantic Africa lived in the ministates, because these states were found in the most densely populated parts of the region.

Thus, one can say with confidence that political fragmentation was the norm in Atlantic Africa. By this account, the "typical" Atlantic African probably lived in a state that had absolute sovereignty but controlled a territory not exceeding 1,500 square kilometers (smaller than many American counties, perhaps the area occupied by a larger city). Populations might vary considerably; in the sparsely inhabited areas of central Africa, such a state might have 3,000–5,000 inhabitants, but on the densely inhabited Slave and Gold coasts it could control as many as 20,000–30,000 people. Virtually all the land from the Gambia River along the coast to the Niger delta was in states of this size, and much of the land stretching into the interior. In areas like Angola, ministates like these occupied the mountainous land between Kongo and Ndongo and the area of the Kwanza River between Ndongo and the larger states of the central highlands.

In short, enlargement of scale does not seem to have been a priority for leaders. Historians, anxious to assert that Africans did build large states, have to some extent focused too much attention on the empires and the medium-sized states, and thus the point is often overlooked. But the reasons for Africa's small states were probably not the result of some sort of backwardness that prevented them from seeing the advantages of larger units.

One reason for the smallness of scale (not necessarily the only one) may derive from the legal system, which did not make land private property, and may also explain why the Americas, the other world area without landed property, was also the home of small and even tiny states (outside its own few dramatic empires). In Eurasia, control over large areas of land was essential, because it was through grants of land that one rewarded followers, and this land was normally worked by tenants of one kind or another. Eurasians were relatively less interested in controlling people, for without land, the people's labor could not be assigned or its reward collected by landowners. African states were not concerned with land – for as long as there was no population pressure on the land, more people could always be accommodated. Hence, African wars that aimed at acquiring slaves were in fact the exact equivalent of Eurasian wars aimed at acquiring land. The state and its citizens could increase their wealth by acquiring slaves and did not need to acquire land, unless they were short of land at home (which was not the case, as far as we can tell).

The acquisition of slaves instead of land in wars had other advantages. Whereas conquest of land necessarily required administration of larger areas and expansion of military resources, the acquisition of slaves only required a short campaign that need not create any new administrative conditions. Moreover, conquest of land and its subsequent government usually required sharing the proceeds of land with existing landlords, state officials, and other wealthy members of the defeated state, who might be defeated but usually still had to be coopted. Slaves, on the other hand, were unable to bargain as wealthy landlords might have and could be integrated individually or in small groups into existing structures.

We can see these processes in operation in the case of Sierra Leone. The Sapes, as the early Sierra Leone inhabitants were called in documents of the time, were not creating empires or even larger states. They seem to have exported many slaves, however, for although the Sapes did not apparently enter into the trade immediately, by 1500 they accounted for a large proportion of the slaves imported into Europe. If the frequency of the ethnonym in bills of sale is any guide to relative volume, early sixteenth-century port records have them as the third most common group, behind Jolofs (which probably also includes exports from Songhay and some from Mali) and Mandinkas (Mali exports).[21] The Sape slaves, according to Fernandes's informant Alvaro Velho, were the result of "constant wars" of the region.[22]

These wars do not appear to have been waged for territorial expansion; although we lack the chronicle sources of the Sudanese region to confirm this, certainly there was no consolidation in Sierra Leone as a result of warfare.[23] But as Velho also testified, slaves were used in the domestic economy to increase the ruler's personal income,[24] and perhaps this in itself can explain the propensity for wars that did not in-

[21] P. E. H. Hair, "Black African Slaves at Valencia, 1482–1516: An Onomastic Inquiry," *History in Africa* 7 (1980): 132 (1498); Alfonso Franco Silva, *Registro documental sobre la esclavitud sevillana, 1453–1513* (Seville, n.d. [1979]), no page number: entry for 1502.

[22] Fernandes, "Descriçã," fols. 125–125v; see also the legend of the Cantino Atlas (1502), in Cortesão and Teixeira da Mota, *Monumenta* 1:10, pl. 5. Note that this evidence tends to discount the idea advanced by Rodney (*Upper Guinea Coast*, pp. 60–70) and based on early seventeenth-century Jesuit "complaint" literature that the Sapes were peaceful until the Mane invasion of ca. 1545, whose ambitions for expansion increased warfare and slave raiding.

[23] The area may have undergone some consolidation in the late sixteenth century as a result of the Mane invasion, which is mentioned in numerous contemporary accounts. See the dated account of Rodney, *Upper Guinea Coast*, pp. 39–70, and a partial, but better, account of the resulting kingdom in Jones, "Kquoja Kingdom."

[24] Fernandes, "Descriçã," fol. 129.

crease wealth by the annexation of territory but by the annexation and transport of people.

This feature can also explain the existence, already in Velho's time (1499), of small raids being conducted in the "Rivers" region, composed, according to Fernandes, of Falup raiding parties in canoes penetrating all the rivers of the region.[25] In the sixteenth century the Falup were joined by the Bissagos Islanders, who were soon renowned for their naval attacks on the mainland.[26] This type of war was very common in that region in the sixteenth and seventeenth centuries, where a host of visitors describe canoe-based parties that would move silently and strike suddenly (sometimes at night) and carry off people.[27]

In these instances, the slaves could well have been used either by the rulers of the small states of the area to increase their personal dependents and thus strengthen their power base or by private citizens, merchants, or aristocrats to increase their wealth or to increase their power vis à vis the rulers. Although some of these raids may also have been undertaken to supply European demand, this demand was in addition to the greater African demand for slaves to be used domestically as well as for export.

Many Africans retained females from the raids and sold off males, because the Atlantic trade often demanded more males than females. The Bissagos Islanders held many female slaves, and observers believed that virtually all the productive labor was done by women.[28] Lemos Coelho, a Cape Verdian merchant, believed that many societies held large reserves of slaves who could be sold but who would work for their owners in the meantime.[29] Naturally enough, the Portuguese in Angola fell into the same pattern, retaining many slaves on their plantations along the major rivers, and still selling off many, especially males.[30]

Increasing wealth through warfare and enslavement was of course a cheap way of increasing power. Slaves could be captured in wars and in raids and carried back to the home territory by the victors and put to work, without the attacking armies having to conquer and occupy territory. For small states with small armies, this was a logical way to become richer. But of course, in the medium-sized states and empires, territorial expansion also took place. We have already discussed the wars of expansion in Songhay and Jolof and noted that in addition to increasing terri-

25 Ibid., fol. 117v.
26 De Almada, "Tratado breve," *MMA*^{2} 3:315–20.
27 Ibid., pp. 288, 315–20; Francisco de Lemos Coelho, *Duas descrições seiscentistas da Guiné de Francisco de Lemos Coelho,* edited by Damião Peres (Lisbon, 1935), pp. 42–5.
28 Thornton, "Sexual Demography," pp. 39–48.
29 Pierre Cultru, ed., *Premier voyage de Sieur de la Courbe, fait à la coste d'Afrique en 1685* (Paris, 1913), p. 252.
30 Thornton, "Slave Trade in Eighteenth Century Angola," pp. 417–27.

tory, their wars also resulted in capturing slaves. For the expanding empire, enslavement of the conquered population allowed the rulers of the expanding state to increase their personal wealth and also to build armies and administrative corps of direct dependents, just as the revenues from the conquered territories provided continuous new income. Thus, external expansion could also increase wealth, and the slaves that were a by-product of the wars of expansion could increase centralization at home.

All these factors resulted in an enormous slave population in Africa at the time of the arrival of the first Europeans and during the whole era of the slave trade. They meant that the necessary legal institutions and material resources were available to support a large slave market, one that anyone could participate in, including Europeans and other foreigners. Those who held slaves and did not intend to use them immediately could also sell them, and indeed, this is why the number of African merchants who dealt in slaves was large.

Central African data corroborate this process very well. Although there are few useful records for the pre-1483 period, it is clear that Kongo was expanding territorially during the initial period of Portuguese contact, because it was regularly cited as fighting frequent wars.[31] However, we have also already seen that one of the most important aspects of Kongo's centralization was the development of a large urban center with numerous slaves, giving the ruler an advantage over other members of the coalition that began the kingdom. Political motives such as increasing territory, revenues, and a loyal power base played a role in Kongo as in Jolof.

Thanks to Portuguese participation in some of Kongo's wars, we can find out how slaves were used. As in the other areas, the ostensible motive for wars was quite strictly political. For example, Kongo made war against islands in the mouth of the Zaire River in 1491 to bring them back to obedience.[32] The instructions of the king of Portugal to Gonçalo Rodrigues in 1509 strongly support the idea that slaves were captured in such wars. Rodrigues was given orders concerning how to sell whatever slaves the king of Kongo might choose to grant him for participation in the campaign.[33] A still better description concerns a campaign conducted in 1513 or 1514 against Munza, an enemy south of Kongo. This war was apparently a defensive war, for Munza was said to have attacked

[31] Zorzi, "Informatiõ," fol. 131 (ca. 1515); de Enciso, *Suma*, p. 110 (1519); Saintogne, *Voyages advantureux*, fols. 54, 55 (1536); Saintogne, *Cosmographie* (ed. Musset), pp. 339–40; Letter of Jacome Dias, 1 August 1548, *MMA* 2:180.

[32] Rui de Pina, untitled MS, 1492, fols, 97vb–98va.

[33] Instructions for Gonçalo Rodrigues, *MMA* 4:61.

Afonso's son, the Mweni Mbamba, and the war was to relieve him and punish Munza. King Afonso and the Portuguese in his service sent at least 600 slaves back to the capital during the war (and when the army returned, they brought at least 190 more), of which 510 were diverted to the Atlantic trade. Of all these slaves at least 90 remained in Kongo, and Afonso complained that the Portuguese whom he had entrusted with disposal of the slaves in the war had done so improperly, leaving too few in Kongo and, moreover, among them only those who were "old and thin."[34] Afonso was clearly concerned with both domestic use and foreign exports and, at least in this case, believed that his interests were not served by the export of too many, but he was also clearly willing to allow a substantial number to be sold outside the country.

Perhaps one of the reasons that the central African region was a rich source of slaves was that there were several states like Kongo for whom slaves were both a by-product of wars of expansion and useful in themselves for increasing centralization and loyalty. Beginning around 1520, Kongo ran into the growing power of Ndongo, which like Kongo was expanding and using slaves to support centralization. That such wars as developed in the mid-1520s worked in this way is suggested by several letters of complaint written by Afonso in 1526; in one of his bitterest he deplores the (unofficial) help that the Portuguese gave the ruler of Ndongo,[35] which resulted in the capture and sale of Afonso's subjects, even the nobility.[36] A similar struggle seems to have been waged earlier against the Nziko kingdom, which continued exporting slaves itself, becoming a major exporter by the 1530s.[37] Even the countries that were not leading the expansion might export slaves as a result of this warfare; the inhabitants of the islands in the mouth of the Zaire River, called "Pamzelungos" in sixteenth-century sources, also exported slaves, perhaps taken in unsuccessful attempts by Kongo to suppress their revolts.[38] On the basis of the available evidence it is possible to make a very strong case for a simple political explanation of slave-producing wars, even when these wars did not have expansion as a goal and in spite of the Portuguese involvement and the Africans' own strong interests in exporting slaves.

34 Afonso to Manuel I, 5 October 1514, *MMA* 1:314–15.

35 Not named in the letter but presumably the "vassal" whom Afonso complains of; see John Thornton, "Early Kongo–Portuguese Relations," pp. 192–4; cf. Afonso to João III, 6 July 1526, *MMA* 1:470.

36 Pacheco Pereira, *Esmeraldo*, bk. 3, chap. 2 (ed. Silva Dias), p. 134.

37 João III to Afonso I (ca. 1529), *MMA* 1:526 (noting that the northeastern region was the main exporter of slaves).

38 Afonso to António Carneiro, 5 March 1516, *MMA* 1:359. On the location of the "Pamzelungos," see François Bontinck, "Les 'Pamzelungos' ancêtres des Solongo," *Annales Aequatoria* 1 (1980): 59–86.

Domestic use versus the export of slaves

This interpretation of African politics has reemphasized the importance of domestic slavery in Africa. Obviously, slaves were sufficiently important that one could find many in African societies. Likewise, as we have suggested, exports tended to be drawn from those slaves who were recently captured and had not yet found a place in the society of their enslavers. This aspect of slavery obviously places emphasis on the African decisions concerning which slaves to sell to Europeans and when. These decisions were in turn a product of the specific situation in each country, including price and availability of slaves. In large measure, the decision to participate in the Atlantic trade required that specific conditions be met, and countries often entered and left the trade.

The factors that caused an African region to desist from selling slaves to European buyers are dramatically shown in the case of Kongo and Benin. Both countries were early exporters of slaves, both for São Tomé and for the European trade, where a few people from both regions appear in port records.[39] Yet, Ryder has shown that beginning perhaps as early as 1520 the state of Benin began to restrict the slave trade, finally cutting it off by perhaps 1550.[40] In any case, bills of sale and inventories from the New World do not list Benin slaves in the late sixteenth and seventeenth cunturies.[41] Visitors to Benin in the late sixteenth and seventeenth centuries speak of the area as producing cloth and pepper but do not speak of slave exports.[42] Although it must be considered speculative, it is possible that the demands for labor in these industries conflicted with European demands, and local interests put pressure on the state (or the state itself decided) to restrict exports.

In the case of Kongo, the export of slaves continued longer, for it was only in the late sixteenth and early seventeenth centuries that Kongo began to stop exporting slaves – though most early seventeenth-century sources speak of Kongo as a source for a few slaves.[43] Kongo slaves do not disappear from inventories in part because, unlike Benin, it was still a shipping point for slaves (traded from the interior) and in part because Kongo was still being attacked by its neighbors, either the Portuguese (as in their major war of 1622),[44] Matamba (after Njinga moved her capital there about 1635), or its northern neighbors.

In both cases, the decision to stop exporting slaves may have come as

39 Hair, "Black African Slaves," p. 131; Franco, *Sevillana.*
40 Ryder, *Benin and the Europeans*, pp. 56–90.
41 Bowser, *African Slave*, pp. 40–43.
42 Ryder, *Benin and the Europeans*, pp. 82–5.
43 Thornton, *Kingdom of Kongo*, p. xv.
44 Described in Mateus Cardoso, "Relação da morte," fol. 175–75v (*MMA* 15).

a result of a change in political direction as well as from economic considerations. Both countries seem to have stopped expanding at about the time they stopped their exports, Benin in the 1550s,[45] and Kongo at the end of the century.[46] Less frequent wars may have meant fewer enslaved people and a subsequent increase (at least domestically) in prices for slaves. Both states had also, perhaps, met their domestic demand for labor and both states had developed suitable exports to pay for any imports they desired; these exports, moreover, were items that were labor-intensive and this may have driven slave prices up. In Benin, the goods for export were cloth and pepper, and in Kongo, cloth – the conquest of the cloth-producing eastern regions seems to have been instrumental in Kongo's change.[47] Neither state seems to have been impelled by pressure, either commercial or military, to continue trading in slaves. It was only in the late seventeenth and early eighteenth centuries, under the pressure of civil wars, that slave trading resumed in both places.[48]

We can apply a similar logic when we examine those regions that did not participate in the slave trade immediately. For example, the Gold Coast region exported few slaves during its first century and a half of contact with Europe, in spite of the substantial trade taking place elsewhere. Moreover, the Gold Coast was divided into many states, had many wars,[49] and was characterized by social and political structures similar to those of Sierra Leone, which did participate much more fully in the trade. The Gold Coast states surely used slaves in their domestic economies, and probably to support centralization as well, but they were perhaps less willing to export slaves. Indeed, the Gold Coast states imported slaves from their neighbors and from the Portuguese to meet their needs for labor and political dependents and paid for them in gold. Slightly different economic situations thus led to substantially different strategies for accomplishing the same things.

Some similar sort of logic must also have applied in the northern part of the Gabon coast, north of Loango, where, as on the Gold Coast, there were small states and many wars. Here, too, the decision not to sell slaves in any numbers to Europeans was matched by a decision to im-

45 Ryder, *Benin and Europeans*, pp. 15–18, 73–5.
46 Thornton, *Kingdom of Kongo*, p. xv.
47 See the observations made by Hilton, *Kingdom of Kongo*, pp. 104–19.
48 Ryder, *Benin and the Europeans*, pp. 167–9; Thornton, *Kingdom of Kongo*, pp. 95–6.
49 Wars are mentioned in 1502 (ANTT, Cartas Missivas, 2/180), 1510 (ibid., CC I/9/60, Factor and Officials of Mina to King, 2 September 1510), 1519 (Order of Fernão Correia to Factor, 26 September 1519, *MMA* 1:427), 1520 (ANTT, CC II/91/92, Order of Pacheco Pereira to Factor of Mina, 12 November 1520), a lengthy one in 1548 (ibid., I/80/74, Gonçalo Francisco de Almeyda to King, 14 April 1548), and another protracted war that ended in 1557 (Afonso Gonçalves de Botafogo to Queen, 18 April 1557, fol. 3v, published with English translation in Teixeira da Mota and Hair, *East of Mina*).

port slaves in exchange for supply services and exports of cloth.[50] It was perhaps the fact that cloth was exported that meant that the long stretch of coast between the Volta and Benin rivers, later to be called the Slave Coast, did not immediately export slaves, although two slaves called "Lucumies" (Yoruba) did appear in a 1547 inventory from Española; perhaps they were captives of the wars that disrupted Oyo and its neighbors in the first half of the sixteenth century.[51] Only in the later sixteenth century, as we shall see, when a shadowy series of events led to the rise of states such as Allada and Popo (and perhaps also the Oyo Empire), did this region begin to export slaves.

Thus, the evidence strongly suggests that it was the decisions of African states that determined participation in this particular branch of trade and not so much European pressure. These decisions were the product of processes that our sources can reveal only dimly to us – they probably concerned the relative price of slaves versus the prices of other commodities, competing demands for labor, or the relative price of European imports versus exports other than slaves. Of course, Europeans always had a good market for slaves and naturally they were a preferred commodity, but the Europeans would not abandon trade and relations with a country simply because it would not or could not sell slaves. As long as some exchange was possible, trade occurred. At the same time, however, they were perfectly willing to buy slaves whenever an African country decided to sell them, and they always hoped they could get more.

African warfare and European military technology

Although I have shown that African wars led to enslavement on a large scale and that African politics can explain even slave raids that seem to have no political motive, the hypothesis that Europeans influenced African behavior through control over military resources must still be addressed. Given the significance of warfare for expansion of wealth in Africa, the military case must be carefully examined.

Certainly, Europeans did participate, wherever possible, in African politics, often as "military experts" or advisors, occasionally as armed mercenaries. They did this both officially through government-sponsored

50 See David Patterson, *The Northern Gabon Coast to 1875* (London, 1975), pp. 1–22.

51 "Escriptura que enbio el liçençiado çerrato sobre la hazienda de gorjon," 21 September 1547, in J. Marino Incháustegui Cabral, ed., *Reales cédulas y correspondencias de gobernadores de Santo Domingo*, 5 vols. (Madrid, 1958), 1:237–8. Both men were forty years old in 1547, strongly suggesting enslavement after 1525. On the wars in Oyo, see Robin Law, *The Oyo Empire, c. 1600–c. 1836: A West African Imperialism in the Era of the Atlantic Slave Trade* (Oxford, 1977), pp. 37–9.

assistance programs, such as the aid that Portugal gave to Kongo in 1491, 1509, 1512, and 1570, or unofficially and without authorization, as in the support for Ndongo in the 1520s, the help that gunners gave to the Mane in the 1550s, and perhaps the assistance to Benin in the 1510s and 1520s.[52] Other foreigners of European origin also provided assistance – Hawkins's help in Sierra Leone and Ulsheimer's in Benin are two more sixteenth- and early seventeenth-century examples. Acceptance of this assistance might simply be seen as the desire of centralizers to make use of foreign, rather than local, officials and dependents as a means of keeping local political debts to a minimum and of creating a dependent bureaucracy. But it is also clear that Europeans provided new military techniques and technology as well, perhaps at the price of demanding more vigorous participation in the slave trade than their patrons wished.

However, the kind of military assistance that Europeans in the sixteenth and seventeenth centuries could render in Africa was not as decisive as much of the writing on the "gun–slave" and "horse–slave" cycles implies. For example, Elbl has examined records of Portuguese horse imports into Senegambia and found that they can scarcely be considered numerous enough to be crucial to the military survival or even success of Jolof cavalries.[53] Moreover, as Law has pointed out in a detailed study of the horse problem, much of the Sudanese region was capable of breeding fairly large numbers of horses by the fourteenth century.[54] Thus, the Atlantic trade coincided with a period when demands for horses were declining, and perhaps the trade must be seen in much the same light as the trade in other commodities – as supplementing or even complementing an existing trade and production.

Firearms and other personal weapons (as in the gun–slave cycle) are even more problematic. European firearms and crossbows, the missile weapons that differed most from those in use in Africa, were designed to counteract armored cavalry or for naval warfare in Europe. Although they had great range and penetrating power (capabilities that developed out of a long-standing projectile-versus-armor contest), they had a very slow rate of fire.[55] For Africans, who generally eschewed armor, the

[52] See documentation cited in Chapter 3.

[53] Elbl, "Portuguese Trade."

[54] Robin Law, "Horses, Firearms and Political Power in Pre-Colonial West Africa," *Past and Present* 72 (1976): 112–32. Law also makes a case for a horse–slave cycle operating within the West African region between northern horse-breeding areas and southern horse-using areas, especially in regard to the famed cavalry of Oyo. Whatever validity there may be for this case, it is not applicable in any clear way to the Atlantic horse trade.

[55] Some of this technology is examined in H. A. Gemery and J. S. Hogendorn, "Technological Change, Slavery and the Slave Trade," in C. J. Dewey and A. G. Hopkins, eds., *The Imperial Impact: Studies in the Economic History of Africa and India* (London, 1978), pp. 246–52. They distinguish an earlier (pre-1650) period with its matchlock technology from a later period when the flintlock musket was in use.

advantages of range (penetrating power being relatively unimportant) were more than offset by the disadvantages of the slow rate of fire, except in special circumstances.

Such circumstances were found in naval warfare, for example. As we have seen, in the initial encounters between da Mosto's ships and Mandinga craft in the Gambia, the crossbowmen in the tops were able to fire to good effect against the attacking forces, protected as they were by the high sides of their ships. This particular feature of the ship may be one of the reasons Kongo favored Portuguese assistance in its wars with the Zaire islands, where African craft, Portuguese ships, and the long-range weapons of the Europeans could be used to good effect.

Likewise, artillery would be useful for attacking fortified locations. European artillery was used in Sierra Leone in the 1560s[56] and in Benin, probably in 1514, when the king of Benin seized a Portuguese bombard,[57] but certainly in 1601, when Ulsheimer joined Dutch sailors who used a gun to blast down the gate of a rebel town.[58] In these cases, as in those of the naval engagements, however, the new weapons were hardly of such overwhelming decisiveness that they tipped the scales of warfare strongly.

European ships could be employed only as a supplementary force, for we have already seen that unsupported European ships were helpless close in to shore. Only slight changes in fortifications could greatly reduce the effectiveness of artillery. In the Benin area, artillery was not effective, because most of the fortifications were largely earthworks. Indeed, it is only because they could not defend their gate that the defenders of the town that Ulsheimer helped attack were defeated. The stockades of Sierra Leone were perhaps more vulnerable, but earthworks could render them much safer. The common use of earthworks and hedges of living trees in fortifications probably explains why the cannon had such little value as a siege engine in the Angolan wars of the sixteenth and seventeenth centuries.[59]

In this instance the Portuguese operations in Angola after 1575 are especially informative, for here the Portuguese attempted direct conquest with their own weapons and, at least in some instances, with their own soldiers. If European military technology and techniques were of special merit, surely this would be demonstrated in Angola. Portuguese operations might then be of the simple slave-raiding model that many scholars prefer, in which an all-powerful state conducts systematic wars

56 De Almada, "Tratado breve," *MMA*² 3:375.

57 Mina Officials to Contadores of Portugal, 29 April 1514, ANTT, CC II 46/165.

58 Ulsheimer, "Raysen," fols. 32a–32b.

59 Thornton, "The Art of War in Angola, 1570–1680," *Comparative Studies in Society and History* 30 (1988): 360–78.

on its weaker and ill-organized neighbors to gather slaves, relying on the strength of its weapons and the organization and size of its armies to ensure victory and minimize losses. If European weaponry or military organization were indeed superior, given their strong motivations to acquire slaves for export, one would surely expect this model to describe the Portuguese attacks in Angola.

Certainly, the early exports of slaves from Angola were clearly linked to the operations of the Portuguese army. This can been seen in customs data from Luanda covering the period 1579–85, when great surges of exports in 1579–80 and lesser ones in 1581 and 1583 are correlated with wars (described in great detail by contemporary Jesuit observers), and the periods of relative peace in 1580 and 1584–5 show almost no exports.[60] Similarly, Beatrix Heintze has estimated that the wars promoted by Mendes de Vasconcellos, Portuguese governor from 1617 to 1622, resulted in the export of over 50,000 slaves in just a few years – though this ferocious rate of export was not kept up.[61]

But the documentation cannot support the idea that the Portuguese wars in Angola were simply raids of a militarily dominant European power against its weaker neighbors. Cadornega, the chronicler of the Angolan wars of the seventeenth century, was quick to point this fact out. His campaign and battle descriptions are lengthy and show a soldier's eye for military detail. He often records fairly small-scale Portuguese operations conducted, one might easily say, simply for obtaining slaves, that ended in failure and disaster. After recounting one particularly difficult campaign, he asserts that this was far too difficult to be simply a "guerra de negros" (war for slaves). Although one can discount this comment in part as simply a reply to critics who believed that all the Angolan wars were just slave raids, with no political or diplomatic gains in mind (and perhaps running counter to such gains), the detail of his documentation does confirm that whoever conducted war to capture slaves was in no way guaranteed success and might well be killed by his quarry. Cadornega reports an apt saying in this context: "He who would singe another man's whiskers had better look out for his own."[62]

Portugal's African enemies often possessed skilled and well-equipped armies and very often constructed strong fortifications. Cavazzi described in detail the complicated operations needed to attack one of these fortified locations during a campaign that he accompanied in

60 "Papéis vários pertencentes as Conquistas de América e India," Biblioteca do Palácio de Ajuda (Lisbon), MS. 52-VIII-58, fols. 152–7v. See a survey of wars in Pero Rodrigues, "História," in *MMA* 4:565–77.

61 Heintze, "Ende," pp. 204–9.

62 Cadornega, *História* 1:81, 204, 390.

1659.[63] This particular campaign, moreover, continued after taking the town, only to lose badly in another battle, with the result that virtually all its Portuguese members were killed.[64]

Likewise, although the Portuguese played the role of a heavily armored infantry in many of the campaigns, their presence was not decisive, and in most respects their tactics were identical to those of their enemies. Portuguese soldiers could not win unsupported by Africans and were regularly massacred when they tried to do so.[65] If Angola was a major participant in the Atlantic slave trade and the source of export for many thousands of people, it was not through the superiority of European arms.

In summary, we can say that although European arms may have assisted African rulers in war in some cases, they were not decisive. It is unlikely that any European technology or assistance increased the Africans' chances of waging successful war (as the Portuguese in Angola could surely have attested) or that it made the attackers suffer fewer losses. Therefore, Europeans did not bring about some sort of military revolution that forced participation in the Atlantic trade as a price for survival.

The rapid growth of slave exports and innovations in military technology and warfare

It is possible to conclude that European influence over the slave trade may not have been significant in the first century and a half of the trade simply by acknowledging that Africans had slaves and a slave trade already, and that early forms of European military technology and organization were not critical to the success of African armies. But it might still be possible to argue that ultimately Europeans forced Africans to exceed their capacity to deliver slaves at a later period when high demands for slaves and improved military technology played a more important role.[66]

One potential piece of evidence is the dramatic increase in slave exports after 1650. This increase is roughly correlated both with the explo-

[63] MSS Araldi (Papers of the Araldi Family, Modena), Giovanni Antonio Cavazzi da Montecuccolo, "Missione evangelica al regno de Congo" (MS of 1665–8), vol. B, pp. 508–30.

[64] Cadornega, *História* 2:157–63.

[65] Thornton, "Art of War."

[66] Gemery and Hogendorn ("Technological Change," pp. 248–51) attempt to assess this hypothesis but by and large do so by showing that the musket was a "good weapon" or at least was a useful weapon, without really comparing it with its closest competitor as a missile weapon – the bow and arrow. Moreover, they also do not examine exactly how muskets were used in actual fighting or deal with how the musket would fare in action with hand-to-hand, rather than missile, tactics.

sion of growth of plantation economies under northern European control in the Caribbean and with the large-scale arrival of northern Europeans on the African coast. These newcomers brought with them improved weapons technology and a generally greater industrial capacity than Portugal had. Could these events have signaled the arrival of a new and potentially more disruptive group of merchants and resulted in Africans being forced to expand the existing trade against their will? My research suggests, however, that the changes were more of quantity than quality, and that although the increased demand (and subsequent rise in prices) may have persuaded more Africans to part with their slaves, it did not force them to do so against their will.

African exports of slaves expanded dramatically beginning in the mid-seventeenth century, to the point where the number of exported slaves grew from being a relatively small number relative to the total population of the African regions from which they were taken to having a major demographic impact. Virtually all the work on the volume of the slave trade shows that the total number of slaves exported increased relative to the total areas or to the (estimated) African populations involved. The negative demographic impacts, although somewhat apparent in the beginning of the period in some areas (such as central Africa), intensified and spread to virtually the whole of Atlantic Africa. In the late eighteenth century much of Africa reached demographic exhaustion.

It is possible to trace the growth in slave exports in considerable detail for most of the seventeenth century. Even allowing for a fair margin of error, it is obvious that exports did indeed grow significantly. Thanks to the detailed data on shipping available in the archives of Seville and the union of the Spanish and Portuguese crowns in 1580, which brought much of Portuguese trade in Africa under Spanish supervision,[67] we have a detailed picture of trade in the last years of the sixteenth century to 1640, when the ending of the union once again clouds the picture. Table 4.1 gives some idea of the distribution of slave exports in time and space.

Several points are worthy of note. First of all, it is clear that there was dramatic growth, increasing from a rate of 0.6 percent per annum in the sixteenth century to well over 1.5 percent per annum by the second half of the seventeenth century, with exports nearly doubling between 1650 and 1700. However, this growth was uneven, for some regions exported more slaves, while others maintained more or less the same level.

For example, the trade of the western regions, such as Senegambia,

[67] Excluded is the Angola–Brazil and Angola–São Tomé trades, for which we have some spotty customs records, most from the 1620s in Portuguese and Brazilian material, analyzed by Mauro, *Portugal et l'Atlantique*, p. 180.

Table 4.1. *Estimated annual exports of slaves from Africa, 1500–1700*

	1500	1550	1600	1650	1700
Coastal region					
Western coast[a]	2,000	2,000	2,500	2,500	5,700
Gulf of Guinea[b]	1,000	2,000	2,500	3,300	19,400
West central[c]	2,000	4,000	4,500	8,000	11,000
Total	5,000	8,000	9,500	13,800	36,100

[a] From the mouth of the Senegal River, but including Arguim, to Sierra Leone.
[b] From the "Malaguetta" and "Kwakwa" coasts to Cameroon.
[c] From Cameroon to the Cape of Good Hope.
Sources: For the period around 1500, see documentation in Chapter 3. For the period around 1550 I have relied on Magalhães-Godinho, *Economia* 2:205–7. For the period 1600–50, basic data on shipping are compiled in Chaunu and Chaunu, *Séville et l'Atlantique,* 5:70–3, 138–41, 156–7, 188–9, 208–9, 218–19; summarized in Curtin, *Atlantic Slave Trade,* pp. 106–7. Various estimates by Chaunu and Chaunu and by Curtin are based on multiplying tons of shipping by presumed numbers of slaves per ton. Their estimates rely on a ratio of 1.8 slaves per ton; mine rely on an estimate of 4 per ton, hence the much higher figure. This higher estimate is based on my accepting the argument advanced in Bowser, *African Slave,* pp. 34–44, 363, n. 24, and Duncan, *Atlantic Islands,* pp. 200–1, that the slavers of the seventeenth century, unlike those of the eighteenth, tried to overload ships with slaves (both cite documentaion showing that this was a problem), rather than use the right to trade in slaves as a subterfuge for smuggling in other commodites. I have added data on the Angola and São Tomé trades according to Mauro, and include figures on the Dutch trade, based on shipping data, compiled by Johannes Postma, "The Origin of African Slaves: The Dutch Activities on the Guinea Coast," in Stanley Engerman and Eugene Genovese, eds., *Race and Slavery in the Western Hemisphere* (Princeton, 1975), p. 49. This procedure has produced slightly different estimates from those of Lovejoy, *Transformations in Slavery,* pp. 53, 54, 56, 58–9. For the 1700 figure, I have used an average for the decade 1700–9 found in David Richardson, "Slave Exports from West and West Central Africa, 1700–1810: New Estimates of Volume and Distribution," *Journal of African History* 30 (1989): 17 (Table 7).

hardly grew at all throughout the period. Angolan trade grew more, but still modestly, during the same period. Angola's total exports moved from something on the order of 2,000–3,000 slaves in the early sixteenth century to 4,500 by century's end, continuing to 8,000 by 1650 and eventually 11,000 by century's end. The growth increased the Angolan share of the trade from approximately half in 1500 to better than 65 percent by 1650.

But Angolan growth was eventually eclipsed by the dramatic rise of exports from the Gulf of Guinea. In 1500 most slaves from this area came from Benin, but by the end of the sixteenth century Benin had ceased selling slaves in any appreciable number. This loss was more than compensated for by the rapid growth of the slave trade of Allada in the last half of the sixteenth century and throughout the seventeenth century.[68] Slaves from this area first appear in American inventories about 1550: a "Lucumi" (Yoruba) slave first appears on Hispaniola in 1547,[69] and "Ardras" (Allada) first appear in Peru in the 1560s.[70] All such groups become increasingly numerous in the seventeenth century, both in absolute terms and relative to slaves from other areas in American data.

Continued growth from the region of Allada and its immediate neighbors eventually earned the area the title of "Slave Coast" in the late seventeenth century. From virtually no exports in 1500, this region was exporting over 19,000 slaves per year, more than half the entire African total, by 1700. But the seventeenth-century growth of slavery in Lower Guinea (Gold Coast to Cameroon) was also enhanced by the entry of the Gold Coast states into the slave trade after 1630, and especially after 1650. This growth is particularly dramatic because the Gold Coast began the seventeenth century as a net importer of slaves and exporter of gold and ended it as a net exporter of slaves and was even importing gold.[71]

Thus, in order to understand why the numbers of slaves increased so dramatically in the seventeenth century, we really need to focus on Angola and the Lower Guinea region. For Angola we must seek the causes of the continued growth of slave trading, and for Lower Guinea the reasons for its people's decision to participate in the trade and expand their exports toward the end of the century.

There are several possible explanations for the growth of the slave trade in these areas. Both Curtin and Lovejoy have suggested that increases in the price of slaves, which can be documented for the period, might have enticed more slaves from their owners. It may have encouraged more "economic model" wars, and it may have persuaded owners that it would be better to forgo domestic use in exchange for the higher price available from the Atlantic trade. Also, owners of slaves living far from the coast might be willing to bear the transport costs of moving

[68] The proportion of the Gulf of Guinea slaves in the trade is exaggerated, in my view, in Philip Curtin's discussion in *The Atlantic Slave Trade: A Census* (Madison, 1969), pp. 103–4, because he has assumed all ships declaring "Guinea" as their destination went to the Gulf of Guinea. Yet in seventeenth-century nomenclature, Guinea could be any African destination, from Senegal to Angola, and these slaves cannot be said to come certainly from the Gulf of Guinea only.

[69] "Escriptura" of Licenciado Cerrato, in Incháustegui Cabral, *Reales cédulas* 1:237–8.

[70] Bowser, *African Slave*, p. 40.

[71] Rodney, "Gold and Slaves on the Gold Coast" *Transactions of the Historical Society of Ghana* 10 (1969): 13–28.

slaves to the coast if a higher price were offered.[72] This explanation does give European merchants a role in the growth of enslavement in Africa, but it clearly places the economic decisions in the hands of Africans.

Other explanations focus simply on the increase in wars caused by African political dynamics, discounting the role of trade. The connection between African trade, control over the trade, and politics is a complex and controversial one, but for our purposes, such an explanation still rules out European coercion.

Finally, of course, there is the idea that European coercion, either direct or indirect, is responsible for the increase in warfare, which resulted in more slaves for the Atlantic. In the late seventeenth century the musket was developed into a more effective weapon. Moreover, very large numbers of such weapons were produced as European armies re-armed into bodies in which every infantryman carried a musket.[73] Naturally enough, larger quantities of the improved weapons were also available to ship to Africa, where, it is argued, they may have revolutionized warfare. Thus, by directing weapons selectively to those willing to supply slaves, European merchants may have been able to effect the gun–slave cycle.[74]

A detailed examination of both Angola and the Gulf of Guinea can shed some light on probable causes for the transformation of slave exports. In both cases, however, it seems clear that economic motives and political motives not directly connected to the slave trade were far more important than European coercion or influence.

In Angola, the growth can be explained in large measure by the fact that the same areas continued supplying slaves, and slaves whose capture took place farther and farther east joined the exodus from central Africa. For example, the war of the Ndongo succession really only ended in 1672, though hostilities between Matamba, Angola, and Kasanje (in various combinations, not always involving Portuguese participation) continued sporadically, as, for example, in 1679–85.[75] If supplies of slaves captured in the wars of the Ndongo succession were lost with the ending of the war, the Kongo civil wars (1665–1718) surely contributed more than Kongo had earlier in the century, for all the central African slaves in the Remire plantation in Cayenne (French Guiana) acquired from Dutch traders between 1685 and 1690 were baptized Christians from Kongo.[76]

72 Lovejoy, *Transformations in Slavery*, pp. 49–52; Curtin, *Economic Change*, pp. 156–68.

73 The flintlock musket was a much improved weapon over the earlier matchlocks, especially in that it had roughly twice the rate of fire and nearly half the number of misfires (see David Chandler, *The Art of War in the Age of Marlbourough* [New York, 1976], pp. 76–9).

74 This is the underlying argument of Inikori, "Import of Firearms."

75 Cadornega, *História* 2:403.

76 Thornton, *Kingdom of Kongo*, pp. 68–113; MS Montbret 125, Bibliothèque Municipale de Rouen (hereafter BM Rouen), fols. 86–90.

But, as we have already seen, the big wars were not the only source of Angolan slaves, for smaller campaigns (which some thought were no more than slave raids) also continued in the same areas as before. Cadornega's chronicle, which provides detailed documentation on the operations of the Portuguese army up to 1681, mentions several such wars directed against the usual enemies: the Ndembu and Mbwila region to the north; Kisama, Benguela, and the central highlands to the south; and the lands bordering Matamba on the east. The effects of these eastern wars and similar operations by Matamba's army were noted by several late seventeenth-century travelers. The absence of comprehensive chronicles, like Cadornega's, for the period after 1681 obscures the exact direction and nature of these wars, but they surely seem to have continued.[77]

If improved musketry was somehow a factor in the conduct of any of these wars, great or small, it is not visible in these records. Portuguese military success seems no better in 1680 or even 1700 than it was a century earlier, whatever rearmament or reorganization may have taken place as a result of the entry of muskets.

To these sources, which supplied much of the earlier slave trade, came others from far in the interior. It seems reasonable to suggest that the motive for the capture and transport of these slaves, who often came from hundreds of kilometers east of the positions of the Portuguese, may well have been the higher prices paid for slaves in the late seventeenth century. Cadornega mentions contacts between Kasanje and the emerging Lunda state of the far interior that took place before 1680 but does not mention slaves as among Lunda's exports. Nevertheless, Lunda did begin exporting slaves soon afterward, soon contributing a large supply, and capturing many during its wars of expansion and consolidation.[78] It is interesting to note in this regard that Lunda's armies were not reliant on guns from the Atlantic, for as late

77 Cadornega, *História* 2:380–3, 347–9; also Manoel Ribejro to Antonio de Souza, 15 January 1674, *MMA* 13:254–65 passim; Bernardo da Firenze to Propaganda Fide, 22 June 1705, Archivio "De Propaganda Fide," Scritture originali nelle congregazione generale, vol. 552, fols. 64v–65v; Filippo Bernandi da Firenze, "Ragguaglio del Congo" (1714), Archivio Provinciale dei PP. Capuccini, Provincia da Toscana, fol. 685. The evidence cited here convinces me that the earlier pattern of warfare and enslavement was unchanged throughout the seventeenth century, which would invalidate the idea advanced by Joseph Miller in "The Paradoxes of Impoverishment in the Atlantic Zone," in Birmingham and Martin, eds., *History of Central Africa*, 1:141–3; 145–50, that the expansion of warfare and enslavement to the east was the product of the exhaustion of those areas near Luanda and Ndongo that had formerly supplied the Atlantic and an increasing search eastward for fresh supplies of slaves.

78 For this period, see John Thornton, "The Chronology and Causes of Lunda Expansion to the West, c. 1700–1852," *Zambia Journal of History* 1 (1981): 6–9.

as the mid-eighteenth century they still eschewed muskets as cowards' weapons.[79]

We have much less information about the causes of the sudden surge of slave exports from Lower Guinea. The region around Allada, first of the states of the Slave Coast to begin large-scale exports, is very poorly documented by sixteenth- and early seventeenth-century sources, and it is not really until well into the seventeenth century that this situation is remedied. Oral traditions collected in the nineteenth century suggest that this period was characterized by the rise of the powerful Oyo Empire, which is perhaps in some way correlated with the surge of exports.[80] That many of Allada's exports were slaves captured during Oyo expansion is suggested by the fact that Capuchin visitors of the 1660s believed that many of the slaves Allada exported came from the interior and were purchased at markets.[81] Allada and its subject states and neighbors fought numerous wars during the later seventeenth century, even as the kingdom of Dahomey came to dominate the interior and then the coast.[82]

The local African politics of the Gold Coast, the second region to enter the slave trade from Lower Guinea, involved a complicated series of wars between the local states, whose motives are not clear to us and were equally unclear to the Europeans, although the more perceptive observers, such as Willem Bosman, the Dutch factor, provided detailed historical background for some. In total, however, the complexities of local politics and the steady rise of the interior kingdoms of Denkyira, Akwamu, and ultimately Asante overwhelmed the petty politics of the area – the result of deep-seated social changes in the interior kingdoms that owed little to coastal influences, at least as it has been analyzed by Kea.[83]

The military reorganization of Lower Guinea that led to the rise of the great interior powers, such as Asante and Dahomey (and perhaps even the late seventeenth-century expansion of Oyo), has often been blamed on imports of European firearms. But Kea, whose study of this period for the Gold Coast takes such military factors seriously, notes that al-

79 Manuel Correia Leitão, "Viagem que eu, sargento-mór dos moradores do distrito do Dande, fiz ás remotas partes de Cassange e Olos, no ano de 1755 até o seguinte de 1756," in Gastão Sousa Dias, ed., "Uma viagem a Cassange nos meados do seculo XVIII," *Boletim da Sociedade de Geografia de Lisboa* 56 (1938): 20–21.

80 Studied in detail by Law, *Oyo Empire*, pp. 33–53. On our documentary knowledge of the Slave Coast, see idem, "Problems of Plagiarism, Harmonization and Misunderstanding," pp. 337–58.

81 Biblioteca Provincial de Toledo, Coleción de MSS Borbón-Lorenzana, MS. 244, de Zamora, "Cosmografia," fol. 61.

82 The period after 1680 is well documented in I. A. Akingogbin, *Dahomey and Its Neighbors, 1700–1828* (London, 1966).

83 Kea, *Settlements*, pp. 158–64.

though the methods of warfare were revolutionized by the interior kingdoms, it was mainly by their use of mass-recruited armies, and firearms had very little effect. The development of these mass armies was the product of social changes and was not determined by the availability of new military technology. Indeed, he argues that the early expansion of Asante was accomplished by mass armies armed with missile weapons, but these were bows and arrows in the crucial early phases, and only later were the troops re-armed with muskets.[84]

It is worth noting that the creation of mass armies and their subsequent re-arming with firearms may have done a great deal to increase the numbers of people enslaved. If earlier wars involved relatively small professional armies, and the majority of the slaves were taken from the military captives, then obviously the group of people vulnerable to enslavement would be fairly small. But with the rise of mass armies, battles were likely to involve more soldiers, thus increasing the number of potential slaves accruing to the victor. However, the simple correlation between imports of firearms and exports of slaves is not a causal relationship. It is more likely that African demands for guns increased simply because they were creating larger armies, which itself had complicated internal, social causes. The availability of European weapons did not provoke an increase in warfare.

As African armies re-armed and became accustomed to the tactics of musket warfare it became harder to go back to some other "art of war," thus ensuring continued demand. This certainly helped European business in general, but it did not deliver to any European power the capacity to engage in weapons blackmail against states that might wish to refuse to sell slaves. This is because no European country or group of merchants came close to having control over the supply of arms to any African state, at least in any but the very shortest run. Europeans could therefore not freely decide to supply arms or not to supply them to force Africans into any decisions. In any case, the only real form of influence available to merchants would be withholding the very means to make war, and such a strategy would be more likely to inhibit than encourage warfare.

As historians learn more about warfare in Africa in this period, and as they probe more deeply into the political and social structures of African states, they realize that warfare needs to be explained in terms of the internal dynamics of the state or state system. As such dynamics are understood, the role of Europeans in causing war (as opposed to benefiting from it, either as a vehicle to sell arms or to buy slaves) begins to diminish. Thus, for example, the study of the Kongo civil wars of the

84 Ibid., pp. 97–117.

late seventeenth century yields explanations for the wars that lie in the politics of the country and not in Portuguese machinations, as was previously believed.[85]

The same conclusions can be drawn from the study of the Slave Coast and Gold Coast, where the explosion of slave exports and growth of arms imports are the clearest. The numerous surviving letters of Dutch and English factors on the Gold Coast from about 1680 onward certainly tell of a willingness to buy slaves, at least "if the price is right," as one factor wrote in 1683,[86] but there is nothing to suggest that they could or did exercise actual pressure to get the local people to sell them.[87] They did certainly encourage and occasionally bribe local rulers in the multistate system of the coast to fight, including supplying them with arms and even soldiers, but it was normally to get military help in driving other European rivals from their posts and not simply to get slaves.[88] One of the best examples of such an event was the Komenda war of the 1690s, detailed in several contemporary sources. Its origins lay in the complicated politics of African trade, or, as the Dutch factor Bosman said, in "bad government and absurd customs." All sides obtained mercenaries from the Europeans.[89] The relatively small size of African states and the prevalence of professional armies along the coast (it was only in the interior that the mass armies were forming) made small bodies of mercenaries potentially effective, and consequently Europeans frequently hired themselves out in this way. The practice of acting as mercenaries was not restricted to Europeans; several states on both the Gold Coast and the Slave Coast routinely supplied mercenaries in the wars of the period.[90] Robin Law has recently proposed that the kingdom of Dahomey served first as a sort of mercenary state.[91] Their role as suppliers of mercenaries did not give the Europeans much power on the coast; rather, one

85 Thornton, *Kingdom of Kongo;* Hilton, *Kingdom of Kongo.* Though these two works differ substantially in their approach and conclusions on the causes of the civil wars, both assign essentially domestic causes and see European influence as peripheral at best.

86 Ralph Hassel to Elmina, 5 May 1683, Bodleian Library, Oxford, MSS Rawlinson, C 745, fol. 191v.

87 See especially the reports of English factors in ibid., passim, and in the Dutch records preserved in the Algemeen Rijkisarchiv, Nederlands Bezittung ter Kust Guinea. See the sample of such correspondence published in English translation by Albert van Dantzig, *The Dutch on the Guinea Coast: Select Documents* (Accra, 1978).

88 Hassel to Cape Coast, 5 May 1683, Bodleian Library, Oxford, MSS Rawlinson, C 745, fol. 191; Thomas Pearson to Cape Coast, 22 May 1683, ibid., fol. 201v–2 (but retelling events back to 1667); Mark Bedford Whiting to Cape Coast, 18 August 1683, ibid., fol. 281.

89 The political background is outlined in Bosman, *Description,* pp. 175–83 (quotation, p. 164).

90 On mercenary armies of African origin, see Barbot, "Voyage," pp. 319–22, 351; Bosman, *Description,* pp. 362a, 395–6.

91 "Dahomey and the Slave Trade: Reflections on the Historiography of the Rise of Dahomey," *Journal of African History* 27 (1986): 237–67.

gets a much stronger impression of European weakness and helplessness in the face of local African politics.[92]

African rulers continued to engage in wars, not unlike those of previous centuries, and naturally, as the new weapons figured more prominently in warfare, acquiring supplies of the weapons became important. Thus, in the late seventeenth century and into the eighteenth century, civil wars troubled the Senegambian states, and often pretenders sought and acquired weapons in order to make their claims. But it would be incorrect to say that somehow Europeans had persuaded the potential candidates to seek power in order to get slaves, even if they did delight in the prospect of increased slaves as a result.[93] Senegalese state leaders built up substantial armies of slave soldiers, and often these armies engaged in local raiding (frequently without royal permission), which proved quite disruptive,[94] but neither the origin of these armed forces nor their kings' lack of ability or desire to control them was the result of European policies or pressures.

In conclusion, then, we must accept that African participation in the slave trade was voluntary and under the control of African decision makers. This was not just at the surface level of daily exchange but even at deeper levels. Europeans possessed no means, either economic or military, to compel African leaders to sell slaves.

The willingness of Africa's commercial and political elite to supply slaves should be sought in their own internal dynamics and history. Institutional factors predisposed African societies to hold slaves, and the development of Africa's domestic economy encouraged large-scale trading and possession of slaves long before Europeans visited African shores. The increase in warfare and political instability in some regions may well have contributed to the growth of the slave trade from those regions, but one cannot easily assign the demand for slaves as the cause of the instability, especially as our knowledge of African politics provides many more internal causes. Given the commercial interests of African states and the existing slave market in private hands in Africa, it is not surprising that Africans were able to respond to European demands for slaves, as long as the prices attracted them.

92 David Harper to Cape Coast Castle, 20 April 1683, Bodleian Library, Oxford, MSS Rawlinson, C 754, fol. 189; David Harper to Cape Coast Castle, 5 May 1683, ibid., fol. 192; Hugh Shears to Cape Coast Castle, 21 May 1683, ibid., fol. 199v and passim.

93 See the detailed study, focusing on the early eighteenth century, in Charles Becker and Victor Martin, "Kayor and Baol: Senegalese Kingdoms and the Slave Trade in the Eighteenth Century," (trans. Linda Zuck) in Inikori, *Forced Migration*, pp. 100–25.

94 Ibid., pp. 120–2 (dealing with the eighteenth century); for an analysis of internal dynamics, see James Searing, "Aristocrats, Slaves and Peasants: Power and Dependency in the Wolof States, 1700–1850," *International Journal of African Historical Studies* 21 (1988): 475–504.

Part II

Africans in the New World

5

Africans in colonial Atlantic societies

In the first part of this book, we saw how African political and institutional structures and African economic developments made the trade in slaves possible. This internal dynamic was far more responsible for the development of the African trade with the Atlantic than any pressure that European merchants or political authorities could exert, directly or indirectly. Africa was therefore a full partner in the development of the Atlantic world, and that development cannot be understood without appreciating African history and culture.

In the second part of the book, the emphasis shifts from the dynamic, independent African societies to Africans outside Africa, residents in the new Atlantic world that began in the offshore islands of São Tomé or the Cape Verdes a few miles from the African coast and extended to the vast American continents (see Map 4). Although a few Africans migrated to the Atlantic world voluntarily (mostly high-status diplomats or students and occasional settlers and sailors),[1] the majority came as slaves. The role they played in the formation of the Atlantic world was perhaps just as profound as that of the people who remained in Africa, but it was quite different.

The impact of the African slaves was twofold. On the one hand they came into the Atlantic to work and serve, and by their efforts and numbers made a significant contribution to the economy. On the other hand, Africans brought with them a cultural heritage in language, aesthetics, and philosophy that helped to form the newly developing culture of the Atlantic world. The elements of this twofold contribution of Africans were also related to each other. In many ways the nature of the role of Africans as workers and their place in the economy and societies of the colonial Atlantic also helped to shape their role as cultural actors by

[1] For a description of some of these early high-status Africans, see Thornton, "Kongo–Portuguese Relations," pp. 183–203.

permitting or denying them access to time, raw materials, and supervision of production.

The chapters that follow will analyze these two contributions, with a particular emphasis on how the African role as workers and servants shaped and conditioned their role as transmitters of African culture to the Americas and developers of a new Afro-Atlantic culture, which they shared to some degree with Native Americans and Euro-Americans. This chapter will explain how the African role as laborers and servants came to be defined for the Atlantic world and particularly how their economic centrality for European settlers increased their impact even in areas where they were a minority of the population. Chapter 6 will then show how the labor conditions of Africans in the Atlantic world varied and how African communities developed and sustained themselves throughout the Atlantic world.

In Chapter 7 the emphasis shifts from labor to culture; this chapter examines the process by which African culture developed and changed after it crossed into the Atlantic world, shaped as it was by the conditions of the slave trade and laboring life. Chapter 8 will continue the same theme by examining African religion in detail as a case study in the development and transformation of African ideas in the Atlantic world. In the final chapter the themes of cultural transition and labor reunite in an examination of the special world of the rebels and runaways, viewing them in their role as workers (or as rebel workers) and in their role as cultural and political actors in the Atlantic world.

Africans' role as a labor force was crucial in shaping the ways in which they influenced the Atlantic world. In some areas, such as the Spanish colonies, they provided a dependent group of colonists, who might serve the European colonial society in certain specified ways in a world where most of the basic labor was performed by the conquered Native American population. In other areas, such as the offshore African islands, Brazil, and the colonies of the northern Europeans in the Caribbean, they were the only labor force available in thinly inhabited or uninhabited areas. In still other areas, such as North America, they served the wealthier colonists as a labor force that supplemented the indentured and free labor of European immigrants. In each of these areas, the African worker played a different but, as we shall see, central role in both economy and society.

Africans and Native Americans in the Iberian colonies

Both the Spanish and the Portuguese made extensive use of Native American labor in their Atlantic empires. Sometimes this labor was available through existing Native American states that fell under the control of invading Europeans; in other cases Native American slaves provided the labor force. In both situations, African slaves were used and came to play a more central role than the often more numerous Native Americans in shaping the culture of the Atlantic world.

The earliest Spanish conquerors in the Atlantic world (and all major conquests of the indigenous people were made by the Spanish) used existing Native American systems of tax and tribute to draw labor supplies and finished goods from the local laboring population. This was because the nature of the conquest allowed the Spanish to take over and rule existing American states, complete with their fiscal apparatus, and use them for their own purposes, simply replacing some of the Native American administrators with Spanish colonial officials. The institutional arrangements by which the Spanish converted native political systems to accommodate their own government were complex and varied from region to region, depending on the exact nature of indigenous fiscal arrangements, but Latin Americanists have normally discussed them under the Spanish terms *encomienda* (grant of tribute payers to a Spanish recipient) and *repartimiento* (division of lands or tribute payers among Spanish recipients).

Most Native American fiscal systems provided both for taxation in kind and money and for unpaid public labor to be performed for aristocracies or the state, although like African systems, they did not have landed private property.[2] When the Spanish acquired the rights of the state, either through alliance, blood brotherhood, and inheritance as in parts of Hispaniola[3] and in some fringe areas such as Venezuela[4] or through conquest of the state itself as in Mexico and Peru, they immediately adopted this fiscal system. Although Spaniards were interested in tribute payments in kind, they were ultimately much more interested in the labor tribute. They needed people to work in mines, produce non-American crops such as wheat or sugar, and raise livestock of European origin. The Crown provided Spanish settlers with uncultivated and uninhabited land through land grants and allowed them to use their rights over the Native American peasant class to recruit workers.

However, the Crown was also mindful of its own rights and opted ultimately to remove Native American political authorities from private control and place the Native American communities directly under its

2 For a useful summary of Native American labor arrangements, see James Lockhart and Stuart Schwartz, *Early Latin America: A History of Colonial Spanish America and Brazil* (Cambridge, 1983), pp. 37–44.

3 On these alliances, see Juan Pérez de Tudela Bueso, "La quiebra de la factoría y el nuevo poblamiento de la Española," *Revista de Indias* 15 (1955): 208–10; Floyd, *Columbus Dynasty*, pp 22–3, 35–7.

4 Such arrangements are reported in the sixteenth-century account of Venezuela in Enrique Otto, ed., *Cédulas reales relativas a Venezuela, 1550–1650* (Caracas, 1963), pp. 244–52.

own rule. Private exercise of the right to recruit labor was replaced by Crown distributions of labor to needy settlers. This system in turn eventually evolved into a system of semifree labor in which Native Americans paid taxes to the Crown with money earned as wage workers for European settlers. Although the process was fairly long, and was never completely realized in some places, the end result was that Spanish immigrants and *indios* (Native Americans) were placed under separate jurisdictions, with the Spanish obtaining private land tenure on vacant lands that they made economically useful, and the Native Americans remaining on their traditional land (normally without rights of private property in land) often under their own rulers, *caciques,* but typically under the supervision of missionary orders. Tax obligations and wage receipts defined the mature Spanish colonial economy, although occasional state-sponsored forced labor remained, epecially in the Peruvian mining economy.[5]

The development of the Spanish colonies was shaped by political and economic forces. The legal separation of Native American workers from Spanish landowners and mine owners was intended to prevent European-style serfdom and its accompanying noble privileges, but the nature of debt bondage (peonage), wage labor, and economic development in each region was the product of economic forces. Africans, arriving as slaves, played an important interstitial role in these economies as a result of this pattern of development.

The laws of Spanish America made it impossible for Spanish settlers to enjoy full-time labor from the vast majority of the Native American population. The requirements for separate residence, "just wages," and often limitations on the length of time that native workers could serve (sometimes determined by the Crown and at other times by the competition of the religious orders for the same workers) made the Native American into a perpetual migrant worker. Such workers often worked poorly and were not always available when they were most needed, especially in the agricultural economy. Consequently, the earliest Spanish settlers turned to slavery as a source of permanent labor, sometimes evolving into free wage labor, other times remaining as slave labor.

Slaves made up a permanent work force and thus were especially useful for the continuous activities required by some agriculture and most stock raising as well as the majority of artisanal, skilled, and domestic employment. Their condition of servitude limited their ability to participate politically in the process of government. In Iberian America,

[5] An immense literature is summarized in Lockhart and Schwartz, *Early Latin America,* pp. 68–73, 92–6, 113–18.

where most European settlers received political rights and did not hesitate to return to Europe if they found they could not become well off, there was a great need for a permanently dispossessed and politically powerless class. Legislation had limited the free Native American labor force; opportunity, the European one. Slaves and their descendants could fill the gap.

Many of the slaves, especially in the earliest periods of colonization, were Native Americans, but over time circumstances combined to favor ever larger number of slaves drawn from Africa. Many Native American societies had the institution of slavery, and the earliest permanent workers and servants on Spanish American estates were Native American slaves, sometimes drawn from the slave groups of the conquered societies but often drawn from Spanish raiding or trading. Spanish estates in the Caribbean in the sixteenth century engaged in voracious raiding of the entire basin in search of slaves, sometimes tapping local Native American sources (such as the joint raiding in modern Venezuela),[6] sometimes proceeding on their own.[7] Although the conquest of Mexico yielded substantial numbers of local slaves for use throughout their possessions, the Spaniards still obtained thousands from Central American before the mid-sixteenth century.[8] In Peru the situation duplicated that of Mexico, and in other areas, such as New Granada (modern Colombia), a permanent state of war and rebellion kept a continuous supply of slaves available for Spanish owners.[9] Spanish settlers on the northern coast of South America tapped a long-standing slave trade from the Orinoco for longer than many of the other sources lasted.[10]

The Portuguese conquests in Brazil bear some similarities to the Spanish New World conquest. Although the Tupinambá of Brazil, with whom the Portuguese first came into contact, did not have the elaborate state systems of the Mexicans or Peruvians or even the larger Caribbean islands, they were a settled agricultural people. When the Portuguese succeeded in conquering some of the Tupinambá in Bahia after 1549, they created a fiscal system based on villages of "surrendered" or conquered Native Americans.

6 For a firsthand account, see Girolamo Benzoni, *History of the New World*, trans. W. H. Smyth (London, 1858), chap. 2, passim.

7 For a general account, see Sauer, *Early Spanish Main*.

8 Murdo MacLeod, *Spanish Central America: A Socioeconomic History, 1520–1720* (Los Angeles and Berkeley, 1973), pp. 50–5.

9 Monique Lepage, "La gobernación de Popoyán et le nouveau royaume de Grenade entre 1536 et 1573," *Caravelle: Cahiers du monde hispanique et luso-brésilien* 33 (1979): 19–47.

10 Rodrigo de Navarette, "Relacion de las provincias y naciones de los indios Arauacas" (1570–75), in Moreno, *Relaciones geográficas de Venezuela*, pp. 84–5.

The Portuguese Crown placed these villages under missionary control, paralleling the Spanish Crown's attempt to exercise regular control over various Native American groups. Subsequently, these Tupinambá became wage workers under conditions that resembled those of the Native Americans in the Spanish areas.[11] As in Spanish America, the Portuguese still needed slaves for continuous operations and domestic service, and like their Spanish counterparts, Portuguese forces often raided the numerous still-unconquered people that surrounded their colonies along the Brazilian coast.[12]

In both Spanish and Portuguese America, however, the European rulers took steps to replace this early Native American slavery with African slavery. The reasons for this are complex, involving both demographic and political variables. Native American populations were not numerous or accessible enough to meet all the demands of the settlers for slaves, and moreover, economic and political policies of the Iberian monarchs favored the replacement of Native American slaves by ones from Africa.

Most of pre-Columbian America, outside the core areas of the Andean and Mesoamerican empires, was fairly sparsely populated, and the introduction of Old World diseases reduced that population even more.[13] Furthermore, the majority of the Native American societies that were not conquered in the earliest wave of Spanish activity were militarily strong and not easy to raid. In areas such as the Guyanas or the Amazon many slaves were obtained not by direct European attack but through commerce or through assisting Native American allies in their own wars.[14] Therefore, ultimately the number of Native Americans who could be purchased as slaves or enslaved directly was insufficient to meet the demand for slaves.

For example, the fairly large number of Native American slaves in Brazil helped to fuel Bahia's sugar economy, but their numbers were diminishing already in the 1570s, and by the early seventeenth century

[11] Lockhart and Schwartz, *Early Latin America*, pp. 196–8; for more detail, see Stuart Schwartz, "Indian Labor for New World Plantations," *American Historical Review* 83 (1978): 43–79; and Urs Hörner, *Die Verskavung der brasilianische Indianer: Der Arbeitsmarkt in portugiesich Amerika im XVI. Jahrhundert* (Zurich, 1980).

[12] For a thorough survey of this activity, see John Hemming, *Red Gold: The Conquest of the Brazilian Indians, 1500–1750* (Cambridge, Mass., 1978).

[13] For a recent discussion on the size of the pre-Columbian population and its decline, see William Denevan, ed., *The Native Population of the Americans in 1492* (Madison, 1976). For a dissenting view of the type of calculations typically used for assessing population decline, see David Henige, "On the Contact Population of Hispaniola: History as Higher Mathematics," *Hispanic American Historical Review* 58 (1978): 217–37.

[14] For operations within Brazil, see Hemming, *Red Gold*. For the Guyanas and Orinoco valley, see Marc de Civrieux, "Los Caribes y la conquista de la Guayana Española," *Montalban* 5 (1976): 875–1021.

virtually all the slaves in Bahian estates were Africans.[15] Similarly, in New Granada, a survey of the mines in 1573 shows that in spite of the very substantial numbers of Chibchans captured during the wars and rebellions of the period, African slaves were already passing them in numbers in mine work.[16] Such examples could be multiplied everywhere that Native American and African slaves were imported.

The particular skills that African slaves possessed favored African as opposed to Native American slavery. In the early days of the conquests, Native Americans, who owned no large domestic animals, would be unsuitable for raising cattle or riding horses, although obviously, in time many Native Americans learned to deal with these animals, eventually becoming feared as cavalry. But in early times such tasks might fall to African slaves. It is perhaps no wonder that all the *vaqueros* and *ganaderos* (cowboys) on the mid-sixteenth-century Hispaniola estates were not only Africans but from Wolof, Fula, and Mandinga areas, where there was a strong equestrian and cattle-raising tradition.[17] The value of Africans from these regions did not diminish as Native Americans learned the skills, though; in the mid-seventeenth century the Cape Verdian sailor Lemos Coelho noted the demand for slaves from the Senegambian area because of their skills with horses and cattle.[18] Angolans also possessed cattle-raising (though not equestrian) skills; the cattle raisers of Venezuela in the mid-seventeenth century were from Mbundu groups.[19]

Africans from the Gold Coast were skilled divers. Pieter de Marees, who observed them swimming and diving there, also noted that masters from the "Pearl Coast" (Venezuela and Trinidad) purchased them to fish pearls in the late sixteenth and early seventeenth centuries.[20] Although Native American slaves may well have possessed these skills, the ones who did have them may not have been available in sufficient numbers, for certainly the entire pearl-fishing industry was conducted by African slaves, up to and including the supervisory tasks.[21] Similar dynamics may

[15] For the evolution of Native American slavery in Bahia, see Stuart Schwartz, *Sugar Plantations in the Formation of Brazilian Society: Bahia, 1550–1835* (Cambridge, 1985), pp. 28–70.

[16] Lepage, "Gobernación de Popoyán."

[17] "Escriptura de Licenciado Cerrato," in Incháustegui Cabral, *Reales cédulas.*

[18] Francisco de Lemos Coelho, "Description of the Coast of Guinea (1684)," trans. P. E. H. Hair (Liverpool, 1985), fol. 7 (original MS, 1684).

[19] Empadrimiento de los negros de estancia de la valle del Chama (1656), Ermillia Trochis de Veracoechea, *Documentos para el estudio de los esclavos negros en Venezuela* (Caracas, 1977), pp. 193–5.

[20] De Marees, *Beschrijvinge,* p. 94a. See also Acosta, *Historia natural y moral de las Indias* (Seville, 1590), bk. 5, chap. 15.

[21] Antonio Vázquez de Espinosa, *Compendio y descripción de las Indias Occidentales* (c. 1634; modern ed. and trans., Charles Upson Clark [Washington, 1942 (English); 1948 (Spanish)], nos, 127–30, 936). A modernized Spanish edition was published by B. Velasco Bayón in Madrid in 1969. The paragraphs are numbered the same in all editions.

have been behind African involvement in the coastal and riverine trade of Brazil (where they dominated offshore fishing)[22] and Cartagena.[23]

A third reason that Africans often filled the need for slave labor was that Crown policies favored it. Although the formal reasons for favoring African over Native American slaves were often couched in humanitarian terms (Africans could stand the work better than the Native Americans), fiscal concerns were also important. By ensuring that slaves were acquired only from outside, the Crown could control, rent, and tax the trade, which would have been more difficult for local trade.

Ever since the early sixteenth century, Spanish memorials had argued that Native Americans could not stand the heavy labor required by many forms of work in mines and plantations while contending that Africans ought to be imported for the task. The most vociferous champion of these ideas was Bartolomé de las Casas, the indomitable defender of Native Americans from slavery and outspoken opponent of slave raiding within the Americas. Yet it was not slavery itself he opposed, only the slavery of Native Americans. This is clearly seen in his plans to establish a model colony on the Venezuelan coast, which would allow maximum freedom for the Native Americans. In this colony, 10,000 Cumanagotos, organized in three towns under their own missionary-supervised government, would have perpetual rights to land. But if the Cumanagotos were to be free, this did not mean there would be no slavery, for he also anticipated that the Spanish settlers, in addition to tapping Cumanagoto wage labor, would each have three African slaves for their service, a number that could increase to seven with clerical permission.[24] This plan was to serve as a model for many others to follow, like the sixteenth-century suggestion that the mines of Potosí be worked entirely by African slaves in order to protect the Native Americans.[25]

Thus, it was not slavery or the slave trade that the Spanish Crown opposed, but rather slave raiding and trading among Native Americans. The Crown not only wished to limit the use of Native Americans as slaves but to end the Native American slave trade. From 1503 onward, the Crown sought to limit the areas from which slaves could be captured, typically to more distant and remote regions.[26] This may have been to force slave raiding into large and easily taxed ventures under Crown control.

Equally or even more important, however, by insisting that such wars

[22] Dierick Ruyters, *Toortse der zee-vaert* (Vlissinghen, 1623) p. 140. The original pagination is given in the modern edition of S. P. L'Honoré Naber (The Hague, 1913).

[23] Nicholas del Castillo Mathieu, *La Llave de las Indias* (Bogotá, 1981), pp. 201–2.

[24] Bartolomé de Las Casas, *Historia de las Indias,* 3 vols. (Mexico City, 1951), bk. 3, chap. 34.

[25] Memorial cited in Alberto Crespo R., *Esclavos negros en Bolivia* (La Paz, 1977), pp. 101–7.

[26] MacLeod, *Spanish Central America,* pp. 50–5, for a review of relevant legislation up to the 1540s.

be conducted for just reasons (typically to capture cannibals), the Crown required that only its officers could lead them, thus securing the potential revenues to be gained by the raids and ensuring that taxes would be collected, taxes that might not be forthcoming from private campaigns.

The Portuguese monarchs seem to have adopted a similar policy in Brazil. Legislation from the 1570s onward argued that Native American slaves in Brazil, like those of their Spanish counterparts, could be taken only in "just wars" against people who were alleged to be cannibals or practitioners of human sacrifice, typically in remote areas.[27] Thus, the Crown could protect its own subjects or potential subjects in nearby areas while ensuring that the revenues from the slave trade remained in royal hands or the hands of their appointed agents. Yet in Brazil there was surely no attempt to abolish slavery or the slave trade, for this was an area that would receive thousands of Africans annually as slaves.

The Brazilian historian Fernando Novais has argued that the Crown also had fiscal considerations in mind when it supported the import of African slaves, for it could draw income, at the planters' expense, from its monopoly of the African slave trade.[28] The ability to control, tax, or otherwise extract revenue from the slave trade clearly played an important role in Spanish legislation as well. It was probably for reasons of financial gain and control rather than simply a desire to protect Native Americans as a people weaker than Africans that led to the policies.

Nowhere is this more strongly suggested than by Portuguese policy in Angola. Because the slave trade from the colony in Angola involved Africans, attempts to limit it could not be framed in terms of racial protection as they were in the Americas. Furthermore, Angola was a preferred source of slaves for the Atlantic, by all accounts. Yet Angolan policy exactly mirrored the policies of Brazil. In the earliest phases of the conquest (1579–1602) individual Portuguese soldiers received the obedience of African rulers (*sobas*) and collected revenue and labor from them or their subjects.[29] In 1607, however, the monarchy removed all conquered African groups in Angola from private jurisdiction and placed them under its own control or that of its representatives, just as the Spanish had done earlier in Hispaniola. Furthermore, the same legislation required all slaves to be secured in "just war" and limited commercial acquisition to specified markets under royal supervision.[30]

Finally, beyond these fiscal matters, African slaves, even when freed,

[27] Fully discussed in Hemming, *Red Gold*, pp. 72–3, 147–55.

[28] See his argument in *Portugal e Brasil na crise da antigua sistema colonial, 1777–1808* (São Paulo, 1979).

[29] This system is described in Andrew Battel, *Strange Adventures of Andrew Battel in Angola and Adjoining Regions*, edited by E. G. Ravenstein (London, 1901), pp. 64–5.

[30] Regimento do Manuel Pereira Forjaz, 26 March 1607, *MMA* 5:268–9, 269–70, 274.

formed a readily identifiable part of the population that was typically dependent and lacked opportunities that other groups often had. The average manumission contract in most of Iberian America often stipulated continued service and dependency. Several studies of manumission practices show that most freed slaves continued in closely bound dependency, freedom amounting to little more than a reduction of the master's responsibility.[31] Even when free of their former masters, ex-slaves had fewer political rights than other free people, for legislation routinely barred them from political participation and the holding of public office.[32] In the Americas, this legislation tended to be racial in outlook, specifying the color (*negro* or *pardo*) as an identifying characteristic, but the spirit of the law was probably based more on the issue of legitimate birth (which was held against mestizos or mulattos, who were all assumed to be illegitimate) or former servitude.[33] Thus, in São Tomé, people of African ancestry routinely held office, generally claiming ancient privileges or noble and free African birth.[34]

The combined pressure of Native American demography, the terms of conquest and its legislation set down by the Iberian royal authorities, and the fiscal policies of the monarchs all contributed to make African slaves the main providers of long-term labor, whether it was in agriculture, mining, crafts, or domestic service, in the areas of America where there were large and conquered populations of Native Americans. In many of the areas where Spanish conquest had brought a large Native American population under their control (which was proportionately large even after the early colonial epidemics reduced the numbers of Native Americans considerably) African slaves might still be the majority of the settler population.

Thus, for example, the Mexican Inquisition conducted a census in 1595 listing the population of many of the towns where Europeans lived. This census is unusual in that it gives the numbers of people of African

[31] Frederick Bowser, *The African Slave in Colonial Peru, 1524–1650* (Stanford, 1974), pp. 298–300; Colin Palmer, *Slaves of the White God: Blacks in Mexico, 1570–1650* (Cambridge, Mass., 1976).

[32] For a survey and overview, see Rout, *African Experience*, pp. 126–61, and Katia M. de Queirós Mattoso, *To Be a Slave in Brazil, 1550–1888*, trans. Arthur Goldhammer (New Brunswick, N.J., 1986 [original French ed., 1979]), pp. 151–212.

[33] In this book I use "mulatto" to mean a person of mixed African and European descent and "mestizo" to mean a person of mixed Native American and European ancestry.

[34] For a telling discussion of this point in a primary source, see Manuel Rosário Pinto, "Rellação do descubrimento da Ilha da San Thome . . . (1734) (modern ed., António Ambrósio, "Manuel Rosário Pinto [a sua vida]," 3/31 [1970]: 205–329), fol. 60, in which an attempt on the part of the settlers of partial European ancestry (*mestiços*) to disenfranchise the wealthier of those of pure African ancestry (*pretos*) on racial grounds was firmly defeated at the Portuguese court by relying on birth and service.

descent, and it clearly shows that such people were the most common element in every Spanish town in Mexico, even outnumbering the mestizos (among whom were usually included many people who had only Native American ancestry but found legal advantage in claiming partial European descent).[35] In Mexico, Peru, and most of Central America, persons of African descent were greatly outnumbered in the population as a whole by Native Americans and mestizos.

Records of mines and plantations also clearly show that the majority of the population that resided on such establishments permanently were also of African descent. Some mines, such as those of Mexico and Peru, employed numerous Native American wage earners (and occasionally slaves and forced workers, depending on the location); in most American mines the majority of the underground work was actually done by Native Americans.[36] But even in these mines, such as Potosí, slaves of African descent often filled supervisory, skilled, and administrative positions, as well as dominating domestic service among the owners and Spanish workers, and were more likely to be permanent residents than the Native Americans.[37] In other mines, such as those of New Granada, slaves of African descent might make up virtually the entire population, from the miners to all the support personnel, or share jobs with Native American slaves and tributary or wage workers.[38] The copper mines of Venezuela also employed both types of labor, with Afro-Venezuelans making up a major portion of the work force, especially in the skilled positions.[39]

In sugar milling, the other great agro-industrial establishment of Iberian America, slaves were the permanent work force from almost the beginning. Ward Barnett's detailed study of the sugar haciendas of the Cortés family estates in the Marquisado de la Valle in Mexico, which covers the entire colonial period, makes it clear that Native American labor was employed only seasonally and much of the year-round work

35 Dr. Lobo Guerrero and Licenciado Alonso de Peralta to Inquisition, 29 November 1595, fols. 54–57, in Georges Baudot, "La population des villes du Mexique en 1595 selon une enquête de l'Inquisition," *Caravelle: Cahiers du monde hispanique et luso-brésilien* 37 (1981): 5–18.

36 D. A. Brading and Harry Cross, "Colonial Silver Mining: Mexico and Peru," *Hispanic American Historical Review* 52 (1972): 545–79; on mines in Central America, see MacLeod, *Spanish Central America*, pp. 58–60; 257–8.

37 For Potosí, see Crespo R., *Esclavos Negros*, pp. 25–31.

38 For the New Granada mines, see Vázquez de Espinosa, *Compendio*, nos. 964 (*cuadrillas de negros y indios*), 980 (*negros y indios*), and 1047 (mine located in area of considerable tributary population of Native Americans), all suggesting both groups working in all phases. For a detailed study of one mine employing mostly Afro–New Granadian labor, see Robert C. West, *Colonial Placer Mining in Colombia* (Baton Rouge, 1952), pp. 83–90.

39 Miguel Acosta Saignez, *Vida de los esclavos negros en Venezuela* (Caracas, 1967), p. 157.

(skilled labor, household service, and support labor) was performed by a slave staff on several of the estates.[40]

What was true on most Spanish American sugar estates was also true for Brazilian sugar mills, the most important revenue earner for Portugal in America. Stuart Schwartz has studied the many mills of Bahia during this period and come to the same conclusions. Tupinambá labor was critical in the early formative stages, and late sixteenth-century slaves were mostly Tupinambá, though even then, smaller numbers of African slaves were employed in the house and as skilled labor. By the early seventeenth century, African slaves had more or less completely replaced them in domestic service, skilled labor, and even fieldwork. Tupinambá workers, now working for wages and recruited from nearby Jesuit-run villages (*aldeas*) provided only seasonal labor at the peak of the harvesting and milling season or for general maintenance.[41]

African slaves were therefore at the center of the conquered part of the emerging new Atlantic world. Their importance in the towns where most European immigrants and their descendants made their homes, in domestic service, and as year-round residents on mines and estates ensured their proximity to the centers of power and wealth, even if they did not share in that wealth and power. For many Europeans and Euro-Americans (any persons of European ancestry born in the Americas), it was the African presence in towns, farms, mines, and estates that was their only contact with Atlantic people who were not of European descent, the Native Americans being sequestered in rural areas and under tight missionary supervision. Thus, the development of Atlantic culture was ultimately a Euro-African phenomenon in many parts of Iberian America, with the Native American presence being felt strongly only in their home areas.

This geographic centrality was reinforced by the African slave role as supporters of the Europeans, sometimes against the Native American inhabitants, sometimes as an intermediary with them. During the earliest phases of the conquest, African slaves augmented the numbers of Europeans and provided assistance in exploration and conquest. Few conquests were accomplished without African participation. Perhaps the

[40] Ward Barnett, *The Sugar Hacienda of the Marques de la Valle* (Minneapolis, 1970), pp. 74–92.

[41] Schwartz, *Sugar Plantations*, pp. 28–70. These conclusions are also supported by direct examination of one of the most important series of documents used by Schwartz, the various inventories and daybooks of the Engenho Sergipe do Conde in the late sixteenth and early seventeenth centuries, published as Instituto de Açucár e Alcool, *Documentos para a história do Açucár*, 3 vols. (Rio de Janeiro, 1953–6), vol. 2, *Engenho Sergipe do Conde: Livro do Contas (1662–53)*, and vol. 3, *Engenho Sergipe do Conde: Espólio de Mem de Sá (1569–79)*.

most famous of these early Africans was Juan Valiente, who participated in the conquest of Chile and Peru.[42]

Frederick Bowser has pointed out the significance of this African presence in his study of the African slave in Peru. Bowser shows that the African slaves were not only economically important to European settlers and their descendants, but they were intermediaries between the Europeans and their Quechua and Aymara subjects as well.[43] Slaves augmented the military might of the Iberians whenever there was danger from Native Americans. For example, on early Hispaniola, royal instructions demanded that Spanish settlers arm their most trusted slaves (normally those with a family), called "secure blacks" (*negros seguros*), in case of a revolt by the Tainos,[44] and later still to protect various colonies against foreign incursions.[45] Slaves also served in the Portuguese army in Brazil, both against the Tupinambá and Tapuya and against European rivals such as the French and Dutch.[46]

Nowhere is the proximity of the African slaves to the European community more clearly demonstrated than in the relationship of the two subordinate groups to the Spanish Inquisition. Whereas the Native American population was placed under episcopal supervision and their crimes and religious beliefs put under the special purview of the religious orders, the Africans were judged by the same tribunals as the Europeans.[47] African slaves were subject to European cultural norms, but this allowed the Africans to influence those norms as well.

African slaves in uninhabited or unconquerable areas

If the African slave was likely to be very important even in areas where the majority of the population and work force was Native American, how much more important would they be in areas where there were no indigenous inhabitants or where the local population could not be conquered. These areas can be grouped into two types of settlements: areas

[42] William F. Sater, "The Black Experience in Chile," in Robert Brent Toplin, ed., *Slavery and Race Relations in Latin America* (Westport, Conn., 1974), p. 16.

[43] Bowser, *The African Slave in Colonial Peru*.

[44] Documents cited in Wright, "History of Sugar."

[45] Carlos Esteban Dieve, *La esclavitud del negro en Santo Domingo*, 2 vols. (Santo Domingo, 1980), 1:99. Documentation for Cuba can be found in "Papers Bearing on the Negroes of Cuba in the Seventeenth Century," *Journal of Negro History* 12 (1927): 55–56.

[46] E.g., the forces of Diogo Dias (Vicente do Salvador, *História*, bk. 3, chap. 22). Also Thales de Azevedo, "Indios, brancos e pretos no Brasil colonial," *América indigena* 13 (1953): 119–32.

[47] For an excellent overview see Solange Alberro, "Noirs et mulâtres dans la société coloniale mexicaine, d'après les archives de l'Inquisition," *Cahiers d'Amerique Latine* 17 (1978): 57–88.

like the offshore islands of Africa (the Cape Verdes, São Tomé, and Príncipe) and Barbados in the Caribbean, where the land was uninhabited before the arrival of the Europeans; and areas like North America or the eastern Caribbean (including the Guyanas), where there were Native American inhabitants, but their conquest proved impossible. In these last areas, Native American slaves (from near or farther away) might be integrated into the laboring and serving population, but for the most part the Native American society was not actually conquered and integrated into the society of the settlers as it was in much of Spanish America or even in sections of Brazil.

These two divisions can be further subdivided into those in which European immigrants were brought to provide some or all of the work force, such as North America and the eastern Caribbean, and those where the climate was judged too harsh or dangerous for Europeans, such as Cape Verde or especially São Tomé. Although the demographic mixture that resulted in all these areas varied widely, African slaves proved to be an important element, at times serving simply as a minority of the labor force coexisting with other workers and at other times gradually becoming virtually the only people who labored or served.

Historians have been divided as to why the African slaves became so important in all these areas. For some, disease and climate have been of great significance. Just as Old World diseases often made it impossible to use Native American workers or slaves because they died off too quickly (at least in the Caribbean Islands and perhaps in lowland mainland regions as well), so too the tropical climate of the Caribbean and the Gulf of Guinea with its hostile disease environment made it impossible for Europeans to labor there.[48] Indeed, the prevalence of disease in São Tomé is best illustrated by the observation of the papal nuncio in Portugal that in the 1530s the Portuguese government circumvented papal injunctions against civil authorities inflicting capital punishment on clerics by simply exiling them to São Tomé, knowing that within a short time after their arrival on the island they would be dead.[49]

But if the epidemiological argument works fairly well for explaining why not only the entire laboring population but even most of the settler population was of African origin in the Gulf of Guinea, it is somewhat less successful for the Caribbean, where European workers played an important role in colonies of all the northern European nations for the

[48] A worthwhile analysis is Philip Curtin, "Epidemiology and the Slave Trade," *Political Science Quarterly* 83 (1968): 190–216.

[49] Marco Vigerio della Rovere to Amborsio Riacalcato, 7 October 1535, in Charles-Martial de Witte, ed., *La correspondance des premiers nonces permanents au Portugal, 1532–1553*, 2 vols. (Lisbon, 1980), 2:156.

first fifty years of colonization.[50] Furthermore, it does not work at all well in North America, where, by all accounts, the climate was fully suitable for European workers, though the first generation found it difficult.[51]

Other historians have focused on the issue of race and national origin as a means of supplementing or supplanting arguments based on epidemiology. Following the lead of Winthrop Jordan, numerous historians have suggested that deep-seated European prejudices against non-Christian and dark-skinned people have predisposed them to selecting their labor force, especially the most oppressed and vulnerable segment of the labor force, from among this group rather than from among Europeans. Thus, because Europeans were valued more, they tended to hold the skilled laboring positions or set themselves up on small farms, whereas Africans and to a lesser extent Native American slaves were consigned to the dirty, difficult, and dangerous work.[52]

More recent scholarship has placed heavier emphasis on economic factors. African slaves and European indentured servants bore different costs to their masters and were available for immigration depending on a number of factors. European immigration especially was governed by the ability of the immigrants to obtain legal freedom and rights in the future, by the wages and land available in Europe, and by opportunities in the Americas. In Africa, as well, local conditions determined the price of slaves, and shipping and mortality factors affected their price and utility in the Americas. Then, depending on characteristics of the colony – its choice of exports, the agronomy of export crops, the profitability of one or another export, and the degree of concentration of capital – the economic decision makers would determine what sort of work force was preferable: slave or free, European or African.[53]

At the very beginning of colonization, when Europe still had feudal relationships, at least in some areas, European immigration might not have

[50] For a good survey of this era in the British Empire, see John J. McCusker and Russel Menard, *The Economy of British America, 1607–1789* (Chapel Hill and London, 1985), pp. 211–57.

[51] See ibid. and the careful study of the situation in Virginia by Allan Kulikoff, *Tobacco and Slaves: The Development of Southern Cultures in the Chesapeake, 1680–1800* (Chapel Hill and London, 1986), pp. 30–44, 54–63, 167–203.

[52] Winthrop Jordan, *White over Black: American Attitudes towards the Negro, 1550–1812* (Chapel Hill, 1968), esp. pp. 71–82. Also Leon Higginbotham, *In a Matter of Color: Race and the American Legal Process: The Colonial Period* (New York, 1978), esp. pp. 7–14. For the English Caribbean, see Gary Puckrein, *Little England: Plantation Society and Anglo Barbadian Politics, 1627–1700* (New York, 1984), pp. 146–69. For an extension to Native Americans, see Aulden T. Vaughn, "From White Man to Redskin: Changing Perceptions of the American Indian," *American Historical Review* 87 (1982): 917–53.

[53] See also McCusker and Menard, *Economy of British America*, pp. 35–70. A recent comprehensive attempt to analyze the choices between various types of labor is in David Galenson, *Traders, Planters and Slaves: Market Behavior in Early English America* (Cambridge, 1986).

been different from that of Africans. For example, a mid-fifteenth-century contract for workers for the Azores tendered by a German specifies that the contractor will deliver workers, perhaps from his own estates.[54] Similarly, some of the workers in the Spanish Canaries who had emigrated from Portuguese Madeira in the early sixteenth century seem to have been day laborers working for a wage, suggesting that a European-style labor force had developed there.[55] Similarly, Portugal frequently deported criminals and other elements deemed undesirable (Gypsies and Jews, for example) to their overseas colonies to serve as common workers.[56] But these relationships were relatively insignificant, and in any case, were not available to the northern European settlers in the Americas, for whom the choice between European and African labor forces was posed.

Rather, for northern Europeans, it was a choice between European workers, recruited through a contract of indenture, or African slaves, acquired by purchase on the African coast or from another part of the Americas. The indenture contract typically gave the holder the right to full use of the workers' labor in exchange for paying the workers' passage and food, minimum clothing, and a grant of land plus sufficient capital to begin life as a petty agricultural producer at the end of the contract term (three to seven years). Such terms were often glowingly set out, along with equally impressive descriptions of the colony to be settled, in advertisements for workers.[57]

These contracts were generally beneficial to the workers, if they could survive the rigors of travel, the change in climate, disease, the difficult work, and the illegal attempts on the part of the holders of the contracts to withhold pay, freedom, or other stipulated items. This beneficial contract, framed to attract the landless or marginal European peasant or town dweller, was not at all to the liking of many of the colonists, who wished to use the American colonies to make their own fortunes, often as quickly as possible. Such people preferred slave labor, because it involved no legal restrictions on the master, was indefinite, and was inheritable.

For example, in 1631, a young English squire, Henry Colt, complained that planters in Barbados (wealthy settlers hoping for quick profits) could not adequately control an indentured labor force under conditions that allowed the workers easy access to freedom.[58] Some years later, in

54 Contract of 29 March 1457, *Monumenta Henricina*, 13:93–4.

55 Armesto-Fernádez, *Canary Islands*, pp. 16–21.

56 Serrão, *História de Portugal*, 2:

57 E.g., *A Publication of Guiana's Plantation* (London, 1632) (sample contract, pp. 19–21), or the Dutch announcement, *Pertinent Beschrijvinge van Guiana, gelegen aen de vaste Kust van America* (Amsterdam, 1676), sample contract, pp. 5–11.

58 Henry Colt, "The Voyage of Sir Henry Colt" (1631), in Vincent Harlow, ed., *Colonising Expeditions to the West Indies and Guiana, 1623–67* (London, 1924; reprint, Lichtenstein, 1967), pp. 65–6.

1647–50, Richard Ligon found the same complaint echoed by the larger Barbados planters, who were now becoming wealthy from newly introduced sugar production.[59] These complaints were not limited to Englishmen, for the Jesuit priest Jacques Bouton, among the pioneer settlers in the French Caribbean, made exactly the same complaints in 1640, noting that the main problem with indentured servants was that one "lost them every three years" (the term of service in the French indenture contracts).[60] These sentiments were expressed in similar terms by his successors in the 1650s and 1660s, as the French islands turned to sugar production as their main crop and needed larger labor forces.[61] Dutch settlers in New Netherlands (modern New York) also complained, for a much poorer settlement in the temperate regions of North America, that "farm servants must be bribed to go thither with a great deal of money and promises"[62] and hoped to replace them with slaves.

Given these complaints, one should not be surprised that the wealthier sought by whatever means to limit and revoke the contracts that they had made to obtain European labor. When the Dutch pirate Esquemeling came to the Caribbean in the 1660s as an indentured servant himself, he met in his own experience and in the tales of other pirates with similar backgrounds many examples of contracts being extended, broken, or abused by the wealthy, who sought to maximize the labor they received from their indentured workers.[63] These tactics were often resisted by the workers not just by running away and joining pirate gangs but by work stoppages, revolts, petitions, and labor action.[64] The situation had reached such a point when Ligon visited Barbados that he believed that the potential for violent confrontation was greater every day.[65] The problems of the indentured servants, seeking legal redress in often hostile courts (which were controlled for the most part by holders of indentured labor), and competition over land between freed indentured laborers

59 Richard Ligon, *A Trve and Exact History of the Island of Barbados* (London, 1657), pp. 43–5.

60 Jacques Bouton, *Relation de l'establissment des Francois depvis l'an 1635 en l'isle de la Martinique* (Paris, 1640), pp. 98–9.

61 Charles de Rochefort, *Histoire naturelle et morale des Iles Antilles de l'Amerique* (Rotterdam, 1658), pp. 319–21; Jean-Baptiste du Tertre, *Histoire generale des Antilles habitées par les François*, 4 vols. (Paris, 1667), 2:545–7.

62 Report of Board of Accounts on New Netherlands, 1644, in E. B. O'Callaghan and Berthold Fernow, eds. and trans., *Documents Relative to the Colonial History of the State of New York*, 15 vols. (Albany, 1856–87), 1:154.

63 John Esquemeling, *The Buccaneers of America*, 2d ed. (London, 1684; reprint, New York, 1987), pp. 52–4.

64 See the overview by Hilary Beckles, "Rebels and Reactionaries: The Political Response of White Laborers to Planter-Class Hegemony in Seventeenth Century Barbados," *Journal of Caribbean History* 15 (1981): 1–19; also Jill Sheppard, *The "Redlegs" of Barbados* (New York, 1977).

65 Ligon, *History of Barbados*, pp. 43–5.

and wealthier proprietors shaped Barbados politics for much of the mid-seventeenth century.[66]

Although the competition was less acute in North America, the contests between indentured servants and the holders of their contracts were important there as well. Even those former indentured servants who had acquired land found that pressure on them by their wealthier neighbors threatened their position. Bacon's rebellion in 1676 can rightly be viewed as a major expression of these political tensions.[67] All in all, this situation made the use of European indentured labor difficult for those who wished to employ it, especially on larger estates.

There were, therefore, some institutional reasons that made slave labor more attractive, at least to those wealthier planters who could afford the higher initial cost of purchasing slaves rather than importing contract labor. Slaves had no way of automatically obtaining liberty, and the owner was not bound by a contract to give them anything, though obviously owners had to provide subsistence if they expected them to work effectively.

Some historians, largely using data from Virginia, have argued that northern European law, unlike that of southern Europe, had no provision for slavery, and that originally African slaves were simply seen as bondsmen and bondswomen, to be freed after a specified period of time. In this scenario, some see racial attitudes as creating the conditions both for the development of a slave law and for imposing this on the Africans.[68]

But a wider view of the colonies of the northern Europeans does not support these ideas as a whole. Although the English and Dutch may not have held slaves at home in any numbers, most English and Dutch merchant companies and colony founders had concrete experience in the Spanish and Portuguese colonial world long before setting out to the Americas. Furthermore, the laws of these countries were not codified (as was, for example, Spanish law) and thus tended to grow somewhat haphazardly in all cases. However, canon law and biblical literature included discussions of slavery that may well have substituted for a more specific set of legal precedents.

66 Puckrein, *Little England*, pp. 25–31. For a detailed outline of these issues, which shows in how many respects indentured laborers were like slaves, see Beckles, "Rebels and Reactionaries."

67 Wilcomb E. Washburn, *The Governor and the Rebel: A History of Bacon's Rebellion in Virginia* (Chapel Hill, 1957); and more recently, Edmund S. Morgan, "Slavery and Freedom: An American Paradox," *Journal of American History* 59 (1972–3): 20–4.

68 This long debate originates with Oscar Handlin and Mary Handlin, "Origins of the Southern Labor System," *William and Mary Quarterly* 7 (1950): 199–222; for a more recent view and survey see Russel Menard, "From Servants to Slaves," *Southern Studies* 16 (1977): 355–90. The emphasis on racial attitudes in the shift is found in Carl Degler, "Slavery and the Genesis of American Race Prejudice," *Comparative Studies in Society and History* 2 (1959): 49–66, and Jordan, *White over Black*.

Whatever the legal case, the earliest settlers certainly understood that the Africans they purchased were legally different from the indentured servants they brought from Europe, long before the first slave codes were promulgated in Virginia or the West Indies. The Dutch settlers in New Netherlands insisted on the right to import slaves from the very start of their settlement in 1626[69] and were upset that they were having to use indentured servants rather than slaves in 1644, precisely because they recognized the legal impediments to the fullest long-term use of the labor of their indentured servants.[70] In 1631 the English settler Colt realized that slaves could be held for their lives, and their descendants for theirs,[71] as did the French colonists who informed Bouton in 1635 and later.[72]

These choices were made concerning the legal status of their workers and show a clear understanding that there was a crucial difference between a European indentured servant and an African slave. Ultimately, too, legal status rather than race determined the choice of slaves over indentured servants for many colonies, as is well illustrated when people of African descent came to America as indentured servants rather than slaves. There were several cases where such persons were wrongly enslaved and sought redress in courts in Virginia[73] and, in at least one case, that of Thomas Hagelton in Maryland in 1676, successfully defended their rights as former indentured servants and free people.[74]

But in the end, it may well have been economic conditions rather than simply legal status that determined the choice of labor force. Wages and conditions in Europe went a long way toward determining who would be willing to undertake the task of settling. Adverse publicity concerning conditions for indentured servants in the Americas may also have shaped the decisions, all tending to make indentured servants more expensive.[75] At the same time, the Dutch expulsion from Brazil in 1644 may have cheapened slaves for North America and the Caribbean as the Dutch sought to dispose of their slaves from African sources more cheaply.[76] The organization of the French and English slave-trading companies in the 1670s and 1680s also ensured a certain supply of slaves at

69 E. B. O'Callaghan, ed., *Voyage of the Slavers St. John and Arms of Amsterdam* (Albany, 1967), p. xiii.
70 Remonstrance of 1644, ibid., pp. 200–1; and remonstrance of 1649, in O'Callaghan and Fernow, *Documents* 2:213–14.
71 Colt, "Voyage," pp. 65–6.
72 Bouton, *Relation*, pp. 98–9.
73 Kulikoff, *Tobacco and Slaves*, p. 360
74 Decision of 24 May 1676, William Hand Browne, ed., *Archives of Maryland*, 72 vol. (Baltimore, 1883–1972), 66:291.
75 See the discussion in Galenson, *Traders, Planters and Slaves*.
76 Dunn, *Sugar and Slaves*, pp. 60–6.

low cost.[77] Thus, the two tendencies of more expensive European labor and cheaper African labor when combined with the advantages of slave labor over indentured labor for a long-term work force contributed to the gradual replacement of one by the other.

Other economic factors of significance also concerned the development of profitable export crops. In Barbados, for example, once sugar took off as an export crop, it made fortunes for those who invested in it, allowing them to replace their indentured work forces with the more expensive but more satisfactory slaves, and then to buy up suitable land from the remaining free farmers, gradually transforming the demography of the island from one of European settlement to one of African slaves and European owners.[78] In general, the same sort of cycle took place in Virginia with the tobacco farmers, where the wealthier farmers reinvested their incomes in slaves and replaced their indentured servants, even though they were not as capable as their West Indian counterparts in driving out the competition from small holdings.[79]

In all the areas of settlement without Native American workers, the conditions favored the placement of African slaves in crucial positions, thus enhancing their ability to make a cultural impact. Obviously, in the uninhabited islands of the Gulf of Guinea and the Caribbean, they formed virtually the entire labor force (expecially after the sugar cycle forced the indentured workers out, after about 1660) and the majority of the population. But even in the areas where they were not the largest demographic element, they tended to be well placed in the society.

In North America, for example, slaves were most likely to be found in the largest estates and wealthiest households. William Byrd, living in Virginia in the 1680s, in land occupied by his estate and the smaller farms of former indentured servants, still felt that he was living in a "great family of Negro's [*sic*]."[80] Byrd's slaves not only worked fields but provided domestic service, in close proximity to the European master. This same situation prevailed in New Netherlands. The wealthiest had large estates of slaves, where everywhere else European indentured

77 For the English case, see Davies, *Royal African Company*, and Galenson, *Traders, Planters and Slaves*.

78 Dunn, *Sugar and Slaves*, outlines the process. See also Robert Carlyle Batie, "Why Sugar? Economic Cycles and the Changing of Staples in the English and French Antilles, 1624–54," *Journal of Caribbean History* 8 (1976): 1–41; and for a slightly different perspective, Matthew Edels, "The Brazilian Sugar Cycle of the Seventeenth Century and the Rise of the West Indian Competition," *Caribbean Studies* 9 (1969): 24–44.

79 Kulikoff, *Tobacco and Slaves*, pp. 30–44.

80 William Byrd to Warham Horsmandon, 31 March 1685, in William Tinling, ed., *The Correspondence of the Three William Byrds of Westover, Virginia, 1684–1776*, 2 vols. (Charlottesville, Va., 1977), 1:32.

servants prevailed. Thus, only West India Company officials and the governors had as many as forty slaves each in New Netherlands.[81] Slaves also provided most of the domestic service in the homes of the elite, even though some visitors may have preferred Europeans, believing that "Angolan slave women are thievish, lazy and useless trash."[82] But whatever the overall Dutch opinion of them, they were virtually ubiquitous in domestic service among the better households.

Owners of slaves could also engage in large-scale nonagricultural enterprises without the problems contingent upon using indentured servants, especially in some skilled tasks, where the loss of a trained servant might be hard to make up. This might explain why one Virginia master, Samuel Matthews, was reported in 1648 to have some forty slaves whom he "brought up to trades" so that he could hire them out as skilled workers and, moreover, enjoy that right perpetually.[83] Such strategies often had the effect of undercutting free workers, and not surprisingly, free workers in both Boston and New York complained of the practice of masters employing skilled slaves and hiring them out.[84] Even where the slaves were less skilled, a master might hire them more cheaply than a free person would be willing to work, undercutting free labor even in unskilled tasks. Certainly this practice was undertaken in Dutch New Netherlands, though the documents do not reveal the attitudes of free workers to it.[85]

As in Spanish and Portuguese America, the earliest settlers found African slaves valuable military allies, especially in those colonies where hostile Native American groups were constant threats. French accounts of the settlement of Cayenne (French Guiana) mention frequent use of *nègres* to fight the local Carib inhabitants.[86] The Dutch governor of New Amsterdam told the heads of settler families in 1641 that he would use

81 Stuvysant letter, in O'Callaghan and Fernow, *Documents* 2:474, 504; Esther Singleton, *Dutch New York* (New York, 1909; reprint, 1968), p. 152.

82 Michaelus to Smoutius, in J. Franklin Jameson, ed., *Narratives of New Netherlands, 1609–64* (New York, 1909), p. 129.

83 *A Perfect Description of Virginia . . . Being Sent from Virginia at the Request of a Gentleman of Worthy Note* (London, 1648).

84 Town meeting minutes, in *A Report of the Records of Commissioners of the City of Boston*, 13 vols. (Boston, 1881–1909), 7:5; Minutes in *Minutes of the Common Council of the City of New York, 1675–76*, 8 vols. (New York, 1905), 1:179.

85 Dutch documents on the case of a certain Bastian Jansen in the 1670s reveal the dynamics of the process, which might be complicated; see sessions of 1 February 1670 and 2 May 1671 in Peter Christopher, Kenneth Scott, Kenneth Stryker-Rodda, eds. and trans., *New York Historical Manuscripts: Dutch: Kingston Papers*, 2 vols. (Baltimore, 1976), 2:459, 465. For more evidence, though from a later period, see Edgar J. MacManus, *Black Bondage in the North* (Syracuse, 1973), pp. 45–7.

86 Antoine Biet, *Voyage de la France Eqvinoxiale en l'isle de Cayenne* (Paris, 1654), p. 103; du Tertre, *Histoire* 2:498.

the "strongest and fleetest Negroes" to fight the Native Americans with hatchets and the half-pike,[87] and Pieter Stuyvesant requested in 1658 that the Dutch West India Company send "clever and strong Negroes" to work and to fight Native Americans, either directly or as adjuncts in carrying supplies.[88] Likewise, in 1652 the Massachusetts assembly ordered that all the inhabitants of the colony, including "Scots and Negroes," be armed and trained for war.[89]

The problem of having adequate soldiers was an acute one as more and more slaves arrived, however. When the slaves were not numerous and there were relatively few Europeans as well, arming slaves to stand and fight side by side against Native American or European rivals might be practical. But as slaves gradually replaced indentured servants as a labor force, and fears of slave revolt rose, most colonial legislatures decided to end slave military service, as happened in Barbados. In Barbados, however, the colony had to accept (at a cost in local self-government) the protection of the royal army and navy because the elimination of poor Europeans and slaves from the military left it defenseless.[90] Alternatively, when European indentured servants or their free descendants were sufficiently numerous to fill the militia, slaves were phased out so that the militia could police slaves as well as defend the colony. This took place fairly rapidly in Massachusetts, which banned slaves from militia service in 1656,[91] but a bit more slowly in Virginia, which did the same in 1680.[92]

In the Atlantic colonies of the northern Europeans, as in the Spanish colonies, freed slaves and their descendants could also form a permanently dependent group. Their owners could grant them freedom without necessarily losing control over them, because the owners could control exactly how they wished freedom to be given. The Dutch West India Company granted many of its slaves freedom but in exchange for payment of perpetual dues, and it retained the right to reenslave the children of the original slaves. Several such slaves appeared in a legal inquest of 1644,[93] and the

87 Director to Heads of Families, New Amsterdam, 1 November 1641, in van Laer, *New York Historical Manuscripts: Dutch*, 4 vols. (Baltimore, 1974), 4: fols. 104–5.

88 Stuyvesant to Curacao, 1658, in O'Callaghan and Fernow, *Documents* 13:142–3.

89 Ordinance of 27 May 1652 in Nathaniel B. Shurtleff, ed., *Records of the Governor and Company of the Massachusetts Bay in New England, 1628–74*, 5 vols. (Boston, 1853–4), 3:268.

90 For the complexities of this situation in seventeenth-century Barbados, see Puckrein, *Little England*, pp. 118–20, 175–80.

91 Ordinance of May 1656 in Shurtleff, *Records* 3:420.

92 For a detailed discussion of armed slaves and legislation in Virginia, see T. H. Breen and Stephen Innis, *"Myne Owne Ground": Race and Freedom on Virginia's Eastern Shore, 1640–1676* (New York and Oxford, 1980), pp. 24–8.

93 Hearing of 25 February 1644 in van Laer, *Historical Manuscripts* 4: fols. 183–4.

practice was condemned as being "contrary to all humanity" in a remonstrance of 1649.[94]

As in the Spanish and Portuguese colonies, legislation also tended to retain the former slaves as a dependent and powerless group, though this may have been fairly slow to develop in some areas. T. H. Breen and Stephen Innes, for example, have recently shown that former slaves in Virginia enjoyed considerable political rights in the early and mid-seventeenth century,[95] although eventually laws restricting the political liberty and rights of people of servile and African descent predominated.[96] Certainly, these restrictions caused former slaves on French St. Christopher to complain to the Jesuit priest Jean Mongin of their condition as being little better and perhaps even worse than that of the slaves in 1682.[97]

Thus, African slaves even in North America, where they made up a small minority of the overall population, were placed near the center of visibility and power in settler society. They were not marginalized or banished to backwoods areas. Indeed, the marginal areas were the places they were least likely to be found, for only the wealthiest owned them in any numbers, though of course, a large percentage of the African slaves lived in rural areas, and most worked all day in the fields rather than in the houses of the rich.

94 Remonstrance of 1649 in O'Callaghan and Fernow, *Documents* 1:343. For more such cases, see Singleton, *Dutch New York*, pp. 154–5.

95 Breen and Innis, *"Myne Owne Ground."*

96 Higgenbotham, *Matter of Color* (for North America); Jerome S. Handler, *The Unappropriated People: Freedom in the Slave Society of Barbados* (Baltimore, 1974) (for Barbados).

97 Jean Mongin à une personne de condition du Languedoc, St. Christophe, May 1682, in Marcel Chatillon, "L'évangélisation des esclaves au XVIIe siècle, lettres du R. P. Jean Mongin," *Bulletin de la Société d'Histoire de la Guadeloupe* 60–2 (1984): 77.

6

Africans and Afro-Americans in the Atlantic world: life and labor

A combination of political, demographic, and economic circumstances delivered African slaves to the heart of the new Atlantic world in the centuries after 1450. As workers, African slaves and their descendants (Afro-Americans) were a crucial part of the exploited labor force of every Atlantic colony. Their labor was vital for building the Atlantic world, and they made cultural contributions of great significance. This cultural impact was itself a product of the way in which they were integrated into the Atlantic world, for it gave them a geographic position of importance in those areas where culture change was most significant.

However, the nature of their cultural impact depended very much on the social conditions created by their role as exploited slaves in Atlantic economies. Slaves, however centrally located socially or geographically, may well make a very small cultural impact if their living conditions are bad enough and their position degraded enough. Those scholars who have argued that slaves made a minimum impact have often emphasized how their position as exploited and dependent laborers took them socially out of the mainstream of Atlantic culture, even if they were present geographically. An early position, for example, held by such scholars as Franklin Frazier and Stanley Elkins, maintained that the dynamics of the slave trade and the conditions of labor in the Atlantic world had the effect of traumatizing and marginalizing them, so that they became cultural receptacles rather than donors.[1] Although few modern scholars would accept this position in its more extreme form – for the slave condition was anything but uniform in any case – most acknowledge that the nature of Africans' enslavement had a crucial role to play in the way in which they were able to function as cultural actors.

Sidney Mintz and Richard Price, for example, have produced an expla-

[1] E. Franklin Frazier, *The Negro Family in America* (Chicago, 1966), pp. 7–8; and *The Negro Church in America* (New York, 1964), pp. 1–16; Elkins, *Slavery*.

nation of the slave experience that attempts to describe their potential for cultural influence within the conditions of slavery. Their study focuses on the role of the slave trade and plantation labor as shaping forces, which were extremely disruptive to the slaves.[2] As they saw it, the slave trade had the effect of permanently breaking numerous social bonds that had tied Africans together and of forcing them to rebuild a society in the conditions of the New World. Furthermore, plantation life, with its harsh labor regimes, unstable family units, and high mortality, often did not permit this rebuilding to be accomplished easily.

Atlantic social systems provided a vast array of possible lives and careers for the African and Afro-American slave. Some of these were harsh plantation agricultural systems where slaves were mostly male, rarely formed families, died quickly, and perhaps never had the chance to alter an African culture to apply it to a new environment or transmit either the original or the revised culture to future generations. But in other cases, even within plantation systems, the African and Afro-American slaves rapidly formed village communities, and although they were exploited for their labor and often suffered high mortality, their communities became culturally self-sustaining. Likewise, although in some areas of the Atlantic world slaves were thrust into household service among Europeans and cut off from other Africans, thus being more or less forced to readjust to the new environment, in many areas where slaves performed domestic work they had plenty of contacts with other Africans and might still develop and transmit an African-based cultural pattern outside their home environment.

This chapter will focus first on the slave trade, a common experience, and its effect on the slaves, and then on the wide variety of labor situations of African slaves in the Atlantic world, paying special attention to their ability to form a viable community, to their prospects for passing on their changing cultural heritage to a new generation through training their own offspring, and the possibilities that they had, in any given labor regime, to associate with each other.

The Middle Passage: a common experience

Historians have sometimes seen the passage of slaves across the Atlantic on the slave ships as a first and crucial step in their deculturation. As some scholars have seen it, the passage was a psychological shock from which they never recovered, rendering them docile and passive and thus receptive to whatever limited cultural inputs their masters or the slave situation might provide.

[2] Mintz and Price, *An Anthropological Approach to the Afro-American Past*.

Certainly the Middle Passage was the starting point for most of the Afro-Atlantic world. With the exception of a few voluntary migrants from Africa to the Atlantic islands and perhaps a few African sailors on European vessels, slaves joined the Atlantic world through the Middle Passage. Although the nature of the crossing varied widely, it was a common experience that nearly all newly arrived slaves shared.

The voyage was at the very best extremely unpleasant, and for many it was a slow and painful death. For those in the sixteenth century who made the passage from Kongo or Benin to São Tomé, the trip was perhaps tolerable, taking only about two weeks, although sixteenth-century ships' books clearly reveal that for some even this short trip was fatal.[3] For those who made the much longer trip from Angola to the Spanish port of Cartagena from the late sixteenth century onward or, thanks to the Dutch West India Company's policies, from Angola to New Netherlands (New York) – a substantial number by the mid-seventeenth century – the trip pushed a significant number of the cargo to the brink of death and routinely killed up to a third of them.[4]

Alonso de Sandoval, who took great pains to discover exactly how the trade to Cartagena was carried out in the early seventeenth century, including interviews with the slaves themselves, provides us with an excellent description of the life on the ships. While still on shore in Africa (de Sandoval was particularly knowledgeable about conditions in Angola), slaves were chained together on long chains (*corrientes*) in groups of six, to which were added foot shackles for each pair to prevent them from running away (when loading and unloading) or throwing themselves into the sea. Once on board, they were put below decks, "locked from the outside, where they saw neither sun nor moon," and placed head to foot, still chained in long rows.[5] Jean Barbot, who traveled on the French ship *Soleil d'Affrique* in 1678–9, noted that the general practice was to separate the sexes by a partition, with the men forward and the women aft.[6]

Slaves might not stay below for the entire trip – indeed conditions below decks would make that impossible. The air was so close and circulation so bad that ships' surgeons could not work below decks because candles would not stay lighted, and the heat made it impossible

3 The existing ships' books show mortality among the slaves: ANTT, CC II/128/3, Book of *Conceição* to Kongo (28 August 1525), fols. 13–14; Book of *Santo Espirito* to Kongo, 10 January 1535, *MMA* 15:101–2; Book of *Urbano* to Kongo (30 April 1535), *MMA* 15:117; Book of *Conceição* to Kongo (21 July 1535), *MMA* 15:126–8. For the voyages to Benin, see Ryder, *Benin and the Europeans*, pp. 56–67, and idem, "Trading Voyage," for a voyage from the Forcados River near Benin.

4 De Sandoval, *Instauranda*, p. 107.

5 Ibid., p. 107.

6 Barbot, "Voyage," p. 546.

for them to work.[7] Barbot gave specific details on the regime that was followed by the most successful French slavers – slaves were brought on deck every day, men for limited times, women whenever they wished. Men might return to deck in small escorted groups as well, though the possibility of revolt kept the male slaves more closely watched.[8]

Merchants who carried slaves had a strong interest in packing as many slaves as possible into their ships, and this practice contributed substantially to making the trip both uncomfortable and dangerous, as work by Joseph C. Miller on this and later periods clearly reveals.[9] Barbot also agreed that slow voyages (due to poor sailing planning) and packed ships made for higher mortality as well.[10] Although the physical crowding might have been frustrating and difficult for the cargo, cramped as they were on benches and chained facing head to foot, it was the necessary reduction of supplies of food and water that loading extra slaves entailed that made the greatest danger for the trip. Portuguese regulations after 1519, important because Portuguese vessels carried virtually all slaves that made the trip to the islands or America before 1620 or so, required that adequate supplies of both food and water be carried,[11] and documents from royal ships in the 1520s and 1530s studiously certified that these requirements had been met.[12] If royal captains documented compliance, many private captains did not, for captains were anxious to make as much profit as possible, and overloaded ships were a standard item of complaint from most observers of the sixteenth- and seventeenth-century trade.[13]

The result was that, according to de Sandoval, slaves were fed only once in every twenty-four hours, and then a miserly meal composed of "no more than a medium-sized bowl of corn or millet flour or raw millet

7 Ibid., p. 547.

8 Ibid., p. 546.

9 Joseph C. Miller, "Overcrowded and Undernourished: The Techniques and Consequences of Tight-Packing in the Portuguese Southern Atlantic Slave Trade," in Serge Daget, ed., *De la traite à l'esclavage, Ve au XIXeme siècle: Actes du Colloque International sur la Traite des Noires, Nantes 1985*, 2 vols. (Nantes and Paris, 1988), 2:395–424. Although most of Miller's examples and data come from a later period, the concepts are undoubtedly applicable to this earlier period as well.

10 Barbot, "Voyage," p. 545.

11 Regimento of São Tomé trade, 8 February 1519, *MMA* 4:124–33.

12 E.g., ANTT, CC II/128/3, Book of *Conceição*, fols. 15–16; *Santo Espirito, MMA* 15:100–1; *Urbano, MMA* 15:115–16; *Conceição, MMA* 15:126; on the Kongo run. Food was loaded in *quereillas* (from the Kikongo for "sack," *kidila*), and on the *Urbano* each set of slaves was assigned a number of sacks. Similar certificates were issued for slaves from São Tomé bound for Mina (book of the *Santa Maria do Cabo*, 24 April 1535, *MMA* 15:112; *São Cristóvão*, 13 July 1535, *MMA* 15:121).

13 See Tomás de Mercado, *Suma de tratos y contratos de mercaderes y tratantes decididos y determinados* (Seville, 1569), pp. 63–8; de Sandoval, *Instauranda*, p. 107. See the further discussion in José Gonçalves Salvador, *Os magnates do tráfico negreiro (séculos XVI e XVII)* (São Paulo, 1981), p.108.

gruel," and water rations were simply a "small jar of water."[14] De Sandoval's descriptions dealt with the Portuguese trade, which was virtually the only one when he wrote. After the 1620s, however, an increasing number of Dutch merchants engaged in the trade, supplying not only their own holdings in Brazil, Surinam, and New Netherlands but also most of the English and French colonies in the Caribbean and North America until the 1670s.

Dutch merchants sought to emulate what they saw as ideal Portuguese practices. Thus, the Dutch commander of Luanda, Pieter Mortamer, writing in 1642, noted that slavers on the Luanda–Brazil run (then in Dutch hands) gave the slaves only "a little palm oil and a bit of cooked corn." He placed the blame for their mortality on poor food and believed that increased food would reduce mortality and increase profits. He proposed measures to improve Dutch methods based on what he believed was common Portuguese practice, according to what he was told by a certain Luis, a former slave of the Portuguese captain António Bruto, who had taken several trips to Brazil and managed the slave cargoes. The proposal included larger rations of maize meal, alternated with beans and elephant or hippopotamus meat and dried fish.[15] A similar proposal, again based on alleged Portuguese practice, suggested cleaning the holds periodically "with bad vinegar" and caring for sick slaves and – a significant point – providing "water in abundance."[16]

Barbot's description of French practices confirms this: The Portuguese, he felt, provided more for the slaves' comfort, including sleeping mats. The French fed slaves twice a day, at 10:00 a.m. and 5:00 p.m. (the Dutch, he believed, fed their slaves three times), with some snacks of manioc meal, corn, and tobacco in between. Food included beans and mush made from one or another grain, with occasional grease, fat, or lard.[17] Although such practices might have been ideal and indeed carried out by some captains, they were probably still more honored in the breach. If Mortamer and Barbot had discovered something good in Portuguese ship management, we should remember that de Sandoval was also describing common Portuguese practice.[18]

The dangers of undernourishment, severe but probably not fatal, were coupled with the much greater dangers of dehydration, implied by the small water rations and the fact that the slaves were kept in poorly venti-

[14] De Sandoval, *Instauranda*, p. 107.

[15] Pieter Mortamer to Council of Brazil, 14 October 1642, in Jadin, ed. and trans., *L'ancien Congo* 1:353–4.

[16] Pieter Mortamer to Zeeland Chamber, 29 June 1643, ibid. 1:359.

[17] Barbot, "Voyage," p. 546.

[18] On the legal and practical struggles involved in treatment of slaves in the Portuguese slave trade, see Salvador, *Magnates*.

lated quarters in a tropical climate. The potential for dehydration from inadequate water rations was increased because Africans traveling on the high seas for the first time suffered seasickness and vomited frequently, creating an environment that rapidly became nauseatingly odorous. More important, widespread diarrhea inevitably occurred because of poor food and inadequate preservation measures, complicated by the impossibility of adequate hygiene, even when diseases had broken out. Witnesses, including slaves who had traveled on such ships, testifying in an inquest of 1658, spoke of the routine presence of "flusso" – a medically inspecific term, which probably included simple diarrheas as well as more dangerous diseases – on incoming slave ships.[19]

Such conditions were an inevitable and unavoidable consequence of making the transatlantic journey in the routinely overloaded ships, and there were very few slaves indeed who escaped them. For many, however, there was the much worse situation created when serious epidemic disease – especially waterborne diseases of the intestinal tract – embarked with the slaves. Typhoid fever, measles, yellow fever, and smallpox were deadly diseases that could kill virtually all the slaves (and the crew) of an unfortunate ship and, moreover, might spread an epidemic in the port in which it called. For example, António Fernandes Brandão observed that slaves from Kongo and Allada had introduced epidemics into Brazil in 1616 and 1617 from which slaves and native Brazilians, rich and poor, had died.[20] Two hundred and forty of those slaves died on the estates of Pero Garçia, who eventually renounced God for doing this to make him so poor.[21]

Many more Brazilian epidemics arriving on slave ships damaged Brazil in the years to come, as documented in a recent survey by Dauril Alden and Joseph C. Miller.[22] In the same vein, Jamaican officials complained of smallpox reaching the island from a ship from Allada in 1680.[23] David Chandler has documented the numerous epidemics that arrived in Cartagena via slave ships.[24] Not surprisingly, such ships were

19 Biblioteca Nacional de Colombia (henceforth BN Colombia), Claver Inquest, fols. 32, 102, and passim.

20 Fernandes Brandão, *Diálogo* (ed. Conçalves de Mello), p. 59.

21 Investigation of Pero Garçia, 17 September 1618, in Eduardo d'Oliveira França and Sonia da Siqueira, eds., *Segunda visitação do Santo ofício as Partes do Brasil: Pelo Inquisitor e visidor Licienciado Marcos Teixeira, 1618–20*, São Paulo, Anais do Museu Paulista, 17 (1963), p. 444.

22 Dauril Alden and Joseph C. Miller, "Out of Africa: The Slave Trade and the Transmission of Smallpox to Brazil, ca. 1560–ca. 1830," *Journal of Interdisciplinary History* 18 (1987): 195–224.

23 PRO T/70, vol. 1134, Herder, Rould, Molesworth, and Powell to Board of Trade, 20 January 1680.

24 David L. Chandler, "Health Conditions in the Slave Trade of Colonial New Granada," in Toplin, *Slavery and Race Relations in Latin America*, pp. 53–7.

often quarantined, as happened to a ship from Angola carrying smallpox that was forced to land its human cargo on the island at Bordones near Cumaná in Venezuela in 1620. There officials dutifully noted the deaths day by day.[25]

Such dangers spread even beyond the port cities, especially because the nature of the trade often took infected slaves inland and placed them in the centers of population. In Virginia, with its scattered rural population, the arrival of sick slaves in the larger plantations could set off a local epidemic. One planter, William Byrd, observed that two slaves he had purchased from the Gambia in 1686 carried smallpox with them, in the end killing three of his slaves and making fifteen others sick, including his own daughter.[26]

The dangerous conditions created even by uneventful voyages worsened the longer the ship was at sea; mortality was limited and perhaps no more than 5–10 percent on voyages to São Tomé from Benin, whereas it varied from as few as 1 to as high as 16 percent from Kongo and was 15 percent and above on the sixteenth-century Arguim-to-Lisbon route.[27] For the longer trip between Senegambia and the Spanish Indies, mortality reached the 15–20 percent range, at least according to Tomás de Mercado, a late sixteenth-century commentator.[28] The long voyage from São Tomé to Lisbon, which usually took a month and a half or more, might run up to 30 percent or higher,[29] as was the case on long runs like the Angola-to-Cartagena route. Thus, Dutch merchants typically experienced 15–20 percent losses in their transatlantic trade (to all American ports) between 1637 and 1645,[30] as did the Portuguese en route to Brazil.[31] The English Royal African Company suffered slightly higher losses in the late seventeenth

[25] Decision of Cabildo de Cumaná, 25 October 1620, and Declaration of Tomás Muñoz, 5 December 1620, in Trochis Veracoechea, *Documentos*, pp. 173, 185–9.

[26] William Byrd to Sadler and Thomas, 18 October 1686, in Marion Tinling, ed., *The Correspondence of the Three William Byrds of Westover, Virginia, 1684–1776*, 2 vols. (Charlottesville, 1977), 1:65–6, 68.

[27] Ryder, *Benin and the Europeans*, pp. 62–8, on the Benin route to São Tomé, based on ships' books; on the Kongo route, four known ships took a total of 2,099 slaves in 1935. Mortality varied widely. The *Conceição* had 502 slaves with 68 deaths (13.5%) on its first run (*MMA* 15:125, 126–9) and 91 deaths from 550 slaves (16.5%) on its second run (ANTT, CCII/128/3); the *Santo Espirito* had 9 deaths from 380 slaves (2.3%) (*MMA* 15:100, 101–2); the *Urbano* had 8 deaths from 667 slaves (1.1%) (*MMA* 15:115–16, 117). For the Arguim-to-Lisbon route, see Saunders, *Black Slaves*, p. 14.

[28] De Mercado, *Tratado*, p. 66. Note, however, that an early seventeenth-century merchant considered 17% mortality on one voyage "a punishment from God," implying that lower rates were expected (Bowser, *African Slave*, p. 50).

[29] Saunders, *Black Slaves*, p. 14.

[30] Ernst van den Boogaart and Pieter C. Emmer, "The Dutch Participation in the Slave Trade, 1596–1650," in Gemery and Hogendorn, *Uncommon Market*, p. 367.

[31] Curtin, *Atlantic Slave Trade*, p. 277.

century in their operations, which mostly connected the Gold Coast with the Caribbean.[32]

It was probably to reduce the increasingly high rates of mortality experienced toward the end of the long voyages to Cartagena, Portobelo (in Panama), and Vera Cruz that both Spanish Jamaica[33] and Portuguese Maranhão[34] were often used as stopping points for the longer voyages where supplies could be replenished and slaves rested. But even with rests included, the longer voyages were physically very demanding, for slaves arriving in Cartagena were generally, in de Sandoval's words, "reduced to skeletons."[35]

North American settlers often bought slaves from the Caribbean (the English from Barbados and the Dutch from Curaçao), rather than obtain slaves via the direct route from Africa. Thus, one Virginia planter, Edmund Jennings, noted that before 1680 only a few slaves arrived directly from Africa and most were purchased from Barbados after a shorter or longer stay there.[36] Likewise, English settlers in New England sold Native Americans captured in wars there to Barbados in exchange for African slaves after 1637.[37] The Dutch West India Company, which supplied New Netherlands with slaves (and also, directly or indirectly, the English colonies to its north and south), decided to supply its North American colonies with Angolan slaves,[38] much to their cost, and consequently the settlers, anxious over the high mortality rate and bad condition of newly arrived slaves, began to purchase slaves from Curaçao.[39]

In order to deal with the serious health conditions of the newly arrived slaves, the Jesuits of Cartagena gave them fruit, sweets, preserves, and water – an appropriate initial diet for persons suffering from severe dehydration and, almost inevitably, scurvy.[40] Heavier food, indeed, tended

32 Davies, *Royal African Company,* p. 292.
33 Vázquez de Espinosa, *Compendio,* para. 328.
34 Mauro, *Portugal et l'Atlantique,* pp. 167–8.
35 De Sandoval, *Instauranda,* p. 108.
36 Edmund Jennings to Board of Trade, 27 November 1708, in Elizabeth Donnan, ed., *Documents Illustrative of the History of the Slave Trade,* 4 vols. (Washington, D.C., 1930–5), 4:89. See also statistical details and notes on the practice of the Royal African Company in Davies, *Royal African Company,* pp. 38–44.
37 Plymouth Colony meeting minutes, 15 September 1646, in Nathaniel Shurtleff and David Pulsifer, ed., *Records of the Colony of New Plymouth,* 12 vols. (Boston, 1855–61), 9:71; Edward Downing to John Winthrop, August 1645, quoted in note in Robert Moody, ed., *The Saltonstall Papers, 1607–1815,* 2 vols. (Boston, 1972–4), 1:138.
38 Documents cited in Singleton, *Dutch New York,* p. 156.
39 Pieter C. Emmer, "De slavenhandel van en naar Nieuw Nederland," *Economische en Sociaal-Historische Jaarboek* 34 (1974): 114–15.
40 De Sandoval, *Instauranda,* p. 108; BN Colombia, Claver Inquest, fols. 20, 100–101v, and passim. Moortamer also noted the ideal practice of including preserved fruits in slave rations (Report to Brazil Council, 14 October 1642, postscript in Jadin, *L'ancien Congo* 1:354).

to kill them, a common problem of rehabilitating people suffering from dehydration and severe malnutrition.[41] Arrival in port did not stop the mortality – the Spanish Jesuit Pedro Claver's first action on boarding the ships in Cartagena was to ask the slaves (through his interpreters) which ones were in imminent danger of dying so that he could baptize them and give them Last Rites.[42]

Moreover, still more were irrecoverably sick. The Jesuits of Cartagena set up a makeshift hospital for them right on the docks, where many more died. Others, sold to busy merchants, were simply left more or less uncared for in private prisons, where they went to "populate the cemeteries."[43] One slave who knew these conditions well was Isabella Folupo, from the "Rivers of Guinea," for she lay herself some time in the Jesuit hospital after her arrival in the 1630s, cared for by the indefatigable Pedro Claver. She believed she was at the point of death when Claver miraculously cured her while giving her the Last Rites.[44] Although both nutritional and health care in even the worst of the private prisons were probably superior to those of the ships, they were sufficiently bad that many more slaves, who might have recovered, died while awaiting customs clearance and sale.[45]

For many, the transatlantic crossing was not the end of their journeys, and subsequent travel can properly be seen as a continuation of the Middle Passage. For those who landed in the Caribbean Islands or Brazil, where the settlements that would purchase them were relatively close to the shore, this journey was fairly short and not particularly arduous. Those who were bound for Spanish settlements in Peru (whether illegally by the route passing through Rio de Janeiro and Buenos Aires or legally through Cartagena or Panama), however, faced a new journey that could be almost as difficult and sometimes more likely to be fatal as the crossing of the Atlantic, especially because many were not fully recovered from their passage.[46] Records of one merchant who worked the Cartagena–Lima route suggest that mortality ran in the 10–15 percent range.[47]

Thus, this complex process of shifting people from Africa to the Americas was full of horrors and might well last several months, during which most slaves would witness the maximum in human degradation, while suffering it themselves. Vomit, urine, feces, and perspiration made the

[41] De Sandoval, *Instauranda*, p. 108.
[42] BN Colombia, Claver Inquest, fols. 20–2, 100–1, and passim.
[43] De Sandoval, *Instauranda*, p. 108.
[44] BN Colombia, Claver Inquest, fol. 165v.
[45] See the detailed discussion of health conditions in Chandler, "Health Conditions," pp. 58–9.
[46] Bowser, *African Slave*, pp. 64–8; Chandler, "Health Conditions," pp. 72–80.
[47] Bowser, *African Slave*, p. 66.

holds of the ships intolerable by the end of the voyage, even on such ships that took precautions to clean them. Indeed, it was the foul smell that wafted over New Amsterdam in 1655 that announced to the inhabitants that a slave ship had arrived,[48] and the Cartagena Jesuits believed that spending even an hour in the holds would make a person sick.[49]

Therefore, while enduring these conditions, they would be driven to the brink of death, see others die, often horribly, and at all times live under conditions of extreme deprivation. No doubt many were driven insane, and others suffered severe psychological shock. One wonders if the depression and shock contributed to the slaves' devotion to Pedro Claver, for he was willing to stay as long as necessary below decks, kindly inquiring about their needs and tending to the dying.[50]

This psychological shock was noted by some of the witnesses as well. De Sandoval heard that upon their departure from Luanda, slaves from Angola were "full of sadness and depression." If it were not enough that they had just been advised to forget their homes and former lives, they were convinced, from the time they left Africa, that they were unwilling participants in a "form of witchcraft" in which "upon their arrival they would be made into oil and eaten."[51] This was a near universal opinion: the Kongo slave Jose Monzolo, a Christian at the time of his enslavement, testified that he thought that the Spanish would kill him to make oil and that "the flags of the ships, when they were dyed red . . . had been made from the blood of the slaves."[52] Isabella Folupo noted that she, a slave from the Rivers of Guinea in modern Guinea-Bissau, had once held the same beliefs as a group of slaves from Allada (modern Benin) that she helped Claver attend to: "that the Spanish carried them to this land to eat them or to make them into oil or to make gunpowder from them."[53]

In this situation, it is hardly surprising that Jesuits like Claver tried to overcome their fears. Claver greeted every slave, embraced them, and welcomed them to the New World, while constantly assuring them that the Spanish intended to make Christians of them and not oil.[54] Although his reassurances may have been a bit naive and surely did not reveal the

48 Herren XIX to Pieter Stuyvesant, 23 March 1654, in O'Callaghan, ed., *Documents Relative to Colonial New York* 14:304–5; and Emmer, "Slavenhandel," pp. 114–15.

49 De Sandoval, *Instauranda*, p. 107.

50 BN Colombia, Claver Inquest, fols. 20 (testimony of Nicholás González, his companion), 99 (Manuel Moreno, a slave), 101v (Andreas Sacabuche, a slave), 140 (Jose Monzolo, a slave), and passim.

51 De Sandoval, *Instauranda*, p. 107, and testimony of traders made in Tucumán, 21 December 1622, in ibid., pp. 348–9.

52 BN Colombia, Claver Inquest, fol. 141v.

53 Ibid., fol. 166v.

54 Ibid., fols. 20, 100–101v, and passim.

Spaniards' real intentions for the new arrivals, his words may well have helped them to cope, at least temporarily, with their new situation.

Thus, the factors that led historians like Frazier and Elkins to view the impact of the entire process as a major first step in deculturation or in the creation of a highly dependent personality are evident. Nevertheless, although these experiences were never to be forgotten, they do not seem on the whole to have been more than temporarily debilitating. We cannot really penetrate the slave psychology on the bases of such limited sources and theoretical statements about psychological trauma. In the end, the real measure of the effects of the slave trade on slaves must be seen in their subsequent situation and behavior in the Americas.

Slave life in the Atlantic world: labor on rural estates

It is impossible to generalize about the way of life in the Atlantic world for slaves, given the vast array of duties that slaves performed. Even within one type of work, such as plantation labor, conditions varied widely depending on the personality of the master, on the agronomy of the plantation, and on the availability of various types of labor. Thus, statements dealing with the cultural impact of slaves that stress the nature of their work environment necessarily must address the characteristics of each region.

Earlier historians tended to focus on the extremes: life as highly exploited workers on some plantations and the pampered existence of the domestic slave. It was the first of these prospects that one found in the rural enterprises as the main work force, and it is in their case that the most extreme statements about the deculturizing process, development of dependent personalities, and eradication of Afro-Atlantic culture have been made.

Conditions on some plantations certainly inhibited the development and transmission of a full cultural life. For example, where most slaves were male, were housed in barracks, worked for very long hours, and lived short lives, their opportunities for cultural interaction were limited, just as their prospects of forming a family and socializing children in this culture were limited. On the other hand, where conditions permitted slaves to build their own houses and live in families and raise children, the chances for continuing African culture, creating a new Afro-American culture from the blending of African and European elements, and subsequently transmitting this culture through generations were kept alive.

We will now examine life under various labor regimes and labor systems with a special eye to determining the degree to which Atlantic societies permitted slaves the opportunities for cultural interaction, community development, and socialization of children, first on rural estates and then in the special case of domestic service and urban life.

Although conditions in rural life varied widely, the evidence never shows life there being easy. Even on the best of these estates, working conditions were hard, and life was precarious. The French priest Antoine Biet, visiting Barbados in 1654, recorded with horror the harsh beatings that were given to slaves for the smallest offense on the sugar estates – an observation that many others repeated.[55] Likewise, most descriptions of the labor emphasize the long hours and danger inherent in the work, especially the milling operations, where slaves were working around machinery under the pressure of twenty-hour workdays.[56] Schwartz's careful examination of Brazilian work records, especially the well-documented plantation of Sergipe do Conde, confirms the casual observations of other visitors.[57] Records of the Remire plantation in French Guiana (Cayenne) show that virtually all the slaves who died between 1688 and 1690 did so as a result of accidents, though these accidents happened off the estate when the slaves were required to perform public works.[58] Miners also faced the dangers of accidents, and it is surely significant that most of the deaths recorded in the books of the Cocorote mine in Venezuela in the mid-seventeenth century were from accidents.[59] These situations were found in virtually all types of mills and mines, a universal in the Atlantic world.

If virtually all such work was dangerous and involved exploitation of the labor force, the degree to which these dangers and exploitation affected the processes of family, community, and intergenerational cultural transmission still depended on other elements in the labor regime. Some labor regimes tended to inhibit the kind of community that would allow the slaves a full cultural life, especially those that had high mortality, unbalanced sex ratios, and high work loads. But, even on the worst of estates, the evidence supports the idea that slaves managed to form communities that maintained and reproduced themselves and thus that could develop and transmit their culture. On other estates, however, conditions were much more favorable, and the cultural development process was more advanced.

Conditions that made for hard conditions on estates varied widely. On

55 Biet, *Voyage de la France Eqvinoxiale*, pp. 275–91; Pierre Moreau, "Histoire des derniers troubles du Brésil . . .," in Augustin Courbé, *Relations veritables et cvrievsaes de l'isle de Madagascar et du Brésil* (Paris, 1651), pp. 40–2; Nieuhof, *Brasilianense*, p. 215.

56 Andriaan van Berkel, *Amerikaansche voyagien, behelzende en reis na Rio de Berbice . . . Guiana* (Amsterdam, 1695), pp. 63–5; George Flecknoe, *A Relation of Ten Years' Travel in Europe, Asia, Affrique and America* (London, 1656), pp. 79–80.

57 Schwartz, *Sugar Plantations*, pp. 131–60, analyzing eighteenth-century material as well.

58 BM Rouen, MS Montbret, Goupy des Marets, "Voyage," fols. 91–2.

59 Acosta Saignes, *Vida*, pp. 164–6.

some estates, for example, especially those in the Spanish Indies, African slaves formed a small and fairly specialized work force that could be employed continuously, with many other types of work being left to Native Americans. Such estates often had mostly male work forces, a condition that limited the strength of the community and worked against the development of a self-sustaining population and culture. For example, the sugar estate of Hernando Gorjón on Hispaniola, served in part by the labor of a native encomienda, had forty-six male and twenty-six female African slaves in 1547, an imbalance that surely limited family formation. Moreover, many of the skilled positions lay in the hands of Europeans, and the slaves, though performing some skilled labor, generally had positions as simple field hands, with few privileges.[60]

But other estates producing sugar and using outside labor did employ slaves for skilled labor, and in many of these cases, the skilled slaves clearly had advantages in their ability to form families, even though the overall sex ratios were sometimes unbalanced. The Schetz estate of southern Brazil shows a similar imbalance among the African slaves in the 1540s (though they dominated skilled positions), although its Native American slaves (the Brazilian equivalent of a Spanish *encomienda*) had much more balanced sex ratios and hence the probable benefits of a community life denied the Africans, especially the unskilled ones.[61] The earliest inventory of Sergipe do Conde in Bahia (1569–71) shows nineteen males and only one female (who was not married to any of the men), and like the Schetz estate, it had a force of Tupinambá slaves with a clear community life. The seven African slaves who were married in Sergipe do Conde (some to Tupinambá, others to wives whose residence is unknown) were either skilled workers or engaged in cattle raising (a job that few Native Americans could do at that time).[62] Likewise, the one married male slave (of six) at the nearby estate of Sant'anna (in 1572) was a skilled worker.[63] These conditions clearly were typical of larger Brazilian estates in the seventeenth century as well, as Schwartz's survey of existing inventories shows.[64] The Cortés sugar estates also were served by Native American labor, and inventories and purchases again show a strong preponderance of male slaves, but at the same time skilled slaves possessed greater opportunities to have stable families and raise children.[65]

It was not just in estates located in areas where Native Americans could provide a supplementary work force that such conditions existed.

[60] Dieve, *Exclavitud* 1:235.
[61] Stols, "Primeiros documentos," pp. 407–20.
[62] Inventory de Engenho de Sergipe," in *Documentos* 3:40–1.
[63] Inventory of Engenho Sant'anna, in ibid. 3:89.
[64] Schwartz, *Sugar Plantations*, pp. 346–8.
[65] Barrett, *Sugar Hacienda*, pp. 79–84.

They might also be evident in more mature societies where various support and occasional tasks were performed by labor forces, some of them possibly slaves, who resided off the estate. Perhaps this situation is reflected by the seventeen Cuban sugar estates inventoried in a survey of 1602. On these estates a total of 199 male slaves were matched by just 37 females.[66] Even Jesuit estates in Mexico, where there were ideological commitments to creating families (even if it was not strictly rational from an economic point of view), showed sexual imbalances, at least in the early seventeenth century, though the ratios did balance out later.[67]

Records from mining establishments show a pattern similar to those of plantations, at least in cases where the slaves were used as a specialized labor force with support from Native Americans. Mayer's study of the life of African slaves on the mining frontier of northwest Mexico suggests that as many as 72 percent of the slaves shown in purchases and inventories were males, in a situation with mixed free and slave workers of both African and Native American origin.[68] The records of the copper mines at Cocorote in Venezuela confirm this for enterprises with a mixed Native American and African labor force. There, where slaves and Native Americans performed the same type of labor, among the slaves the males made up 78 percent of the total labor force.[69]

Of course, not all slaves were purchased by the owners of sugar estates or mines, either in Iberian America, where there were often sources of Native American labor, or in other slave-using American economies. There were many other productive enterprises besides these, though mines and sugar mills did produce most of the wealth of the Atlantic zone. But many estates produced other crops, less important in the overall wealth of the zone but significant in their own region, such as cacao, tobacco, or food crops; other enterprises specialized in cattle ranching, fishing, or logging. Conditions in such estates are illustrated by the fairly well documented North American tobacco estates.

Owners of tobacco farms in Virginia and Maryland seem to have had ample access to labor from indentured servants, who upon becoming free could often perform roles like the Native Americans in Iberian America, but whose wage demands were sufficiently high as to prevent them from being attractive as a labor force. Thus, planters who owned large estates with indentured servants as well as slaves often kept their slaves

66 Studied in Isabelo Macías Domínguez, *Cuba en la Primera mitad de Siglo XVII* (Seville, 1978), pp. 52–4.

67 Herman W. Konrad, *A Jesuit Hacienda in Colonial Mexico: Santa Lucia, 1576–1767* (Stanford, 1980).

68 Vincent Mayer, Jr., *The Black on New Spain's Northern Frontier: San José de Parral, 1631 to 1641* (Durango, Colo., 1974), p. 14.

69 Acosta Saignes, *Vida*, p. 157.

as a specialized work force, as is revealed in Menard's study of inventories in the Chesapeake region. The wealthier tobacco growers with larger estates had gangs of slaves with sharply unbalanced sex ratios, just as in the mines and mills of Iberian America.[70] William Fitzhugh, one of the largest Virginia planters, was quite explicit when on one occasion in 1682 he instructed his agent to buy up to six slaves, with "as few women as possible, not above two." His other correspondence shows the constant purchase of new slaves, suggesting that hard work and unbalanced sex ratios took their toll, and slaves were constantly having to be replaced.[71]

These conditions may also have prevailed among the company slaves of the Dutch West India Company in nearby New Netherlands. At least their labor was hard, for malefactors of all statuses were occasionally forced to labor alongside company slaves as a punishment.[72] Private owners who possessed numerous slaves and used them for production of food crops may well have managed their slaves like their tobacco-producing colleagues to the south, although details are lacking.[73]

Similar dynamics probably existed in lesser enterprises in the rest of the Americas also, though details elude us. Bowser's study of inventories of food-growing estates in Peru suggests that these estates on the whole had unbalanced sex ratios and small numbers of children, suggesting problems with forming families on them.[74] Similarly, the labor forces of cacao walks (the local term for "farms") in Venezuela were almost entirely male, and although these men may have been able to take Native American wives, the documents of the church for the 1650s do not show them as living in families.[75] Such cacao workers, like their colleagues in Central America, where a similar situation prevailed, may have been the ultimate in a specialized labor force in an economy dominated by Native American labor.[76]

If the sex ratios on an estate were unbalanced, it would, of course,

70 Menard, "Maryland Slave Population," pp. 32–3.

71 William Fitzhugh's Instructions to John Withers, 5 June 1682, in Richard Beale Davis, ed., *William Fitzhugh and His Chesapeake World, 1676–1701: The Fitzhugh Letters and Other Documents* (Chapel Hill, N.C., 1963), p. 119 and passim.

72 Hearing of 16 November 1641 and 26 June 1642, in van Laer, *New York Historical Manuscripts* 4: fols. 101, 129.

73 Pieter Stuyvesant had a group of forty slaves (a large number by North American standards) engaged in intensive labor; see Stuvysant Fish, "Peter Stuvysant," pp. 14, 32, 32; Stuyvesant Letter in O'Callaghan, *Documents Relative to Colonial New York* 2: 474, 504. At least one other settler of the time, Frederick Philipse, owned forty slaves (Singleton, *Dutch New York*, p. 152).

74 Bowser, *African Slave*, p. 95. The children under fifteen compose 279 per thousand (expected: 377 per thousand) even when sex ratios are evened out by eliminating adult males and by doubling females.

75 See the documents in Tronchis Veracoechea, *Documentos*, pp. 197–207.

76 This labor regime is documented for the early eighteenth century but probably prevailed earlier; see Olien, "Black and Part Black Populations," p. 19.

limit the number of families that could be formed and undermine the stability of those that did form. These two factors might combine with the high rates of mortality to cut back on the number of slaves that survived and reproduced as well as the size and care of the succeeding generation born into slavery.

One effect of high mortality and a limited ability to reproduce was the constant importation of new slaves to replace those who had died. Sergipe do Conde in the 1622–53 period required importation of some five slaves per year to keep its staff up to a strength of about seventy.[77] Self-reproduction on the Mexican sugar estates owned by the Cortés family was sufficiently low that at any given time about one third of the slaves were imported.[78] The relative absence of children on the larger estates of wealthy Virginians, noted in Menard's study, suggests that fertility and mortality were affected by the unbalanced sex ratios and lack of family formation.[79] The needs of all such estates were such that they affected the whole Atlantic trade, causing the demand for males to greatly outnumber the demand for females. After 1524, for example, contractors delivering slaves to the Spanish New World were required to deliver two males for every female.[80]

But it is easy to exaggerate the overall impact of even the worst conditions. Just as we can demonstrate unbalanced sex ratios, low rates of reproduction and family formation, and high rates of mortality, at the same time we can also document, even for the worst conditions, the emergence of a creole generation who must have had some input from their parents in their socialization. Sometimes this group emerged from the privileged segment of the plantation work force, such as the skilled workers, who, as noted, often could form families and have children, while the field hands could not; in other cases, even the field hands still managed to do so occasionally. The fact that such a creole generation did not replace all those who died does not negate the fact that they were transmitters of African culture, even if they did not become the majority of the society.

The significance of an emerging creole generation can be demonstrated even on the estates with unbalanced sex ratios and unfavorable conditions for family formation. On the Tuxtla estate of Mexico an inventory of 1566 showed that children under twelve made up 188 per thousand in the population,[81] while Angolan populations at about the same

77 "Livro de Contas," in *Documentos* 3:21, 55, 83 (15 new slaves), 91 (seven more in the same year), 139, 144, 222, 299 (12 slaves in one lot), and passim.

78 Barrett, *Sugar Hacienda*, pp. 79–81.

79 Menard, "Maryland Slave Population," pp. 40–42.

80 Gonzalo Aguirre Beltrán, *La población negra de México* (Mexico City, 1946), p. 18.

81 Data given in Palmer, *Slaves of White God*, p. 46.

time would have as many as 315 children under twelve per thousand.[82] In large measure, however, this imbalance was caused by the fact that males outnumbered females (64.5 percent of the adults were male). If one corrects for this imbalance by doubling the number of females and calculating as if sex ratios were normal, then the children made up 352 per thousand, which suggests that fertility and infant–child mortality were normal. Thus, although unbalanced sex ratios limited the number of families that could form and children that were born, a substantial number of children did manage to survive.

From such a background, one could expect a steadily increasing creole population and certainly a reasonably large generation to pass a heritage on to. Thus, in the Cortés estates with its sex ratio imbalance and high mortality, deaths could never quite be replaced by births, but still, by the mid-seventeenth century between half and two thirds of the slaves were creoles.[83] Likewise, although Sergipe do Conde in Brazil had to import slaves constantly to keep its labor force up to strength, the birth rate among the slaves almost equaled the death rate.[84]

The development of self-sustaining families, reproducing themselves demographically and creating and transmitting a culture, is not the only feature of interest in the impact of labor regimes on the cultural development of African slaves. While slaves were living, the ability to produce for themselves, develop their own housing styles, design their own clothes, and the like would affect the spheres in which their cultural impact would be felt. On some estates, for example, the master provided slaves with most, perhaps all, of their food and shelter, so that they were deprived of all sense of self-sufficiency and community feeling. The Sergipe plantation regularly records purchases of clothing, cloth, sleeping mats, and all types of food, showing that these slaves were not expected (or allowed) to support themselves.[85] They must have had relatively little free time. Barrett has made the same case from the records of the Cortés estates,[86] and it can also be seen in the records of the copper mines of Venezuela, where Native Americans received no food or clothing, but the African slaves received a full set of rations.[87]

Such slaves might not even choose their own style of housing. The housing provided the slaves in Brazil, at least, is known from the striking illustrations of landscapes published in Kaspar van Baerle's descrip-

[82] The Angolan figure is postulated from my reconstruction of the age pyramid for Kongo in the seventeenth century; see Thornton, "Demography and History," pp. 516–19.

[83] Barrett, *Sugar Hacienda*, pp. 78–86.

[84] Schwartz, *Sugar Plantations*, p. 59.

[85] "Livro de Contas," in Tronchis Veracoechea, *Documentos* 2:21, 93, 139, 144, 145, 199, 222, 250, 299, and passim.

[86] Barrett, *Sugar Hacienda*, pp. 93–7.

[87] Acosta Saignes, *Vida*, pp. 159–62.

tion of the 1640s, which were engraved from the brilliant, attentive paintings of the Dutch masters Albert Eckhout and Zaccharis Wagner. The illustrations show plantations with a mill, owner's residence, and a small quarter set aside for the "workers," which appears to be a barracks built for the accommodation of a gang, and certainly not individual houses for families.[88]

Similar conditions seem to have occurred among the wealthier estate owners in North America as well. A Huguenot traveler in Virginia in 1678 noted that on one estate he visited, the master kept large barracks for both his slaves and his indentured workers, presupposing little community life and close discipline for both types of workers.[89] When Jasper Danckaerts, a Dutch traveler, visited Virginia in 1679 he was likewise impressed with the rigor of tobacco farming, at least on large estates, where overseers demanded long hours of hard work from their slaves "as if planting [tobacco] were everything." The slaves and servants returned from the fields exhausted but still had to pound maize for their food, which was mostly hominy and poor in meat.[90]

These were the conditions on the harshest of the estates, but not all estates, even sugar mills and mines, were managed in this way. Some owners allowed slaves to build a community and encouraged family formation. There were numerous such mines and estates all over the New World and the Atlantic islands, even in areas where other establishments did not adopt similar policies. Sugar estates in sixteenth-century São Tomé, uninhabited at the time of its colonization, reveal the situation fairly well. In 1528 João Lobato was ordered to start four mills there for the king of Portugal. Lacking workers, he had to begin by acquiring 270 slaves from the royal account. He divided them into areas to begin growing food and building watercourses for irrigation, thus creating a whole economy preparatory to starting sugar production. Indeed, some of the slaves ran away to other estates nearby where there was on-going food production, because he could not provide them with enough.[91]

The dynamics of community building in this situation are seen in later accounts, such as that of an anonymous Portuguese pilot who visited the island five times between 1520 and the 1540s. As he described it in an account sent to an Italian gentleman, rich men of São Tomé had large groups of slaves ranging from 150 to 300 who had the "obligation to

[88] Casparis Barlaei [Kaspar van Baerle], *Rervm per octennivm in Brasilia* (Amsterdam, 1647), map following p. 24 and map no. 46. On the background of the paintings, see Clarival do Prado Valladares, Luis Emygdio de Mello Filho, *Albert Eckhout, Pintor de Maurício de Nassau no Brasil, 1637–1644* (Recife, 1981).

[89] *A Hugenot Exile in Virginia; or, Voyages of a Frenchmen Exiled for His Religion with a Description of Virginia and Maryland*, ed. Gilbert Chinard (New York, 1934), p. 120.

[90] Danckaerts, *Journal*, pp. 133–4.

[91] João Lobato to João III, 13 April 1529, *MMA* 1:505–6.

work for their master every day of the week except Sunday, when they worked to support themselves." The masters "gave nothing to the said blacks," neither food nor even clothing, which they had to make for themselves from local products in their own time.[92] In this regard the labor regime of São Tomé was similar to that of some slave regimes in Africa, such as Jolof, where slaves were also said to work one day per week on their own account.[93] Carmelites who visited São Tomé in the 1580s noted the same custom and expressed concern that the slaves had to work on feast days and Sundays to produce for themselves, which they argued should be days of rest.[94]

The absence of clothing rations meant that the Africans had to produce their own cloth and clothing, perhaps a burden but an opportunity to be self-sufficient and express themselves. Indeed, a royal order addressed to Manuel Cão, the bishop of São Tomé in 1559, expressed concern that the slaves were wearing clothing that was considered indecent and its style sufficiently African that they were denounced for the "custom of wearing their clothes in the manner of heathens."[95] But the bishop was aware of the limitations of the local economy to provide clothing, for he replied to the king that the people were simply too poor to dress better.[96] Poor or not, this sort of production presumed that however badly they were treated the slaves formed a community that produced for itself as well as its masters.

Similarly, the anonymous pilot noted that the slaves built their own houses and moreover were settled in family units. Settlers bought "black slaves and their wives" from Benin and Kongo and put the slaves "and their wives" to clear fields for subsistence crops.[97] As the Carmelites saw the situation in the 1580s, each master had one hundred female slaves for each one hundred males, so that each male slave had "a wife or two as concubines" (i.e., not married with the Church's approval), and these wives, in turn, had "a baby each year." Although the Carmelites thought that it was good to form families in this way, they were concerned that the masters did not have the slaves' marriages conducted according to Christian rites.[98]

Thus, in São Tomé, where slaves had to form the entire labor force, planters were encouraged to apply different management techniques,

[92] "Navagazione de Lisbona all'isola di San Tomé, posta sotto la linea dell'equinoziale, scritta per un pilotto portoghese e mandata al magnifico conte Rimondo della Torre . . .," in Ramusio, *Navigazioni* (ed. Milanesi) 1:579, 581.

[93] Fernandes, "Descriçã," fol. 92v.

[94] Biblioteca Vaticana, MS Latina 12516, trans. in Cuvelier and Jadin, *L'ancien Congo*, p. 155.

[95] Alvará of Sebastião I, 9 November 1559, *MMA* 1:445.

[96] Manuel Cão to Sebastião I, 28 April 1560, *MMA* 1:463.

[97] "Navigazione" in Ramusio, *Navigazioni* 1:579, 581–2.

[98] Biblioteca Vaticana, MS Latina 12156, in Cuvelier and Jadin, *L'ancien Congo*, pp. 154–5.

which gave the social structure a very different tone. Indeed, Brazilian historians have often followed the lead of Ciro Flammarion Cardoso, who noted the existence of this sort of labor regime in many parts of the Atlantic world, and have spoken of it as being a "peasant breach" because the conditions were more those of peasants and thus a "breach" in the usual treatment of slaves.[99] It was once assumed that the peasant breach was characteristic only of the nineteenth century, but more recent research has generalized it to the whole period.[100]

The conditions that allowed the peasant breach were determined by the absence of other labor forces or by economics, compassion, or abolitionist sentiments (as in the nineteenth century). This did not mean that the slaves were well treated, or even that they lived well, but only that they were capable of maintaining a good deal of their African culture, creating a new Afro-Atlantic culture and transmitting it to the next generation.

This type of management was not restricted to São Tomé or to Portuguese colonies. It was found in all the colonies either where there was not outside labor force, whether Native American or indentured servants, or where conditions caused estate owners to concentrate the entire producing population on their estates. Thus, the English had to start this way in Barbados. Richard Ligon, a careful observer of the early days of the sugar boom (he lived in Barbados from 1647 to 1650), noted that masters imported equal numbers of male and female slaves and encouraged them to form households and reproduce.[101] Statistical information confirms Ligon's comments,[102] and a good series of inventories for Jamaica, where a similar situation existed, confirms this as general seventeenth-century practice in Jamaica.[103] Likewise, although the slaves were fed communally on Barbadian plantations, much of the food was produced on the estate itself, and only items such as meat and fish were provided by the master from imports.[104] Archeological data from slave burials confirm the local production by slaves of domestic items such as pottery.[105]

The slaves built their own homes, forming villages located on the estate. Antoine Biet compared the plantations of Barbados to villages when he visited the island in 1654, and a later visitor to Jamaica, Thomas

99 See Ciro Flammarion Cardoso, *Agricultura, escrivadão e capitalismo* (Petropolis, 1979), chap. 4. See a survey of literature in his "The Peasant Breach in the Slave System: New Developments in Brazil," *Luso-Brazilian Review* 25 (1988): 49–57.

100 Alice Piffer Canabrava, *O açucár nas Antilhas (1697–1744)* (São Paulo, 1974).

101 Ligon, *History*, pp. 47–8.

102 Jerome Handler and William Lange, *Plantation Slavery on Barbados: An Archaeological and Historical Investigation* (Cambridge, Mass., 1978), p. 36.

103 Studied in Dunn, *Sugar and Slaves*, pp. 251–2.

104 Ligon, *History*, pp. 31, 37, 43.

105 Handler and Lange, *Plantation Slavery*, pp. 139–42.

Trapham (1679), included more details of the same sort.[106] It was not just the structures (individual houses) that struck these visitors as conveying the sense of community.

The same system had to be adopted in the French Caribbean, where the unconquerable Caribs would not provide a labor force, and so French masters were required to build communities as their English counterparts had. The French priest Jean Baptiste du Tertre, writing in 1667 after long experience in the islands, recorded a system that provided the slaves with nothing save sufficient ground on which to plant food crops, build a house, and produce some other subsistence items and, of course, the time off to do these things.[107]

The French masters were careful to establish slave families, encouraged by a vigorous policy of French priests and royal ordinances,[108] even going so far as to allow slaves to select their own wives or husbands, typically from their own language group, from arriving slave ships.[109] A census of properties on Guadeloupe conducted in 1664 reveals that about one quarter of all masters listed their slaves by family groups. In 1680 Jean Mongin conducted a more careful census of slaves in the quarter of Guadeloupe where he lived and found that over 70 percent of all slaves lived in families, whether formally or informally constituted.[110] The biggest barrier to the formation of families seems to have been the small size of many properties, especially in the earliest years, for there were many estates in which the total population was unbalanced by sex, though this does not seem to have been a barrier to fertility, for many estates that had only women still had children.[111]

Slave families settled in their own villages in houses of their own construction. One such town, created by the French governor du Poincy, was known as the "city of Angola" and was surrounded by a wall. Children built homes near their parents, so that by the 1660s there might be several generations living in the slave settlement.[112] Clodoré, who was governor of the islands in the 1660s, believed that these communities, which were not only self-sufficient but produced considerable goods for other plantations or for the market in towns, sold by the slaves

[106] Biet, *Voyage de la France Eqvinoxiale*, p. 281. Thomas Trapham, *A Discourse on the State of Health of the Island of Jamiaca* (London, 1679), p. 26.

[107] Du Tertre, *Histoire* 2:515–16; Clodoré, *Relation dece que s'est passé dans les Isles et Terre-Ferme de l'Amerique*, 2 vols. (Paris, 1671), 1:45–65.

[108] Arlette Gautier, *Les soeurs de Solitude: La condition féminine dans l'esclavage aux Antilles du XVIIe au XIX siècles* (Paris, 1985), pp. 63–5.

[109] Du Tertre, *Histoire* 2:504–6.

[110] Gautier, *Soeurs de Solitude*, pp. 73–6.

[111] Ibid., pp. 74–5.

[112] Du Tertre, *Histoire* 2:518.

for their profit, were very like the rural communities of his native France.[113]

Various records of the Remire plantation in French Guiana (Cayenne) compiled by its overseer Jean Goupy des Marets from 1688 to 1690 give an intimate view of life on such a French sugar plantation. Inventories confirm the attempts to balance sex ratios and create families: The inventory of 1675 (included in des Marets's collection) listed the initial adult personnel of seventeen males and seventeen females, and included twenty-one children, although it did not specify if these were found in families.[114] The inventory of 1690 is much more specific and lists all the ninety-two slaves by families, along with biographical details showing that some families had been in existence since 1678.[115] A bird's-eye sketch of the estate, probably drawn in the 1680s, shows that like du Poincy's estate of a somewhat earlier date, Remire had a slave village of individual houses, surrounded by a stockade (and another stockade surrounded much of the estate).[116] More detailed census records from Guadeloupe and Martinique in the period 1664–80 reveal that French policies did favor childbearing, even if regular families (which in French practice usually meant Christian married families) were not formed.[117]

English and Dutch settlers in Surinam faced a similar situation, for the Arawak and Carib inhabitants of that region were as intractable as the inhabitants of the islands. Not surprisingly, these settlers controlled slave labor in much the same way as their French and English colleagues in the islands. This is revealed in English and Dutch descriptions of the colonies.[118] A survey of Dutch Surinam in 1684, for example, showed that while males outnumbered females among all slaves in the colonies, the larger planters, especially the Jewish ones, had a close balance of sex ratios. Likewise, in the detailed records drawn up at about the same time of the clerical estate of Johannes Basseliers, there were twenty-eight adult males and twenty-three adult females.[119]

Sugar estates managed as communities were necessary in areas where

113 Clodoré, *Relation*, pp. 45–7; du Tertre, *Histoire* 2:515–16; 519–20.

114 BM Rouen, MS Montbret 125, fol. 3, des Marets, "Voyage," an inventory of 28 February 1675.

115 Ibid., fols. 83–93.

116 Ibid., front matter, sketch C. Sketch B shows another estate in Cayenne, which has a similar layout.

117 Gautier, *Soeurs de Solitude*, pp. 71–2.

118 Adriaan van Berkel, *Amerikaansche voyagien, hebelzende een reis na Rio de Berbice . . . Guiana* (Amsterdam, 1695), p. 126 (based on travels in 1670–4 and 1680–9); George Warren, *An Impartial Description of Surinam upon the Continent of Guiana in America* (London, 1667), p. 19.

119 Data summarized in Jan Marinus van der Linde, *Surinaamse suikerheren en hun kerk: Plantagekolonie en handelkerk ten tijde van Johannes Basseliers* (Wageningen, 1966), p. 75.

Native Americans were absent or unconquered. But even within areas where there were conquered Native Americans, some of the estates might not have access to them, perhaps because the Native Americans were bound to other estates or the estates did not have sufficient influence to obtain any. Thus, even there, estates might resemble the estates of São Tomé and the English and French Caribbean. In Brazil, where, as we have seen, it is possible to document harsh plantation conditions and the use of Native American labor in the seventeenth century, there were plantations run on the community system. Pierre Moreau, describing Brazil in 1646–8 under Dutch administration, observed that many of the plantation slaves had "little pieces of land on which, during the limited time they have for rest (after a twelve-hour day) they sow peas, beans, millet, and maize." They also did a little marketing, selling a drink called *grape* (probably *garapa,* a strong cane wine), which was made from adding water to the waste of the sugar mills.[120]

The Dutch and Portuguese New Christian and Jewish refugees from Brazil who fled with the Dutch in the 1640s brought this labor system when they settled in Surinam and the Caribbean. Du Tertre noted that in the French Caribbean there was a system of labor control he called the "Fernambuco [Pernambuco] system" that gave the slaves so much community life and freedom of movement that some French planters feared the consequences.[121] This system, probably related to the one noted by Moreau in Pernambuco Province in Brazil, would work in the Caribbean, of course. Obviously, then, it is not enough to know just that Africans were slaves or even that they were settled upon sugar-producing estates to be able to say that they were incapable of sustaining a cultural and social life.

The same observations can be made about those slaves who were made to work in mining. As in the case of sugar production, the absence of an outside labor force might alter the regime of labor management. Thus, we find communities developed in the gold-producing lowland New Granada (modern Colombia). Vázquez de Espinosa's survey of the region in the early seventeenth century, probably based on more detailed government surveys (*relaciones topographicas*) noted that Native American labor served in mines like the Vetras de Oro and in the Cucarica valley, where encomiendas of Native Americans provided labor and perhaps created a situation like that of the Cocorote copper mine in Venezuela. But in other areas, such as mines around Zaragoza and Pirura, the natives were unsubdued and thus unavailable. This situation may have

[120] Pierre Moreau, "Histoire des derniers troubles du Brésil . . .," in Courbé, *Relations veritables et cvrievsaes,* p. 41.

[121] Du Tertre, *Histoire* 2:151–6.

stimulated community organization of the labor force.[122] West's classic studies of mine labor in New Granada provide evidence of community formation. In the Remedios mine, for example, inventories of 1632 show there were balanced numbers of males and females. Both men and women engaged in the mine work and on holidays were permitted to mine on their own account. Such operations were self-sufficient in food, half of the gang being put to work on small plots growing food, although owners did import meat items and other commodities.[123]

Such situations were not confined to mines in Colombia. The royal mines of Prado in Cuba, established by the king between 1598 and 1620, were organized from the very start to use families engaged in self-production as well as mining, employing slaves almost entirely from Angola (a region that produced and exported considerable copper). The governor was especially pleased that this system resulted in relatively low mortality and a sense of community.[124]

Other agricultural enterprises also allowed communities to develop. Poorer Chesapeake Bay planters, for example, lacking the income to replace indentured servants with slaves or to engage in what might be more expensive means of provisioning might also decide to develop slave communities on their properties. Menard shows that on smaller estates in this area with poorer owners, sex ratios were more balanced and the numbers of children relative to adults higher, suggesting some family life. For example, slaves living on the Ridgly estate in Maryland in the middle of the seventeenth century were simply settled on sections of the estate and told to farm and sell their produce, sharing the profits with their master.[125] Another example is that of William Evans, a Virginian, whose slave John Graweere was allowed to raise pigs on his own and sell them as he saw fit, in exchange for "one half the increase."[126]

On occasion, such slaves would even be given their legal freedom, sometimes in exchange for production of set amounts of tobacco; at other times they would receive partial freedom, such as the "half freedom" of Dutch areas, which carried the sort of dues appropriate to tenant farmers.[127] In these situations, clearly, slaves had some mobility and could form families and socialize their children. That they might not choose to forget their African background is revealed in the fact that one of the most successful of these small-holding former slaves, Anthony Johnson, named his farm "Angola."[128]

122 Vázquez de Espinosa, *Compendio*, nos. 960–1, 1027–9, 1035.
123 Robert C. West, *Colonial Placer Mining in Colombia* (Baton Rouge, 1952), pp. 83–90.
124 Domínguez, *Cuba*, p. 100.
125 Menard, "Maryland Slave Population," pp. 40–2, 36.
126 Helen T. Caterall, ed., *Judicial Cases Concerning Slavery* (Washington, D.C., 1926), 1:77.
127 Examples are documented in Breen and Innis, *"Myne Owne Ground,"* pp. 68–109.
128 Breen and Innes, *"Myne Owne Ground,"* p. 17.

Advice to intending cacao planters in Jamaica in the mid-seventeenth century also suggested that one should buy equal numbers of males and females and establish provision gardens before commencing production.[129] Unlike the cacao producers of Central America and Venezuela, where an almost entirely male labor force lived in an economy dominated by Native American labor, the early Jamaican planters could not yet rely on any outside labor force and thus chose to create communities of slaves.

Such dynamics may well have applied in cattle ranching as well, though in these enterprises, as in many others that were not the purview of the great elite of colonial society, detailed records are often lacking. Venezuelan ecclesiastical documents of the 1650s show that most such slaves were married,[130] and the nature of the work clearly made it easy for slaves who might live far away from each other to socialize. If the presence of several "negro" and "mulatto" proprietors of modest cattle ranches in Hispaniola in the early seventeenth century is any indication, such slaves were likely to have considerable freedom to develop their lives and to gain their freedom.[131] Like their Venezuelan counterparts, they might well have also had family lives and perhaps have been responsible for socializing their children.

The formation of families and communities, wherever it was found, resulted in the rapid growth of creole populations. Thus, although the more difficult conditions on other estates, with unbalanced sex ratios and specialized labor forces, managed to produce a creole generation, the more community-oriented management schemes produced such a generation much faster. By 1620 in the Prado mines of Cuba, the 85 families had produced between them 70 children, or 292 children per thousand, a slightly below normal figure if "niño y niñas" meant children under 12 (expected 315 per thousand) but above normal if it meant children under ten (expected 275 per thousand).[132] Bassliers's estate in Surinam in 1684 had normal rates of reproduction and mortality for

[129] "Description de l'isle de Jamaique," in Sieur H. Justel, *Recuil de divers voyages faits en Afrique et en l'Amerique* (Paris, 1674), pp. 7–8. This text (written before 1669, when the royal license to publish was issued) is said to be a translation of an original by "Sir Thomas, governor of Jamaica," probably Thomas Modyford, whose account of establishing a cacao walk was available in English in Richard Blome, *A Description of the Island of Jamaica . . .* (London, 1672), pp. 16–21, but differs from this one in details.

[130] Documents in Tronchis Veracoechea, *Documentos*, pp. 197–203.

[131] Dieve, *Esclavitud*, pp. 93–4, 107–9.

[132] Domínguez, *Cuba*, p. 99. Note, however, that the population also included ninety unmarried males and nine widows or widowers, so that the actual age structure was still heavily unbalanced in favor of adult males, with resulting low actual reproduction rates.

children,[133] as did the Remire sugar estate.[134] Gautier has calculated, on the basis of census returns from Martinique and Guadeloupe between 1669 and 1685, that slaves had a birthrate of 51 per thousand in the French islands, which would make these rates even higher than African rates, though infant mortality was high, of course.[135]

Sometimes one did find sugar estates or mines where fertility and survival rates for children were below normal. One such was the Remedios mine, where despite a favorable sex balance, children under ten made up 117 per thousand, as against an expected rate of 275 per thousand.[136] Perhaps this was the result of famines that occasionally struck these mines. Ligon's observation that masters ought to expect to import 5 or 6 slaves per hundred every year to make up for "wastage,"[137] repeated by other guides to management,[138] may reflect an unfavorable demography, but because his advice was for planters starting out, it is obvious that for at least fifteen or twenty years no owner could expect the children born in captivity to replace dead adults as workers.

The special case of slaves in urban areas and domestic slaves

Domestic slaves and urban workers might in many ways be considered the most fortunate and the most likely of all slaves to be able to live a full cultural and social life. The contrast between the life of a domestic servant, residing in the owner's house, perhaps well dressed and not necessarily overworked, and that of the plantation slaves and field hands is well illustrated by the case of two Brazilian domestics, Ines and Juliana. These two pampered slaves, raised among the Europeans and sharing in their lives, testified against their master, Paulo Affonso, to the Inquisition of Bahia in 1613–14, and in reprisal, their master ordered them transferred as field hands to his sugar estate at Itapianga. There, a short time later they were both dead, victims of "many whippings and bad life and labor."[139]

Domestic servants were joined as a generally privileged group by

133 Van der Linde, *Surinaamse suikerheren*, p. 75. Correcting for a slight imbalance of males to females by dropping adult males from the total and doubling the females, children under twelve make up 294 per thousand (expected: 315 per thousand).

134 BM Rouen, MS Montbret 125, Goupy des Marets, "Voyage," fol. 91. For a tabulation, see Debien and Houdaille, "Sur une sucrerie," p. 188.

135 Gautier, *Soeurs de Solitude*, p. 76.

136 Data in West, *Placer Mining*, p. 86.

137 Ligon, *Trve and Exact History*, p. 115.

138 E.g., see Howard Littleton, *The Groans of the Plantations* (London, 1689), pp. 6, 18.

139 Marcos Teixeira, "Livro das Denunciações que se fizerão na Visitação do Santo Oficio à Cidade de Salvador . . . em 1618," in *Anais da Biblioteca Nacional do Rio de Janeiro* 49 (1927): 112.

many slaves who resided in urban areas. Some were skilled artisans; others were day laborers who were purchased as an income-bearing investment by owners who then hired them out in exchange for a share of their wages. Joined to this group were the numerous slaves, mostly female, who were employed by their masters as retailers and vendors in exchange for a share of their profits.

In urban areas, the conditions of life were such that many slaves had considerable control over their own time and, thus, could have contact with other Africans, even if, as domestic slaves, for example, they normally moved in the world of the Europeans and Euro-Americans. Ines and Juliana, mentioned above, were considered to be *ladina,* having been "raised among whites" and versed in European language and culture,[140] as were many domestic slaves, but as residents of Bahia they would have had ample opportunity to socialize in a wider Afro-Brazilian community as well.

A portion of this larger African community was made up of the numerous slaves working semi-independently. One such group included slaves, usually women, put out by their masters to make money any way they could. The early settlers of Hispaniola at the start of the sixteenth century commonly did this as soon as towns large enough to support markets developed. The system was lucrative enough that it survived several attempts to eliminate it through legislation. Similar accounts describe it in other areas, such as urban Peru and Cartagena. Towns in English and Dutch North America exhibited the same tendencies.[141]

Artisan slaves existed throughout the Americas and are well documented for Peru by Bowser and for Mexico by Palmer.[142] Such slaves, as well as those hired out as day laborers and those performing unskilled labor, had considerable control over their time and the pace of their labor. Documents occasionally cast some light on the conditions in urban areas. Witnesses in the Claver inquest, for example, often mention slaves socializing at taverns or on the streets, often meeting at well-frequented hangouts.[143] A particularly interesting text comes from the Mexican Inquisition records concerning Diego de la Cruz, a slave of a cacao merchant, who spent many days visiting friends, socializing, and sometimes spending the night out.[144] There were often troops of pam-

140 Teixeira, "Livro de Denunciações," p. 111.

141 For Hispaniola see Dieve, *Esclavitud* 1:307–10. For Peru see Bowser, *African Slave,* pp. 278–90; for Cartagena see de Sandoval, *Instauranda,* pp. 135–44. For English and Dutch towns see McManus, *Black Bondage,* pp. 45–7, who cites later evidence of what was probably true earlier.

142 Bowser, *African Slave,* pp. 106–109; Palmer, *Slaves of the White God,* pp. 44–5.

143 BN Colombia, Claver Inquest, fols. 39–39v, 108–108v.

144 Solange Alberro, "Noirs et mulâtres dans la société coloniale mexicaine, d'après les archives de l'Inquisition (XVI–XVII siècles)," *Cahiers d'Amerique Latine* 17 (1978): 64–5.

pered slaves who surrounded successful businessmen or planters. They were also the most likely to be freed unconditionally in such a way that freedom was clearly a reward for service.[145]

But if life might provide some opportunities for slaves in these conditions, one should not imagine that they were not exploited or mistreated. De Sandoval, for example, paints a grim picture of the life of many domestic slaves and urban workers in Cartagena in the early seventeenth century. Domestics were frequently beaten. Even short absences might be brutally punished, and sometimes such slaves were even killed as a result of them, as was the slave of one "great and noble lady" of his acquaintance. Many, he noted, were fed little and dressed in such poor clothing as to be almost naked. Some had to work on days off or festival days to earn money to purchase clothing that a master refused to provide. Sometimes, sick slaves were freed when gravely ill, so that the master would not have to pay the cost of their burial, and "the street became their grave," even those who "were very good in Spanish [*muy ladino*] and long serving."[146] This last point finds some confirmation in contemporary records of manumission, where old slaves are freed without any clear means of supporting themselves.[147]

Surely a harsh master could make life for domestic slaves miserable, and the Inquisition records many instances of it in testimony against slaves who "renounced God" as a result of bad treatment or beatings.[148] The Mexican Inquisition archives hold many documents that provide detailed discussion of mistreatment of slaves by their masters, sometimes driving them to suicide and often causing them to run away, plot their master's death, or blaspheme.[149]

Although much of de Sandoval's testimony relates to household servants, some of the same problems also apply to slaves whose masters simply sent them out to earn a living on their own and who were required to share profits with the master. Masters often believed that such slaves withheld profits or cheated them but had little recourse save beating to obtain what they believed was their share. Claver was noted for his intervention in the case of shopkeepers whose masters threatened them. Isabella Folupo specifically noted that he sought justice for women forced to work as street vendors, for she noted that if "female slave vendors lacked the money she needed to give her master, he would give her the money she lacked or go to the master on her be-

145 Palmer, *Slaves of the White God*, pp. 173–5.
146 De Sandoval, *Instauranda*, pp. 195, 197.
147 Palmer, *Slaves of White God*, p. 174.
148 Ibid., pp. 150–2.
149 Alberro, "Noirs et mulâtres," pp. 66–8.

half."[150] But just as in the case of the slaves employed on the large estates, harsh treatment and bad life did not necessarily prevent slaves from bearing and raising children and having a social and cultural life. Many slaves had a fairly good life.

Slaves in urban areas and domestic service probably had a higher rate of survival than many other slaves, although this is difficult to document securely. Certainly there seems to have been a better chance for marriage and raising children, although even here data present problems. In Iberian America, towns often had fairly equal numbers of men and women and therefore afforded at least the possibility of marriage. Bowser has shown that the sex ratios in bills of sale and other data support the idea that Peruvian towns had roughly equal numbers of each sex and that this was true in most urban areas.[151] Furthermore, the freedom of movement and even of residence that many slaves in urban areas enjoyed meant that finding a suitable mate and maintaining a family were easier there than elsewhere.

On the other hand, slaves in conditions typical of urban areas were still subject to the whims of their masters, and they seem to have had few qualms about opposing marriages or separating families if it suited their interests. Indeed, Bowser has shown that a remarkably small number of slaves represented in bills of sale or the inventories of estates in wills or of urban slaveholders were actually married.[152] Although this suggests that masters discouraged formal marriages among their slaves, it may well be that such slaves still maintained families, especially those with some freedom of movement, but did so without contracting a Christian marriage that required the master's blessing. In urban settings, especially, even if slaves were sold frequently or not allowed to marry, the concentration of people was likely to allow informal families to have regular contact with each other. The documents of the Mexican Inquisition often make reference to these informal marriages, not sanctioned by the Church but often involving a father who at least visited his children.[153] Moreover, the Church, which was much more active in urban areas than in rural estates and mines, used its influence to prevent owners from separating families. Palmer and Bowser have shown this to be the case in both Mexico and Peru, and Claver was noted for his diligent attempt to preserve marriages in Cartagena.[154]

[150] BN Colombia, Claver Inquest, fols. 39–39v, 107–8, 166, and passim.
[151] Bowser, *African Slave*, pp. 81, 337–41.
[152] Ibid., pp. 255–7, 261.
[153] Alberro, "Noirs et mulâtres," pp. 62–5.
[154] Palmer, *Slaves of the White God*, pp. 56–60; Bowser, *African Slave*, pp. 254, 157–60. Also see Alberro, "Noirs et mulâtres," p. 64; BN Colombia, Claver Inquest, fol. 40.

Such slaves often had intimate contact with their masters, including in the case of female slaves (and some males) sexual liaisons. The large American mulatto group was the obvious result of these liaisons, which sometimes worked to the slaves' advantage. Dierick Ruyters, a Dutch captain visiting Brazil in 1618, noted that the Portuguese were good to the slaves who were concubines and especially to their children.[155] Indeed, several Brazilian planters were denounced before the Inquisition for repeating the widely held belief that "it was not a mortal sin to sleep carnally with single women or slaves [*negras*]."[156]

As in virtually all societies with social stratification and inequality, women could make use of physical attractiveness to serve powerful men in exchange for privileges and advancement. Take the case of Magdeleine, originally named Aoua (Awa) and nicknamed Victoire, an attractive Fula slave on the Remire plantation in 1690. Her first master, the *sieur* Gaudais, had treated her as a wife (and nicknamed her Piaquenine, perhaps a form of "pickaninny"), as had two subsequent Frenchmen, Boudet and Dupuis. All the while, though, she was also married to a slave named Etienne (originally Bony), a Bambara who came on the same ship with her. Goupy des Marets, who recorded these details, believed that she might be a good worker, but as she had served as wife to three Frenchmen, she was "good for nothing at all today except to play the lady [*faire la demoiselle*]."[157] Certainly there is ample evidence of an attempt to reward such service with freedom, for the most common reason for unconditional manumission for females was bearing children for their masters, at least from the data from Lima and Mexico studied by Bowser.[158]

Occasionally such affairs could even lead farther, for French records noted that in Martinique in 1660 two slave owners married their slaves, a number that rose to eight in 1680.[159] These numbers are very small compared with the large population of slaves, of course, representing the most extreme case of relationships that benefited slave women.

But the benefits of this sexual game could be transitory, and no doubt many women did not welcome the sexual advances of their masters. French laws against interracial contacts passed in the 1660s were clearly intended to prevent violent sexual abuse and rape rather than to limit

155 Dierick Ruyters, *Toortse de Zee-Vaert* (Vlissinghen, 1623), pp. 4–5. This pagination is marked in the modern edition of S. P. L. L'Honoré Naber (The Hague, 1913).

156 Teixeira, "Livro de Denunciações," p. 177.

157 BM Rouen, MS Montbret 125, Goupy des Marets, "Voyage," fol. 86.

158 Frederick Bowser, "The Free Person of Color in Mexico and Lima: Manumission and Opportunity, 1580–1650," in Stanley Engerman and Eugene Genovese, ed., *Race and Slavery in the Western Hemisphere: Quantative Studies* (Stanford, 1975).

159 Gautier, *Soeurs de Solitude*, p. 169.

interracial love or marriage.[160] Cases of rape cannot be documented particularly well, although the Inquisition records in Brazil give us some insight into homosexual liaisons. Because any homosexual contact was considered a crime and a sin, the Inquisition recorded details that might be overlooked in heterosexual relations. On some occasions slaves appear to have been raped by their masters; in others it was apparently a voluntary participation.[161]

Clearly, however, these household slaves had the opportunity to socialize, develop friendships, and be involved in cultural activities. Some, such as the mistresses or lovers of their masters, may have been almost totally acculturated, which seems to have been the case of the Brazilian slaves Juliana and Ines, slaves who were "*ladinas* and raised among the whites." However, sometimes masters may have preferred what they considered exotic and encouraged African norms of conduct. It is clear that no matter how exploitative the institution of slavery was, or how traumatic the Middle Passage and subsequent enslavement were, the condition itself was unlikely to result in a permanent state of psychological shock. Furthermore, even in the most brutal of slave systems, slave communities formed, children were raised, and culture was maintained, altered, and transmitted. Clearly, the condition of slavery, by itself, did not necessarily prevent the development of an African-oriented culture.

160 Ibid, pp. 154–9.

161 Luiz R. B. Mott, "Escravidão e homossexualidade," in Ronaldo Vainfas, ed., *História e Sexualidade no Brasil* (Rio de Janeiro, 1986), pp. 33–40.

Culture?

7

African cultural groups in the Atlantic world

Clearly the condition of slavery, however bad it was, was not sufficiently bad to prevent the development of a reasonably self-sustaining slave community. This community, though often demographically unbalanced, nevertheless managed to create a creole generation and thus had the potential to maintain and transmit its own culture. But what type of culture developed among the slave societies of the Atlantic basin?

Historians have traditionally been divided on this issue, some arguing that the slaves maintained an African culture and that African influence was significant in the resulting Afro-Atlantic culture, others maintaining that the cultural disorganization of slave society made them much more dependent upon the culture of the Europeans or Euro-Americans.[1] Modern research has dispensed with the original dichotomous positions of the 1940s. Current thinking, while hardly reaching a consensus, can be well represented by the work of Mintz and Price, anthropologists who have sought to understand the dynamics of the formation of Afro-American, and specifically Afro-Caribbean, culture.[2] They begin by arguing that the conditions of the slave trade and slavery prevented the direct transmission of African culture to the Americas. In the first case, African culture was not homogeneous enough to constitute a single cultural block; instead, dozens, if not more, independent cultures were involved (Map 5). Second, the slave trade tended to randomize slaves, grouping those of disparate cultures together, unlike European migration, which tended to occur in blocks of people from the same area traveling and settling in the Americas together. African immigrants were not a group (homogeneous culture) but a "crowd" (disparate cultures with no prior contact), and an entirely new social structure and organiza-

[1] Melville J. Herskovitts, *The Myth of the Negro Past* (Boston, 1941); Frazier, *Negro Family;* Frazier, *Negro Church.*

[2] Mintz and Price, *Afro-American Past.*

tion had to be created, starting with the "dyad" of two slaves sharing the same space on the slave ship.[3]

Lacking the ethnic and cultural specificity necessary to maintain or re-create their African culture in the Americas, the slaves necessarily had to form a new culture. To be sure, this new culture had African roots, from a sort of least common denominator of the many and varied African cultures that served as its building blocks, but it was built in a context in which elements of the European culture served as linking materials. Moreover, not only was European culture pervasive in the slave society, but it was much more homogeneous than the various African cultures, giving it a coherence that the Africans lacked. The resulting mixture was distinctly European and Euro-American oriented, with the African elements giving it flavor rather than substance.[4]

An evaluation of the role of African slaves in forming American culture must consider all these issues. First, how culturally heterogeneous were the slaves who came to America? Second, how successful were Africans in interacting with other Africans who shared their culture (in a culturally heterogeneous situation) in the American setting of plantation, mine, or town? Finally, what were the dynamics of cultural development and change that transformed the various African cultures into Afro-Atlantic cultures? This chapter examines the first two questions; the issue of cultural transformation and change will be discussed in the two chapters that follow.

Cultures and cultural interactions in Africa

In the early development of the history of African culture in the Atlantic, scholars divided on the degree to which African culture was homogeneous. Herskovitts, for example, tended to see many broad similarities among the disparate cultures of Atlantic Africa, whereas his opponents stressed the numerous differences. On the whole, modern research has tended to side with Mintz and Price, who argue that there were major differences among the cultures of the Atlantic coast of Africa.[5]

Seventeenth-century Europeans recognized the ethnic diversity of Africans, just as modern scholars do. To them, especially those who encountered the Africans as slaves in the Americas, Africans were divided into so many "nations" or "countries."[6] In its primary form, the nation

[3] Ibid., pp. 4–6, 9–10, 21–4.
[4] Ibid., pp. 24–6.
[5] Mintz and Price, *Afro-American Past*, pp. 5–8.
[6] Spanish and Portuguese used terms such as *nación* (*nação*) and *generación* (*geração*) or *casta*. In French-speaking areas the most common term was *terre* ("land"), and English-speaking countries employed "country."

was recognized by language, as is clear from Alonso de Sandoval's lengthy inventory of the linguistic situation on the Atlantic coast of Africa, but it also included other marks of group identity, such as scarifications.[7] In all, de Sandoval identified over thirty nations in Atlantic Africa, and surveys of inventories of estates, especially in Spanish America, show that his list was a bit more complete than can be compiled by consulting these notarial classifications.[8] The number of distinct languages might be somewhat less, for Pierre Pelleprat, a French Jesuit working in the Caribbean some twenty-five years later, complained of thirteen distinct African languages.[9]

The term "nation" in Europe at the time was also essentially an ethnolinguistic one, and not a political one, and de Sandoval, aware of this, often points out that for his informants, some nations or castes were divided into multiple states, while other states contained members of more than one nation.[10] A missionary could catechize to all Brans in the same language, but if asked to what nation they belonged such people would give smaller groups: Cacheo, Baberral, Bojola, Papel, and Pesis. This too was similar to the ideas of seventeenth-century Europeans, who recognized the concept of a German nation when Germany was divided into many different states, or that boundaries were indistinct but might include loosely related ethnolinguistic units, just as seventeenth-century Dutch sometimes called their nation "Duytsen" (and not "Nederlanders," as today), which linked them with the "Deutschen," their German neighbors.[11]

Like the seventeenth-century observers, one can use linguistic diversity as a measure of cultural diversity but doing so may exaggerate the importance of these differences. One can use language or nation as a first-line indicator of culture, where every language represents a new

7 De Sandoval, *Instauranda*, pp. 90–7. De Sandoval's discussion of African nations is also an excellent guide to American concepts, for in the end, it was the American identity that concerned him. His guide can equally serve to analyze the ethnonyms found in thousands of Spanish documents, wills, estate records, bills of sale, and court records that govern most modern research on slave ethnicity in the Spanish Indies.

8 Ibid., pp. 14–17 and 91–6; the precise number of distinct "*castas*" or "*naciones*" identified by de Sandoval is not easy to ascertain, for his text makes it evident that both his informants and he were uncertain of exactly what made for a homogeneous nation. For a good survey of mid-seventeenth-century national names found in inventories and notarial documents and estate records, see Bowser, *African Slave*, pp. 42–4. De Sandoval's book was widely read and owned in America, and the Jesuit's ethnography may well have influenced notarial determinations.

9 Pierre Pelleprat, *Relation des missions des PP. de la Compagnie de Iesus dans les Isles, et dans la terre ferme de l'Amerique Meridionale* (Paris, 1655), p. 53.

10 E.g., de Sandoval, *Instauranda*, p. 92.

11 See the usage in Ruyters, *Toortse*, p. 329, "Duytsche natien" in reference to Dutch ships in Kongo (modern Dutch and some seventeenth-century writers use "Nederland" to describe this nation), among others.

culture. In this case, western and central Africa was a very diverse area, having as many as fifty languages according to modern classification. But few scholars would argue that every linguistic or national unit on the West African coast possessed a culture entirely different from its neighbors, and there was fundamental similarity over a fairly wide area.

Moreover, as every linguist knows, the usual definition of a language is a speech community in which all members can understand each other. Thus, when people cannot understand each other, they are speaking different languages. Yet in closely related languages there is a variation in the degree of difference. Multilingual people can understand a wider variety of speech than monolingual people can; some people can understand different dialects better than their friends and neighbors can. Thus, linguistic boundaries are always a bit flexible and confused, particularly in the days before national educational programs defined standard languages.

In addition to this objection, one could also add that language is not the sole mediator of culture. In many parts of western and central Africa people of diverse language groups interacted with each other from day to day as a result of residential proximity or commerce. In the course of these interactions they might exchange many cultural ideas even if they did not exchange languages. Thus, they might share religious ideas or aesthetic principles to such a degree that they possessed a common religious or artistic heritage despite their linguistic diversity.

Viewing culture from aspects other than language shows how important proximity and economic systems can be for creating cultural similarities in diverse zones. This is seen clearly in the field of aesthetics. The aesthetics of ceramics has sometimes been used as an indicator of a culture as much as language (sometimes the two are incorrectly used as substitutes for each other). But Posnansky notes that West Africa has vastly diverse pottery traditions; sometimes quite different traditions coexisted within a few miles of each other. Just as the production of pottery often showed variety, so did its consumption, in that items produced in one area often traveled some distance to other areas, and potting villages sometimes produced several "ethnic" styles for export.[12] Jan Vansina, using modern data, shows that the same sort of cultural mixing took place freely in other artistic production, so that the idea of an ethnolinguistic unit with its own unique culture tends to break down.[13]

Using language, we can divide the parts of Atlantic Africa that participated in the slave trade into three culturally distinct zones, which can be

[12] Posnansky, "West African Reflections," pp. 9–10.

[13] Jan Vansina, *Art History in Africa: An Introduction to Method* (London and New York, 1983), pp. 29–33, 44–7, 50–2.

further divided into seven subzones. From this analysis one can then say that although Africans may have been linguistically diverse, there were only three different cultures that contributed to the New World, and among them only seven distinct subcultures. Although this is not Herskovitts's uniformity, it is not nearly so diverse as to create the kind of cultural confusion posited by those who see African diversity as a barrier to the development of an African-based American culture.

The first of these cultural zones can be called, following European geographical practice, Upper Guinea. It covered the area reaching from the Senegal River down to the area just south of Cape Mount in modern Liberia.[14] It was the most linguistically diverse of the zones, two completely different language families being represented: the West Atlantic family and the Mande family. Of the two language families, West Atlantic had the greatest variation. It included Wolof (and closely related Serer) and Harpulaar (the language of the Fula) in the north and the Mel language of Sierra Leone and Guinea-Bissau in the south. These languages had split off from each other in the very ancient past and were quite different. Mande, on the other hand, was extremely homogeneous; the forms spoken in Gambia, along the Niger, and even in Sierra Leone and Liberia were almost mutually intelligible, at least in the seventeenth century. On strictly linguistic lines, therefore, the Upper Guinea region contained three distinct groups of quite different languages: Mande, which dominated the interior and the coast in Gambia and Sierra Leone; the northern West Atlantic languages (Wolof and Harpulaar) along the Senegal River; and the southern West Atlantic languages along the coast from the Gambia River to Cape Mount.

In fact, American observers like de Sandoval recognized that some nations were ethnically and linguistically closer to each other than were other nations, an important point to this Jesuit who was interested in catechizing slaves in languages they could understand.[15] One can see this clearly in de Sandoval's description of the linguistic situation of the "Rivers of Guinea" (modern Guinea-Bissau), the area of greatest diversity in his opinion of the whole Atlantic coast, where all the languages are from the West Atlantic group. He noted, for example, that Banhuns could easily understand the languages of Fulupos and Bañons, because

[14] In discussing linguistic items, I have relied on Joseph Greenberg's classic linguistic study, *Languages of Africa* (New York, 1963). More detailed study has outdated Greenberg's work for some areas, however. Greenberg's classification relies on simple vocabulary comparisons of representative languages to build a family tree that appreciates the degree of linguistic similarity between languages. Whatever its value as a tool for historical linguistics, it is especially valuable in that it gives a rough indicator of mutual intelligibility, ideal for our purposes here.

[15] This is why he compiled his linguistic data in *Instauranda* (pp. 91–6). The information was also to guide other missionaries.

their kingdom was between the two, whereas all Bañons (because they were bilingual) could understand Cazangas, who served as kings among them. Sometimes, these languages were indistinct linguistically. According to de Sandoval, Balantas, for example, sometimes could not understand other Balantas from remote areas; clearly, though, all could understand Balanta well enough to understand the catechism, whereas Biafaras, though speaking a different language, could usually understand Nalus, because the two were so closely related.[16]

Even where linguistic differences tended to separate the zone into culturally different societies, economic factors tended to unite it. The rivers and coasts of the area in particular gave the zone a strong set of commercial interconnections, and Mande commercial and political dominance helped to lessen cultural distance in other ways. For example, the "Rivers of Guinea" in modern Guinea-Bissau was a complex series of creeks and lagoons that connected not only the various parts of the country but also allowed frequent communication with the Gambia farther north and Sierra Leone to the south.[17] The fact that water transportation is cheap made the movement of bulk commodities possible and contributed to the extensive market networks that brought together people from linguistically diverse regions on a routine basis to exchange not only luxury goods but agricultural surpluses, salt, fish products, and the like.[18]

The frequency of the contacts and the numbers of people from all walks of life participating meant that cultural sharing and multilingualism would be widespread. De Sandoval shows this clearly: Brans, located in this aquatic crossroads region, could generally understand many languages – specifically, Bañons, Fulupos, Balantas, Mandingas, and Biafaras. Although most of these are closely related West Atlantic languages, Mandinga is not linguistically similar; however, it was a commercial and political lingua franca. Bañons located near the Fulupos could speak with Fulupos much more often than they could with other, more remote Bañons because they had much more contact with the Fulupos, by reason of their commercial relations. As noted, Bañons could also understand Cazangas, who in turn often spoke Mandinga and Bran among themselves.[19]

It was not just in language that commerce resulted in convergence; de

[16] Ibid., p. 92.

[17] These points were first noted by Fernandes, "Descriçã," in the early sixteenth century, but repeated by most of the later writers, such as Alvares de Almada, Donelha, and Lemos Coelho.

[18] On the markets and specialized division of labor, see Rodney, *Upper Guinea Coast*, pp. 16–22, and sources cited.

[19] De Sandoval, *Instauranda*, pp. 91–2.

Sandoval believed that the Mandingas, Jolofs, and Fulas, though of "diverse castes" could "understand each other because of the great communication they have through having received together the cursed sect of Muhammed."[20] Even in religion beyond the pale of Islam, the people of the region shared broad philosophic concepts with each other, and even with the Moslems, who still accepted much of the local world view.[21] These factors converged to give the zone a homogeneity that might be otherwise unexpected from linguistic study alone.

In addition to its commerical integration, Upper Guinea was also politically integrated by the Mande group, especially speakers of Mandinga. The Mande group was linguistically quite distinct from both of the West Atlantic groups, but Mandinga conquests under the Mali Empire and the Mane (who spoke a closely related language and who claimed connections to Mali as well)[22] invasion of Sierra Leone in 1560 had given them great political dominance. In some places Mande officials ruled over subjects who spoke different languages, while everywhere Mande merchants plied their trade.

The second great zone was what European geographers called Lower Guinea. It stretched from the lagoons of western Ivory Coast roughly over to Cameroon. On the west it was separated from Upper Guinea by a long stretch of coast, the so-called Kwakwa Coast of older geography (mostly modern Liberia and Ivory Coast), where there was only intermittent trade and few slaves were ever obtained.[23] On the east, it was separated from the Angola region by another stretch of coast reaching from modern Cameroon down to northern Gabon, which was so rarely visited that there are virtually no seventeenth-century descriptions, and like the northern part of the Angola coast (as far south as Loango) it exported few slaves.

Linguistically, the Lower Guinea region was more homogeneous than Upper Guinea, for all the people spoke languages of the Kwa family. But the Kwa family is an ancient one, and its westernmost branch, Akan, is quite distinct from its easternmost one, Igbo. It can be subdivided on this account into two groups: the Akan group on the west and the Aja group (including Fon, Yoruba, Edo, and Igbos on the east). De Sandoval believed there was even less diversity: "Minas (Akan), Popoos, Fulaos, Ardas, Arares [all Aja] are all one." Although they spoke several differ-

20 Sandoval, *Instauranda*, p. 91.

21 E.g., BSGL, Manuel Alvares, "Etiopa Menor," passim, for descriptions of religion and interactions (including, in his day, Christianity and Islam).

22 Ibid., fols. 76–90; Donelha, *Descrição da Serra Leoa*, fols. 11v–12; Alvares de Almada, "Tratado breve," *MMA*[2] 3:360.

23 E.g., see Pacheco Pereira, *Esmeraldo*, bk. 2, chap. 4, (ed. Silva Dias, pp. 109–10); de Marees, *Beschrijvinge*, pp. 6b–7b.

ent languages, many were so similar in grammar and vocabulary that multilingualism was not particularly difficult. This fact was duly noted by de Sandoval, who clearly felt that work in this area was easier. He noted that sometimes Ardas (Fon speakers from the Aja group) could understand catechism for "Caravales puros" (Kalabari), from opposite ends of the zone.[24]

As in the case of Upper Guinea, good transportation networks brought the linguistically diverse people into close economic and cultural contact and tended to force linguistic accommodations. Water transport was the key here, as in Upper Guinea, especially the complex coastal lagoon system that made the towns along the Gold Coast and eastward as far as the Niger delta specialized producers of fish, salt, and agricultural products. This extended inland waterway was linked to the interior by a series of rivers that prolonged it inland.[25] A gap in the waterways between the Volta and Allada hampered transportation and created what was probably the most significant internal division in the zone, between the Gold Coast and the area east of Allada.

These numerous commercial interactions tended to promote cultural intercommunication. By the 1630s, for example, Yoruba had emerged as a lingua franca along the coast from the Volta to Benin, though other lingua francas functioned both east and west of this.[26] Yoruba traditions and even deities were worshiped on the coast, even in the absence of Yoruba political domination.[27] In the east of the zone, Benin domination performed a similar integrating role: In fact, Benin's expansion westward had carried its soldiers and administrators as far as Allada and created a cultural unity like that created by the Mande in Upper Guinea. Benin and Yoruba traditions merged as well, perhaps because so many Yoruba served in the Benin court, and art styles were freely exchanged in the entire zone.[28]

Finally, there was the Angola coast. By 1680 this zone stretched inland

[24] De Sandoval, *Instauranda*, p. 94. He also pointed out that not all Lucumies (Yoruba) could understand each other, but his Lucumie group included Baribas, who are indeed of a distinct, non-Kwa, language family. Their inclusion in the Lucumie family might reflect their political situation relative to Yoruba-speaking states.

[25] See Law, "Land behind Lagos," and Kea, *Settlements*, pp. 11–96, passim. An excellent near-contemporary source on the economic specialization along the whole coast can be found in Bosman, *Description of Guinea*. On boat traffic going inland along the rivers, see Biblioteca Provincial de Toledo, MSS Bourbón-Lorenzana 244, de Zamora, "Cosmographia," fol. 53.

[26] De Sandoval, *Instauranda*, pp. 94–5; Colombino de Nantes to Prefect of Propaganda Fide, 26 December 1640, *MMA* 8:465 (information collected from Piersec, who visited there in the 1630s).

[27] John Thornton, "Traditions, Documents and the Ife-Benin Relationship," *History in Africa* 15 (1988): 357–9.

[28] On the Yoruba Benin connections in ideology, see ibid.

at least as far as the Lunda Empire of Shaba province in modern Zaire, although Lunda had only recently become involved in the Atlantic world. The linguistic diversity of this zone was much less pronounced than in Upper Guinea, and even less than in Lower Guinea. Not only did all the people speak languages of the Bantu group (itself more homogeneous than the Kwa group), but all were drawn from the Western Bantu subgroup, in fact from only two sections within that group.[29] Kikongo and Kimbundu, the two languages spoken in the zone by the vast majority of the slaves, were as linguistically similar as Spanish and Portuguese, according to Duarte Lopes in the late sixteenth century.[30] Most of the people from the more linguistically diverse interior (Malembas, Monxiolos, Angicos) could also speak, according to de Sandoval, "Angola" (probably Kimbundu, but perhaps Kikongo), which served as a lingua franca far into the interior.[31] It was probably possible for a speaker of one language in the region to learn another without much special instruction in about three to five weeks, and even from the beginning they possessed numerous items of vocabulary in common.[32] Likewise, they possessed many common items of religion, artistic canons, and the like.

It was only in politics that the Angolan zone was genuinely diverse. Two kingdoms, Kongo and Ndongo, were preeminent, each playing a role in the other's traditions and in the traditions of the smaller states that formed a band between them. But in the seventeenth century, politics created far more a feeling of rivalry among the elites than among the ordinary persons who were likely to be sold as slaves, in Angola and elsewhere. For most of them, they cared little what their kings or rulers thought of nearby kingdoms and would trade and interact in wartime as readily as in peace.

To sum up then, we must conclude that the degree of diversity in Africa can easily be exaggerated. The older anthropological tendency to see each ethnolinguistic group as a separate "tribe" and to ignore such factors as multilingualism or nonlinguistic cultural sharing have tended to force the real diversity beyond its true limits. At most we have three truly culturally diverse areas, and the seven subgroups are themselves

29 For a discussion of linguistic relations within this group, see Jan Vansina, "Western Bantu Expansion," *Journal of African History* 25 (1984): 129–45.

30 Filippo Pigafetta, *Relazione del Reame di Congo* (ed. Georgio Cardona; Milan, 1978) (French trans., Willy Bal, *Description du royaume de Congo et des contrees environnantes* [Louvain, 1965]), both editions with original (1591) pagination.

31 De Sandoval, *Instauranda*, p. 96.

32 This is true for Bantu languages in general. Zambians often informed me (in 1979–81) from their own experience that they could learn another Zambian language in about this time period, though they would not obtain fluency so quickly. I am assuming that the task was no more difficult in the seventeenth century.

often quite homogeneous. In addition, as we shall see, the slave trade took some groups far more frequently than others and often had the effect of bringing people of similar backgrounds together more than a maximum-diversity hypothesis will allow.

African cultural groups and the slave trade

The issue of the cultural homogeneity of Africa has often been debated, but many scholars now side with Mintz and Price in arguing that whatever the African cultural situation might have been, the process of acquiring slaves and placing them in various economic establishments had the effect of randomizing them.[33] The results of this randomizing might still be serious even if we reduce the number of distinct African cultures involved to three or a maximum of seven.

Randomization did not occur with the Middle Passage. Slave ships drew their entire cargo from only one or perhaps two ports in Africa and unloaded them in large lots of as many as 200–1,000 in their new Atlantic homes. It was in the interests of slave-ship captains to gather as many slaves as quickly as possible to reduce expenses and to keep down mortality. Once slaves were on board in one location, the captain had little choice but to keep them on board, even if he went to other points of the coast. But if the slaves were gathered in one place, he could keep them on shore until he had to depart. Not only would this improve the health of the cargo, but it might allow him to shuffle some of the loss due to death onto the sellers.

Early slave voyages generally confirm this. For example, the *Santiago*, a Portuguese ship visiting virtually the entire Upper Guinea coast in 1526, nevertheless obtained all its slaves (as opposed to other elements of the cargo) at one point – Sierra Leone.[34] The several Benin–Forcados rivers voyages by Portuguese ships in the 1520s that have left records confirm the same thing – slaves bought at one point and at one time.[35] Finally, all four of the voyages to Kongo in the 1520s and 1530s for which we have records also show the entire cargo taken in at one point.[36]

The same pattern is confirmed for slaving voyages in the seventeenth century. In only one area, Lower Guinea, was it fairly routine for ships from Britain, France, or the Netherlands to draw slaves from two points on the same coast, but this situation was created by the peculiarity of trading there. Many captains and the companies that sent them wished

[33] Mintz and Price, *Afro-American Past*, pp. 8–10.

[34] Ship's book of *Santiago* (ed. Teixeira da Mota).

[35] Ryder, *Benin and the Europeans*, pp. 62–8; and idem, "Trading Voyage."

[36] Kongo ships' books: *Conceição* (1525), ANTT, CC II/128/3; *Santo Espirito* (1535), *MMA* 15:98–102; *Urbano* (1535), *MMA* 15:115–18; and *Conceição* (1535), *MMA* 15:124–30.

the ships to visit the Gold Coast to buy gold. But since an entire ship could scarcely be filled with gold, captains rounded out their cargo space by taking on slaves. When the Gold Coast did not supply enough slaves, captains would typically go on to Allada (soon the center of what was to be called the Slave Coast) to finish filling the ship.

Thus, it was possible that even though most visitors to Lower Guinea drew their slaves from only one point, many others drew them from two (though both in Lower Guinea). When Jean Barbot visited Africa in the *Soleil d'Affrique* in 1678–9, for example, his captain purchased most slaves at a single point on the Gold Coast, although some of the cargo was drawn from Allada.[37] Given the fairly strong cultural difference between the Gold Coast and the areas east of the Volta, these might have been slaves of two distinct cultural subgroupings (Akan and Aja). Other French ships seem to have done the same when dealing with this part of Africa, and Goupy des Marets, whose experience on the matter stretched from 1675 to 1688, confirmed that this was a general procedure for French captains on that coast.[38] English ships seem to have proceeded the same way at times, for the Royal African Company's ledgers and ships' books (as well as instructions to captains) all show that the usual procedure was to visit the Gold Coast and then to "round out" the cargo by visiting Allada.[39]

But it was also common, even in voyages to Lower Guinea, for ships to proceed directly to the Slave Coast (Allada) and skip taking on gold. This strategy was suggested to the Royal African Company by one of its agents, John Mildmay, in 1680.[40] For example, John Philips, a Royal African Company captain, got his cargo only at Allada in 1694, and apparently French practice was often the same, for as early as 1671, the Sieur d'Elbée obtained his entire cargo at Allada.[41] Ships that called further east, in the Niger delta region (usually Kalabar), typically acquired all their slaves there.[42]

However, this two-stop strategy, often called "coasting," was largely restricted to the Lower Guinea region. In the other two regions, the one-stop approach was far more common (though not without its occasional

37 Gabriel Debien, Maracel Delafosse, and Guy Thilmans, eds., "Journal d'un voyage de traite en Guinée, à Cayenne et aux Antilles fait par Jean Barbot en 1678–9," *Bulletin, Institute Fondamentale d'Afrique Noire* B, 40 (1978): 25–35 (pagination of the original MS).

38 BM Rouen, MS Montbret 125, Goupy des Marets, "Voyage," fols. 151–4.

39 Davies, *Royal African Company,* p. 227.

40 John Mildmay to Royal African Company, 13 October 1680, PRO T/70, vol. 1134.

41 D'Elbée, "Journal du voyage," in Clodoré, *Relation,* p. 383; Philips, "Voyage," in Churchill, *voyages,* p. 230.

42 See, e.g., the log of the *Arthur,* visiting New Calabar in 1667, in Elizabeth Donnan, ed., *Documents Illustrative of the History of the Slave Trade,* 4 vols. (Washington, D.C., 1930–5), 1:226–7.

exceptions, of course). In Senegambia, for example, on-shore factors ensured that slaves could be acquired in one-stop visits by gathering slaves over a period of time, tapping trade routes that led into the interior: Factors were located near the Senegal and Gambia rivers and along the coast of Sierra Leone down to Cape Mount. Thus, the Sierra Leone and Gambian posts provided the Royal African Company's ships that visited their areas with their entire cargoes,[43] as did the French post at Gorée near the Senegal.

On the Angola coast, northern countries typically made the single stop at the ports of the kingdom of Loango or the ports of Malemba, Kabinda, or Mpinda (in the kingdom of Kongo). Here the trading was not normally handled by an on-shore factor, but African merchants ensured a steady supply, because the slaves normally came from other parts of the zone; before 1680 they usually came from Angola or Kongo.[44] Further south, the Portuguese colony of Angola, with its ports of Luanda and Benguela, served as a factory for the Portuguese trade with the Atlantic. Ships typically made single stops in this area as well.

In short, with the exception of the Lower Guinea voyages that followed the two-stop pattern, virtually all slaves were taken from a single point. The slaves actually boarding at that point would be drawn from whatever slaves merchants based there had acquired, and this would not necessarily be just the immediate hinterland of the port. But it was probably from a restricted and culturally quite homogeneous zone nevertheless.

These ports were served by trade routes that reached various distances into the interior. However, the same trade routes that served the ports also served local trade. As we have already seen, commercial interaction was an important element creating homogeneity, and hence virtually all slaves exported from a port would be from the cultural zone that was already united by commerce in other goods. Ships reaching Upper Guinea, for example, might stop at the Senegal, Gambia, Rivers of Guinea, or Sierra Leone ports. Each of these ports, in turn, served a distinct hinterland: the Senegal basin, the Gambia basin, the creek and lagoon network of the "Rivers," or the coastal waterways and river routes of Sierra Leone. Jula merchants might send slaves from the interior out any one of these ports, using various routes, as Curtin shows they surely did, but they were all from the quite homogeneous Mande interior.[45] Otherwise, the slaves were drawn from the commercial circuit that served both the port and the region.

43 See ample documentation in Letters from Agents of the Royal African Company in Africa and America, 1680–3, PRO T/70, vol. 1134.

44 The supply and purchasing situation on the coast is discussed and detailed at length in Martin, *External Trade*.

45 Curtin, *Economic Change*, pp. 168–82.

Likewise, although Capuchin visitors to Allada noted that many of the slaves exported from that port in the 1660s were from inland and brought down by rivers,[46] their usual source, according to Barbot, was still the kingdom of Lucumie (Oyo) or other Aja-speaking groups of the near interior.[47] These states were already commercially and culturally linked to Allada in the same zone. Not only would all the people in this port's interior have cultural interaction, but slaves from the same groups that were exported were also likely to be retained by those in Allada society who held slaves, and their integration into Allada society would increase the people of Allada's familiarity with them. This last point might hold true for every part of the zone but can be clearly shown for the Gold Coast, where, for example, one could meet many slaves acquired in Allada in private hands.[48]

Other circumstances of enslavement might well make the slaves placed in individual ships extremely homogeneous. For example, slaves captured in wars were extremely likely to be from the army of the defeated country, recruited from a very restricted group of people. In 1678, the French captain Barbot noted that they were sure to find slaves at Coremantyn because the king of that region had just won a war over his enemies.[49] The point is often confirmed in records of the English Royal African Company.[50] An entire ship might be filled, not just with people possessing the same culture, but with people who grew up together.

Obviously, then, the slave trade itself did little to break up cultural groupings. The breaking up of cultural groupings was likely to occur in the process of sale and subsequent employment in American estates. Slaves were rarely sold all in one block once they reached America, and hence one might reasonably expect plantations and estates to mix up slaves from many different ships and cargoes. In some cases, masters tried deliberately to mix slaves from different origins in the belief that this would hinder attempts at rebellion, a tactic that was common enough in mid-seventeenth-century Barbados that Ligon commented on it.[51] This might then have served to hinder the direct establishment of an African culture in the Americas.

46 Biblioteca Provincial de Toledo, MSS Bourbón-Lorenzana 244, de Zamora, "Cosmographia," fols. 62–62v.

47 Barbot, "Voyage," p. 356 (probably based on notes of his 1682 visit). De Sandoval, who knew the ethnic makeup of the coast very well from his work in catechisms, was unaware of any nation lying inland of the Lucumies, though of course modern historians do. Presumably, de Sandoval's ignorance was due to very few, if any, such slaves coming to Cartagena.

48 Examples cited in Kea, *Settlements*, pp. 105–6.

49 Barbot, "Journal," p. 29.

50 Davies, *Royal African Company*, pp. 226–8, 278.

51 Ligon, *History*, p. 46.

But not every master shared these sentiments. French masters in the Lesser Antilles, for example, sought to get as many slaves as possible from the same nation (*terre* in French sources) and to encourage them to marry each other, in the hopes that the stability of the community thus developed would improve efficiency and limit rebellion.[52] Other masters may well have seen the value of such an approach as well, even in Barbados, for sugar estates on seventeenth-century Barbados, like the French colonies at the same time, were managed on the idea of building a self-sustaining community among their slaves. Other regions where the slave economy was characterized by the so-called peasant breach (see Chap. 6) might also have sought to unify nations rather than to diversify them.

Even if owners really did hope to randomize slaves, however, it might prove impossible to do this effectively. Of course, such a strategy would be immediately limited by the relative lack of diversity among arriving Africans, so that at best one might have seven different groups – perhaps an effective deterrent to rebellion with the side effect of limiting the growth of an African culture.

But patterns of the slave trade might well hinder such an attempt at maximizing diversity. How could Brazilian masters in the seventeenth century mix their slaves if, as Dutch accounts tell us, over 15,000 slaves a year came only from Angola between 1620 and 1623?[53] Indeed, given that Angolans made up some 50–60 percent of the slaves exported from Africa throughout the period, how could any master expect to avoid having a concentration of Angolans on his estate?

English and French masters might face similar problems simply because conditions in Africa and the politics of the slave-trading companies dictated that the bulk of their operations would be centered on one or two points in Africa. The English and French Africa Companies drew most of their slaves in the late seventeenth century from the Gold Coast and Allada because that is where they had their factors and most of their ships went. They might draw on Senegambia or the whole Upper Guinea coast as well, through factors in Senegal or Sierra Leone, but in the end, that coast did not supply nearly as many slaves as the Lower Guinea region, and thus many a master would have to choose between buying no slaves at all or buying from the many Coromantis (Akans) or Alladas arriving in ship after ship.

Thus there were limits on the ability to achieve a random linguistic distribution of slaves, and what this meant was that most of the slaves on any sizable estate were probably from only a few national groupings.

[52] Du Tertre, *Histoire* 2:504–5.

[53] De Laet, *Jaerlick verhael*, Portuguese edition, p. 239.

These circumstances operated to ensure that most slaves would have no shortage of people from their own nation with whom to communicate and perhaps to share elements of common culture. These groupings of slaves served as a base from which many elements of African culture could be shared, continued, and developed in America and perhaps even transmitted into the next generation.

Take, for example, the Remire estate in Cayenne (French Guiana) at the end of the seventeenth century. The estate is exceptionally well documented, perhaps unique among sixteenth- and seventeenth-century estates because of the very detailed inventory of it left by Jean Goupy des Marets, its manager from 1688 to 1690. He recorded the exact provenance of each slave (often including the name of the village in Africa where they were born) and some biographical details on marriages, time of arrival, age, name of ship that brought the slave and other occasional information. It is difficult to generalize from the details of this inventory to other regions where different national policies, management schemes, or estate structure functioned, but at least it gives us a rich source of data on cultural groupings.

Supplied by both French and Dutch shipping, Remire probably had a better "mix" than most estates in other areas, and indeed slaves came from all three of the coasts and six of the seven subgroups. But the core of the labor force was composed of twenty-eight slaves from the region right around Allada, complemented by an additional nine slaves from Lower Guinea (three Gold Coast and six Kalabari). Moreover, eleven slaves came from the Angola coast region, all certainly from the kingdom of Kongo, because the inventory records that all had been baptized in Africa.[54] Finally, nine slaves derived from the Upper Guinea region, but all from its northern part (Senegal) and not from either the Rivers area further south or Sierra Leone.[55] There were probably few estates in the New World that had greater diversity.

Thanks to Goupy des Marets's detailed knowledge of African geography, acquired in several visits to Lower Guinea before coming to supervise the Remire estate in 1688,[56] and his willingness to give biographical details, we can get some idea of the interaction of nations in an American setting. Certainly slaves tended to cluster around members of their own nation, as is seen in the six Kalabari slaves, who formed a tight group,

54 One might add that these slaves were all acquired in the 1680s, at the height of the Kongo civil wars, and were thus in all probability the victims of the frequent small-scale wars and raids of the time. See Thornton, *Kingdom of Kongo*, pp. 95–106.

55 Data from BM Rouen, MS Montbret 125, Goupy des Marets, "Voyage," analyzed in Debien and Houdaille, "Origines," p. 181.

56 BM Rouen, MS Montbret 125, Goupy des Marets, "Voyage," fols. 151–5.

went around together, and intermarried.[57] The same closeness was exhibited by the group from Allada and its neighbors (Whydah, Grand Popo, Little Popo, Fon, and Oyo), probably as a result of the way the ships were supplied. Two of this group were from Allada town itself, two more from the village of Weme (in Fon), and two more from the village of Saito. It is quite likely that these people either knew each other before their sale in America or at the very least had common friends and family. The Whydah slaves, five in all, came from towns within fifteen kilometers of each other in this tiny ministate, and unless they spent all their time at home may well have had much knowledge of each other's background and family in Africa. Of course, they also spoke the same language as Allada, Little and Grand Popo, and Fon slaves, even though the slaves from this part of Africa came at different times on no less than five different ships.

Records and inventories that give ethnonyns of slaves for the sixteenth and seventeenth centuries are fairly rare, so it is not always possible to determine the degree to which the situation in Remire is duplicated elsewhere. But the distributions on surviving inventories show how patterns of the slave trade and the distribution of slaves over time tended to produce sizable blocs of slaves on one estate from the same nation, and even larger groups from a fairly small region like the Rivers of Guinea, the Senegal valley, or the like. Sixteenth-century Spanish inventories show how the connection to Upper Guinea produced concentrations of slaves from there on their estates. Of slaves in the estate of Gorjón (1547 on Hispaniola) for which there are identifiable ethnonyms, one can find several blocs: 4 Zapes from Sierra Leone; 5 Brans, a Bañon, and a Biafara from the Rivers of Guinea; 2 Jolofs and 2 Mandingas from the Senegal valley; making a total of 15 slaves from the Upper Guinea region. The remaining group was from Lower Guinea: 2 Kalabaris and 2 Lucumies (Yorubas).[58] Slaves on the Cortés estate in 1549 showed a similar grouping: The Senegal valley produced 30 slaves (Jolof, Mandinga, Siine, and Tukulor), and the Rivers produced no less than 47 (Bañon, Zape, Bran, Biafara, and Cazanga); the estate had no Lower Guinea slaves and only 2 from Angola. Two were from Mozambique.[59] A similar grouping is evident on another Hispaniola inventory from 1606. Here 10 were Zapes from Sierra Leone, and the Rivers region was represented by 8 Beafadas, 9 Brans, 1 Bioho, and 1 Cazanga, forming a single bloc of 29 members. There were also 1 Fula, 6 Mandingas, and 1 Jolof from the Senegal basin, a total of 37 Upper Guinea slaves. Lower Guinea

57 Ibid., fols. 85 and 89.

58 Escripta de Licenciado Cerrato, 17 December 1547, Incháustegui Cabral, *Reales cédulas* 1:236–9.

59 Published in Aguirre Beltrán, *Pobolación negra*, pp. 244–5.

had few representatives (1 Yoruba and 1 Benin), and Angola had only 2 Angolas and 1 Kongo.

On large estates, therefore, slaves would typically have no trouble finding members of their own nation with whom to communicate, and they would have even less trouble finding those of other nations with whom they were linked through commerce and other interaction in Africa. This was true even if the estate was small or if slaves were scattered on several small estates. For example, in the middle of the seventeenth century, the slaves around Lake Maracaibo in Venezuela were distributed on estancias of 2–3 slaves each intermixed with larger estates with 6–10 (17 being the largest number on any one estate). Lists of these slaves who received religious instruction in 1656 give ethnonyms revealing their origins. The largest estancia, that of Arraez de Mendoza (17 slaves), had 9 Angolan slaves and 4 from the Rivers (2 Brans, 1 Bañon, and 1 Fulupo), and the rest were listed as "creoles." Of the Angolans, 3 were from Matamba and 1 was from the province of Malemba (then under Matamba's sovereignty). A fifth, Melchior Enbuyla, was from Mbwila in the "Dembos" region some distance away.[60] The Matamba and Malemba slaves were probably born within fifty kilometers of each other and could no doubt share much in common, even if perhaps less than the Allada group on Remire.

Big plantations concentrated slaves in the hundreds, but on small estates in areas such as Venezuela, Virginia, or Central America, the lack of numbers did not mean that slaves from adjacent estates had no communication with each other, as long as plantation management did not inhibit occasional travel or visiting. Thus, in the Maracaibo area, the small group of Angolans on Arraez de Mendoza's estate might have been able to visit Pascal Enbuyla (from the same small state as Melchior Enbuyla) and Juan Andala (from Ndala, which was close to Matamba and Malemba), who lived on the adjacent estate of Pedro Fernández. Or, if Francisco Narara, the only Allada slave on the estancia of Ana de Quiroz, wanted to meet people from his nation, he could visit Hernando and Juan Arara on the estancia of Diego de Cuervo de Valdez, nearby.[61]

The documents do not tell us if these slaves in Venezuela visited (or were allowed to visit) each other, however. But French documents do suggest that slaves often visited others from the same nation, and this pattern was probably true everywhere that off-estate visiting was permitted. According to Charles de Rochefort, writing about the Lesser Antilles in the middle of the seventeenth century, people often visited others

[60] Padrón de negros del Valle de los Borbures, 22 November 1656, in Trochis Veracoechea, ed., *Documentos*, p. 205.
[61] Ibid., pp. 205–6.

from the same "terre" (nation), specifically for cultural activities, such as celebrations or funerals.[62] This seems to have been the case in Jamaica as well, in spite of the policy of some English masters to mix slaves on their estates. Hans Sloane, visiting Jamaica in 1688, noted that "when they die their country people [people from their nation] make lamentations and mourning."[63]

National loyalty might be reinforced by marriages as well, if circumstances permitted. French masters in the Lesser Antilles, as part of their strategy of allowing family formation, encouraged slaves to marry within their own nation, going so far as allowing the slave to pick a bride or husband from the cargo of an incoming ship. This preference is revealed in the records from Remire. Twelve of the twenty-four married couples on Remire were from the same nation, and two were from the same village (Weme), though they had arrived on different ships. Three more slave couples came from nations in the same national grouping, such as a Bambara married to a Fula.[64]

Some were married before they arrived in America and may well have been married before their enslavement. A Kalabari slave named Ouanbom came on the same ship with a Kalabari woman named Aunon. They were both forty-two years old in 1690. As Goupy des Marets described their relationship, "she came, was bought and sold with her husband, and has never left him up to the present day." Another slave, Aguinon, in 1690 a seventy-year-old man from Fon, had another type of relationship with Bassi, aged seventy-three in 1690, who although she came on the same ship with him was from Grand Popo and probably did not know him in Africa. He had relations with other women, however, for he was said to be like a husband to sixty-two-year-old Ouapay, from Saito (a town in Fon), and was actually married to Sanon, from Allada.[65] All these slaves spoke the same language, and perhaps the original relationships had been formed on board ship, although the possibility that the Kalabaris had been married before they left Africa cannot be ruled out in the manuscript as it reads.

We do not possess information of equivalent detail for the seventeenth century, but some research on Brazil in the mid-eighteenth century suggests that marriages between people of the same nation were common there, or at least had become common at some earlier point. Schwartz's analysis of several sources suggests that there was a very high rate of

[62] Rochefort, *Histoire naturelle*, pp. 321–2.
[63] Hans Sloane, *A Voyage to the Islands Madera, Barbados, Neives, S. Christopher and Jamaica*, 2 vols. (London, 1707–25), 1:xlviii.
[64] Du Tertre, *Histoire* 2:504–5; BM Rouen, MS Montbret 125, Goupy des Marets, "Voyage," fol. 84.
[65] BM Rouen, MS Montbret 125, Goupy des Marets, "Voyage," fol. 85, 87, 88, 89.

intermarriage among the same nation in general, but interestingly enough, as at Remire, it was those from Lower Guinea (Yorubas and Kalibaris) who were most prone to this type of marriage, whereas central Africans seemed indifferent to it (more than half of Remire's Kongos were not married to other Kongos).[66]

These marriages that linked people of the same nation obviously had cultural implications. Not only could they communicate with each other in the same language and share the same religious and aesthetic concepts, thus continuing their African culture in America, but they could even develop a national culture in the next generation. For example, in the late 1680s Guiaon, from the village of Alamba in Whydah (of the Fon nation), married an eighteen-year-old named Marie Doré, who was listed as "creole" (born in America) in the estate records. But Marie Doré was both creole and a member of the Fon nation, for both her parents, Agouya and Phillipe, were from Fon.[67] Her marriage to a man from Whydah would continue that tradition, as they were both of the same language and nation.

The formation of national blocks on estates, intermarriage, and visiting undoubtedly helped to foster an idea of national identity in most American areas, which is not surprising considering that people would naturally prefer interaction with others who shared their heritage. The idea of national identity was sufficiently strong among slaves in rural America that it even affected them when they decided to rebel or run away. The slave plot on Guadeloupe in 1656 involved Angolans and Senegambians (called Cape Verdians in the sources), and they were sufficiently conscious of their differences that the Senegambians pulled out when the Angolans insisted that leadership in the resulting society should be held by Angolans.[68] Slaves plotting on Barbados in 1675 conceived of a "Coromanti" (Akan) state.[69] Runaways often segregated their communities by nations. Among the runaway communities around Cartagena in the late seventeenth century the Akan slaves had a separate community,[70]

66 Schwartz, *Sugar Plantations*, pp. 391–3. A similar analysis by Francisco Vidal Luna and Iraci del Nero da Costa of marriages in Minas Gerais from 1727 to 1826 showed that 77% of all females and 64% of all males in the group he called "Sudanese" (Upper and Lower Guinea combined) were married within the same group; but the rates for "Bantus" (Angola) were somewhat lower, 67% for females and 44% for males. Tight groupings were also partially explored: Among Minas (probably the Allada group) 56% of the men and 68% of the women were married to someone of the same nation; among Angolas the proportions were 34% for men and 51% for women ("Vila Rica: Nota sobre casamentos de escravos [1727–1826]," *Africa* [*São Paulo*] 4 [1981]: 108–9).

67 BM Rouen, MS Montbret 125, Goupy des Marets, "Voyage," fols. 83, 85.

68 Du Tertre, *Histoire* 1:500.

69 See the plot discussed in Craton, *Testing the Chains*, pp. 108–14.

70 Memorial de Gobernador de Nueva Granada, 1693, summarized and quoted in Arranzola, *Palenque*, p. 195.

as did the Angolan slaves in the Brazilian runaway community of Palmares, who had their own leader.[71]

The development of African nations in America was not just the result of concentrations of slaves from one area on individual estates or patterns of visiting in rural areas. Patterns of shipping and residence clearly put slaves of the same nation together: This process was reinforced by marriage and the natural association based on common language and heritage. But it was not long before more formal national organizations developed. Girolamo Benzoni, writing about Hispaniola in the early 1540s, noted the African nations of that island each had "its own king or governor" and were somewhat jealous of each other. He specifically mentioned the Kongo, Wolof, Sape, and Berbesi nations.[72]

National organization was especially strong in urban America, where the lower levels of day-to-day supervision and greater freedom of movement allowed nations to create semiformal and formal organizations. One of the earliest references to such national organizations in urban areas comes from de Sandoval's description of early seventeenth-century Cartagena. He complained that masters in Cartagena had the unconscionable practice of freeing their slaves on the point of death, leaving it to their "nation" to see to their burial, implying a sort of self-help organization that took care of funerals, at least.[73] Other Jesuits provide more details. Nicolás González, a Jesuit companion of Pedro Claver, testified at the inquest of 1658 that such funerals were social occasions, where "certain assemblies of Moors of the same nation [*stripe*] meet when someone of their nation dies." These were not just informal assemblies, for they had *capitoli*, or "chapters," as if they formed a brotherhood, such as was common in Latin countries.[74]

These institutions sometimes frightened authorities, who thought they might be conspiratorial. It was probably the celebrations of one such assembly that prompted a panic among government officials in Mexico in 1609 and again in 1612, for they elected a "king" and "queen" as well as distributing other mock offices in those years.[75] From what little information is available in seventeenth-century sources, it seems probable that the institutions did have some sort of formal organization, in which annual festivals, recognition of certain feast days, the election

71 "Relação das guerras feitas aos Palmares de Pernambuco no tempo do Governador D. Pedro de Almeida de 1675 a 1678," *Revista do Instituto Archaeologico e Geographico Pernambucano* 10, no. 56 (1859): 303.

72 Benzoni, *History of the New World* (trans. Smyth), p. 92.

73 De Sandoval, *Instauranda*, p. 195.

74 BN Colombia, Claver Inquest, fol. 40.

75 Juan de Torquemada, *Monarchia Indiana*, 3 vols. (Mexico City, 1943), 1: bk. 5, chaps. 70, 74.

of kings and queens, and various mutual aid functions (such as funerals) figured prominently.

When officials in Cartagena feared a slave plot in 1693, they interrogated a certain mulatto named Francisco de Veas for days about life in the city's Afro-Colombian community. Among their questions to him were "if he knew that the Negroes of the Arará, Mina, and other newly arrived [*bozales*] nations [*castas*] have their kings, governors, and captains, and if they meet in their councils [*cabildos*] to deal with the problems of their nation or caste, and have their parties and festivities in which they join together." De Veas expressed surprise at the question, for he thought it was common knowledge that the nations had "coronations" annually at which officials were appointed.[76] Indeed, it was; nations had taken out licenses to dance in the streets and play their drums since 1573,[77] and the city's European and Euro-American population enjoyed the festivities as well.

Brazilian sources noted that the Kongo nation had elected a king and queen since the early seventeenth century, a time when central African slaves dominated the Brazilian trade.[78] By 1674 nations were playing a significant role in the social life of Brazilian slaves, with annual elections of a king and queen over the entire slave community as well as governors for each nation and numerous other positions forming a whole administration.[79] Although the government of Brazil paid little formal attention to these organizations, as was the case elsewhere in the Americas, they probably exercised considerable informal power.

These national organizations probably preexisted the better-known lay brotherhoods, such as the Brotherhood of Our Lady of the Rosary, to which so many Afro-Americans belonged, and which probably gradually emerged as the formal leadership of the nation, whether they were members of the brotherhood or not. The brotherhoods were organized by the clergy to attempt to regularize the slaves' social life and attracted mostly the more fortunate and free among the Afro-American community; they were often organized along national lines, being only for Minas or Angolas or Alladas, and so on.[80] In Brazil, at least, the first elections of kings and queens for the Kongo nation were conducted by

76 "Testimonio de la culpa," in Arranzola, *Palenque*, p. 163.

77 Act of Cabildo of Cartagena, 9 January 1573 in ibid., p. 22.

78 R. C. Smith, "Manuscritos da Igreja de Nossa Senhora do Rosário dos Pretos do Recife," *Arquivos* 4/10 (1945–51): 55, footnote.

79 Réné Riberio, *Cultos afro-brasileiros de Recife: Um estudo de adjustamento social* (Recife, 1952), pp. 29–32.

80 Bowser, *African Slave*, pp. 247–50; for Brazil, see Patricia A. Mulvey, "Slave Confraternities in Brazil: Their Role in Colonial Society," *The Americas* 39 (1982): 39–68.

the brotherhood of Nossa Senhora do Rosário,[81] and the brotherhoods played a role in other elections as well. Some scholars have seen the membership along national lines as an attempt on the part of the clergy to "divide and conquer" the African population,[82] and perhaps it did contribute to preventing plots or maintaining control, but it more likely simply co-opted a larger, preexisting organization. It is probably more correct to say that the missionaries' interest in national organizations was a way of controlling the alleged sexual immorality of the slaves. Certainly Claver believed that funerals often involved immoral dancing and sought to break them up.[83]

Although brotherhoods were characteristic of large Iberian towns, some were organized in rural areas, among the slaves on estates as well. Jesuit sources mention the organization of lay fraternities in rural Brazil as early as 1587,[84] although the sources do not reveal whether they were organized along national lines as in the cities.

Thus, wherever more than a few slaves from the same nation were concentrated, in towns or on estates, the possibility of cultural transfer was possible. Presumably the several dozen Fon-speaking Allada slaves on Remire could maintain many of the cultural traditions of their homelands. Although some slaves might well find themselves in a relative minority, such as Kongos on the estate of Cortés in 1549 (there were only two), on most estates one or more nations had sufficient numbers to create a community. This community could transmit, develop, or maintain the African culture they brought with them. If they married among themselves they stood a chance of transmitting it on to the next generation. Even if the numbers from a single nation were small, larger groups composed of nations from the same general vicinity in Africa, nations that certainly had considerable intercommunication before their enslavement, could continue that communication in America. No doubt in all American situations, communication between nations was more intense than in Africa, with interesting results for the African culture in the Atlantic world.

The slave trade and subsequent transfer to New World plantations was not, therefore, quite as randomizing a process as posited by those who argue that Africans had to start from scratch culturally upon their arrival in the New World. Quite the contrary, though the process of enslavement, sale, transfer, shipment, and relocation on a plantation was certainly disruptive to the personal and family lives of those people who endured it, its effect on culture may have been much less than

81 Smith, "Manuscritos," p. 55, footnote.
82 E.g., see Bowser, *African Slave*, p. 249.
83 BN Colombia, Claver Inquest, fol. 180v.
84 Serafim Leite, *História* 2:234.

many suggest. Slaves, although no longer surrounded by their familiar home environment, village, and family, were nevertheless not in a cultural wilderness when they arrived in America. They could easily find others who spoke their language and shared their norms in the new environment, especially if they were on a large estate or in an urban area. The Remire data even show that they might even meet relatives, friends, and associates whom they had known in Africa, thanks to patterns of enslavement and the slave trade that served to concentrate, rather than disperse, people, though such cases might be rare and were probably not typical.

8

Transformations of African culture in the Atlantic world

African slaves arriving in Atlantic colonies did not face as many barriers to cultural transmission as scholars such as Mintz and Price have maintained. However, they probably also did not simply recommence an African culture in the New World. If they met sufficient people from their nation to keep language and culture from dying out, this did not mean that they maintained them intact. They were, after all, in a new environment, with a new political and economic system. They had communication with people who did not share their heritage or that of their near African neighbors, including Europeans and Euro-Americans. Even if they were able to transmit their culture to a new generation, the culture passed on was not the original African culture. Afro-Atlantic culture became more homogeneous than the diverse African cultures that composed it, merging these cultures together and including European culture as well. The evidence suggests that the slaves were not militant cultural nationalists who sought to preserve everything African but rather showed great flexibility in adapting and changing their culture.

Culture change in the Atlantic world: dynamics of culture

In order to understand the process of cultural maintenance, transformation, and transmission, one must first understand something about what is meant by culture and particularly cultural dynamics. Anthropologists define it as a total lifeway for a society, including among other things kinship, political structure, language and literature, art, music and dance, and religion. But all these elements are not equally fixed. Some are highly sensitive to conditions in a particular area and might change rapidly; others are much more fixed and change slowly.

Certainly, historical research shows that African political structures have evolved and changed over time. Kongo, for example, went from a strongly centralized authoritarian kingdom in the seventeenth century to a much more weakly centralized system ruled collectively in the early eighteenth century.[1] As it changed, the ideology of kingship altered as well, from one emphasizing the absolute power of the founding king and his descendants, expressed by their ability to kill anyone freely without challenge, to one stressing the founder as a kind and generous blacksmith who mediates disputes.[2]

Similarly, family structure and kinship can be highly variable. We know fairly little about family structure among commoners in seventeenth-century Africa, but research into the elite shows that African kinship and social organization were flexible, encompassing multiple principles that were sometimes at odds with each other and altered as the social environment changed. For example, it is possible to show that the Kongo possessed a matrilineal system of kinship through the study of kinship terminology in seventeenth-century vocabularies,[3] but it is also obvious that real descent for the elite was reckoned bilaterally, in a lineage structure that was very fluid.[4] Interesting parallels can be found in Wolof society, where elite matrilineality was also abandoned in favor of more flexible patterns.[5] Anthropologists now recognize that African kinship is not a fixed system but one with multiple possibilities, able to accommodate rapid change in the twentieth-century world.[6] Studies of kinship in the early modern European world have reached the same conclusions.[7]

But other elements of culture are much more stable, changing much more slowly. For example, languages change only at a very slow rate. A modern speaker of Kikongo, for example, can fairly easily understand the language of the Kikongo catechism of 1624,[8] and can translate the sermon found at the back of the Flemish Capuchin Joris van Gheel's copy of the Kikongo dictionary of 1652.[9] Similarly, speakers of Kim-

1 Thornton, *Kingdom of Kongo*, pp. 84–115.

2 Ibid., pp. 117–20.

3 This is done in Hilton, *Kingdom of Kongo*, pp. 19–23 and Appendix 3.

4 See ibid., pp. 19–23, 88–90, 212–14; for a very different account that emphasizes flexibility of a single system rather than systematic change over time, see Thornton, *Kingdom of Kongo*, pp. 31, 47–51. The differences in these two accounts do not affect the general argument made here, however.

5 For sixteenth- and seventeenth-century Wolof kinship, see Jean Boulègue, *Les anciens royaumes wolof: Le Grand Jolof* (Paris, 1987), pp. 58–60.

6 One of the pioneers in dealing with central Africa is Wyatt MacGaffey, who stresses the flexibility of real (as opposed to theoretical) kinship systems. See his *Custom and Government in the Lower Congo* (Berkeley and Los Angeles, 1970).

7 A classic statement is Emmanuel LeRoy Ladurie, *The Peasants of Languedoc*, trans. John Day (Urbana, 1974), pp. 29–36.

8 See the modern edition of Bontinck and Nsasi, *Le catéchisme kikongo*, introduction.

9 A translation to French was in fact made in the modern edition of the dictionary: C. Penders and J. van Wing, *Le plus ancien dictionaire Bantu* (Brussels, 1928).

bundu and Fon could do the same with seventeenth-century materials in those languages.[10] Furthermore, languages easily survive numerous changes in the social and political environment, as can be seen in the American forms of English, Spanish, French, German, and Dutch, which are still understandable by speakers in the original country. In large measure, this is because languages are complex systems of arbitrary sounds, which when arranged in particular patterns communicate thoughts and convey messages. In order to work at all the system has to be fixed and change little, because people literally spend years learning the system. This rigidity of structure and content is probably why language is the preeminent method of identifying a culture, and why linguistic comparison and grouping provide a guide to cultural distance and interaction. It is also because of this rigidity that the speakers of a language must either change their own language or learn a new one when they enter into communication with speakers of another language.

Between these two extremes of stability and changeability of culture are a wide range of other possibilities. Religions and philosophies, for example, are quite changeable, though in many ways less so than kinship and political structures, because like languages they involve complex systems of symbols, depend upon a community who can understand them to function, and require considerable time to learn. Often change was possible through manipulating ambiguities or contradictions in philosophical principles; for example, several seventeenth-century kings of Kongo cited completely contradictory political philosophies in order to justify their rise to power and discredit claims of their rivals.[11] Nevertheless, the most stable elements of family and political structures tend to be the basic underlying ideological principles rather than the relationships themselves. In contrast to languages, too, discourse between people of differing religious and philosophical backgrounds is possible without either party necessarily altering their own system.

Principles of aesthetics (including art, music and dance, literature, decoration, and even cooking) also fall in the middle of the spectrum. Unlike languages, a symbol system, although often arbitrary, can still be appreciated by a larger community than the one that originally created it and, moreover, requires no particular effort to learn (at least on the part of those who appreciate rather than perform). One can appreciate another culture's art and music, its cooking, or its decoration without prior

[10] Do Couto, *Gentio de Angola* (Kimbundu catechism of 1642); and anon., *Doutrina christiana* (Allada/Fon catechism of 1658).

[11] Thornton, "Correspondence of the Kongo Kings," pp. 414–18.

training and without necessarily making direct reference to one's own culture's aesthetics.

Another intermediate category of culture is material culture, broadly speaking. The design of houses and tools, the inventory of useful plants and medicines, and use of the environment are elements that are somewhat fixed in that a single tool might have several possible and effective designs, but they are also changeable in that many tools and other elements of material culture are dependent upon a particular environment. Africans migrating from tropical regions to temperate zones like North America might well find that much of their material culture had to alter simply due to lack of proper materials, different demands from the climate, or a different botanical and zoological regime (Africans brought relatively few African crops and useful plants with them). Within this set of limits they might still exercise some choice; for example, they could change the standard billhook to a machete (closer to the African type of bush knife) or convert European-style long-handled hoes into African-style hoes with shorter handles.[12]

Anthropologists, who typically study particular societies at particular times, have often viewed cultures as bundles of traits that correlate with each other in a given society. Language, aesthetics, philosophy, family structure, and political systems all coexist and, moreover, are harmonized with each other. It is only recently that anthropologists have come to realize that these correlations do not hold together well in circumstances of change over time or migration. When these factors are taken into consideration, the different elements of the bundle behave differently over time and through interaction, some apparently being completely lost or transformed and others surviving intact or nearly so.

This explains why African culture in the Atlantic has so frequently been examined through "traits," often considered in isolation from each other, and why some anthropologists criticized this approach.[13] Whether these traits were seen as "survivals" from the previous cultural system, as Herskovitts's acculturation model proposed, or "extensions," as has been recently suggested by Kubik, authors have tended to examine specific "Africanisms" in American life rather than the cultural totality.[14]

In larger measure, this has also been because the study of African traits, survivals, or extensions among the Atlantic population of African

12 Merrick Posnansky, "West African Reflections on African-American Archaeology," paper presented at "Digging the Afro-American Past: Archaeology and the Black Experience," University of Mississippi, 17–20 May 1989, p. 14.

13 Mintz and Price, *Afro-American Past*, pp. 1–10 and passim.

14 Herskovitts, *Negro Past*, pp. 9–32; Gerhard Kubik, "Extensionen afrikanischer Kulturen in Brasilien," *Wiener Ethnohistorische Blätter* 22 (1981): 33–51.

descent has been wedded to larger political and ideological concerns, whether it be to establish a "Negro Past" (in Herskovitts's terminology) that extended past slavery or to meet Pan-Africanist concerns of modern nationalist intellectuals.[15] Denying the survival of African culture among Afro-Americans has constituted a denial of the Afro-American past and a possible Pan-Africanist present; affirming it accepts the past and the prospect. But, as Mintz and Price point out, the real issue is the nature of cultural interaction and change.

As we have already suggested, cultures as a whole are constantly changing, some elements faster and more radically than others to be sure, but changing and evolving nevertheless. This change takes place in two ways. First, cultures change through their own internal dynamics as political forces shift, the environment changes, the population grows, fashions come and go, intellectual potentials are worked out, and so on. Posnansky, an archeologist, points out in a recent discussion of the African roots of American culture that in the period of the slave trade there were several major changes in the pottery traditions of some of the West African societies that have been studied in depth by archeologists.[16] Even languages gradually change over time, so that Latin has given way to French and Spanish, and Chaucer's English is different from that of Shakespeare or of today, and the Kikongo of the catechism of 1624 sounds archaic and contorted to a modern speaker.[17]

Second, cultures change through constant interaction with other cultures, due to trade, politics, or perhaps alliance. For example, DeCorse's excavations at Elmina in modern Ghana, where Europeans interacted intensely with Africans, have uncovered a large number of imported European items as well as new items of local manufacture (like smoking pipes) that had not been made before.[18] These in turn diffused out in all

[15] E.g., the recent discussion by Sterling Stuckey, *Slave Culture: Nationalist Theory and the Foundations of Black America* (Oxford, 1987).

[16] Posnansky, "West African Reflections," p. 10. Posnansky cites studies of the Begho region of northern Ghana, where a continuous pottery sequence has been built up from the twelfth century to modern times (Merrick Posnansky and Leonard B. Crossland, "Pottery, People and Trade and Begho, Ghana," in Ian Hodder, ed., *The Spatial Organization of Culture* [London, 1978]).

[17] This feature caused some nineteenth-century missionaries to argue that the authors of the older materials did not understand the language correctly (e.g., W. Holman Bentley's comments concerning the Capuchin materials in Kikongo, *Pioneering in the Congo* [London, 1889]). Wyatt MacGaffey, in conversations with me, also suggested that the old catechism sounded stilted to him, a speaker of Kikongo, though it was grammatically correct (according to modern rules). However, scholarship has established that these materials were composed and checked by native speakers of Kikongo, not Europeans trying to write in a foreign language, and we must assume that they represent authentic versions of the language as spoken in the mid-seventeenth century.

[18] Christopher DeCorse, "Historical Archaeological Research in Ghana, 1986–1987," *Nyame Akuma* 29 (1987): 27–31.

directions in West Africa, affecting societies that had no contact with Europeans.

These changes in African society had their impacts on the type of cultural change that took place among those Africans who found themselves, mostly as slaves, living in the Atlantic world outside Africa. First of all, their Atlantic environment was so different from the African one, socially, ecologically, politically, and the like, that the internal dynamic of each African culture, if it operated at all in this disruptive environment, was altered. Given that even Europeans who migrated across the Atlantic in much more homogeneous blocks under their own authority still experienced considerable culture change and altered dynamic, it is obvious that Africans experienced even more severe changes.

Second, Africans in the Atlantic world had interactions with other Africans from a much wider variety of African societies than at home. In America, Angolans might work side by side with Senegambians, whereas in Africa they would have had no contact at all. Finally, the enslaved Africans would have interactions with European culture, though the European presence in Africa made this less a foreign element than might be expected at first glance. However, this interaction in the Atlantic would be much more intense and different. In America, Europeans were numerous and in positions of political authority, whereas in Africa they were a rarity and existed at the pleasure of African governments.

In all these aspects of cultural change, too, the dynamics would impact differently on different elements of culture. Political systems, family structure, aesthetics, religion, philosophy, and language would all respond to the various changes in different ways and at different speeds depending on the specifics of each interaction and the nature of each element. Out of this mass of interactions would gradually emerge an Afro-Atlantic culture, not necessarily homogeneous throughout the Atlantic, in fact, displaying substantial regional variations, but shaped by these new forces into a new creation.

With this background established, we can turn to examining the way in which various elements of culture changed through interaction between different African groups, relationships with Europeans in Africa, the transatlantic migration, and intercultural contact in the Atlantic world. In this chapter the discussion will focus on language and aesthetics, and the following chapter will devote its attention to religion and philosophy, since more abundant source material allows a fuller picture of developments in religion than in the others.

Culture change in the Atlantic world: language

Cultural elements can be arranged from the most stable to the least stable, and in such a system, language is the most stable. Yet African languages were, on the whole, the least likely element of African cultures to survive and develop in the Atlantic world. In fact, everywhere except perhaps in a few runaway communities, unusual situations, such as the resettled slaves of the nineteenth-century English and French Caribbean,[19] or in inaccessible areas, African languages all but disappeared, replaced at least by a creole language and often by a more or less standard form of a European language.

The usual explanation for this, that the slave trade and slavery broke up speech communities, is not wholly adequate. Although speakers of minor languages (at least from the point of view of their contribution to American populations) might find themselves linguistically isolated, some African languages existed in large speech communities. Kimbundu, for example, was spoken by thousands of Americans, sometimes by virtually the entire population of an estate, and nearly one third of the Remire slaves spoke Fon. It is possible to understand the disappearance of some of the minor languages, but not of these major ones.

This paradox can be explained by the essential arbitrariness of languages. In order to participate at all in linguistic intercourse, two persons must have considerable and extensive knowledge of the entire system, including grammar and at the very least several hundred vocabulary items. If numerous languages are in contact and are quite dissimilar in structure and vocabulary, the most likely result will be for a lingua franca to develop so that each speaker need only learn a second language in order to communicate with the others.

Conditions on every estate and in every town therefore promoted the growth of a lingua franca. Most estates had multiple nationalities, often from very diverse African nations. Kikongo has very little in common with Fon in either vocabulary or structure, and neither are intelligible to or even easy to learn for a native speaker of Temne. Furthermore, although some marriages involved partners from the same nation, many slaves married outside their nations. The Kongos on Remire, for example, married people from such diverse regions as Senegambia and Allada. In fact, one half of all the marriages involved culturally diverse partners. For them, the parents would have to communicate in a common third language, typically a lingua franca, or learn each other's native language. This clearly caused creole slaves, especially those of nationally mixed marriages, to opt for a lingua franca as their native speech. Indeed, intercommunication on any estate required that all slaves be able to communicate with each other and with their master and overseers. Consequently there were strong practical reasons for the lingua franca on American estates to be based on European languages.

[19] For an exploration of one such situation, see Monica Shuler, *"Alas, Alas, Kongo": A Social History of Indentured African Immigration into Jamaica* (Baltimore, 1980).

This tendency in the Americas was further reinforced by the fact that many parts of Atlantic Africa had already adopted European lingua francas as a result of the Atlantic trade. These lingua francas, however, whether spoken in Africa or the Americas, were not standard forms of European languages but creoles. Creoles are typically characterized by drawing virtually all their vocabulary from one language but having grammatical structure that is atypical of that language. After all, the most arbitrary aspect of any language is its vocabulary, whereas grammar is less so. It is much easier to understand someone whose grammar is faulty but who uses vocabulary one can comprehend than someone with perfect grammar but an entirely foreign vocabulary.

In dealing with creole grammar, linguists have debated two theories. Some have contended that the grammar of the Atlantic creoles was based on the grammatical forms of African languages. Thus, native speakers of African languages could focus their attention on learning vocabulary only, fitting the new words into their own grammar. Native speakers of European languages would find the grammar of this language difficult and sometimes puzzling, but could probably adjust to it in a few weeks' time, and hence communication could continue. Other scholars argue that creoles are based on a "universal human grammar" that is found in deep psychological structures common to all languages, not specifically African grammars.[20] This technical matter need not concern us very much, however, as long as the overall relationship between grammar and vocabulary in creoles is understood.

The Atlantic creoles probably emerged in the fifteenth century as a pidgin – that is, a language that allows minimum communication between speakers of different languages. Pidgins are simple languages and often do not have the full range of linguistic expression, but if a community develops that uses this language as a native speech, then it evolves into a creole, which does have full capacity. Creoles probably developed first among the settlers of the offshore Atlantic islands near Africa, such as Cape Verde and São Tomé, as early as the middle of the sixteenth century.[21]

Some of the earliest hints of the development of the pidgin or early creole form can be found in the letters of King Afonso of Kongo, where a locally trained literate group produced a secretarial body as early as 1491.[22] Afonso's own clerk, João Teixeira, a Kongo, was a product of this

20 The debate is aired in Luiz Ivens Ferraz, *The Creole of São Tomé* (Johannesburg, 1979), pp. 106–15. Ferraz, however, opts for the first interpretation.

21 Ibid., pp. 15–19.

22 The first letter of a Kongo king, authenticated by João I in September or October 1491, is known only in an Italian translation, in Rui da Pina's untitled MS, fols. 99rb–100vb in Leite de Faria, "Relação." This letter was probably written by the literate Kongo mentioned in the Portuguese manuscript version of da Pina's chronicle (ca. 1515) who had studied in Portugal (*Crónica del Rey d. Joham* in *MMA* 1:152).

early school and wrote several of Afonso's letters.[23] These letters are often in quite standard forms of Portuguese, but several display grammatical irregularities typical of Atlantic creoles, most notably the use of the infinitive or third-person singular form of verbs for all persons.[24]

Creole forms of the language probably developed more rapidly among the settlers of the offshore islands or among the slaves from Africa living in European cities, where the need to communicate with each other and the larger European population undoubtedly put pressure on them to adopt a lingua franca, which was known at the time as *fala de Guiné*. A number of European playwrights, fascinated by this language, had their slave and African characters speak in it in theatrical productions of the mid-sixteenth century. Garcia de Resende published a collection of songs in this language, including one allegedly written by a king in Sierra Leone in the fifteenth century but probably reflecting Lisbon versions of the language in the early sixteenth century.[25] The master of this language, however, was the Portuguese playwright Gil Vicente, who delighted in reproducing Portuguese regional accents (with suitable nonstandard spelling) as well as *fala de Guiné* in his plays.[26] Other European playwrights, perhaps inspired by Vicente, included African and Afro-European characters in their work who also used *fala de Guiné*.[27] Even Castillian writers had slaves speaking this language, faithfully reproducing the language even though its vocabulary was Portuguese.[28]

Vicente's language is a creole rather than a pidgin, and his characters can express themselves fully, suggesting that at least in Lisbon, it had reached linguistic maturity. Such maturity might never have been reached on the Atlantic coast of Africa, where conditions would not favor it being learned as a native language by anyone. However, it probably did become the language of the islands offshore, and given their extensive commerce with the mainland, including long-term settlement, probably came to be a lingua franca rather than just a contact pidgin.

This creole was widely spoken as a trade language along the African coast, both in Portuguese settlements and as a second or third language by Africans who had dealings with these Portuguese. The French trav-

[23] Afonso to Manuel, 5 October 1514, *MMA* 1:322–3, for a summary of Teixeira's background.

[24] See, as an example, Afonso to Manuel, 31 May 1515, *MMA* 1:335–8, with grammatical irregularities pointed out by the editor, António Brásio.

[25] Garcia de Resende, *Canconeiro geral (1516)* (mod. ed. A. J. Gonçalves Guimarãis, 5 vols., Coimbra, 1910–17), 1:204–5.

[26] Paul Teyssier, *La langue de Gil Vicente* (Paris, 1959), pp. 227–50.

[27] Ibid., pp. 249–50, for a list of such plays.

[28] F. Weber de Kurlat, "El negro como tipo cómico en el teatro español del siglo XVI," *Romance Philology* 17 (1963): 387–8.

eler Alexis de Saint-Lô found that Portuguese was spoken all over coastal Senegal when he visited in 1635,[29] and some years earlier de Almada noted how widely it was spoken in the Gambia and Rivers of Guinea.[30] Many people could speak and understand this language; Nicholas Villaut believed that all the people of Kayor, both men and women, could speak it in 1667.[31] Portuguese was still the normal language of trade in the Gambia when the Royal African Company set itself up there in the 1660s,[32] and Villaut found it spoken in Sierra Leone and Cape Mount, farther south.[33]

Although most of these writers do not mention much about the form of the Portuguese they are describing, a few comments suggest that it was the creole form. Villaut, for example, called the language a "kind of corrupt Portuguese."[34] Alonso de Sandoval notes that long-standing contact with the people of São Tomé caused the people of the Lower Guinea coast to speak "a type of language that was very corrupt and perverted [*revesado*] Portuguese that they call the *lengua de San Tomé*."[35] Spanish Capuchins who visited Allada in 1660 recorded the form of the speech, giving short quotations in the language as they heard it from "Captain Carta" who, according to José de Naxera, "spoke Portuguese and understood Spanish," which have some of the creole grammatical elements.[36] Both Dutch and French travelers at the time found that they had to communicate in this Portuguese in Allada, and perhaps elsewhere, too.[37]

However, when other European nations began to trade extensively in Africa, new pidgins and eventually creoles evolved, especially in areas where the long-term establishment of factories made for a population that had to communicate on a daily basis in the European language. In the early seventeenth century Manuel Alvares complained that the French had begun trading so heavily around the Cape Verde peninsula (Senegal) that the people there were speaking French "like natives."[38] Pieter van

29 Abridged version in C. A. Walkenaer, *Collections des relations de voyages par mer et par terre en différentes parties de l'Afrique* (Paris, 1842), 2:322.
30 De Almada, "Tratado breve," *MMA*[2] 3:325–6.
31 Villaut, *Voyages*, p. 23.
32 Cambridge University, Pepysian Library (Magdalen College), MS 2698, "Captain Robert Holmes, his Journalls of voyages into Guynea . . . 1660–61 and 1663–64," no foliation, entry of 4 March 1660.
33 Villaut, *Voyages*, pp. 27, 46, 57.
34 Ibid., pp. 23, 57.
35 De Sandoval, *Instauranda*, p. 94.
36 De Naxera, *Espejo mystico*, p. 239. The passage is written in a rough phonetic equivalent, rather than in an attempt to render it in Portuguese orthography. This hinders analysis, but the use of verbs seems appropriate for a creole grammar system.
37 UBL:BPL, MS. 927, "Beschrijvinge," fol. 12v; d'Elbée, "Relation," pp. 395, 446.
38 BSGL, Manuel Alvares, "Etiopia menor," fol. 6.

den Broecke was pleased to see that people in the same area could speak English, French, and Dutch when he visited in 1606.[39] Samuel Brun made similar observations a few years later – at Cape Mount the ruler could speak French and his wife could speak Dutch.[40] By the time Barbot visited the Gold Coast in 1678, the people all around Elmina could speak "good English," and those at Commenda, French; in fact, the ruler of Commenda had even sent two of his subjects to La Rochelle.[41]

Thus, European languages were widely understood by at least the commercial community in coastal Atlantic Africa. Creole Portuguese had become a lingua franca in many regions as well. This linguistic background would help to provide a common lingua franca for slaves in the New World, who found many reasons for taking up such a language. Of course, we have no reason to believe that any more than a minority of the slaves crossing the ocean had occasion to learn a creole language in Africa, but this group may well have played a major role in spreading the language to other slaves. Given that masters did not consider themselves in the business of giving language lessons, the growth and development of American creoles may have relied heavily on creole-speaking slaves who could teach the others.

De Sandoval provides some evidence of this in his comments on language problems in the Cartagena mission. He noted that in order to speak with slaves from Lower Guinea it was best to address them in the "lengua de San Tomé," which no doubt helped to spread knowledge of the language to other slaves.[42] In the same mission, Pedro Claver sought out creole-speaking slaves to assist him. Francisco Jolofo, for example, knew both Portuguese and Wolof when he arrived in America, and for that reason Claver bought him from his original master, Pedro de Vera. A slave like Francisco Jolofo was especially useful, because like others of the Jesuit catechists, he had probably been involved in the local commercial community in Africa, and indeed could also speak Mandinka and Serer.[43]

French missionaries also sought to extend the creole forms of language that they met among incoming slaves to the rest of the community. For example, early missionaries such as Pierre Pelleprat, working in St. Christopher before 1655, found the fact that as many as thirteen different African languages were spoken by the incoming slaves very frustrating and decided to conduct instruction in French (unlike their compatri-

[39] Van den Broecke, *Reizen*, fol. 3.
[40] Brun, *Schiffarten*, p. 51.
[41] Barbot, "Journal," p. 32.
[42] De Sandoval, *Instauranda*, p. 94.
[43] BN Colombia, Claver Inquest, fol. 177.

ots in Cartagena who sought numerous interpreters). In order to do this, however, Pelleprat said, "we tried to accommodate ourselves to their manner of speaking," which, according to examples he then cited, included only using the infinitive form of verbs.[44] The accommodation that these Jesuits made seems to be a creole form of the language, then deliberately propagated.

If creoles originated in Africa and the offshore islands, however, their immediacy was much greater in the Americas. Africans probably never spoke the creoles as native languages, but soon Americans, the children of the first generation of slaves, did. As this speech community grew and developed it would no longer need to rely on imported bilingual or multilingual speakers to propagate, though obviously such people might find their lives made easier if they spoke the language. At the same time, the creole became the normal language for everyday speech, even among African-born slaves, and served to limit the potential for national groups to preserve their original African languages.

Nevertheless, some linguistic survival did take place. Nations, especially in urban areas, appear to have had sufficient pride in their national languages to preserve them, at least on ceremonial occasions and particularly in song. Slaves often sang in their national languages, even in the rural estates. Sloane, visiting Jamaica in 1688, recorded words and music to two songs, one Koromanti and the other Angola.[45] A few years earlier, French Jesuits observed their slaves also singing in their own languages.[46]

Singing allows languages that are essentially foreign to be remembered and preserves them, even independently of understanding,[47] although no doubt the relatively frequent influx of new native speakers also helped to preserve the linguistic purity of the songs. Songs and ceremonial occasions are also suitable opportunities for expressing the kind of nationalism that can engender pride but does not require the kind of disruption of normal life that learning or continuing to speak the whole national language would require. That languages can serve as patriotic symbols may explain why, in the mid-eighteenth century, one Brazilian lay brotherhood sought to petition the Crown to allow them to continue to sing songs in "the Angola idiom" as had been a long-honored custom.[48] It is also not surprising that the survival of African

44 Pierre Pelleprat, *Relation des missions des PP. de la Compagnie de Iesus dans les Isles, et dans la terre ferme del'Amerique Meridionale* (Paris, 1655), pp. 53–4.

45 Sloane, *Voyage*, 2 vols. (London, 1707–25), 1:l–li.

46 Du Tertre, *Histoire* 2:526–8.

47 Consider, for example, that many Americans who know no German or Latin may be able to sing "Stille Nacht" ("Silent Night") and "Adeste Fidelis" ("Oh, Come All Ye Faithful") in those languages.

48 Document cited in Mulvey, "Slave Confraternities," p. 46.

languages in the present-day Caribbean and Brazil is often in the context of song or religious chants.[49]

Culture change in the Atlantic world: social structure

Most anthropologists who stress the loss of African culture in the Atlantic crossing note that African social structure was completely broken by enslavement and transportation. The issue is particularly important given the anthropological emphasis, in general, on studies of kinship and their important discovery that kinship was a critical organizing principle in African societies.[50] Obviously, kinship played a role on those estates where families formed and a creole generation developed, though its structure might be different from the structure in Africa. Insofar as marriages were within a single nation, however, one might reasonably expect such indications of kinship as naming patterns to continue just as members of that nation used it in Africa, though the kind of deep lineage investigation necessary to establish such patterns cannot be documented, at least for the seventeenth century.[51]

An approach based on kinship, however, tends to overlook the fact that the widespread institution of slavery in Africa meant that most African societies had developed mechanisms for integrating foreign people as slaves, often using the idiom of kinship. Given that Africans sold into Atlantic slavery may well have already been slaves in Africa or even owned slaves themselves at the time of their enslavement, the new "false kinship" of an estate or American household might not be unfamiliar. It was noted earlier that both Africans and Europeans regarded slaves legally as a species of junior kin, a point firmly entrenched in the American custom of referring to slaves by names indicative of children or the frequent use of diminutive forms of words.

Important, too, was the fact that within African societies there were numerous ways of organizing people without reference to kin or kinship groups. Organizations of this type could obviously flourish in an environment where many people who were separated from their kin might arrive. For example, most African states were not kinship organizations, as demonstrated earlier. Instead they were corporate organizations whose leadership was often chosen by election, even if the

[49] For example, the "Lucumi" language used in Santeria in Cuba (see Joseph Murphy, *Santeria: An African Religion in America*). My knowledge of this has been increased by speaking with Maureen Warner-Lewis of the University of the West Indies (Mona), a long-time researcher on African languages in the Americas.

[50] E.g., Mintz and Price, *Afro-American Past*, pp. 11–12, 32–7.

[51] For an example of one attempt to do this, see Cheryl Ann Cody, "There Was No 'Absalom' on the Ball Plantations: Slave-Naming Practices in the South Carolina Low Country, 1720–1865," *American Historical Review* 92 (1987): 563–96.

electorate was severely restricted or if senior lineages of kin groups had come to "own" or to dominate it. Nevertheless, the ideology of the state could govern an organization of Africans without reference to kinship.

Often African armies were organized as corporate units that also did not take kinship into consideration. A good example of this is the Imbangala army of central Africa, which may have had as its original inspiration hunting or initiation camps. Imbangala recruitment was often violent, but within it, the idea of kinship was absent, and promotion, even to positions of high leadership, was done on a system of merit or patronage.[52] Other armies, both in central Africa and elsewhere, probably also recruited people in this way, especially if the army was professional and required training and skill to function. Given that many of the enslaved Africans had served in armies (often as the initial step to their enslavement), such institutions would be of great significance.

In addition to these political organizations, African religions produced many societies devoted to religious affairs, which nevertheless provided a good set of flexible organizational principles outside the bounds of kinship. The various societies of Sierra Leone and Guinea-Bissau described in seventeenth-century documents, such as the Ve'i Poro (Belly-paaro) society mentioned by Dapper,[53] or the *contuberia* of farther north found in descriptions of Alvares de Almada and Manuel Alvares,[54] were organizations (often known in anthropological literature as "secret societies") dedicated to serving religious purposes. However, this documentation also reveals that they played important roles in settling disputes, especially across state boundaries and, from an elite perspective, helped to give coherence to the upper class.

In central Africa, such societies were a routine part of life in the Mbundu areas. Cavazzi's description of "idols" (territorial deities) mentions that the priests formed "congregations" devoted to their worship, and he recorded the initiation rituals of several. Though less concerned with the social than the religious aspects of these congregations, he noted in passing several social and political functions that they served.[55] In Kongo, Catholic lay congregations often integrated elite society.[56] The *kimpasi* society in Kongo was a religious organization that served the lower classes in which kinship was specifically abolished among its mem-

52 The classic study is Joseph C. Miller, *Kings and Kinsmen: The Imbangala Impact on the Mbundu of Angola* (Oxford, 1976). An excellent contemporary account, based on intimate knowledge, is MSS Araldi, Cavazzi, "Missione evangelica," vol. A, bk. 1.

53 Dapper, *Naukeurige beschrijvinge*, pp. 418–9.

54 De Almada, "Tratado breve," *MMA*² 3:351–2; BSGL, Manuel Alvares, "Etiopia menor," fols. 67–70, 134v–135v.

55 MSS Araldi, Cavazzi, "Missione evangelica," vol. A, bk. 1, pp. 91–9.

56 Thornton, *Kingdom of Kongo*, pp. 49–50, 53.

bers, who kept in touch with each other as a special society, once they were initiated.[57]

Modern anthropologists have documented secret societies widely in Africa, the best known probably being those of the Igbo and Kalabari areas. Seventeenth-century descriptions do not include much discussion of these, save for a merchants' society mentioned by de Marees,[58] but they were probably functioning at an early date.

When Africans arrived in the New World as slaves, organizations modeled on these African examples, or at least following their principles of organization, could provide a substitute kinship organization that could give them coherence. Examples of all of these organizations are hinted at in documentation concerning African nations in the New World. For example, we have already seen that nations elected kings and queens and were often governed by officials who met in various types of councils. Although the nations were clearly not states, they functioned much as African states did, though undoubtedly without the class and status ideologies, hereditary kinship, and military potentials of African states. Often the ideology underlying states could survive though such states did not exist in America. The fact that each organization was composed of slaves from one nation meant that its ideology and iconography were linked to the specific ideology of the African state. This is clearly revealed in the plot by Akan-speaking "Koromanti" that was uncovered in 1675 on Barbados. The testimony reveals the use of an Akan oathing ceremony and the enthronement of an elected king on a stool "exquisitely carved and wrought after their own mode."[59] American nations probably looked to an ideal African state that did not conform to its African reality. The election, for example, points to a more democratic institution than the reality may have been. Thus it was an ideal Africans were striving for, not simply a re-creation.

Not all nations were constantly conspiring to overthrow the system or create African kingdoms, in spite of the fact that they were routinely accused of doing so by colonial authorities. In most cases, nations elected their kings and queens publicly in festivals and served as mutual aid societies, as we have already seen. Given their role as burial societies, they may also have served as religious organizations and thus been modeled on the religious societies of their respective homelands. As slaves became explicitly Christian, such societies often merged with

57 The *kimpasi* is often described in missionary literature; see Thornton, *Kingdom of Kongo*, p. 61.
58 De Marees, *Beschrijvinge*, pp. 85b–87a.
59 Puckrein, *Little England*, pp. 163–4, quoting original testimony of the inquest into the plot, found in an anonymous pamphlet, *Great Newes from Barbados*.

the lay brotherhoods, which were dedicated to the worship of one or another saint, in Catholic countries.[60]

African military organizations may also have served as models, often also in a national setting, in the Americas. Obviously slaves rarely formed armies, except in times of revolt or among runaway communities. Fuller discussion of these African nonkinship organizations will be found in Chapter 10. It is enough to say here that sometimes runaway armies appear to have relied on African command systems and military organizations.

Culture change in the Atlantic world: aesthetics

If language and social organization (especially social ideology) are somewhat rooted in a philosophical–ideological model, aesthetics is probably the least anchored element of culture. Aesthetic principles were the element of African culture that survived and endured the best in the Americas. Few scholars today could seriously doubt, for example, that African music and dance lay at the root of Afro-American music and dance and, moreover, that this part of the African aesthetic sense is the one that is most appreciated and appropriated by European and American culture. Other elements of aesthetics are less visible but have increasingly been identified by historians. Perhaps the most intriguing research in recent years is that of Robert Farris Thompson on the African and Afro-American aesthetic in art, decoration, and design.[61]

For our purposes here, we can define aesthetics very broadly as deliberate attempts to generate what a culture considers beautiful. This might be decoration or aspects of form of a pot or dish that extend beyond minimum utility. It includes combining food, spices, and heat in cuisine, taking food beyond nutrition and into pleasure. It surely includes decoration of the human body, from styling hair to cutting tatoos to arranging fabrics over the body to selecting colors and designs for those fabrics. It extends to music and dance, home design and decoration, and finally to deliberate works of art in painting and sculpture intended for display.

Each of these items involves imposing an arbitrary pattern on some object or behavior. Humans need to cover themselves, feed themselves, and construct dwellings, and obviously in all of these matters any action

60 Recently, Margaret Washington has argued that slaves in eighteenth-century South Carolina also merged iconography and ideology of the Poro society with that of Baptist institutions to create a new version of this older African society (Margaret Washington Creel, *"A Peculiar People": Slave Religion and Community Culture among the Gullahs* [New York, 1988], pp. 279–84).

61 See particularly, from among his many works, *The Flash of the Spirit: African and Afro-American Art and Philosophy* (New York, 1983).

must meet minimum requirements, but the form and decoration that are pleasing for each of these needs are open to choice. Humans everywhere have danced and created music, but beyond moving one's body or striking and blowing into objects, the patterns of these behaviors are arbitrary. In the manipulation of these possibilities a culture identifies itself as it identifies its aesthetic sense.

That the aesthetic sense in its simplest form can define a culture is well known to archeologists at least. For well over a century and a half, the decorations and forms of ceramics have been taken as the surest evidence of the extent of a culture, and pottery studies remain at the heart of archeological definitions of cultures. Often the aesthetic principles that dictate pottery decoration can be found in other elements of a society as well. For example, central Africans were fond of creating complex patterns of intersecting lines resulting in geometric designs as a mode of decoration, which is well illustrated in Cavazzi's paintings of life in Matamba in the 1660s. Patterns of this sort are shown on cloth, on basketry, on caps and boxes, and on the side of a stool.[62] The Museo degli Argenti in Florence possesses a sixteenth-century Kongo horn of ivory that is also decorated in this pattern.[63] In short, this lozenge and line pattern or variants of it immediately says central Africa to anyone viewing it. Moreover, it is not specifically a national pattern, tied to a specific linguistic group, for it can be found on material of Mbundu, Kongo, or Loango provenance, and no doubt much further inland, where it is still a common motif today.[64]

No doubt the same sort of observations could be made about other elements of culture, and other cultural "trademarks" could be identified, dividing Africa into several aesthetic regions. Muscial patterns, dance movements and steps, culinary combinations, or bodily decoration might all reveal cultural zones, though not all could be so definitively identified in the existing source material as simple decoration patterns might. Tracing these indicators could also reveal something of the patterns of cultural transfer outside Africa as Afro-Americans interacted with each other, developed new traditions, and borrowed from the culture of the Europeans and Euro-Americans.

Nevertheless, tracing the transfer of African aesthetic principles across the Atlantic and their reworking in the Americas requires some thought,

[62] MSS Araldi, Cavazzi, "Missione evangelica," vol. 1, front matter, illustration nos. 17, 23, 7, and 20. Full-color reproductions of all the illustrations, as well as comparative studies of the artistic and material cultural items, are found in Ezio Bassani, "Uno Missionario Cappuccino nell'Africa nera nel seicento: I disegni dei *Manoscritti Araldi* del Padre Giovanni Antonio Cavazzi da Montecuccolo," *Quaderni Poro* 4 (1987), who gives illustration numbers in his photographic appendix.

[63] Shown in ibid., appendix, pl. 21.

[64] Ibid., pls. 14 and 21 (Kongo and Loango from seventeenth century).

for as in the case of linguistic transfer, the situation of the slaves must be considered. After all, work routines and management strategies of slave owners often meant that not every slave was capable of producing objects for aesthetic adornment (or patronizing other African slaves who did). Production that required high levels of skill also required that people possessing those skills be allowed to practice them and support themselves with a clientele able to buy their products. Moreover, many African materials were unavailable.

Some aesthetic production was nearly ubiquitous, insofar as the production of pottery was widespread throughout Africa and its decoration in many hands, and textiles were produced by thousands of rural people working in their own homes, as is at least attested for eastern Kongo, one of the great centers of textile production.[65] Similarly, Africans decorated their own homes and bodies, perhaps having some recourse to specialists, but in most details using their own and their communities' aesthetic principles.

However, much of aesthetic production is the work of specialists, even if these specialists must necessarily accept the general aesthetic ideas of the wider community as their guidelines. Although it might be that virtually every African was engaged in the production of some type of aesthetic material, other types required skills and background that the average person did not have. Posnansky has pointed out that pottery production in West Africa has been traditionally a speciality of women, but the skill takes many years to acquire. Even though many women from families that produced pottery must have been enslaved, many may not have mastered the techniques simply because they were too young, the slave trade generally favoring young women.[66]

This would be even more true for the "higher" forms of art. Curnow Nasara, for example, has shown that it is possible to identify particular artists and workshops from the ivories exported from sixteenth-century Sierra Leone.[67] No doubt other production of high artistic quality, especially that produced for the elite, was also the work of specialists – certainly an artists' quarter was identifiable in Benin.[68] Similarly, every court had its own professional musicians, as is frequently attested in travelers' literature;[69] no doubt every musical performance even in vil-

65 For a thorough review of documents on methods, see Bassani, "Missionario Cappuccino," pp. 41–60.

66 Posnansky, "West African Reflections," p. 10.

67 Kathy Curnow, "The Afro-Portuguese Ivories: Classification and Stylistic Analysis of a Hybrid Art Form" (Ph.D. diss., Indiana University, 1983), pp. 94–153.

68 Dapper, *Naukeurige beschrijvinge*, p. 125–6.

69 For example, MSS Araldi, Cavazzi, "Missione evangelica," illustrations in Bassani, "Missionario cappuccino," pls. 9, 10, 19, 25; de Marees, *Beschrijvinge*, p. 87b; Müller, *Afrikansche*, p. 104.

lages was the work of specialists, even though the community as a whole might join in.

Thus, only if musicians were enslaved and crossed the Atlantic could African music be produced in America – for without the specialist the ordinary slave could not have music and would perforce have to accept whatever music was available, gradually accepting it as his own. Similarly, the "high arts" like sculpture or metalwork that also relied on specialists with high levels of technique would be crippled in the Americas without specialists among the slaves. Such specialists were often valued by their patrons and might avoid Atlantic enslavement even if captured, for their patrons might redeem them.

Even if people possessing the requisite skills did come to the New World, they had to have opportunities to show their abilities. For example, although central Africans may have placed their geometric designs on pottery, musical instruments, baskets, and cloth, what if, as slaves, they never had the opportunity to produce these things? Obviously, the aesthetic principles that guided them would soon be lost, and they would have to accept whatever was available in Euro-American, Native American, or European culture. At best, they might exercise some kind of distinctive choice among a variety of such objects, made with a different set of aesthetic principles.

In many cases the process of enslavement did in fact cause specialists to be retained in Africa, and the conditions of slavery in America limited aesthetic production. But, as we have already seen in our examination of slave life, there were ample opportunities in many American slave societies for a substantial exercise of the African aesthetic on those lines of production available to slaves.

Of course, Africans might well choose to mix or change their aesthetic guidelines. One must consider that the Atlantic world offered intense contact between cultures. There is nothing inherent in aesthetics that holds that people can accept only their own culture's ideas. Unlike language, which can be appreciated only once the whole system is accepted, aesthetic principles can be borrowed, adopted, enjoyed, and combined in an infinite variety of ways. Other than militant cultural nationalists, few people are so committed to the aesthetic of their own societies that they do not enjoy another society's aesthetic performance. Thus, the tight boundaries that allow us to identify languages are lost in aesthetics.

This aspect of aesthetics can be illustrated by considering European reactions to African music. Some, like Cavazzi, had little good to say about it, thinking it without harmony and poorly performed. But even Cavazzi liked the music of the marimba, singling it out as one instrument he thought that Africans could play well and enjoyably.[70] Others, however, were more impressed. Johan Nieman, the Brandenburg factor at Gross Friedrichsburg on the Gold Coast, wrote in 1684 of the local people's love of music and noted that they had "several instruments for this purpose, including a sort of guitar which they can play fairly well and sing pleasantly to."[71]

At the same time the appreciation might go the other way, and Africans took an interest in European music, adapting it to their own tastes. For example, Baltasar Barreira, a Jesuit priest in Sierra Leone, related that in the late sixteenth or early seventeenth century the inhabitants of the Ilha de Idolos seized a pirate ship and captured among the crew a young German. Finding the German to be an "excellent horn player" they presented him to the ruler of Fatema, who ruled the area. The king was pleased with the German, who began playing horn in his own court, and when Barreira met him, he was earning a living giving lessons to many young men of the area.[72] Obviously, the German must have developed his musical sense in Europe, but presumably the people of Sierra Leone found it pleasing enough to allow him to continue practicing it, even seeking to learn his style, and perhaps both the German and his students eventually began to blend German style with local styles.

Aesthetic contact thus involved a complex of borrowing and lending. Many museums in Europe and the United States today contain a large body of objects termed "Afro-Portuguese ivories," produced in at least three different African cultures (Sierra Leone, Benin, and Kongo). These include a variety of objects, horns, saltcellars, hunting knives, boxes, and other items that were carved in Africa to meet European demands.[73] Although the objects were made for a European clientele and are often not found at all in African society, they display recognizably African aesthetic principles. Moreover, each group of items is sufficiently distinctive that an art historian can determine which of the three African cultures an item came from. Unlike the music of the German horn player, modern scholars can see a blending of aesthetic principles that accommodated local and European tastes.

Thus, although aesthetics might be a clear reflection of a local culture, it is that element of culture that is likely to be borrowed or transform

70 Giovanni Antonio Cavazzi da Montecuccolo, *Istorica descrizione de tre' regni Congo Matamba ed Angola* (Bologna, 1687), bk. 1, no. 332, among other places.

71 Johan Nieman to Brandenburg Company, 8 March 1684, in Jones, *Brandenburg Sources*, p. 88.

72 Guerreiro, *Relaçam annual*, fol. 234v.

73 For a thorough study of the ivories with ample illustrative material, see Curnow, "Afro-Portuguese Ivories."

itself in a situation of contact. This transformation would be modified or intensified if, as in conditions of slavery, the Africans were unable to engage fully in their own artistic or aesthetic production due to their work routines, plantation management, availability of materials, or the presence or absence of specialists in the production of aesthetic items.

However rare musicians were in the slave trade, they were certainly sufficient to create a new musical culture in the Americas based on African aesthetic principles. That African music crossed the Atlantic is confirmed by Hans Sloane's record of both words and music of seventeenth-century Afro-Jamaican songs.[74] Richard Rath, who has analyzed this music, points out that a certain Mr. Baptiste, who put this music into European-style notation, was quite sophisticated in accommodating the differences between African and European music. For example, he was able to show microtones, a distinctive feature of African music, by a pattern of sharps and flats, which makes the music hard to play, at least as written, unless one assumes that Baptiste was trying to represent microtones. Rath also argues that the piece labeled "Koromantin" and the piece labeled "Angola"[75] both show characteristics that are distinctive of those two cultures today, although he notes that in one piece both Akan and Angolan music are played in different registers of the same song, suggesting an early cultural blending.[76] Thus, recognizably African music was being performed in Jamaica and undoubtedly elsewhere, and already being mixed and blended to meet new demands of the multiethnic slave community.

African music, then as now, relied heavily on rhythm, and creating the complex rhythms necessarily required a variety of percussion instruments – drums of different shapes and sizes, bells, gongs, and rattles. Cavazzi's illustrations of Njinga's personal band in Matamba around 1660, for example, cannot tell us the music the Africans played, but they surely show their fondness for percussion instruments.[77]

This element of music, which is distinctly African (found in all regions, in spite of the great differences in style and performance), is also found in American contexts. Rath notes that the Jamaican music is synco-

[74] Sloane, *Voyage*, pp. l–li. This is the earliest transcription known to me of what was probably completely African music. It can be compared both with ethnographically recorded music from the late nineteenth century and with modern music of African origin in the Caribbean, such as the music in Maureen Warner-Lewis's corpus (many of which have lyrics in African languages).

[75] A third piece, labeled "Papa" (from Popo or Allada), is too short to be analyzed in any detail.

[76] Richard Rath, "African Music in Seventeenth-Century Jamaica: Cultural Transit and Transmission," *William and Mary Quarterly* 50 (1993): 700–26.

[77] E.g., illustrations nos. 9, 10, 16, 19, in Bassani, "Missionario Cappuccino," and the descriptions found on pp. 62–77.

pated, another distinctly African feature that was captured well by Baptiste's musical notation, and it is probably possible to reconstruct the rhythmic line employed.[78] Although these Jamaicans were not allowed drums for fear of rebellion, other Afro-Americans re-created a good number of African percussion instruments, and of course, singing and dancing required only a body with enough energy to perform. Similarly, as long as there were sufficiently large numbers of members of their own nation among the slaves, musicians could find an audience that would appreciate their performances. Charles de Rochefort noted that slaves in the French Caribbean made their own instruments and sang "in agreeable harmony." They often went off into the woods to do this on Sundays, on feast days, or for funerals (occasionally taking so much time and energy that they could not work on Mondays), and such meetings were typically of people from the same *terre* (nation).[79] Father du Tertre, who occasionally attended these gatherings, noted that they danced and sang "as in their own land" with drumming and singing.[80] In Brazil, the Reformed preacher Soler noted the special music and dance of slave life there, especially at funerals (which were often an occasion for people from the same nation to gather to mourn).[81] The Dutch master Ekhout painted a picture of a slave dancing in the late 1640s, showing a band with African percussion instruments.[82] Similarly, in Colombia, Pedro Claver was famous for breaking up some of these nocturnal gatherings, which he thought might involve some sexual transgressions, and he seized, among other things, their African-style drums.[83]

Of course, the instruments were not just confined to percussion instruments, though the frequency and variety of the latter suggest the kind of percussive musical culture typical of Africa. Sloane, who notes that slave owners restricted the use of drums and trumpets because they had military uses in Africa and might have contributed to the revolts that racked late seventeenth-century Jamaica, described and illustrated several African stringed instruments. He described them as being "in imitation of lutes," but these stringed instruments surely draw on African precedents.[84]

Nocturnal gatherings of slaves where music and dance were per-

[78] Rath, "African Music."
[79] De Rochefort, *Histoire naturelle*, pp. 321–2.
[80] Du Tertre, *Histoire* 2:526–8.
[81] Soler, *Corte ende sonderlinghe verhael*, p. 7.
[82] Reproduced as an engraving in Nieuhof, *Brasiliaense Zee- en Lant-reize*, p. 215.
[83] BN Colombia, Claver Inquest, fol. 180v.
[84] Sloane, *Voyage*, pp. xlviii–xlix. The illustrations are on unnumbered pages between the introduction and the main text in *Voyages*, vol. 1. They are not identical to stringed instruments shown in central African illustrations; see Bassani, "Missionario Cappuccino," pp. 63–78 and pls. 35–46.

formed could be found in the English colonies as well. Several visitors to Jamaica besides Sloane noted the nocturnal funerals there, including dancing and singing with African instruments and in African languages.[85] Settlers in Virginia sought to ban such gatherings in 1680 where the slaves "played on their Negroe drums" as being a danger to public order.[86] A similar complaint heard by the Virginia Council in 1687 noted that slaves met "in great numbers in makeing and holding of Funneralls for Dead Negroes."[87] Thus, national music could be played in the New World, along with related traditions of dance.

This national music must certainly have interacted with other musical traditions, both from other African nations and from Europe. We know little of the first process in the Americas, though one might note that in any large city, especially in Iberian America, nations routinely marched, played their instruments, and danced on various festivals and holy days. As such they would soon come into contact with each other's music and attempt to create a new music, incorporating features of various musical traditions that would be pleasing to members of more than one nation. Even up to today, in some areas of the Caribbean, such as Carriacou, there are specific dances and music associated with a particular nation, but people of all nations perform them as well as hybrid performances specific to the island itself.[88]

The influence of European music is somewhat better documented. This interaction probably begins in Africa and not in the Americas. For example, one cannot tell what influence the German horn player might have had on Sierra Leone music, or the performances of other European musicians who traveled to Africa on the shipping of the time. The conversion of Kongo to Christianity led to the creation of an Afro-European Christian music, influenced by both traditions. Missionaries to Kongo were often impressed by their singing of this music, and samples of it recorded in modern Trinidad show a strongly European tradition of church music with African words and rhythm.[89] Pedro Claver's singing

85 Dunn, *Sugar and Slaves*, pp. 250–1.

86 William W. Henning, ed., *Statutes at Large*, 13 vols. (Richmond, Va., 1819–23), 4:128–9.

87 H. R. McIlwaine, ed., *Executive Journals, Council of Virginia* (Richmond, 1925), 1:86–7.

88 Interview with Margaret Andrews, St. Georges, Grenada, 13 August 1988. According to Andrews, who has organized a troupe to perform "Big Drum" dances peculiar to Carriacou, members of her troupe and she herself have personal membership in a particular nation (she is a Temne), but they perform the music and dance of other nations.

89 Discussion with Dr. Maureen Warner-Lewis, Atlanta, 4 November 1989, and correspondence, December 1989. Dr. Warner-Lewis collected some religious music of this kind from Kikongo-speaking informants in Trinidad in the 1960s and 1970s and generously shared some of her transcriptions and notes with me. Some of the Christian music (judged by the content of the lyrics) is sung in an African style and resembles secular songs in the same corpus, but other pieces are in a distinct and apparently religious style, though the lyrics cannot be traced to any seventeenth-century source, such as the 1624 catechism.

group, which included Angolans as well as members of other nations, sang in parts and played European instruments,[90] perhaps combining a variety of styles.

Of course, the interactions took place in the secular field as well. Musically inclined slaves might play their own national music for other slaves at funerals or at other gatherings, as well as listening to the music of other nations. They would also be likely to play for their masters and somehow had to create a style that was pleasing to their aesthetic sense as well. Even the most hostile European, like Cavazzi, could usually find some instrument or effect of African music pleasing, and the task of the music specialist in this situation was to find what his master liked in African music or, lacking that, to combine his own aesthetic ideas with those of European music, sometimes having to play European instruments. Ligon, visiting Barbados in the late 1640s, asked one musically inclined slave named Macow to play a wind instrument called the theorbo. Macow's playing was competent in Ligon's view, but different from that of a European player, and thus interesting.[91] This experience and that of other slaves who played to both audiences must gradually have amplified and altered the aesthetic ideas in music of both African and European listeners in the Americas, gradually leading to the distinctively African and European blending that characterizes American music as a whole.

Research in both European and American musical history has revealed the results of some of this interaction. For example, in the seventeenth century, court musicians began to play popular music as well as that performed only for the nobility, and the seventeenth-century Church in Europe and the Americas used popular music as a means of reaching the common people. Several European and American pieces whose lyrics are clearly directed at slaves or people of African descent, often even being written in creole languages, probably have African musical traits and are certainly distinct from other pieces from the same time period, though careful study of these pieces is yet to be done.[92]

Opportunity as well as aesthetics characterized the way in which African cultures blended and survived in the Americas. For example, archeologists working in both Virginia and South Carolina have located items of local manufacture that are decorated with distinctively African motifs: Mandinga motifs on clay pipes from Virginia and distinctively central African motifs on pottery from South Carolina.[93] The design patterns on

90 BN Colombia, Claver Inquest, fol. 175, testimony of Diego Folupo.

91 Ligon, *Trve and Exact History*, pp. 48–9.

92 Program notes for the performance of the Waverly Consort at Columbia University, New York, June 1990.

93 Neil Asher Silberman, "Letter from Mississippi: The Black Experience in America," *Archaeology* 42/5 (1989): 70.

the musical instruments illustrated by Sloane include African motifs, especially the kind of line and lozenge pattern typical of central Africa on one.[94] Roderick Ebanks, excavating at Spanish Town in Jamaica, found striking similarities to pottery made in the Shai Hills region of modern Ghana (seventeenth-century Gold Coast).[95]

But interaction made itself felt rapidly in those areas where slaves made their own pottery, for the pottery found in Barbados looks to the excavators like a general African design, but a specific national tradition cannot be determined.[96] This pottery was limited in its variety, possibly because the best potters remained in Africa, clays varied, and conditions of slavery did not permit a full inventory of the best wares to be made. These factors, plus the tendency to blend aesthetic traditions among the several African and European models available, made most slave-produced pottery notable, "not for being distinctively African, but for being distinctively non-European."[97] Although plantation archeology is still in its infancy, many sites have artifact assemblages so uniform that it is hard to identify slave quarters just from them.[98] In many such sites, the slaves may not have manufactured anything themselves, and naturally enough, their aesthetic choices may well not be represented.

The complexity of cultural and aesthetic interaction is best illustrated in the case of clothing and personal decoration. Here interactions in Africa and in America shaped the distinctive dress of Afro-Atlantic peoples. One important feature of African personal aesthetic was the treatment of the head. The tightly spiraled hair of Africans makes it possible to design and shape it in many ways impossible for the straighter hair of Europeans. Consequently, when Europeans first came into contact with western Africa in the late fifteenth century, they commented on the myriad hairstyles worn by the people they met. Various combinations of braids, plaits (often with shells, beads, or strips of material woven in), shaved areas, and areas cut to different lengths to make patterns adorned the heads of people, creating a stunning effect.[99] Pieter de Marees published a plate in 1602 showing sixteen different hairstyles of various classes and genders in Benin alone.[100]

94 Sloane, *Voyage*, vol. 1, illustrations between introduction and main text.

95 Posnansky, "West African Reflections," p. 11, citing a personal communication of 1988.

96 Handler and Lange, *Plantation Slavery*, pp. 219–29.

97 Matthew Hill, "Ethnicity Lost? Ethnicity Gained? Information Functions of African Ceramics in West Africa and North America," in Reginald Auger, ed., *Ethnicity and Culture* (Calgary, 1987), p. 138.

98 Silberman, "Black Experience," pp. 68–71.

99 An early source that makes mention of hair and clothing styles is Fernandes, "Descriçã," fols. 93, 110v, 134, 338. See also de Almada, "Tratado breve," *MMA*[2] 3:239–40, 266, 301, 304, 314, 317–18, 347–50.

100 De Marees, *Beschrijvinge*, pl. 18.

Clothing was typically made from cloth bands wrapped or draped over the body, although in some areas, such as the Senegambian region, males wore trousers of varying design with tailored top parts.[101] African textile industries were active before European contact, and no doubt the early descriptions fall short of giving the full variety of clothing styles worn by the people of Atlantic Africa. However, the elite of African society also adopted some European fabrics and styles, so that soon the two aesthetic traditions began to blend in Africa. These principles, developed in Africa, may also have helped shape the aesthetic ideas of Africans who lived outside Africa.

The infusion of great quantities of imported cloth, at first mostly from Europe and later from India as well, certainly had an impact on clothing, at least insofar as this cloth was often designed, cut, and colored differently from the cloth Africans produced. Africans were critical consumers of this cloth, often confounding the importers with their rapid shifts in demand. These shifts, of course, reflected the African aesthetic sense and their attempts to find cloth that appealed to it or that could be combined with materials of their own manufacture. Müller's minute description of feminine dress in the Gold Coast clearly shows the ways in which imported cloth had become a part of clothing styles that were of local inspiration and answered local aesthetic sensibilities.[102]

It was not just cloth as a raw material that was accepted and modified by Africans. European clothing was also incorporated ready-made into African dress, at least among the elite. Thus, for example, rulers and the elite in Kongo quickly took to European fashion, perhaps starting with the Kongo ambassador who arrived in Lisbon in late 1491,[103] so that by the mid-seventeenth century the possession of European-style clothing was a sign of status.[104] Müller also noted that wealthy Gold Coast merchants began wearing European hats and other items of clothing by the same period. Like the Kongo, they often mixed the two types of clothing together.[105] The residents of the areas around the Portuguese posts in the Rivers of Guinea, both men and women, had begun dressing in European fashion by the 1570s, when Alvares de Almada visited the area.[106] Similarly, Dutch merchants in Sierra Leone noted that rulers and their immediate subordinates often received gifts of clothing from merchants, which they wore proudly, including hats

101 Fernandes, "Descriçã," fols. 93, 338; de Almada, "Tratado breve," *MMA*[2] 3:239–40.
102 Müller, *Afrikansche*, pp. 154–63.
103 Milanese ambassador in Lisbon, 6 November 1491, in Capelli, "Proposito," p. 417.
104 Cavazzi, *Istorica descrizione*, bk. 1, no.
105 Müller, *Afrikansche*, pp. 153–4.
106 De Almada, "Tratado Breve," *MMA*[2] 3: 326.

and suits of clothing,[107] a custom that had become generalized by 1668, when Villaut visited the same area.[108]

Even more dramatic shifts are seen in the new styles of clothing created by the new groups of people living along the Atlantic coast in association with the European colonies or coastal points. These people were capable of drawing fully on both aesthetic traditions and tended to blend them more than did the Africans who remained completely under African jurisdiction. At the start of the seventeenth century, de Marees published illustrations showing the distinctive clothing worn by mulatto women, many of whom were the wives or mistresses of the local Portuguese merchants. The clothing emphasized their Christian conversion, being covered by rosary beads, and unlike the local styles, covered the top part of the body completely.[109] A later illustration from Sierra Leone, drawn by the traveler von der Gröben in 1682, also shows a contrast between the African and Afro-Atlantic dress: A Christian woman is shown with her head partially wrapped in cloth and with a full top garment of European design.[110]

Meanwhile, the distinctive clothing of the island of São Tomé was drawing attention as well. In 1559 the women of the island of "whatever quality" (most were wholly or partially of African descent, however) were ordered not to wear "silks and cloths opened in the front, from the waist to the bottom, as up to now some are accustomed to wearing in the manner of heathens." This order was coupled with another one expelling all prostitutes, and perhaps there was a link between the two.[111]

The São Tomé ordinance is ambiguous, and it is hard to imagine exactly what the costume was, but the description of feminine dress in Cape Verde in 1647, a similar colony, given by Ligon leaves little doubt that various aesthetic traditions had been combined to striking effect. There he met the mistress of Bernardo Mendes de Sousa, owner of most of the Ilha do Sal. She was "a Negro of the greatest beauty and majesty that I ever saw in a woman." His minute description of her clothing included a carefully wrapped head, numerous cloths of various colors that covered most of her body, and a long mantle. His later encounter with some teenage free inhabitants of the island at a well shows the reaction of a European who had some familiarity with African feminine aesthetics to the eclectic fashion of an Afro-Atlantic population. These

107 Anon., *Waerachtich verhael van de gantsche reyse ghedaen byden errsamen Jan Dircksz Lam . . .* (Amsterdam, 1626), pp. 4–5, as translated in Adam Jones, "Sources on the Early History of Sierra Leone (22): The Visit of a Dutch Fleet in 1625," *Africana Research Bulletin* 15 (1986): 42–64.

108 Villaut, *Voyage*, pp. 35–66.

109 De Marees, *Beschrijvinge*, pl. 1.

110 Von der Gröben, *Guineische Reisebeschreibung*, pl. 3b (Jones edition).

111 Alvará of King Sebastião, 9 November 1559, *MMA* 2:445.

girls had their hair plaited in layers around their faces, "not shorn as . . . in Africa, nor in quarters and mazes" (a reference to a plaiting pattern popular in Guinea), and various materials were worked into the ends of each plait. They wore skirts and a mantle so arranged that a "great part of the natural beauty of their backs and necks before lay open to view, their breast[s] round, firm, and beautifully shaped."[112]

Some features of the Afro-Atlantic feminine aesthetic are already prefigured in this account and find full fruition in both the famous "Signares" of Senegal of the eighteenth century[113] and the clothing of the Americas, where the paintings of Wagener and Eckhout attest at least the basic elements by the middle of the seventeenth century.[114] Sloane, for his part, mentions that Jamaican women in 1688 were plaiting their hair (though he provides no illustrations) and cutting designs into it with glass from broken bottles, making a pattern of "Lanes and Walks" as in a garden.[115] The wide-bodiced open dresses, with fabrics, colors, and designs of African, Asian, and European origin, and the wrapped heads (but often coupled with elaborate plaiting styles) have become ubiquitous in Africa today, often as a "traditional" style, and can also be found in the numerous illustrations of women in nineteenth-century Brazilian travelers' accounts, such as those of Debret and Rugendas.[116]

One notes immediately that women in this new Afro-Atlantic community began wrapping their heads, in contrast with the nearly universal bareheadedness of early descriptions of Africa, in which hair design was the most important element of bodily decoration and could still be found among some early slaves, as in Jamaica. Perhaps the covering of the head was a sign of Christian conversion, where heads must be covered in the mass. Perhaps it was the result of the racially mixed new population of the coast and islands, because the hair form was looser and straighter and thus did not hold plaits as well.

The African makers of this Afro-Atlantic fashion were often of high status, or at least had considerable freedom to choose their designs and cloth. They chose between local, European, Asian, and new cloth of mixed traditions. For example, the cloth of the Cape Verde Islands, made

112 Ligon, *Trve and Exact History*, pp. 12, 16.

113 One of the earliest descriptions of this group, who pioneered the high fashion of modern Senegal and the rest of West Africa, can be found in "Mémoires historique sur les différents parties de l'Afrique dépendant de l'île de Gorée . . . M. Doumet, major de Place, 1769," in Charles Becker and V. Martin, "Mémoire inédit de Doumet (1769): Le Kayor et les pays voisins au cours de la seconde moitié du XVIIIe siècle," *BIFAN* B 36 (1974): 45.

114 These are shown as woodcuts in Nieuhof, *Brasiliaense Zee- en Lant-reize*, passim.

115 Sloane, *Voyage* 1:liv.

116 Jean-Baptiste Debret, *Voyage pittoresque et historique au Brésil*, 3 vols. (Paris, 1834–9). João Maurício Rugendas, *Viagem Pitoresca através do Brasil* (1835), trans. Sergio Milliet (São Paulo, 1967).

by Mande weavers imported from the mainland but involving new patterns and use of colors, had great popularity not only among the islanders themselves but in much of Senegambia and other parts of West Africa to which it was exported.[117] Likewise, weavers in Allada were already reworking European "says and perpetuans" into their own cloth to create a new cloth that not only enjoyed an African market but was also exported to America, where according to Phillips, who purchased some in 1694, it fetched a good price in Barbados.[118]

African cloth arriving in Brazil or Barbados may have been worn by women and men of European descent, given its high price. But it seems likely that one way or another it was also worn by the African and Afro-American population. Seventeenth-century descriptions of clothing in Mexico, for example, often refer to "mantas Congas" (Kongolese mantles) as an item of clothing worn by Afro-Mexicans.[119] These texts do not reveal whether such cloth was imported from central Africa or locally produced in the home or by one of the many textile works (most of which employed African slaves) of colonial Mexico. The American consumers of this cloth were often slaves who had few resources, were unable to produce their own cloth, and probably were unable to choose their clothing styles. But even as slaves they could enjoy, appreciate, and thus contribute to the development of an Afro-Atlantic aesthetic among those of their fellows who, through luck or skill, were able to dress well and exercise some choice in clothing. Thus, it is not surprising that one meets the new styles among the free Christian population and among mistresses, concubines, and prostitutes. As the Afro-Atlantic population became richer or freer, the fashions of the minority became generalized and imitated.

117 See António Carreira, *Pannaria Cabo-Verdiano-Guineense (aspectos históricos e socio-económicos)* (Porto, 1969), for a fascinating historical study of the cloth and its demand throughout Africa and in the Americas.

118 Phillips, "Journal," p. 236.

119 Gonzalo Aguirre Beltrán, *Cuijila: Esbozo etnogáfico de un pueblo negro* (Mexico, 1958), chap. 8.

9

African religions and Christianity in the Atlantic world

The dynamics of culture change can be seen in the evolution of African languages, social structures, and aesthetics as Africans moved across the seas or came into contact with Europeans. This dynamic process also affected African religion and philosophy both in Africa and as Africans became Americans in the new Atlantic world. As with the other elements of culture, religion responded both to its internal dynamic and to the new dynamic created by culture contact and physical transfer. The result was the emergence of a new Afro-Atlantic religion that was often identified as Christian, especially in the New World, but was a type of Christianity that could satisfy both African and European understandings of religion.

This new African Christianity allowed some of the African religious knowledge and philosophy to be accommodated in a European religious system and represented a merger of great significance, similar to the creation of Chinese (or East Asian) Buddhism or the Indianization of Islam. In order to understand this remarkable transformation one must first understand the underlying dynamics of religious knowledge (itself the most fundamental branch of epistemology in this period) and from this the mechanisms for religious change, conversion, and transformation in the presence of other systems of religious knowledge. Viewed from this perspective, we can then examine the development of African Christianity, first in Africa and then in the Atlantic world.

The basis for religious knowledge

The merging of religions requires something more than simply mixing forms and ideas from one religion with those of another. It requires a reevaluation of the basic concepts and sources of knowledge of both religions in order to find common ground. Religion as it was experienced in the sixteenth and seventeenth centuries was not simply an intellectual conception, made up by people and subject to reconsideration or debate. Rather, the ideas and the images were "received" or revealed from nonworldly beings in one or another form, and humans' only role was to interpret these revelations and act accordingly. Thus religious philosophy was not the creator of religion; revelations were. Religious philosophy simply interpreted them.

Therefore, strictly speaking, humans were not free to change religions or to question the revelations, and in the end virtually all religious change required at least reinterpretation of existing revelations, at most a new set of stronger revelations. The development of African Christianity in Africa and its transmission to America was in large measure a combination of both factors, used by both Africans and Europeans.

Africans and Europeans had somewhat different systems of religious knowledge, as well as a completely different set of basic revelations, but they still had a number of major ideas in common. Had they not shared these ideas, the development of African Christianity would probably not have been possible. Both cultures accepted the basic reality of religion: that there was another world that could not be seen and that revelations were the essential source by which people could know of this other world.

Thus, sixteenth- and seventeenth-century Africans and Europeans conceived the cosmos as being divided into two separate but intimately interconnected worlds: "this world," the material world that we all live in and that can be perceived by the five normal senses, and the "other world," normally imperceptible except to a few gifted individuals and inhabited by a variety of beings or entities. One could pass from this world to the other world upon death, so that the souls of the dead were among the denizens of the other world.

Europeans, who provide us with the sources necessary to study African religion in this period, were anxious to establish right away that the two cultures shared this fundamental starting point. Sometimes, discovering this shared belief was as far as their inquiries into religion went. For example, Pieter de Marees noted in his early seventeenth-century record of the Gold Coast that the people there believed in another world and that they passed there when they died, a belief that was reported at various times for most of the rest of Africa as well.[1]

The other world was more than a home for the dead, however; it was also a superior world, in that events in this world were governed by the other world. Barbot, describing religion on the Gold and Slave coasts between 1678 and 1682, maintained that all Africans believed in a Su-

[1] De Marees, *Beschryvinge*, p. 36b.

preme Being who ruled the other world, caused accidents, and determined the time of life and death.[2] The Sieur d'Elbée remarked in 1671 that the inhabitants of Allada believed in a higher power that caused accidents to happen.[3] Likewise, when fishing or commerce was bad on the Gold Coast, according to Villaut, who visited in 1668, the people attributed it to the action of the higher powers and made sacrifices, apologizing to the powers of the other world and begging forgiveness.[4]

Both Africans and their Christian visitors from Europe also agreed that the way of knowing about the other world was through revelations, though they disagreed about the validity of many specific revelations. Nevertheless, they did accept the general principle in common that the souls of the dead and those of other inhabitants of the other world, although often omnipresent, were invisible and could not communicate with people in this world on a regular basis. Cavazzi, a priest whose observations of Kongo and Mbundu religion show a high degree of attention to details, related several instances that emphasize the normal inaccessibility of the other world. These anecdotes have an African ring and were probably tales of his African informants. In one case, he noted that a woman had been cruelly sacrificed to the other world by an Imbangala ruler, but in spite of the grievous wound she suffered, she still managed to rise and return to the town. When she saw the ruler, she informed him that she had been to the other world but had not been wanted and was thus returned. Even more significant, Cavazzi related the story of a powerful and haughty prince who wished to know for himself what the other world was like. He thus ordered himself buried alive, but alas, he did not return to tell any tales, confirming that no matter how powerful one is in this world, one must yield to the other world.[5]

Because of the inaccessibility of the other world to normal human senses, every society has its unbelievers, who deny the reality of any phenomenon they cannot perceive. Marcellino d'Atri, a Capuchin priest who traveled widely in Kongo and the Mbundu-speaking regions of central Africa at the end of the seventeenth century, noted that he had met an occasional "Epicurian" (a seventeenth-century term for an atheist or materialist) during his travels and religious investigations, though such people were reasonably rare.[6] D'Atri's Epicurians not only confirm

[2] Barbot, "Voyage," p. 352.

[3] D'Elbée, "Journal," p. 442.

[4] Villaut, *Voyage*, p. 187.

[5] MSS Araldi, Cavazzi, "Missione evangelica," vol. A, bk. 1, pp. 70, 140.

[6] Marcellino d'Atri, "Giornate Apostoliche fatte da me . . . nelle messioni de Regni d'Angola e Congo . . . 1690" (ca. 1705), fol. 129 (modern ed., Carolo Toso, *L'anarchia Congolese nel secolo XVII: La relazione inedite di Marchellino d'Atri* [Genoa, 1984]).

the existence of materialists in Africa but are a direct connection to the existence of similar people and systems of thought in Europe.

Those who did accept the existence of another world did so because they believed that some people had had direct contact with it. Most people could not perceive the other world most of the time, but there were special people endowed with a sixth sense that allowed them to receive messages and images from the other world.[7] These people could then report back to their fellows on the existence, nature, and structure of the other world.

At the same time, the other world also had its own means to make people in this world understand it. Not only could it communicate directly with the limited group of people with a sixth sense, but it could send messages to people in this world through indirect means. These might include dreams or the ordering of events in this world in such a way as to convey messages for all to understand (augury).

All these various communications take the form of revelations. A revelation is a piece of information about the other world, its nature, or its intention that is perceptible to people in this world through one or another channel. Revelations provide this world with its window on the other world. The information thus gathered is then basic data used for constructing a general understanding of the nature of the other world and its inhabitants (a philosophy), a clear perception of its desires and intentions for people to obey (a religion), and a larger picture of the workings and history of both worlds (a cosmology). It is thus through revelations that religions are formed, and it is also through them that they change.[8]

7 Medieval debates between Moslems, Christians, and Jews on the nature of the prophet are particularly revealing about the nature of this sixth sense as it was understood in the broader Mediterranean tradition. See Moshe Perlman, ed. and trans., *Ibn Kammūna's Examination of the Three Faiths: A Thirteenth Century Essay in the Comparative Study of Religion* (Los Angeles and Berkeley, 1971), pp. 13–39 (citing and using similar texts from the tenth to twelfth centuries).

8 Modern discussions of revelation in Western literature are generally confined to Christian and Jewish applications, but there is a wide recognition that the fundamental works of Islam, Zoroastrianism, Hinduism, and Buddhism are also based on revelations of a very similar sort; see R. C. Zaehner, *At Sundry Times* (London, 1958). See also, for a more Christian-oriented theological text that discusses revelation in Eastern religions, J. H. Walgrave, *Un salut aux dimensions du monde* (London, 1970). Scholars of African and other "primitive" religions are less certain about the applicability of the concept; see most notably the work of Jack Goody, who draws a strong distinction between the "revealed religions of the book" of Eurasia and the traditions of Africa on the basis of a complex of material and social traits (private property, dowry payments, intensive plow agriculture, and, above all, writing traditions) (see, among others, *The Domestication of the Savage Mind* [London, 1977]). Other scholars, however, accept the universality of the idea, especially those associated with the concepts of Rudolph Otto, *The Concept of the Holy* (1918), such as G. van der Leeuw, *Religion in Essence and Manifestation*, 2 vols. (1933; New York, 1963).

European travelers, both priests and laypeople, had definite ideas about the role of revelations in forming their own tradition. Christian concepts were founded on a series of revelations, a record of which was contained in the Holy Scriptures. This series began with the revelations to Moses that formed the old Hebrew law (as well as the creation story) and was extended by stories of the Hebrew prophets or their actual writings in the rest of the Old Testament. This in turn was transformed by the revelation of Jesus and further by the inspired testimony of the apostles in the New Testament. Catholics believed that many post-biblical writers ("Fathers and Doctors of the Church") were also inspired and their words were as much revelations from the other world as those in the Scriptures, and all accepted the idea that lesser revelations, in the form of dreams, conjunctions of events, heavenly apparitions, and the like were divine messages as well as the Scriptures.

Africans also recognized the concept of revelation, and their own revelations had much in common with those of Europe, so that Europeans had little trouble in recognizing them, just as Africans ultimately had little trouble in recognizing the content of the Bible or Church histories of the Europeans as being revelations. In the end, where Africans and Europeans did not always agree was on the validity of any given revelation, since both recognized that apparent revelations could be received by the insane or that ambitious and cynical people might feign revelations to increase their own power or prestige. Many Europeans, moreover, believed that although African revelations were genuine messages from the other world, they originated with the Devil and thus ought not to be followed, a point that Africans contested. Africans were less concerned about diabolic revelations but did have difficulty in accepting the validity of many of the revelations that Europeans said were received in the ancient past, for which there were no recent witnesses.

African revelations of the sixteenth and seventeenth centuries can be divided into several categories. Augury and divination involve the study of events to determine otherworldly intentions. Dream interpretation relies on the notion that the other world can sometimes communicate through the unconscious mind. More dramatic revelations came in the form of visions or hearing voices, usually only by people with special gifts. Perhaps the most dramatic form of revelation was given through the spirit medium or possessed object, in which an otherworldly entity took over a human, animal, or material object and spoke through it.

Europeans, familiar with the concept from their own tradition, recognized African augury at once, though many writers regarded it as a diabolic contrivance. In augury, random events of this world are studied to determine the other world's desires or intentions. Cavazzi, himself a firm believer in augury as a valid form of Christian revelation,[9] mentioned that in mid-seventeenth-century Mbundu society, people were attentive to the cries of birds, the behavior of dogs, foxes, and rabbits, the sputtering of fires, earth tremors, the discovery of unusually shaped stones or plants, and celestial phenomena.[10] To a similar list compiled for Gold Coast societies around 1669, the Lutheran priest Müller added birdcalls and human sneezes.[11]

Observation of the course of time (like astrology in Europe) was often a form of augury, for Müller noted that on the Gold Coast in his time people had devised a calendar of lucky and unlucky days. People avoided doing various types of business on specifically unlucky days, and A person's birthday prescribed a personal cycle of good and bad days.[12] A related form of time augury was observed by Cavazzi in central Africa. There, the conditions of a person's birth could sometimes reveal the person's character or govern his or her decisions. Indeed, he noted, Queen Njinga was so named because she was born with the umbilical cord wrapped around her neck. This foreordained her to have a proud and haughty character.[13]

Divination was a variant of augury. In divination, people perform an activity and ask the other world to influence the results in such a way that those of this world can know the other world's intentions. As we shall see, Christian priests often used various forms of divination to determine which saint to direct prayers to or which saint a church ought to be dedicated to, although they also believed that divination in other contexts was consulting with the Devil.

One of the most famous African forms of divination, known most often by its Yoruba name, Ifa, was described in detail in an early eighteenth-century description of Whydah. The priest caused cowry shells to fall on a specially designed board, while asking the other world to influence the outcome of this event in such a way as to allow the diviner to answer questions.[14] The Capuchin de Naxera, visiting Allada in 1660–2, was probably speaking of Ifa or a related sort of divination when he noted that they consulted with "the Devil" through casting "lots."[15] A divination board from Allada, obtained by a curious Euro-

[9] See his own list of omens in the Christian tradition that occurred while he was resident in Angola, MSS Araldi, "Missione evangelica," vol. B, fols. 548–611.

[10] Ibid., vol. A, bk. 1, pp. 122–3, 125, 127–8.

[11] Müller, *Afrikansche*, pp. 99–101.

[12] Ibid., p. 99.

[13] MSS Araldi, Cavazzi, "Missione evangelica," vol. A, bk. 1, pp. 50–1, 125, and bk. 2, p. 20.

[14] Archives Nationales de France, Depôt des Fortifications d'Outre Mer, MS. 104, anonymous, "Relation du Royaume de Juda en Affrique," pp. 56–7.

[15] De Naxera, *Espejo mystico*, p. 278.

pean before 1659, survives today in the Ulmer Museum and is similar to other such boards in use today.[16]

But Ifa did not exhaust African divination by any means. The Jesuit missionary Alvares noted several forms in Sierra Leone, including throwing sticks or stones or choosing lots randomly.[17] Müller has a description of a form of divination used on the Gold Coast as well. This involved throwing specially marked stones, called "obuss ubbues" (*obussù bù*), up in the air and catching them in a basket. Another method was to throw strings of teeth, whose position at landing provided the basic data for interpretation.[18]

This type of divination was typically used to learn the other world's intentions, to find solutions to problems that came from or could be addressed by the other world, or to ascertain how best to gain the favor of the other world. A variant on this was the judicial ordeals found in most Atlantic African societies. In this sort of divination, the other world was asked to influence events in such a way as to reveal the guilt or innocence of a person accused of a crime.

A common ordeal, such as the *bulungu* of Angola,[19] the "red water" ordeal of the Upper Guinea region,[20] and an Allada ordeal observed by the Capuchins in the early 1660s,[21] required giving the accused poison – if he vomited it up, then he was held to be innocent; if not, then he either died of its effects or was held to be guilty. Other ordeals achieved the same purpose. A famous one in Allada involved throwing the accused into a particularly tricky stretch of river that sometimes sucked swimmers down (who were then held to be guilty) or threw them ashore (then declared innocent). José de Naxera declared that even nonswimmers underwent this ordeal when confident that their innocence would save them.[22] Cavazzi also recorded a variety of other judicial ordeals in his careful inventory of African religion in Angola, including plunging hands in hot water or seizing hot irons (the innocent were unburned) or throwing sticks (as in other forms of divination). In addition to testing one ordeal himself (he was badly burned), Cavazzi also noted numerous European parallels to the African practices.[23]

Augury and divination were indirect forms of revelation and some of

16 The board is illustrated and discussed in Vansina, *Art History*, pp. 2–3.

17 BSGL, Alvares, "Etiopia menor," fol. 108.

18 Müller, *Afrikansche*, pp. 62–3; also see Barbot, "Journal," p. 174. These references, as well as modern terminology and ethnographic data, are collected and analyzed in Jones, *Brandenburg Sources*, appendix A19.

19 MSS Araldi, Cavazzi, "Missione evangelica," vol. A, bk. 1, pp. 82–3, 112.

20 BSGL, Alvares, "Etiopia menor," fols. 58v–60.

21 De Naxera, *Espejo mystico*, p. 281.

22 Ibid., pp. 277–80.

23 MSS Araldi, Cavazzi, "Missione evangelica," vol. A, bk. 1, pp. 112–21.

them were ambiguous in their interpretation. This may explain why Africans also relied on more direct revelations. One such direct revelation came from the study of dreams. Because Africans, like people in other areas, often believed that dreams or other altered states of consciousness provided access to the other world, they were carefully attentive to the assumed meanings of their dreams. Since all people have dreams, in many ways they were considered no more remarkable than the study of divination or augury. Dreams employ symbolic language and often require interpretation – a direct, unambiguous revelation in the form of a dream seems to have been rare. Cavazzi noted that people in Angola often reported speaking with the souls of their dead ancestors in dreams, and because these were fairly direct types of communication, people often paid close attention to dreams.[24]

The small number of people who had visions or heard voices from the other world formed an important part of the priesthood. Gold Coast priests reported actually having seen beings from the other world and having communicated with them. They could provide physical descriptions of such beings, and Müller, based on one such description and some dubious biblical exegesis, concluded that the being was none other than the Devil himself.[25] Miguel Cube, a Temne priest in Sierra Leone who upon his conversion to Christianity became an important informant for the Jesuits there at the start of the seventeenth century, also gave them a description of the "demon" who appeared to him.[26] Finally, the king of Allada informed his French guest d'Elbée in 1671 that he had seen such a deity in the form of a white child, and the child had actually predicted d'Elbée's coming.[27]

Such messages, heard or seen by special people, were, of course, very direct revelations, for the priest might actually converse with an otherworldly being. But average people could not have such communication. Instead, they had to rely on the priest or priestess to have the communication and inform the rest of the people of the message. Müller noted this fact in his description of Gold Coast religion. Often priests would go off by themselves and have visions and then return to report them to the community at large.[28]

Surely the most dramatic and convincing of the various revelations were those given to spirit mediums or possessed objects and shrines, revelations that Europeans often associated with the Devil (diabolic possession requiring exorcism) rather than God, but which were revelations

[24] Ibid., p. 126.
[25] Müller, *Afrikansche*, pp. 45–8.
[26] BSGL, Alvares, "Etiopia menor," fol. 64.
[27] D'Elbée, "Journal," p. 434.
[28] Müller, *Afrikansche*, p. 45.

nevertheless. Christians did believe, however, that the Holy Spirit routinely possessed churches during the performance of mass and that Christ was physically present in the host during Eucharist, beliefs that were analogous to possession of shrines, though messages were not received in this way.

In the case of human possession, a being from the other world would enter the medium's body and speak with his or her voice. In the case of a shrine, the being might use a material object for the same purpose. Obviously, anyone in earshot could clearly hear the being and thus the revelation obtained in this manner was perfectly clear and unambiguous. Moreover, the being might engage in conversation and even answer questions while inhabiting the body of the medium. Typically possession would occur after the medium had fallen into a trance, for as in the case of dreams, the other world seems to have found it easiest to communicate with people in an unconscious state or an altered state of consciousness. Such a trance might be induced by drugs or hypnotic dancing, singing, or drumming.

Spirit mediumship would play a role in the merger of traditions in Africa, especially when saints possessed mediums or when ancestors advised their descendants through mediums to take up Christian practice. Central Africa was the land of the spirit medium par excellence, and we have detailed descriptions of possessed mediums from Angola and Kongo. Luca da Caltanisetta, who traveled throughout the area in the last decade of the seventeenth century, provides an excellent description of the medium in operation. When the people want to know the cause of "a death or sickness or a lost item or another thing" they go to the *nganga ngombo* (a spirit medium). Forming a circle around him, they "sing and pray for the Devil to enter the head of that priest" (entering the head being a term for spirit possession). Once the spirit enters, they make their demands, wishing to know all about who has poisoned whom, or how it is that someone has died or something has been lost. The "devil" then "says a thousand lies through the mouth of that witch [*fatuciero*] and if their desire is to have a sickness treated, he also gives them the remedy for it."[29]

Cavazzi gave descriptions with similar details of the Angolan spirit medium, the *xingila*. Like his Kongo counterpart, the *xingila* would typically enter a trance state induced by clapping, drumming, or dancing – a process that in one case that Cavazzi observed took three days to

[29] Luca da Caltanisetta, "Relatione della missione fatta nel Regno di Congo per il Padre Fra' Luca da Caltanisetta . . . 1701," fol. 48. Modern ed., Romain Rainero, *Il Congo agli inizi del settecento nella relazione di P. Luca da Caltanisetta* (Florence, 1974). The original pagination is marked in this edition and in the French translation of François Bontinck (Brussels, 1971).

finish. In one detailed description of a medium in 1657, Cavazzi observed the being, in this case a deceased brother of an Imbangala ruler, enter the medium, speak convincingly in the brother's voice, and then inform the king that he would be well advised to agree to a peace treaty with the Portuguese that had been under discussion for some time. Often such ancestors would berate the living for their lack of attention or their failure to make sacrifices, often making specific demands for more.[30]

Central Africans argued that it was best to attempt this form of mediumship in the presence of physical remains of the ancestor, just as Christians often used relics of saints to address them more strongly. Thus, mediums often performed at the ancestor's tomb or with containers (called *misete*) of relics of the ancestors such as bones or personal possessions. If possession was to be by a deity or by an ancestor who had died so long ago that a tomb was no longer preserved, then the possession might take place near specially constructed shrines.[31]

Possession might give special force to divination as well. Both da Caltanisetta and his frequent companion, d'Atri, wrote about the *nganga ngombo* as a diviner. He would place his staff before him while possessed and then allow it to drop in such a way that its position when it landed would indicate the answers to questions. Alternatively, the staff itself seems to have been possessed, for in d'Atri's description he called it an "enchanted staff."[32]

Possession of items is also frequently referred to in descriptions of West Africa. One of the more dramatic forms of West African revelations seems to have been speaking shrines, in which an otherworldly being possessed a physical item and spoke through it. When de Naxera was living in Allada in 1660–2, he noted the presence of a shrine ("idol") there that spoke with the voice of a deity (which he, of course, assumed was the Devil), which the king himself admitted to hearing.[33] The English captain Phillips, visiting in 1694, also heard of the shrine and was bold enough to attack it, shooting at it and causing some small damage. The king told him that the shrine was not itself a god but was only a vehicle for him to speak to the people, but he would not speak to Europeans.[34]

In Senegambia, shrines that did not speak but that nevertheless represented places where otherworldly entities could channel themselves were common. Alvares noted that one such shrine, called a "tower of

30 MSS Araldi, Cavazzi, "Missione evangelica," vol. A, bk. 2, pp. 85, 86–9.
31 Ibid., p. 85; bk. 1, pp. 29, 60, 90, 93, 98.
32 Da Caltanisetta, "Relatione," fols. 48–48v, 49v; d'Atri, "Giornate apostoliche," fols. 223–4.
33 De Naxera, *Espejo Mystico*, pp. 96, 203.
34 Phillips, "Voyage," pp. 239–40.

bagabaga," was the sometime residence of a local deity who was responsible for rain. During one drought, Christian, traditional, and Moslem religious workers performed their rites around one.[35]

Animals could be possessed as well as material objects, although they did not necessarily deliver messages. Typically, possessed animals were agents of the other world seeking revenge or obedience. Shortly after the death of queen Njinga in 1663, for example, the people of Matamba were troubled by rogue leopards, who they believed were possessed by the dead queen's soul and whose exorcism required Cavazzi's full attention.[36] Cavazzi's colleague in Kongo, Girolamo da Montesarchio, faced a similar problem with possessed snakes, elephants, and lions at one or another time during his twenty-year sojourn there.[37]

Possessed animals doing the work of the other world were not a central African monopoly. Alvares noted frequent trouble in Sierra Leone with possessed leopards, who might be carrying out the will of the other world.[38]

Finally, the possession of material objects by beings from the other world might not necessarily be a form of revelation, just as the possessed animals were not. Possession of material objects by beings from the other world lay at the root of the efficacy of magical charms, whose use was widespread. Modern descriptions of *nkisi*, the Kongo charms, suggest that the priest might actually fix the being into the object, thus subjugating it to his will (a form of magic exactly analogous to the European magic of the same time).[39] Although seventeenth-century descriptions do not confirm this, Cavazzi did note that when preparing to make such a charm and to give it efficacy, the priest would first sacrifice to the soul of the first person to make the charm.[40] Apparently the soul of this "inventor of the art" provided the otherworldly power that made it possible for an entity to be captured.[41]

35 BSGL, Alvares, "Etiopia menor," fols. 10, 103v.

36 MSS Araldi, Cavazzi, "Missone evangelica," vol. A, bk. 2, pp. 222–3. The text actually says "tigers," but there are no tigers in central Africa. Presumably Cavazzi meant large feline predators, and thus might have referred to leopards.

37 Da Montesarchio, "Viaggio," fols. 50v–53.

38 BSGL, Alvares, "Etiopia menor," fol. 28. This is perhaps an early mention of the jaguar society that was held responsible for many murders during the early colonial period.

39 See the detailed discussion based largely on Kongo testimony of the early twentieth century in the Laman notebooks and more recent field observation by Wyatt MacGaffey, *Religion and Society in Central Africa: The Bakongo of Lower Zaire* (Chicago, 1986), pp. 137–48.

40 MSS Araldi, Cavazzi, "Missione evangelica," vol. A, bk. 1, pp. 77, 81.

41 Of course, in contemporary European ritual magic, "demons" were captured in magical instruments, but again only because the magician had enlisted the support of God or other divine agents (saints, angels, etc.). For a general discussion, see Norman Cohn, *Europe's Inner Demons: An Enquiry Inspired by the Great Witch Hunt* (New York, 1975), pp. 168–70.

Thus, Africans had a variety of types of revelations by which they could learn the desires of the other world or ask it to use its power over this world to assist them. The information of these revelations could then be assembled into a comprehensive cosmology and philosophy, and the instructions, rewards, and punishments received compiled into a code of behavior and a religion.

Both Christianity and African religions were constructed in the same way, through the philosophical interpretation of revelations. Africans, however, unlike Christians, did not construct these religious interpretations in such a way as to create an orthodoxy. Thus, Africans might agree on the source of religious knowledge in the abstract and hence accept philosophical or cosmological descriptions, but they might not agree too fully on all the specifics. When Africans came into contact with Christians, this lack of orthodoxy facilitated conversion, and usually the relations between the two traditions were not hostile, at least as Africans saw it.

This absence of orthodoxy in Africa had two causes. The first was the relative lack of power of the priesthood, which lacked the means to force the whole population to accept a uniform cosmology. The second reason was that Africans received revelations continuously, and without a strong priesthood that enforced a certain type of interpretation, rigid cosmologies or philosophies could not survive the constant addition of new data.

The precariousness of the position of each priest derived from the fact that many forms of revelation relied on human agency. For many types of revelation, no one could be sure whether priests genuinely had a revelation or whether they were deluding the people for their own enrichment or prestige. Validation of revelations is a problem for all religious traditions that rely on them, and such traditions all require some form of it.

In the Western tradition, miracles were the means of validation. If a prophet demonstrated power or knowledge that would have been unavailable to him through normal physical laws (as they were then understood), then this was taken as a sign (the root of the word "miracle" ultimately refers to a demonstration) that the revelation he reported did indeed come from the other world.[42] This explains why miracle stories are so central (and so important) to the Christian Scriptures, for they were intended to provide validation of the revelations reported in the same passages.

42 For an excellent philosophical discussion of this for the whole Mediterranean tradition, see Ibn Kammūna, *Examination* (ed. Perlmann), pp. 20–4 (the notes of this edition specify other texts as well).

In Africa, priests were typically required to provide more or less continuous proof of their capacity to receive or transmit revelations as well. Typically, this proof was not so much the performance of miracles as the efficaciousness of their advice. If they predicted the future accurately, provided efficacious cures, or located clearly guilty parties, then their claims were validated; if not, they might be subject to rejection or scorn. In an extreme case, they might be punished. In 1563, the king of Ndongo had eleven rainmakers put to death because they failed to deliver rain and were thus charged with chicanery.[43]

This requirement for constant validation rendered the African priests' position precarious. They derived their support from payments by clients, one of the reasons that Cavazzi believed that they were tricking people to fill their purses. He noted that those who did well were well paid and lived handsomely; those who were less effective might actually live in poverty or give up their profession altogether.[44]

A really successful priest might rise to great heights and obtain an immense following. For example, one named Sucequo came to the attention of Portuguese authorities in Angola around 1642. He claimed to be able to work miraculous cures, bless crops and the like, interpret dreams, and be possessed by anyone's ancestors. His career was brief, for the Portuguese captured him and burned him at the stake, but his fall was ultimately taken simply as evidence that his powers had deserted him.[45]

Such cases were not restricted to central Africa. Müller related the case of a famous priest on the Gold Coast who won great support from the English settled around Kormantin after 1665 because he made significant and correct predictions. He soon won a large clientele drawn from all the people in the area, but later his powers left him, and he ended up "scorned and despised by both Blacks and Whites."[46] Once again, we see that the claims had to be continuously verified, and reputation was worth little in maintaining a following.

Given the potentials for rewards, there were undoubtedly cases of trickery, and such cases as were discovered were immediately grounds for the priest's being abandoned and impoverished. Danish traders successfully exposed one group of tricksters at Komenda in 1668, and they were immediately scorned by all.[47] Some Europeans believed that African priests were tricksters. Other Europeans were convinced that the priests had otherworldly contacts, though the more religious of them

43 Antonio Mendes to Jesuit General, 9 May 1563, fol. 223, *MMA* 2:508–9.
44 MSS Araldi, Cavazzi, "Missione evangelica," vol. A, bk. 1, pp. 78–100, passim.
45 Related at length in Cadornega, *História* 1:367–71.
46 Müller, *Afrikansche*, pp. 76–8.
47 Ibid., pp. 81–2.

attributed the power to the Devil. Cavazzi's attitude is clearly ambiguous, for example, and he alternates between a trickster explanation and a diabolic one.[48] But even Africans seem to have shared their suspicions about the claims of any one priest, and thus in effect all such priests were required to confirm their powers constantly.

The insecurity of the priesthood obviously presented a barrier to enforced orthodoxy in African religions. Moreover, although kings and other powerful people often had their personal and state priests, the absence of landed property meant that an endowed clergy was impossible. Priests lived at the pleasure of their clients, whether they were rulers or simple people paying on a cash-for-service basis. Priests might be able to enforce behavior, Cavazzi believed they certainly did, especially if they insisted that revelations told them certain types of behavior were essential to please the other world. But ultimately their strictures were acceptable only as long as rulers accepted them or people agreed to be bound by them. Religious actors had no independent power to enforce orthodoxy.

By contrast, European Christianity developed with a strong clergy that possessed political power, recruited its own members, had its own law, and at times even threatened the authority of the state. Even in countries like Spain, Portugal, and post-Reformation northern Europe where priests were largely under state control, it was in the interests of both Church and state to continue the institution of an unassailable clergy whose interpretation of revelations could not be challenged. This would be important when Africans converted to Christianity both in Africa and in the Americas. In Africa the Christian clergy remained precarious, and thus conversion always involved questioning of clerical authority. In America the clergy could have their way, although Africans continued to have their doubts about the reality of the clergy's claims.

The second barrier to orthodoxy was an outgrowth of the first condition. Revelations came to Africans in a stream, continuously from day to day, and each one required validation. As long as the clergy were precarious they could not impose their interpretation on these revelations, nor could they control their arrival or institutionalize them. To emphasize, consider the contrasting position of the Christian clergy. Early Christianity also had a stream of continuous revelations, Jesus' revelation being followed by Paul's (and with major implications for how the faith was to be practiced) and others of the early era. But when the Christian Church was co-opted by the Roman Empire under Constantine, the clergy was solidified in an independent position, and moreover, the revelations

[48] MSS Araldi, Cavazzi, "Missione evangelica," vol. A, bk. 1, pp. 79–100, passim.

were canonized, creating, one might say, a discontinuous revelation, in contrast to the pattern of continuous revelation of Africans.[49]

The discontinuous revelation, encapsulated in the Bible (much of it the product of the work of earlier secure priesthoods in Israel), provided the inviolable basis for faith and provided a wide-reaching framework for religion and cosmology. But neither the Church nor laypeople ceased to believe in the reality of continuous revelation. The works of the Doctors and Fathers of the Church, for example, were held to be inspired by the Holy Spirit, and thus a continuous revelation. Moreover, sixteenth-century Europeans believed that a variety of auguries, divinations, and apparitions of otherworldly beings took place constantly, and they regularly consulted astrologers, geomancers, and other diviners and healers.[50]

This was not simply a folk belief; the Church accepted it as well. William Christian, using detailed sixteenth-century Spanish surveys, has been able to show that priests routinely used divination to determine which saints should guide a particular mission or patronize a church or chapel, and many accepted vows as a result of answered prayers to saints.[51] One need only read the work of the priest Cavazzi to see how thoroughly the idea of continuous revelation was fixed in the minds of the European clergy who were selected for mission work.[52]

Nevertheless, the early modern Church was cognizant of the danger that continuous revelation held for their authority, and even though they recognized it, they also sought to contain it. They did this first by insisting on the primacy of the discontinuous revelation (to the point of denying the validity of a revelation if it contradicted the Bible directly) while placing its interpretation in their own hands and second by ascribing revelations with which they did not agree to the Devil.

Scholastic and Humanist philosophy, for example, sought to reinforce

49 This distinction of continuous versus discontinuous revelation parallels but is not exactly similar to that in Christian theology between special and general revelation, where special (or private) revelation, made to an individual, contrasts with general (or public) revelations intended for the whole population. See among others, A. R. Dulles, *Revelation Theology: A History* (London, 1969).

50 For a useful survey of Iberian beliefs, see the sixteenth-century work of Pedro Ciruelo, *Reprouacion de las superstitiones y hechizerias*, 1st ed. (Salamanca, 1530; mod. ed., Alva Ebersole from the 1547 ed., Valencia, 1978); English translation from the augmented 1628 edition by Eugene Maio and D'Orsay Pearson, *Pedro Ciruelo's A Treatise Reproving All Superstitions and Other Forms of Witchcraft* (Cranbury, N.J., 1978). Ciruelo ascribed all such practices to "implicit witchcraft" in arguing that only the Devil could send revelations to nonclerical people, but it is obvious that in his day only a minority of people accepted this position as orthodox, and most did not regard their behavior as witchcraft. For an interesting and influential survey of English practices, see Keith Thomas, *Religion and the Decline of Magic: Studies in Popular Belief in Sixteenth and Seventeenth Century England* (London, 1971) (but with some reservations about the overall argument).

51 William Christian, *Local Religion in Sixteenth Century Spain* (New York, 1981).

52 MSS Araldi, Cavazzi, "Missione evangelica," vol. B, pp. 548–611.

the careful reading of discontinuous revelation as a substitute for accepting continuous ones, to the point where Luther made this, in his dictum *sola scriptura*, a main point of Reformation theology, though neither he nor his Protestant followers ended up taking this literally, as Catholic critics were quick to point out.[53]

The concept of the diabolically inspired continuous revelation formed the second prong in the Church's control over continuous revelation. The Spanish cleric Pedro Ciruelo's popular treatise on this subject carefully delineated the Church's position, ascribing all forms of popular revelations (augury, astrology, divination, etc.) to the Devil, even when the agents of the revelation were good Christians and acting in good faith.[54] All such revelations could then be labeled as witchcraft and their practitioners burned (as indeed thousands were), though the Church still accepted most of the revelations that came under its control or that were not threatening (such as apparitions of saints and the Virgin).

This attack on continuous revelation was successful, however, only because both Church and state authorities accepted the concept of a secure rather than a precarious clergy. Operating from its position of security, the clergy could then use force if necessary to ensure orthodoxy. The witchcraft trials and burnings of the early modern period and the activities of the Inquisition were all manifestations of this enforcement.

Without a secure clergy and with an enhanced place for continuous revelation, African religions had less enforced orthodoxy. Cosmology, the description of the religious universe, is not given in all-encompassing discontinuous revelations received at great intervals and carefully recorded either in writing or in oral tradition for posterity[55] but rather is a constantly updated picture of the other world, which is perceived as being in a state of flux.[56]

53 See, for example, the controversial arguments of St. François de Sales, François Vernon, and the Jesuit Juan Maldonat, who stressed the ultimate requirement of revelation for faith and left the door open for continuous revelation (Richard Popkin, "Skepticism and the Counter-Reformation in France," *Archiv für Reformationsgeschichte* 51 [1960]: 62–6).

54 Ciruelo, *Reprouacion*.

55 The early Christian Gospels, the Quran, and the Hindu and Buddhist scriptures existed in oral form before being written down. In Indian culture, oral transmission was always regarded as being the most appropriate way of passing the "scripture" along, and written forms were eschewed; see C. MacKenzie Brown, "Purana as Scripture: From Sound to Image in the Hindu Holy Tradition," *History of Religion* 26 (1986): 68–86. In this case, oral transmission in a society with a secure priesthood is a means of safeguarding the secret knowledge of a discontinuous revelation. Discontinuous revelation, therefore, is not dependent upon having a written tradition. To this might be added the long retention of esoteric teachings passed on orally among a select elite. The Talmud and many of the principal doctrines of Mahayana Buddhism were preserved orally for generations before being made public.

56 The sudden appearance of esoteric writings may update discontinuous revelations, which is also the function of commentaries, especially the inspired commentaries of mystics or even strictly intellectual writers (the writings of Thomas Aquinas come to mind).

When Müller presented the people of the Gold Coast with the Bible, which he treated as a discontinuous revelation, they were unimpressed. They found Christianity as presented in the Holy Scriptures difficult to accept because the events in question had taken place so long ago and so far away.[57] Instead of consulting a book of revelations like the Bible to determine the course of action in any given situation, Africans would simply approach a priest or spirit medium and could expect an answer on a very specific topic almost immediately. If previous applications to the other world had produced different advice, the person in question would have to assume that the entities of the other world had changed their minds or that the structure of the other world had somehow changed in the interim. Since Africans were in almost constant contact with the other world, the potential for a flowing and constantly changing cosmology and religion was obviously enhanced, contributing to the continuing precariousness of the priests.

Although the primacy of continuous revelation in Africa weakened the priesthood, it did not prevent the creation and maintenance of a fairly stable cosmology. Once a group of revelations had established the existence of a set of relations in the other world and between the other world and this world, it was possible to create a coherent cosmology. Revelations might shape fine points in the cosmology, but it need not change much over time. Thus, scholars studying modern African religions can find great similarities between seventeenth-century cosmologies and those of the twentieth century.

This is quite clear in central African religion, where thanks to a comprehensive description of beliefs in a variety of sources (of which Cavazzi's account is perhaps the best) the cosmology matches modern descriptions quite clearly. Wyatt MacGaffey, comparing his own field notes on Kongo religion in the 1960s, those of literate Kongo in the early 1900s, and descriptions found in missionary sources going back to 1500, was able to identify the same basic religious structure. There were, and are, four categories of otherworldly beings: ancestors (the souls of the formerly living); territorial deities (who modern informants believe were also once living but lived so long ago that they have no specific group of descendants), headed by Nzambi Mpungu, the "first man" from whom everyone descends; lesser spirits that can be captured in charms; and harmful spirits that wander in out-of-the-way places (ghosts).[58] On the other hand, although the general scheme of deities and ancestors is the same, modern informants do not always describe the religion in exactly

57 Müller, *Afrikansche*, p. 91.

58 This whole group is described in MacGaffey, *Religion and Society*, pp. 63–135. My edition of Cavazzi will contain a critical apparatus making specific links between his descriptions and MacGaffey's work as well.

the same way. Whether this is the result of our incomplete knowledge of the earlier period or historical change is unresolved.

In compiling a critical apparatus to Müller's description of Gold Coast religion, Adam Jones has attempted the same task for that region, by matching the older description with ethnographic accounts of the early twentieth century. Though less thoroughgoing than MacGaffey's account, it still demonstrates the basic identity of the two belief systems.[59] In Akan one can identify a group of territorial deities, souls of ancestors, and deities inhabiting charms, as in Kongo.

The accounts of Portuguese Jesuits in Sierra Leone and neighboring regions, as well as earlier accounts (Alvaro Velho's account of religion in Sierra Leone dating to about 1506 is one of the earliest and most detailed), have not been systematically matched with modern ethnography. Insofar as these texts have been published, especially by P. E. H. Hair, the task has been handled in much the same way as it was by Jones. In Sierra Leone, one can recognize a group of territorial deities ("corofims" in Portuguese sources, *krifi* today) and ancestors in the other world; ghosts and charm-spirits are found in other regions.[60]

In Sierra Leone, several writers mention the existence of "secret societies," that is, associations devoted to the worship of particular deities and into which entry was restricted to certain people (often dependent upon wealth or status). There was likely to be esoteric knowledge associated with these societies. Alvares even made note of a "university" of several local societies near Cape Mount.[61] Such societies may have had elaborate cosmologies and governed much of religious life, but our knowledge of them then, as now, is limited.[62]

The cosmology of the Yoruba-Aja group of people (including Allada) has been more deeply studied in modern times than many African religions, and genesis tales and cosmologies have been recorded (many written by Yoruba themselves) since the 1840s. These modern cosmologies contain an important series of distinct, named deities who all have universal power (in distinction to the deities of most other regions, who are more territorially specific), although cosmology also recognized the

59 See the edition of Müller in Jones, *Brandenburg*, pp. 158–81 and appendix A19 (incorporating *Afrikansche*, pp. 43–101). Jones's annotations are especially useful for they also include references to other literature of the seventeenth and eighteenth centuries.

60 See the extensive annotated commentaries on Jesuit sources by Hair (e.g., Donelha, *Descrição da Serra Leoa*) and the numerous shorter extracts of Portuguese documents published in *Africana Research Bulletin* (Sierra Leone).

61 On the "contuberia" society, see BSGL, Alvares, "Etiopia menor," fols. 67–70, and de Almada, "Tratado breve," *MMA*[2] 3:351; for the early mention of various societies, see Fernandes, "Descriçã," fol. 131v.

62 We know even less about the seventeenth-century manifestations of the various secret societies of the Igbo and other Niger delta societies, because descriptive material for that region in this older period is lacking.

existence of a host of lesser spirits and ancestors.[63] The significance of these cosmologies for the Americans is that some modern Afro-American religions, notably Santeria of Cuba, rely heavily on them.[64] The Yoruba were virtually undescribed in the seventeenth century, and relatively few were enslaved at the time, but the general Aja cosmologies could be found among coastal people in Allada and Whydah.

James Barbot's description of Whydah from the late 1670s refers to three classes of gods: a high god who was superior to all others; other major gods, one of trees, one of a snake (probably the cult of Dangbe); and a deity of the ocean, who, as in the modern Yoruba cosmology and in distinction to those of other areas, had universal authority. These gods were in turn manifested in a host of lesser gods, to whom people usually prayed via "idols," all of which is similar to religious beliefs in the region today.[65]

Elements of the Allada cosmology were elaborated in Henri Labouret and Pierre Rivet's edition of the Allada catechism of 1658, which revealed that the godhead in those days (as today) was composed of two elements, then known as Vodu and Lisa, but which the catechism identified as God and Jesus Christ (as in the three-in-one concept of the Western Trinity).[66] Though it is easy to recognize general principles in these older descriptions, changes are also notable. One such change concerning Allada is the introduction of the cult of the god Mawu, who has replaced Vodu (of the earlier sources), an introduction that may have taken place during the eighteenth century as a result of the religious politics of the kingdom of Dahomey.[67]

Continuous revelation and the conversion of Africans

Having established the basis for religious knowledge in both traditions, we can now examine the historical circumstances in which their merger

[63] For a comprehensive account, based on genesis stories, see Peter Morton-Williams, "An Outline of the Cosmology and Cult Organization of the Oyo Yoruba," in Elliot Skinner, ed., *Peoples and Cultures of Africa* (New York, 1973), pp. 654–77.

[64] For an assessment of Santeria as a Yoruba religion, see Joseph Murphey, *Santeria: An African Religion in America* (Boston, 1987).

[65] Barbot, "Voyage," pp. 340–5, 354–6 (for Allada). See the similar description in Archives Nationales de France, Depôt des Fortifications d'Outre-Mer, MS.104, "Relation," pp. 53–4. For some details on the religion of the area in more recent times, see Melville J. Herskovitts, *Dahomey: An Ancient West African Kingdom*, 2 vols. (New York, 1937).

[66] Henri Labouret and Pierre Rivet, *Le royaume d'Arda et son evangélisation au XVIIe siècle* (Paris, 1929).

[67] See the interesting argument of Robin Law, "Ideologies of Royal Power: The Dissolution and Reconstruction of Political Authority on the 'Slave Coast,' 1680–1750," *Africa* 57 (1987): 330. Law asserts, however, that the introduction of Mawu was simply the reemphasis of an existing cult. His sources (n. 30, p. 341) mention a Supreme God but do not name him, whereas the Allada catechism clearly does name him, as Vodu.

took place. Not surprisingly, the merger was not simply a meshing of cosmologies, nor was it an intellectual enterprise, but rather it was a complex examination of revelations conducted by both Africans and Christians. The way in which the revelations interacted and were validated determined the nature of the resulting religion, African Christianity.

African Christianity was a form of Christianity in that its followers accepted as genuine a series of revelations in which various otherworldly beings, primarily saints that were recognized by Catholic Christians through their own tradition of revelations, now revealed themselves and were thus accorded status and worship by Africans. At the same time, however, African Christianity was not identical with that practiced in Europe or by most Euro-Americans, in that the resulting philosophy continued to recognize many other revelations as valid, and moreover, it never fully accepted certain points of Catholic doctrine, especially those that reinforced the power of the priesthood (the primacy of discontinuous revelations such as the Bible or Apostolic Succession and the resulting attitudes toward the Sacrament and the role of the papacy).

Most scholars who have taken an interest in the conversion of Africans to Christianity during this period have focused their attention on the Americas and restricted themselves to the conversion of slaves. To some extent, this is a misleading approach, because the conversion of Africans actually began in Africa, and modern scholarship has largely overlooked this aspect of the problem.

Although only a limited number of slaves were Christians before their arrival in the New World (mostly central Africans), the impact of African Christians was much greater than their numbers. This was especially true because African Christians were often chosen as catechists, both formally and informally. Moreover, even if Africans did not convert in Africa, they probably had a greater knowledge of Christianity before embarcation as a result of missionary endeavors and the proselytization of Christian merchants and other settlers than has usually been acknowledged.[68]

Thus, we should consider the conversion of Africans as a continuous process, commencing in Africa and carrying over to the New World. Moreover, we should understand that it was not entirely dependent upon the slave condition or slave sociology, for at the African end, many of the converts were free and even powerful. Such people often shaped the cosmology and direction of Christianity for all African Christians, especially in areas such as Kongo where there was an existing state-supported church.

[68] For an attempt to rectify this, see John Thornton, "On the Trail of Voodoo: African Christianity in Africa and the Americas," *The Americas* 44 (1988): 261–78.

Most scholars who have looked at the conversion of Africans, whether in Africa or the Americas, have sought to explain the process by trying to match cosmologies. Thus, they have treated African cosmologies as fixed rather than as dynamic and undergoing continuous revelation. In order to explain conversion it has then been necessary to show how one cosmology either merged with or replaced another.

For example, Sobel has presented one of the most comprehensive and far-reaching discussions of the conversion of Africans and their descendants in North America. Sobel writes in general terms about an "African Sacred Cosmos" and a related "Afro-American Sacred Cosmos" that developed in the English colonies in North America. In her analysis, the cosmologies of the Africans were fitted to those of various European Christian denominations. In Latin America and Catholic countries in general, where there was a good fit, there developed a satisfactory syncretism, and conversion (at least nominal conversion) took place rapidly. Where the cosmologies differed, however, as in Protestant countries, Africans developed their own new cosmology (the Afro-American Sacred Cosmos) out of their varying traditions, and only accepted conversion when this cosmos began breaking down over time.[69]

Sobel's work in America is paralleled by Hilton's for Kongo, where the most conversions were made in Africa in this period. Hilton, like Sobel, seeks to understand precisely how African beliefs in Kongo merged with Christian ones. Finding an imperfect fit, Hilton concludes that sixteenth- and seventeenth-century Kongo Christianity was only partially a Christian religion, and it was only through the fostering of misunderstandings of the two traditions that African parishioners could really communicate with Christian priests.[70]

If one approaches the issue of conversion in a different way and stresses the dynamic elements (revelations) rather than the more stable ones (cosmologies) the nature of conversion is changed. Africans became Christians not because the priests or the converts sought to match or replace their cosmologies. Instead, they converted because they received "co-revelations," that is, revelations in the African tradition that dovetailed with the Christian tradition. The conversion was accepted because Christians also accepted this particular set of revelations as valid.

The process of conversion, therefore, was really a process of exchanging and evaluating revelations. This can explain why some Europeans accepted the revelations of African diviners and mediums, just as Africans accepted the revelations of Christianity. One should always remem-

69 Mechal Sobel, *Trabelin' On: The Slave Journey to an Afro-Baptist Faith* (Princeton, 1988).
70 Hilton, *Kingdom of Kongo*, pp. 90–103 and passim.

ber that Church control of the process of continuous revelation in Europe was incomplete, and sixteenth-century Europeans often accepted as valid revelations that the Church did not, though it was precisely in this period that the Church was moving decisively to control the process of continuous revelation.

The process is occasionally manifested in Africa, where, for example, Alvares routinely accused the Portuguese who had settled in Sierra Leone of being bad Christians and even witches for following the continuous revelations of local priests.[71] The English who listened to the oracle at Koromantin who predicted the arrival of ships were likewise accepting these continuous revelations, as were many other Europeans in America, as we shall see.

This view of the status of continuous revelation in Europe would help to shape Christianity's attitude toward other religions. It would be easy to ascribe the revelations that formed the basis of another religion to the Devil and then to introduce the Christian series. But to some extent, this approach was limited by the idea that God must have revealed himself to other people besides the Jews, and thus, potentially at least, other people in the world might have had valid revelations from God and not the Devil.

This idea was especially relevant for non-Mediterranean religions. The Devil might have motivated the Jews who rejected Christ or used Roman beliefs to try to halt the spread of Christianity or made false revelations to Muhammed, but he did so in the struggle against Christ. However, in areas of the world where Christ had never been, many believed God would not have allowed the Devil such a free hand.

This was exactly the attitude of the Spanish clergy in confronting Mexican religion, for example. When they heard Aztec stories of Quetzalcoatl, a good king (deified by the sixteenth century) who had been driven from Mexico by trickery and would return in glory, they decided that Quetzalcoatl must have been the Apostle Thomas, bringing word of Christianity, and those who drove him out must have been inspired by the Devil. Thus, they sought to persuade the Aztecs that they were restoring Quetzalcoatl by bringing Christianity, while at the same time vigorously attacking most current Aztec practices as being diabolically inspired by Quetzalcoatl's enemies.[72]

The degree to which Christian clergy sought to explain the revelations of another religion by seeing them as diabolic or divine determined the degree to which they would tolerate aspects of that religion. If a religion

[71] BSGL, Alvares, "Etiopia menor," fols. 110–12v and passim.

[72] See, among others, Diego Durán, *Book of the Gods and Rites of the Ancient Calendar,* trans. Fernando Horcasitas and Doris Heyden (Norman, Okla., 1971).

were discovered to be founded on diabolic revelations, then the Church had no choice but to adopt what I have called an "exclusive" approach to it. All its wisdom must be denied, a course that was clearly reflected in the destruction of the Mexican codices. but if some of the revelations of a religion were discovered to be of divine origin, then much of its content would be accepted in an "inclusive" approach, if it could be cleansed of the diabolic elements.[73]

The decision as to which approach was most appropriate depended on many factors, of course, and in most mission fields both approaches were at work at once, even where some elements of local religion were seen as valid revelations. But on the whole, considerations of power played a big role, so that the Church tended to be quite exclusive in its attitude toward other religions where it exercised clear political power (such as Mexico) and inclusive where it did not (China). This in turn reflected the degree to which the European priest was secure as opposed to precarious. In Africa, Europeans exercised little power over the local society, and hence, the inclusive approach tended to flourish there.

Continuous revelation played a major role in the development of African Christianity, especially when the revelations were acceptable to both parties. This process can be seen clearly in the most successful of the missions in Africa, the mission to Kongo. The conversion experience in Kongo and its subsequent development were of great significance for the development of African Christianity. Kongo's conversion after 1491 began with a series of co-revelations. Shortly after the first official Catholic priests arrived in Kongo, two Kongo nobles dreamed simultaneously of a beautiful woman who beseeched the Kongo to follow Christianity. Moreover, one of them also found a stone, which was "black and unlike any others in the country" near his house, which was shaped like a cross. When King Nzinga a Nkuwu heard these tales, he asked the Christian clergy present for an explanation. They unhesitatingly explained that the woman in the dream was the Virgin Mary and that she and the stone were "signs of grace and salvation" and that the events were "miracles and revelations."[74]

If Christian clergy regarded these events as miracles and revelations, so did the Kongo. As we have already seen, both dreams and unusual stones represent a form of Kongo augury, and thus an acceptable form of revelation.[75] To prove the point more fully, the first church built in

73 Thornton, "African Catholic Church," pp. 152–6.

74 Da Pina, *Cronica*, chaps. 61, excerpted in *MMA* 1:124–5 (a superior edition to others).

75 For a more detailed discussion of the incident as Kongo augury, see Hilton, *Kingdom of Kongo*, pp. 50–1 (but with reservations about her general reconstruction of the cosmological interpretation).

Kongo was dedicated to the Virgin Mary, who had appeared in the dream, and the stone was placed inside it as an object of veneration.[76]

Within a few years, the augury of the first conversion was reinforced by a more direct revelation. Kongo's second Christian king, Afonso, was struggling for his throne against rivals whom he would later define as pagans when a dazzling vision of Saint James Major appeared over the battlefield and scattered his enemies.[77] As with the first revelation, this one was recognized as miraculous and valid in Portugal as well, for when in 1512 the Portuguese king ordered a coat of arms be registered for Kongo, the events of the apparition were incorporated into it.[78] Moreover, Saint James' day (July 25) became the most important holiday of Kongo.[79]

Such co-revelations recurred from time to time. In the seventeenth century Capuchin priests recorded an apparition of the Virgin to a pious woman of São Salvador[80] and another that gave the Count of Nsevo victory over rebels.[81] Missionaries in Kongo's coastal province of Nsoyo heard that the guardian angel of the province had appeared over the church and spoken to the Count of Nsoyo, demanding that he make peace with his overlord of Kongo.[82] Such apparitions were of great interest to the Kongo, who took them seriously, as they were to the priests, who also regarded them as divine revelations.

Sometimes, the miraculous co-revelations took a different and dramatic form. When Queen Njinga was considering allowing priests to come to her base in Matamba in 1654–5 and convert her people, she sought the advice of the three spirit mediums (*xingula*) who served her.

76 Da Pina, Cronica, chap. 62, in *MMA* 1:130.

77 Afonso described this incident in a letter to the king of Portugal about 1509. It was incorporated in several drafts of letters for him to address to his people, his lords, and the pope (all in *MMA* 1:257, 268) and became the source for literary descriptions of the same event (Martin Fernandez de Enciso, *Summa de geographia* [Seville, 1519], pp. 109–10; de Barros, *Decadas* I, bk. 3, chap. 10). Afonso alluded to the apparition and his earlier letter in his letter to Manuel I, 5 October 1514, *MMA* 1:301. A later tradition (recorded in Pigafetta, *Relazione* [ed. Cardona], p. 52) placed the Virgin Mary in the original apparition.

78 See the explanation of Kongo's coat of arms in Afonso to the Lords of His Country, 1512, *MMA* 1:263, 268. This letter was written for him in Portugal, based on information in Afonso's letter of 1509, reflecting Portuguese acceptance of the vision as an apparition.

79 For the holiday in the sixteenth century, see Pigafetta, *Relazione* (ed. Cardona), p. 52.

80 Biblioteca Nacional de Madrid, MS. 3533, Antonio de Teruel, "Descripcion narrativa de la mission del PP. Capuchinos en el reyno de Congo" (ca. 1664), fol.

81 Da Montesachio, "Viaggio," fols. 25–25v; Biblioteca Nacional de Madrid, MS. 3533, de Teruel, "Descripcion narrativa, fol. 99. These priests considered the apparition significant enough to conduct a formal inquiry into it and take testimony from the lord of Masinga ma Nsessa, leader of the rebels.

82 Biblioteca de Palacio, Madrid, MS. 722, Juan de Santiago, "Brebe relacion de lo sucedido a Doce Religiosos Capuchinos que la Santa Sede Apostolica enbió por missionarios al reyno de Congo" (ca. 1647), p. 136.

Each of the mediums was possessed with a different one of her ancestors, and she put the question of whether she should follow Christianity to each of the ancestors who spoke through the mediums. In each case the ancestor urged her to accept Christianity, even though it meant that she would no longer follow the cult of the ancestors. The event was regarded as a miracle by both Calisto Zelotes dos Reis Magros, the Kongo priest who witnessed it, and Antonio de Gaeta, who recorded it, for as they saw it, the Devil himself (the "real" possessor of the mediums) was admitting defeat.[83]

Clerical augury supplemented these dramatic events as well. By the mid-sixteenth century a chain of churches and chapels had been built throughout the country in all the major provinces. Each of these was dedicated to a saint or other figure of Christian cosmology. Although we do not have details on the dedication rites of these churches, there can be little doubt that the patrons were selected by methods employing divination or augury, as they were done in Europe, and these divinations were surely accepted as co-revelations by the Kongo. This was certainly the way Cavazzi proceeded when building the first church in Matamba in the 1660s, for his account is a long description of miracles and revelations.[84]

Such practices when performed in the presence of Kongo people would surely reinforce the concept of revelation. They might also have the effect of creating a fusion of whatever local deities, ancestors, and otherwordly beings had appeared in the area before the conversion and the Catholic saints or angels who now revealed themselves to the priest or other people. Thus, many Kongo might come to understand that the beings who had long revealed themselves had always been saints or angels and, rather than being the fairly local and particular deities that they had believed to inhabit the areas, were universal saints or angels. In the case of Nsoyo, the concept of a particular guardian angel for each person (or, in this case, territory) could merge with the local ideas of territorial deities. The merger of these deities with saints was more interesting, because in Catholic theology saints were both universal and particular. This concept of a particular saint being specific to a locality and yet possessing an aspect that was universal was found in Europe, where the Virgin of this or that town was recognized as being both specific to the town and universal.

The merger of Kongo deities with Catholic saints and angels was one part of the dialogue opened up by the series of African Christian revela-

[83] Antonio da Gaeta, *La maravigliosa conversione alla Fede Santa de Jesu Christo della Regina Singa* (Naples, 1668), pp. 103–4.

[84] MSS Araldi, Cavàzzi, "Missione evangelica," vol. A, bk. 2, pp. 139–41.

tions. In addition, however, Catholic clergy also implicitly accepted that some of the revelations that had taken place prior to the arrival of missionaries had also been valid. When missionaries decided that the Kongo knew the True God, whom they called Nzambi a Mpungu, as Mateus Cardoso argued in 1624,[85] they were also stating that God must have somehow revealed himself to the Kongo under that name.

The implications of recognizing that prior revelations gave Africans knowledge of the True God before the arrival of missionaries were felt in other areas as well. Thus, for example, when the Capuchins and the Spanish Inquisition decided to print a catechism for Allada in 1658 that used "Vodu" as the term for God and "Lisa" as the term for Jesus, they were also implicitly acknowledging that the people of that region must have somehow known of the existence of both God and Jesus before the arrival of missionaries.[86]

European clergy recognized some sort of local revelation in Warri as well. Warri was converted to Christianity in the 1570s and remained committed to the religion until at least the late eighteenth century.[87] We have very little information on the nature of religious worship there, unfortunately, unlike the missions in Kongo, which are thoroughly documented. However, missionaries to Benin in 1637 noted that the people there called Jesus "Yangemeno,"[88] a term that referred to an otherworldly messenger in Itsekeri (the local language).[89]

However, if European missionaries in Africa adopted an inclusive approach to religious conversion and thus recognized both contemporary miracles and ancient revelations to Africans as being of divine origin, they still might view a considerable part of African religious life as being of diabolic nature. We have already seen that they firmly believed that most of the revelations made in their time that did not have a specifically Christian content were diabolic, much as they believed in Europe when the Virgin or other saints appeared or gave messages.

This attitude naturally carried over to their African missions. Once a church was established, perhaps through revelations, then most continuing revelations would be viewed as diabolic, unless they came specifi-

85 [Mateus Cardoso], *História do Reino de Congo* (1624), fol. 14 (modern ed., António Brásio, Lisbon, 1969). The foliation of the original manuscript is also marked in François Bontinck's French edition and translation, *Historie du royaume de Congo (1624)* (Brussels, 1972), where the authorship of this unsigned text is established.

86 The catechism is reproduced photographically in Laboret and Rivet, *L'evangélisation*.

87 See Alan F. C. Ryder, "Missionary Activity in the Kingdom of Warri to the Early Nineteenth Century," *Journal of the Historical Society of Nigeria* 2 (1960): 1–24.

88 Columbino de Nantes to Capuchin superior, 7 August 1637, *MMA* 8:387.

89 Information supplied by Mr. Vini E. Nakpedia, an Itsekeri student at Howard University, May 1987. He called the being in question a "celestial being, an angel or a messenger of God." He also noted that in modern missionary Christianity, Jesus is called by the name "Otun Oriseh," meaning "Son of God."

cally to the clergy. They therefore had no compunction about describing virtually all the mechanisms of African continuous revelation as being diabolic, "vain," or "superstitious" (terms used in the sense of Ciruelo, rather than modern usage).

This was even true of revelations that involved Christian deities. The celebrated case of Dona Beatrice Kimpa Vita illustrates this well. Beatrice, a former medium (*nganga marinda*), was spontaneously possessed about 1701 by Saint Anthony, who remained in possession of her until her death in 1706. Other saints, known both by their own saints' names and as "Little Anthonies" (*Antoni piccoli*), possessed other mediums. During this time Saint Anthony spoke to the people of Kongo, urging them to reconstruct the kingdom, as well as attacking many local divination practices. Saint Anthony routinely went back to Heaven to consult with God, returning to repossess her otherwise dead (or at least comatose) body.

Although Saint Anthony generally respected the missionaries and urged people to support them and the pope, the missionaries never had any doubt that this was a diabolic possession. They denounced her to the king of Kongo, Pedro IV, and eventually had her executed in 1706.[90] Perhaps because in Europe spirit possession was so closely connected with witchcraft (even in New Testament days; Jesus routinely cast out demons who spontaneously possessed people), or perhaps because a spirit medium represented a fundamental challenge to the priests, they could not countenance her function.

Thus African Christianity was accepted in Africa and in Europe largely on the strength of its revelations, especially those that were allowed by both traditions. But of course there was not a complete overlap. Many Africans continued to support priests whose revelations were not in the Christian tradition or were not recognized by the Church, and although many Europeans accepted some African revelations, they rejected others as diabolic. On the whole, Africans were never particularly moved by the argument of diabolic revelation, though they did understand witchcraft as being a process whereby a person might enlist the powers of the other world to harm others. Hence, they could understand the persecutions of African priests by Catholic clergy for working for evil

[90] This story was recounted in detail in contemporary accounts, especially by Bernado da Gallo, the Capuchin priest who witnessed the whole episode. Most of the original documents are reprinted in Teobaldo Filesi, "Nazionalismo e religione nel Congo all'inizio del 1700," *Africa* (Rome) 9 (1971): 267–303, 463–508, 645–68. A French account and translations of these documents are in Louis Jadin, "Le Congo et la secte des Antoniens: Restauration du royaume sous Pedro IV et la 'Saint Antoine' congolaise (1694–1718)," *Bulletin, Institut Belge de Rome* 33 (1961): 411–615. Interpretations of it are found most recently in Thornton, *Kingdom of Kongo*, pp. 106–12; Hilton, *Kingdom of Kongo*, pp. 208–10; MacGaffey, *Religion and Society*, pp. 208–11.

ends, even if they did not agree that the being who was invoked or revealed himself was inherently evil.[91]

African Christianity in the New World

Much of the Christianity of the African world was carried across the seas to America. In addition to the Africans who were themselves Christians, there were also the catechists who helped to generate an African form of Christianity among the slaves who were not Christian. But Christianity in the New World also had some features of its own that separated it from its ancestor and supporter in the Old World.

For example, in Africa, most people were followers of a particular religion and cosmology that was reasonably fixed and stable. For them, there was a specific body of revelations that they had come to accept as legitimate and from which they had constructed a religion and cosmology. Such religions were fairly particular, being confined to a limited region, though not necessarily to a particular nation or ethnolinguistic group. Even though the people of early eighteenth-century Whydah might also accept Yoruba (Lucumie) revelations,[92] or people all over central Africa might accept the revelations of itinerant Vili merchants as being of value,[93] they would not have come into contact with religions from farther away.

In America, however, people from more distant parts of Africa would be brought together. Except for the slave trade, Senegambians would probably not have encountered people from the Slave Coast, nor people from the Slave Coast those of Angola. Thus, Africans from such disparate areas would encounter cosmologies that were quite different from their own. It might be difficult, for example, for central Africans or Senegambians with their concepts of local deities to accept the more universal deities of the Aja group of the Slave Coast.

French Jesuits in the Caribbean, for example, who took an interest in the African background of their slave parishioners, regularly divided Africa into three broad zones. Mongin, in 1682, designated these zones by the names given to God. In Senegambia, the deity was called Reboucou; in Allada, Boudou (Vodu); and in Angola, Gambi (Nzambi).[94]

91 See Thornton, "African Catholic Church."

92 Archives Nationales de France, Depôt des Fortifications d'Outre-Mer, MS. 104, "Relation de Judas," pp. 21, 53–4.

93 For example, see their reputation in Archivio de Propaganda Fide, Scritture Originali nell Congregazione Generale, vol. 249, fol. 243, Francesco da Monteleone, letter of ca. 1656.

94 Mongin to Personne de Condition, May 1682, p. 85. He also recognized that many of the Senegambians were Moslem and the central Africans Christian. For a similar division, see the scheme of de Perse in Charlevoix, *Histoire*, pp. 501–2

In general, this scheme is a good one, designating three broadly different cosmological patterns, as seen already in the discussion of African religions, and corresponding to the minimum cultural divisions of the three "coasts."

As with other aspects of African culture, the primary context in which these diverse traditions were given expression was within the various functions of the "nation." There were therefore probably several national religions functioning at any given time, though mergers may have begun to take place fairly rapidly. The Mexican Inquisition, for example, examined the case of meetings led by a slave named Domingo during which possessed figures were consulted and, among other things, the participants "danced the dances of their nation" and spoke in Kikongo.[95] Herlein, an early eighteenth-century observer in Surinam who had personal experience in both West and central Africa, specifically noted that many Africans in Surinam practiced religions connected with their nation (*stam*).[96]

National religious concepts probably influenced funeral practices, which as we have seen were almost universally a major part of their social and cultural lives. Dealing as they do with the transition to the other world, funerals have a great deal of religious significance and would thus be the most likely place to practice behavior learned through the original revelations made to specific African nations. Numerous witnesses noted that funerals were also national gatherings, at least where we have documentation on the existence of nations. Therefore, it is not a long step to suppose that these celebrations may well have been occasions to recall national religions.

Yet, on American plantations and in American cities, groups from all the nations of Atlantic Africa were thrown together in close proximity. Interethnic friendships and marriages would, of course, increase the contact between people of different nations as well. No doubt they were acutely aware of the different cosmologies and revelations particular to various nations and might well have sought a reconciliation. There was ample reason in this situation for considerable time and effort to be expended to develop a new cosmology on the basis of these varying traditions.

Sobel has argued that these differences might have been sufficiently great to warrant the emergence of a new cosmology in the New World, which she has dubbed the "Afro-American Sacred Cosmos."[97] Africans

95 Case cited in Palmer, *Slaves of the White God*, p. 164.

96 J. D. Herlein, *Beschryvinge van de Volk Plantige Zuriname* (Leeuwarden, 1718), pp. 106–8, with examples cited from experience in both Surinam and Loango. Herlein had also visited the Gold Coast.

97 Sobel, *Trabelin' On*, pp. 58–75.

arriving in the New World merged their separate cosmologies to arrive at a new, joint cosmology that was neither Christian nor exactly like any particular African cosmology. Instead, it was composed of elements making up the considerable common ground of all Atlantic African religions.

Without denying the probability of such a new cosmology, one needs to look more to the revelations as the basis for cosmologies rather than simply trying to match cosmologies as if they were static entities if we wish to understand the merging of African traditions. Although Africans, particularly those from areas where the cosmos was conceived of as containing local deities and ancestors, might assume that they were now separated from their original otherworldly helpers and enemies, they would immediately begin searching for revelations from whatever otherworldly beings might inhabit this New World.

In this task, they would certainly be helped by the numerous priests who had come from Africa on the slave ships with them. Priests were, in fact, fairly numerous. Cavazzi, for example, no doubt contributed to the development of African religions in the New World when he condemned African priests to "pass salt water" (be deported to America as slaves) for witchcraft or consulting with the Devil. Authorities in the New World did not always appreciate his efforts in this regard. When he condemned the main priest of Matamba to slavery in Brazil around 1660, the governor of Rio de Janeiro, Salvador de Sá, recognized the individual from his earlier term as governor of Angola. He ordered the priest returned, and much to his surprise, Cavazzi encountered the same priest returning to Matamba, two years after his condemnation.[98]

The French Jesuit Jean Mongin gives us our best idea of how numerous these African priests, or at least Africans capable of receiving revelations, were in America. When he took up his mission post on the island of Saint Christopher (St. Kitts) in 1678, he made a careful religious survey of the slaves. He discovered 26 people who were "sorcerers" either by their own admission or by renown in a population of 2,400 slaves – enough to make one priest for every 90 people or so.[99] If we accept that these African priests performed divination, interpreted omens, and acted as spirit mediums, then no doubt they also received a substantial number of revelations that were specific to America. They were surely sufficiently numerous to supply an ample number of revelations from which to build a new cosmology.

We can get some idea of the types of revelations that Africans had in the New World because many of them were persecuted by the Inquisition for witchcraft. Whether the people so accused were actually African

[98] MSS Araldi, Cavazzi, "Missione evangelica," vol. B, p. 470; vol. A, bk. 2, p. 155–9.
[99] Mongin to Personne de Condition, p. 83.

priests or not, they were clearly accepted by African people in the Americas as capable of receiving or interpreting revelations. In the general African concept of precarious priesthood, the distinction between a priest and an inspired or talented layperson would, in any case, not be very significant. But the revelations that they received would be the raw material for a new cosmology.

The Inquisition's persecution of Africans receiving revelations was, of course, a continuation of the European practice of suppressing continuous revelation that was deemed diabolic. In 1618, for example, the Brazilian Inquisition heard testimony about a healer and diviner of African origin named Jorge Ferreira who had been summoned in 1615 to heal a sick child through divination and treatments.[100] In investigating another case concerning an unnamed old African slave whom everyone knew as a diviner "who could know future things," the Inquisitor expressly asked one of the witnesses, Francisco Nugueira of Lisbon, if he was aware "that the Devil could divine future things" and if he knew whether or not the old man had made "an implicit or explicit pact with the Devil," though clearly this reflected the Church's view of his power and not that of his clients, both African and Portuguese.[101] Such diviners were common in Brazil, for Dutch conquerors in the 1640s knew that there were many diviners among the Afro-Brazilian population who could treat sick people (especially those who were bewitched) and could predict the arrival of ships,[102] just as they had on the Gold Coast.

The Mexican Inquisition examined hundreds of such cases, many of which have been carefully analyzed by Gonzalo Aquirre Beltrán. Beltrán attempted to identify religious beliefs and customs in terms of African cosmologies as they were understood by anthropologists, rather than simply focusing on the process of revelation, but his work is still impressive. He is able to show, for example, that the use of grave dirt in various ceremonies mentioned in seventeenth-century texts is related to the concept of the ancestors and that the African concept of soul lies behind accusations of "shadow stealing."[103]

As in Brazil, though, we clearly see that Afro-Mexicans were receiving revelations, not only through divination, which is frequently cited, but also through spirit possession. Lucas Olola, for example, was said in 1629 to have received revelations after dancing and apparently falling

100 Testimony of António da Costa, 17 September 1618, in Eduardo d'Oliveira França and Sonia Siqueira, "Segunda visitação do Santo Ofício as Partes do Brasil: Padre Inquisitor e Visitor Licenciado Marco Teixeira (1618–20)," *Anais do Museu Paulista* 17 (1963): 446.

101 Testimony of Francisco Nugueira, 18 September 1618, in ibid., pp. 452–3.

102 Nieuhof, *Gedenkwaerdige Lant- en Zeereize*, pp. 215–16.

103 Gonzalo Aguirre Beltrán, *Medicina y magia: El processo de acculturación en la estructura colonial* (Mexico, 1963), p. 110 and passim.

dead, when he got up "in a fury" possessed by a spirit. Not only did this case of possession impress the Inquisition authorities (who assigned a diabolic origin to it) but it also impressed the Native Americans of the area, who held the possession to be divine, even though they had no local tradition of spirit mediumship.[104] Domingo, the slave who presided over dances in Mexico, received revelations from figures who spoke in Spanish and Kikongo, the figures acting as possessed or speaking shrines.[105]

The Cartagena Inquisition reported similar cases of "witches," most of whom had come from Angola. Fernando Caramoche was denounced in 1632 for informing all the African slaves in Pamplona that he could be possessed and then was possessed and spoke with the assembled people, which included Spaniards.[106] In this regard, it is interesting to note that several cabals of "white witches" (Euro-Colombians engaged in activities designated as witchcraft by the Church) were led by persons of African descent, even though other Afro-Colombians were strictly forbidden from joining the group.[107] Indeed, just as in Africa and in Europe, Europeans did not always accept the Church's definition of witchcraft and supported continuous revelation from their African slaves, just as in Europe or America they supported astrologers, geomancers, and other nonclerical practitioners.

The content of African revelations in the New World was not necessarily identical to that of the Old. For one thing Afro-Americans were in constant contact with Christianity, both from the African Christians and from the ministrations of missionaries and priests. The Mexican Inquisition records reveal clearly that the revelations that many of the accused witches had contained Christian elements from one or another source. The celebrated case of Leonor de Isla, tried in 1622, is a case in point. She was alleged to have called on the spirit of the sea (perhaps the sea god of Whydah mentioned in contemporary descriptions)[108] and could cause the souls of the dead to speak (spirit mediumship). She also started her prayers with invocations of "Jesus Christ, Son of God, Savior of the World," invoking other saints as well. Another healer, Ana de Pinto, invoked the Trinity and sewed bags containing powders but decorated with the sign of the cross on her patients' clothes. Some of the diviners, when asked where they obtained their power, denied the Inquisition's

104 Ibid., pp. 65–6.

105 Cited in Palmer, *Slaves of the White God*, p. 164.

106 Jose Toribio Medina, *La Inquisicion en Cartagena de Indias*, 2d ed. (Bogotá, 1978), pp. 106–8.

107 Manuel Tejado Fernandez, *Aspectos de la vida social en Cartagena de Indias durante el Seiscientos* (Seville, 1954), pp. 127–30.

108 Barbot, "Voyage," p. 340. This is perhaps a cult of the well-known modern sea goddess in Brazil and elsewhere, Yemanja.

claim that they had made some sort of pact with the Devil and occasionally argued that the power came from a Christian saint.[109]

At the same time that mediums were receiving revelations of both an African and European nature, the priests were accepting the essential validity of some elements of African Christianity that had come to the Americas and even were willing to accept the general African concept of God. Thus, French Jesuits like Mongin were willing to accept that Vodu, Reboucou, and Nzambi, who had revealed themselves to Africans, were in fact manifestations of the Christian God, even if they did not accept as valid more current revelations that made up the basis of much of those religious cosmologies.[110]

Christian priests themselves had revelations in the presence of Africans. In America as in Africa, they practiced divination to determine the saints to whom churches, ships, and plantations were to be dedicated. No doubt the Africans who lived on a plantation knew fully well that it was dedicated to a saint, in whose protection they all were entrusted. Pelleprat noted that slaves in Martinique in the 1650s fasted on the eve of the Epiphany because they had concluded that the black king among the three kings was their patron, as St. Ignatius was the patron of the Jesuits.[111]

Occasionally Africans in the Americas participated in specifically Christian revelations. Certainly a dramatic revelation of this sort took place in Costa Rica in 1635 when a mulatta named Juana Pereira found a dark-skinned image of the Virgin Mary, which was subsequently accepted as a Marian revelation and dubbed "La Negrita" and which remains to this day the patroness of the country.[112]

Less dramatic but just as sure were the revelations of saints who were specific to the Americas. Isabella Folupo, a slave from the Rivers area in Upper Guinea, was not a Christian in her homeland, but she witnessed the miraculous cure of the child of her friend Marianna de Capoverde when he was placed on the grave of Pedro Claver. She had no hesitation in reporting to the inquest of 1658 that the soul of the dead priest had been responsible, in so doing confirming both for herself and those interrogating her that he had helped people in this world from the other world.[113]

Pelleprat noted that one fourteen-year-old slave decided to lead a procession of children to the Jesuit chapel when his brother was sick.

109 As reported in Palmer, *Slaves of the White God*, pp. 161–2, 163, 164.
110 Mongin to Personne de Condition, p. 85.
111 Pelleprat, *Relation*, p. 64.
112 Victor Manuel Arrieta Q., *La patrona de Costa Rica*, 2d ed. (San José, 1960). See also Eliado Prado, *Historia de Nuestra Señora de los Angeles* (San José, 1926).
113 BN Colombia, Claver Inquest, fol. 166v.

Both the Jesuits and the Africans were convinced that the other world was responsible for the boy's subsequent recovery.[114]

In the end, European Christianity may have performed the same functions for the development of an Afro-American Christianity as the European languages did for the formation of creole languages. Just as creole slaves or slaves born of inter-national marriages had to learn creole forms of European languages to communicate, so too did Christianity provide a sort of lingua franca that joined various national religious traditions, though in this case not necessarily replacing them.

Thus, the cult of the saints may have made it easier for Africans from different national traditions to merge their own versions of the cosmos through the revelations of Christian otherworldly beings. For example, if the deities of the Aja group, with their universal jurisdiction, could be merged with Catholic saints (as they surely were, for this is a feature of most modern Afro-American forms of Christianity),[115] then they might also be identified with the same saints who had territorial jurisdiction in central Africa. This would allow central Africans and those from the Upper Guinea coast, with their concept of territorially specific deities (save, of course, for their highest deity), to communicate with the Aja group and their universal deities, by combining the territorial and universal aspects within the Catholic saints.

In Catholic areas of the New World, co-revelations of revelations made it easy for Africans to accept Christian revelations, at least as easy as it had been for their compatriots in Africa. Indeed, most Catholic authorities believed that Africans converted easily and indeed actively sought to be Christians. If the Spanish law of 1545 that said "all negroes by inclination want to become Christians and are easy to convert,"[116] was too general, the specific testimony of the Jesuit Luis de Grã to the same effect in 1554 concerning his experience in Brazil was less so.[117] Indeed, the archbishop of Lima felt that it was sometimes a hardship, because one could not determine which slaves were not baptized, because they all claimed to have been baptized so as not to be taken as "savages."[118]

If clerical opinions were not enough, the slaves themselves expressed this general desire to be Christians, or at least an interest in communicat-

[114] Pelleprat, *Relation*, p. 63.

[115] See, e.g., Roger Bastide, *African Religions of the New World*.

[116] Cedula printed in Richard Konetzke, ed., *Colección de documentos para la historia de la formación social de Hispanoamérica*, 5 vols. (Madrid, 1953–62), 1:239.

[117] Luis de Grã to Diego Mirón, 27 December 1554, in Serafim Soares Leite, ed., *Monumenta Brasiliae*, 4 vols., *Monumenta Historica Societatis Iesu* (Rome, 1956–60), 2:147.

[118] Text cited in Bowser, *African Slave*, p. 238.

ing with Christian otherworldly beings, perhaps as being the specific deities of the New World. There could be no more eloquent testimony than the fact that runaways usually followed the Christian cult in their settlements. Thus, the soldiers who attacked the runaway settlement near Lake Maracaibo in 1585 found one runaway who "went around with a sobrepellia and bonnet and who said mass and baptized the children who were born."[119] A similar priest, practicing Christian rites but not ordained, lived in King Bayano's settlement in Venezuela about the same time.[120]

Dutch reports about Palmares contended that the people followed the "Portuguese religion" in 1647, and a report of 1675 noted a well-tended altar and chapel with images.[121] The clerics in Hispaniola believed that the saints' images in the runaway community there were "idols," but they reported that the runaways said Christian prayers like the Hail Mary and the Lord's Prayer.[122] Yanga, the leader of the runaway community in Vera Cruz, felt sufficiently strongly about the Christian faith that he risked giving away the location of his settlement to secure the services of a priest, and when the Spanish captured him, he was found in his chapel saying prayers.[123]

Of course, whatever the slaves might have felt about becoming Catholics, in Protestant areas there were serious barriers to converting slaves. Settlers from the Netherlands and England refused to believe, whatever their pastors told them, that becoming a Christian did not give a slave freedom, and thus they actively sought to discourage it. Even where pastors continued to preach to slaves, as in Dutch New Netherlands, they doubted that the slaves were truly being converted, believing that the slaves sought conversion to obtain freedom or lighter work loads.[124]

Ligon was severely rebuked when he sought to discuss religion with a slave in Barbados, for example.[125] Maurile de S. Michel, a French priest who knew both Dutch and English policies in the Caribbean, denounced the policy of keeping their slaves from the Christian faith for fear they would thus gain their freedom.[126] As a result, the French constantly tried

119 Luis de Rojas to king, 16 April 1586, in Trochis de Veracoechea, *Documentos*, pp. 79–80.

120 Agudo, *Historia*, bk. 9, chap. 10. Agudo thought his performance of the mass was a parody, but the people seem to have taken it seriously.

121 Barlaei, *Rervm per octennivm*, p. 203; "Relação das guerras feitas aos Palmares de Pernambuco . . . de 1675 a 1678" (ed. Drummond), *Revista do Instituto de Historia e Geographia do Brasil* 22 (1859): 306.

122 Probanza of 22 November 1622 and letter of 1662, cited in Dieve, *Esclavitud*, pp. 491–2.

123 Alegre, *Historia* (ed. Burrus and Zubillaga), 2:175–6 and 180.

124 See the testimony of the pastor Selyns in 1664, in Jameson, *Narratives of New Netherlands*, pp. 408–9.

125 Ligon, *Trve and Exact History*, p. 50.

126 Maurile de S. Michel, *Voyages des Isles Camercanes*, 2d ed. (1651; Paris, 1653), pp. 80–1.

to preach surreptitiously to English slaves whenever possible, which they did when they shared the administration of Saint Christopher.[127]

In addition to the problems created by the resistance of masters to catechizing the slaves for fear it might allow them to sue for freedom, the form of religion may have been more difficult to present. Ever since Luther had proclaimed the formula *sola scriptura,* Protestants had attempted to accept a more scriptural form of Christianity, turning farther away from the concept of continuous revelation than the Catholic church had. Thus, as Müller found, attempting to bring the gospel to the Gold Coast as a book of ancient revelations, Protestants might have found Africans unwilling to accept the word of their masters on the relevance of these messages.

In such Protestant areas, of course, the slaves were less able to receive revelations of Christian beings, or at least to have these revelations recognized by either the religious leaders or the Euro-American settlers. There is little documentation of exactly what such slaves did believe, although if we accept Herlein's testimony on slave religion in Surinam as being typical for other Protestant areas, they probably developed fairly strong American variants of national traditions, which included perhaps revelations of beings of both Christian and Native American origin. They may well have merged these into a uniform Afro-American Sacred Cosmos, as Sobel has proposed, though so far all this must remain speculation. She provides some evidence for revelations taking place within the African and Afro-American community, and if the experience of other parts of the Americas is indicative, surely some of these were Christian, especially in areas such as South Carolina, where African Christians were fairly numerous.[128]

But for North American slaves, conversion that was acceptable by both groups had to await the Great Awakening of the mid-eighteenth century. The Great Awakening's theology relied heavily on personal conversion experiences to create a rebirth and to strengthen faith. These experiences, which were often produced in emotional mass meetings, were, in effect, revelations of the Holy Spirit. The emphasis placed by the Baptist preachers in North America and the Moravians in Jamaica on the mediation of the Holy Spirit provided this Christian tradition with a continuous revelation that both Euro-American Christians and the African and Afro-American slaves could share. Since these revelations appeared from a Protestant source, they gave a different version of the other world than African Christianity or Catholicism. In the end, insert-

[127] Archivum Romanum Societatis Iesu, Francia, vol. 45, fols. 410–412v; Biet, *Voyage*, pp. 276–7, 292.

[128] See Thornton, "Trail of Voodoo," for the significance of African Christians in South Carolina.

ing the Holy Spirit into the act of conversion resulted in the dramatic conversion of slaves in Protestant countries. Now, the Afro-Baptist in North America or Myalist in Jamaica could practice a new form of spirit mediumship and thus accept a set of revelations that was acceptably Christian and yet conformed to their concepts of religious truth.[129]

The changing and merging of religious philosophies in the Atlantic world were thus another example of the complex cultural dynamic that gradually transformed Africans and especially Afro-Americans. Religious conversion, as it is conventionally understood, was therefore not simply a process of Europeans forcing Africans to accept an alien religion, nor did the practicing of traditional African forms of continuous revelation in the New World represent some sort of heroic religiocultural resistance. Instead it was a spontaneous, voluntary act on the part of the Africans, convinced by the same types of revelations that had shown them their own gods that the other world was in fact inhabited by a group of beings who were identical to the deities of the Europeans.

129 For the North American colonies, Sobel, *Trabelin' On*, pp. 99–135. For Jamaica, see Monica Schuler, *Alas, Alas Kongo: A Social History of Indentured African Immigration into Jamaica, 1841–65* (Baltimore, 1980), pp. 34–6. My use of these two books represents a reinterpretation of these secondary works in a way that does not necessarily reflect the analysis of their authors. The period lies outside this study and must be taken as indicative and speculative rather than documented.

10

Resistance, runaways, and rebels

If Africans did manage, in many instances, to re-create and transmit African cultures in the New World, one cannot forget that these slaves still faced exceptionally difficult times. That they might have formed families, socialized with each other, developed self-help organizations, and the like did not take away from the fact that slaves were usually highly exploited. Even when they were more privileged, they were still blocked from full participation in the greater community. Under such conditions there are always people, both exploited and privileged, who see no way to change or improve their overall lot under the normal rules of the system. These people sought to go beyond the circumstances imposed upon them by slavery and demand more than their masters or rulers were willing to give them freely.

These discontented people were the resisters, rebels, or runaways. Each in his or her own way and according to his or her own means sought to alter the system and its rules. For some, it was a way of bargaining for better conditions, for themselves or for their group; for others it was a way of seeking to empower themselves, to break free, or to determine their own destiny; and for a few, a means to turn the tables on their masters and rulers.

Scholars analyzing resistance have generally approached it in several conflicting ways. Historians fired by cultural nationalism, for example, have seen the rebel slaves as seeking to recover African culture and values or to resist racism and deculturation.[1] But others, motivated by economic history or Marxism, have seen resistance and rebellion as be-

[1] See, e.g., Leslie Manigat, "The Relationship between Slave Revolt, Marronage and Revolution in St. Domingue-Haiti," in Rubin and Tuden, *Comparative Perspectives*. Similar attitudes are found in the extensive work of Oruna Lara, "De l'Atlantique à l'Aire Caraïbe: Nègres cimarrons et révoltes d'esclaves," 4 vols. (Ph.D. diss., Paris, 1971); see the summary of his elaborate cultural theory in his contribution to Rubin and Tuden, *Comparative Perspectives*.

ing workplace-related, akin to strikes or walkouts and perhaps to social revolutions. Thus, although most agree that newly arrived Africans were most likely to run away or rebel, there is no agreement on the relative contribution of the African background to dissent.

To some degree, however, resolving the conflicting claims of cultural contribution and direct action in an economic sense must rely on differentiating different types of resistance. In doing this we must distinguish three levels of slave actions that were against their masters' interests. First, there are work slowdowns, low morale, and petty holdups in the work process, what is often called "day-to-day" resistance. The other two levels are what Gabriel Debien calls *petit* and *grand marronnage*.[2] In French, the term *marronnage* includes all forms of absenteeism, from running away to rebellion; the English cognate "maroon" refers only to people who have run away permanently.[3] Petit marronnage refers to slaves who temporarily absented themselves from work either to take an unofficial holiday or, as a means of bargaining, to show their masters their true value. Grand marronnage, on the other hand, involves slaves seeking to break free from the control of their masters either to found their own society elsewhere or to seek refuge in a society that would give them greater freedom and opportunity. The idea of grand marronnage can be extended to include those few rebellions or plots that sought the complete overthrow of the system of colonial slavery and the replacement of the masters' government with one led by the former slaves.

In each of these levels cultural background and class or economic background play different roles. In the day-to-day and petit marronnage forms of dissent, class is predominant, but in grand marronnage, the African background (the cultural factor) plays a much more significant role. In grand marronnage the African background helped to shape the type of resistance slaves would use, the nature of their action, and the attitudes that those who rebelled or ran away would carry to their places of refuge. Thus, in some aspects of resistance and revolt, purely class or situational dynamics apply, but in others, the fact that the slaves came from Africa and not somewhere else gave a special dimension to the resistance. This dimension was a product of particulars of the slaves' backgrounds, the patterns of the slave trade, and ultimately the nature of African society.

2 Gabriel Debien, "Le marronage aux Antilles française au XVIIIe siècle," *Caribbean Studies* 6 (1966): 3–44.

3 English "maroon" derives from the Spanish term *cimarron,* which is used for all sorts of runaways (human and animal) as well as wild forms of plants and animals. Spanish sources often also refer to any rising, even if it aims at no more than escaping slavery, as a "rebellion" and all runaway communities as "rebels" even though these rebels do not necessarily seek to overthrow the existing order.

Day-to-day resistance and petit marronnage

Ever since Raymond and Alice Bauer published their discussion of "day-to-day resistance" in nineteenth-century plantations in the United States in 1942, the idea that planters' descriptions of slaves as lazy and careless might reflect on the slaves' will to resist exploitative labor more than their personal habits has been an attractive one.[4] Although his work is specifically related to the nineteenth-century United States, Eugene Genovese has probably effectively silenced the idea that somehow masters' ideas about slave work habits were rooted in African modes of labor. He argues that such resistance is universal, and examples cited from Africa (mostly modern Africa) are not a special part of African culture but a reaction to modern colonial exploitation. Instead, he sees the slave attitudes toward work and their masters' reactions to it more in terms of typical preindustrial work patterns (though perhaps with underlying class conflict) than as a cultural conflict. If Africans had certain attitudes toward work, it was more a product of their coming from a preindustrial society than any specifically African background, and moreover, the same conflicts could be found in Europe and elsewhere.[5] Present-day scholars thus tend to see the plantation as a workplace in which workers and managers contended with each other over basic conditions, rather than a cultural or revolutionary confrontation.

Therefore, modern researchers have focused on day-to-day resistance as a good example of this type of bargaining chip. Work discipline, tool management, and absenteeism were the weapons available to slaves to require their masters to abolish bad customs, punish sadistic overseers (or reconsider the masters' own sadism), or increase slaves' free time, time available for their own work, rights to visit or live with family members, and the like.

Following the Bauers' lead, many have seen simple malperformance of work as a form of resistance. But perhaps it is not enough, as Genovese suggests, simply to ascribe all poor performance in the workplace to resistance, for one should not necessarily assume that some sort of conscious resistance to slavery or even to exploitation lay behind the slave who performed work unenthusiastically or carelessly.

The data from the sixteenth and seventeenth century broadly support Genovese's position, although we do not possess exact data on the cultural dimension of resistance to exploitation in Africa for the same time period. For example, Jean Goupy des Marets's precious inventory

[4] Raymond and Alice Bauer, "Day to Day Resistance to Slavery," *Journal of Negro History* 27 (1942).

[5] Eugene Genovese, *Roll, Jordan, Roll.*

of the Remire plantation in Cayenne in 1690 provides some interesting information. Goupy des Marets gives a brief assessment of the work performance of each of the slaves in the inventory. He describes no less than twenty-three of the sixty-one able-bodied workers (both male and female) as "malingerers" or a similar term implying that their work performance was substandard by their own free will. The comment is helpful because he also mentions health or physical disabilities that might limit performance.[6]

The number seems large and certainly suggests that at the very least, the workers at Remire were relatively uninterested in the optimum operation of the estate. Chronic malingering was not simply a bargaining tool, perhaps, but an expression of alienation one might find in any situation of exploitation. It is quite possible that under other conditions they might well have worked harder. Remire was a sugar estate, and sugar production was regarded as the most difficult and dangerous work to perform. Perhaps slaves on other types of estates or performing other types of work would be more enthusiastic. However, Remire was an estate on the "Pernambuco model," which allowed slave families and free time for growing provisions and constructing a community. Slaves on the more alienating sort of plantations, such as Sergipe do Conde in Brazil, might not have been even this enthusiastic (though the surviving records of Sergipe do not provide this sort of information).

In the end, perhaps, the idea of resistance through poor work performance is an interesting one, but one that is untestable. There are too many factors that enter into a person's decision to work below his or her potential, even in modern industrial and office settings, for modern scholars, with their limited documentation, to make judgments about broad implications.

Gerald Mullins's work on slave runaways in eighteenth-century Virginia has provided a model that has come to dominate research and influence conclusions drawn from other times and places on the issue of petit marronnage. For him, running away was a means that slaves had to withhold their labor temporarily from their master in order to negotiate for better conditions. In this way it was akin to a strike, but not simply confined to workplace situations, because masters also controlled such things as family formation and time for growing one's own crops and socializing.[7]

6 BM Rouen, MS Montbret 125, Goupy des Marets, "Voyage," fols. 83–90 passim.

7 Gerald Mullins, *Flight and Rebellion: Slave Resistance in Eighteenth Century Virginia* (New York, 1972). For a recent study that emphasizes the bargaining aspects of slavery in the same place and time, see Mechal Sobel, *The World They Made Together: Black and White Values in Eighteenth Century Virginia.* Brazilianists have also begun examining slavery there with the same eye. See the review essay of recent literature, Eduardo Silva, "Por

What little we can see of this phenomenon in the early documentation confirms the existence of petit marronnages throughout the Atlantic world. The Spanish priest Alonso de Benavides, assigned to Vera Cruz in 1609, noted a sort of fluctuating population of people who absented themselves from plantations and went to runaway communities in the hills, later to return. One of Benavides's clients, Francisco Angola, fled to the hills when his master would not let him marry a woman from another estate. He joined other runaways for a time but eventually returned to get Benavides's help in marrying according to Church law.[8] Inquisition documents from Mexico confirm other examples of slaves who apparently came and went freely, sometimes being absent for days, sleeping at friends' houses, only to return later.[9]

In the French Caribbean, laws of the slaveholding society made distinctions between slaves running away permanently and absenting themselves from their place of work for short periods of time and returning voluntarily; the punishments stipulated by law varied accordingly.[10] The English Caribbean obviously faced a similar problem, for a public proclamation of the governor of Barbados in 1656 warned all masters to apprehend "strange negroes and wandering servants that shall come within plantations or houses or wandering abroad." On the basis of this and other evidence, Hilary Beckles has proposed that many slaves enjoyed a sort of semifreedom by leaving one master and taking refuge among slaves belonging to someone else, so that one could conceive of a small community of unattached people (both slaves and bondspeople) who were absent from work but not from the society as a whole.[11]

These "halfway" runaways, who were absent but not trying to get free, were likely to be able to use their behavior as a tool for serious bargaining with their masters. The laws provided stiff, even harsh punishments for runaways, but masters did not have to punish their runaways up to the full extent of the law. A valuable slave might well be

uma nova perspectiva das relações escravistas," *Sociedade Brasileira de Pesquisa Histórica: Anais da V Reunião* (São Paulo, 1986), pp. 141–7. The North American conclusions have been transported to some extent by Stuart Schwartz, whose article "Resistance and Accommodation in Eighteenth Century Brazil: The Slaves' View of Slavery," *Hispanic American Historical Review* 57 (1977): 69–81, has been influential in Brazil.

8 Testimony of Alonso de Benavides to Inquisition, 24 March 1609, in George P. Hammond, ed., *Fray Alonso de Benavides' Revised Memorial of 1634* (Albuquerque, N.M., 1945), pp. 105–6.

9 Cited in Alberro, "Noirs et mulatres," pp. 64–5.

10 See legislation studied in Lucien Peytraud, *L'esclavage aux Antilles Françaises avant 1789 d'après des documents inédits des Archives Coloniales* (reprint ed., Pointe à Pitre, 1973), pp. 348–9.

11 Hilary Beckles, "From Land to Sea: Runaway Barbados Slaves and Servants, 1630–1700," *Slavery and Abolition* 6 (1985): 82–3.

pardoned and even rewarded for his or her return rather than punished for absenteeism.

An excellent case of just such a negotiation is that of Pedro Quiroga, a master founder at the royal copper mines of Cocorote in Venezuela, whose life is documented in the records of that establishment in the 1630s and 1640s. As revealed in Miguel Acosta Saignes's studies of these records, Quiroga was a constant runaway. Yet it is clear that he had no intention of running away permanently, often not leaving the establishment or perhaps only traveling to the city for some days or weeks, often returning of his own accord. Obviously, Quiroga possessed a valuable skill and knew it well. The records show that he was rewarded and welcomed far more than he was punished for his absences, and for him, at least, they were clearly a form of negotiation.[12]

Scattered references in the documents of the estates or of observers confirm that at least some running away elsewhere was also of this sort. Nicholas González, a Jesuit priest and companion of Pedro Claver, testified in the inquest of 1658 that on one occasion an Angolan slave woman came to Claver to announce her intention of running away "to the mountains" (no doubt to the runaway camps that surrounded Cartagena in the mid-seventeenth century) as a result of her "great displeasure with her mistress on some occasion." This slave must surely have known that Claver could not help her and would advise her to return (as indeed he did after showing her a picture of souls burning in hell), but she did manage to enlist his help in interceding with her mistress to improve her condition.[13] Similarly, Claver's superior, Alonso de Sandoval, noted that he was shocked by one mistress who would beat her slave simply for being absent, implying that such absences were not necessarily grounds for punishment but perhaps for negotiation.[14]

It may well be that only slaves who were particularly valuable or important, such as skilled workers or domestic servants, would be able to use such tactics, as seen in the case of the Cape Verdian slave Manuel de Saint-Hyago (Santiago) serving on the Remire plantation in Cayenne in 1690. He was the only one of the ninety-two slaves in Goupy des Marets's inventory who was listed as a habitual runaway, and in 1675 a previous master had cut off his ear for it. But he was also regarded as the best worker on the estate, and as a Cape Verdian may well have also been a linguist and go-between for Senegambian slaves in general, for he had been raised as a Christian and may have had wide contacts through

12 Acosta Saignes, *Vida*, pp. 167–8.
13 BN Colombia, Claver Inquest, fol. 41–41v.
14 De Sandoval, *Instauranda*, pp. 194–7.

commerce in Africa before his shipment to America.[15] Perhaps these factors and the fact that he was a good worker in a gang in which over a third of the able-bodied force was considered to be malingering made him valuable enough to be able to bargain.

For other slaves, running away might be a way of changing masters. Obviously, property laws within most colonies would not allow this to take place, but in Catholic countries such as Mexico, a slave convicted of certain religious crimes could be seized by the Church.[16] Because clerical masters were often perceived as kinder (and certainly would have been more tolerant of the family life of married slaves), some slaves may well have deliberately committed blasphemous acts to take advantage of the law.

More often, however, the slaves would flee from one colony to another, preferably from one national jurisdiction to another. Such flight was common in the Caribbean, where several nations competed for control. Thus, for example, when Dutch freebooters raided Hispaniola in 1626, many slaves took the opportunity to flee to the mountains, and a number joined the freebooters on their further expeditions.[17] Later, the English and French came to share several small islands, and sometimes an easy trip over water was all it took for a slave to go from one island (and nation) to another. The fate of such slaves was often a point of conflict between colonial powers, was dealt with in numerous treaties, and probably was never resolved.[18] When the English drove the French out of Antigua in 1664, for example, the Sieur de Barre was assisted by English slaves escaping with him from the English areas.[19] Even casual travelers might be accosted by escaping slaves complaining of bad treatment, as was Froger, when he visited Brazil in 1696, though he had to deny them help for fear of being accused of stealing them.[20]

Runaways could rarely hope to win complete freedom. They often fled to other slave colonies or ships carrying slaves. Such slaves hoped that by offering themselves to new masters they might obtain a better position. Perhaps they had increased their value by learning a skill or by

15 BM Rouen, MS Montbret 125, Goupy des Marets, "Voyage," fol. 85. The Claver Inquest suggests that Christian Cape Verdians could often serve in such a capacity; see BN Colombia, Claver Inquest, fol. 125v (testimony of Manuel de Capoverde).

16 For examples, see Palmer, *Slaves of White God*, pp. 93–106, drawn from documents of the Mexican Inquisition.

17 See testimony of Pedro Angola, Margarita, 1 March 1626, and testimony of Mateo Congo, Adrian Cornieles, Gonzalo de Bangos, and others, 15 June 1626, in Irene Wright, ed., *Nederlandsche zeevaarders op de eilanden in de Carabische Zee en aan de Kust van Columbia en Venezuela*, 3 vols. (Utrecht, 1934–5), 1:53–4, 79.

18 Du Tertre, *Histoire* 1:502.

19 Journal of de Barre, in Clodoré, *Relation*, pp. 253–4.

20 Froger, *Relation*, p. 147.

becoming fluent in a European language, but their old master would not recognize the new talent or skill, whereas a new master might.

Inter-European warfare offered similar opportunities, with a chance of complete freedom as well. When the Dutch invaded Brazil in 1624, for example, they were greeted by many runaway slaves who offered military service with bows and arrows, old Spanish swords, round shields, and firearms, and they celebrated their victories over their former masters with drumming and dancing.[21] The Dutch did not wish to give them all their freedom, for they felt that their principal motive was to loot and steal, but some did acquire it in reward for their services.[22] Indeed, the offering of military service in this war did become a bargaining tool, for the Portuguese soon found themselves granting freedom to slaves who would serve on their side, and these slave regiments proved decisive in the war with the Dutch.[23] When the French occupied the western end of Hispaniola (modern Haiti) in the late seventeenth century, one slave named Padrejan, later to become a famous rebel, killed his French master and ran away to the Spanish part of the island in 1679 and obtained freedom.[24]

Many slaves therefore sought to improve their situation through running away or at least absenting themselves from work. No doubt many absentees suffered punishment, and many perhaps gained little from returning. For many, running away was closer to a modern strike or work stoppage than an attempt at liberty. Such motives may well have been the reason for runaways staying close to or even within their place of enslavement or running to foreign masters. Surely they may also have been the reason why many returned voluntarily.

On the whole, this evidence strongly suggests that these slaves, whatever their African background may have been, were in fact engaging in economic bargaining. There is no particular reason for us to imagine that this type of bargaining was a uniquely African form of resistance or that the slaves' particular background (unless prior training or experience in Africa gave them skills to use as bargaining chips) should have contributed to it.

21 Johan Gregor Aldenburgk, *Reise nach Brasilien, 1623–26* (modern ed., S. Pl. L'Honoré Naber, The Hague, 1930), pp. 32, 44–5, 51–2.

22 Johannes de Laet, *Jaerlijck verhael van de verrichtinghen der geoctroyeede West Indische Compagnie* (Amsterdam, 1644). Portuguese trans., José H. Duarte Perreira and Pedro Souto Maior, *Historia ou Annaes dos Feitos da Companhia Priveligiada das Indias Occidentaes* (Rio de Janeiro, 1916), p. 235.

23 Barlae, *Rervm per octennivm*, pp. 160–1.

24 Pierre François Xavier de Charlevoix, *Histoire de l'Isle espagnole ou de S. Domingue*, 2 vols. (Paris, 1730–1), 2:126. This text is based largely on memoires of the Jesuit Father Jean Baptiste le Pers, who lived in Saint Domingue for some twenty-five years in the late seventeenth and early eighteenth centuries.

Grand marronnage

However, those slaves who ran away with the intention of completely leaving the slave society and making a life for themselves elsewhere may well have found inspiration, motivation, and perhaps even important skills available from their African backgrounds. The most important contributions of the African heritage were the military training that many slaves had, mostly from having served in African armies. African aristocratic and military culture helped to fire rebellion and provide leadership.

Grand marrons fled to wilderness areas or to Native American communities, sometimes attacking those who stood in their way. Others rose up violently or at least plotted to do so, occasionally causing the slave owners to believe that they intended to take over whole colonies. This was Debien's grand marronnage and was clearly not designed to improve the slaves' position within slave society. It was here that Africans were the most active and where African background was most significant.

Most scholars have noted that rebels and runaways who sought total freedom were more often African-born than not. Some scholars have argued that the destruction of African traditions was essential for the smooth running of American slavery. Thus, the newly arrived Africans, the most vulnerable and least integrated of the American slaves, might provide the intractable element that sought revolt against all odds or sought to escape completely from a society that was too alien to them.[25]

Another way of viewing permanent flight, especially among nationalist scholars, was to see it was a way that newly arrived Africans could reconstruct the lost world of Africa, or perhaps as a sort of cultural nationalism. This might be particularly true of higher-status Africans who were particularly humiliated by their enslavement but could regain leadership roles only by taking charge of a runaway community. Although such views might be regarded as reactionary by modern scholars, especially those who see revolt in terms of class struggle, they do consider the African background as more important than the runaways' present circumstances.[26]

However, present-day scholarship is less impressed with this approach. Rather than see rebels and runaways as unintegrated Africans,

[25] Jean Fouchard, *Les marrons de la liberté* (Paris, 1974), and Manigat, "Revolts." This idea is somewhat developed in Orlando Patterson, *Sociology of Slavery.* Some less romantic interpretations may be found in Monica Schuler, "Ethnic Slave Revolts in the Caribbean and the Guyannas," *Journal of Social History* 19 (1970): 289–325.

[26] Gabriel Debien, "Le marronage aux Antilles françaises au XVIIIe siècle," *Caribbean Studies* 6 (1966): 3–44; Yvan Debbasch, "Le marronage: Essai sur la désertion de l'esclave antillais," *L'Anée Sociologique* 3 (1962–3): 117–95.

they have again stressed class conflicts.[27] Debien has been especially prominent in this approach, and the African factor plays only a small role in the forms of resistance he analyzes. Perhaps, the grand marron was simply a slave who had no particular skills or bargaining power (Africans falling into this position more frequently than locally born slaves) and could not hope to achieve any improvement in status or condition by running away and returning or by being absent. Alternatively, permanent runaways might have committed some serious crime or particularly violent act against their masters in a moment of passion and now feared that they could only be severely punished should they return. If Africans were most frequently rebels, it was because they had fewer opportunities and understood the system less well and not because of their African background.

The evidence of the sixteenth and seventeenth centuries certainly does not support the idea that rebels and runaways were making some general revolutionary statement or even trying to end the institution of slavery. They were members of an exploited class, but they were not explicitly engaging in class warfare. Rebels and runaways seem to have been primarily motivated by fairly limited objectives, principally escape from a system where they saw their prospects limited and the ability to bargain too small.

But at the same time, very often the African background of the slaves did help shape the direction of revolts, influenced timing and tactics, and validated leadership. The runaways certainly did follow African models in shaping new societies when they were in a position to establish themselves permanently in runaway communities. Thus, although not denying the overall class and social forces in shaping the urge for most slaves to revolt or run away, we ought not to forget the role of the African background in the specifics of revolt. Skills, organizations, and outlooks from the African background came to the fore in the more dramatic attempts of rebels and grand marrons, especially since so often these people were drawn from recently arrived Africans. By examining first the runaways who separated from the colonial society and then the rebels, we can see how this background fitted into these strategies.

In order to assess the relative importance of class versus background as factors in grand marronnage, it is important to understand all that went into a successful escape or rebellion. The difficulties of founding

27 See classic statements of C. L. R. James, *The Black Jacobins: Toussaint L'Overture and the San Domingo Revolution* (London, 1937); Herbert Aptheker, *American Negro Slave Revolts* (New York, 1943); Eric Williams, *From Columbus to Castro: The History of the Caribbean* (Thetford, Norfolk, 1970); and more recently, Edner Brutus, *Révolution dans St. Dominque* (Brussels, n.d. [1974]).

wholly new communities, often in inhospitable land, and the challenges of cooperation or conflict with Native Americans and maintaining communities in spite of settler hostility all had to be met before runaways could become independent. The African background of slaves may have been unimportant in dealing with this new environment. Only after we have understood the general dynamics of escape and rebellion can we see the significance of the slaves' background.

Escape from slavery: the dynamics of grand marronnage

In order to escape and found their own, independent and free settlements, or, as Barry Gaspar has termed it, undertake "avoidance protest,"[28] slaves had to find or found a community that could be reached and where runaways would be taken in and given freedom. The vast majority of grand marrons escaped to runaway communities, typically away from European control. A good number of the uprisings aimed, not at overthrowing existing society, but at leaving it – perhaps violently, but leaving nevertheless. Thus many episodes termed revolts in contemporary literature were really no more than armed and violent escapes or, to use prison terminology, "breakouts."[29]

For example, the Hispaniola slave revolt of 1522, often held to be the first major revolt in the Caribbean, seems to have had escape as an objective as much as taking towns or expelling the Spanish.[30] Likewise, the numerous and violent Jamaican revolts of the late seventeenth century generally culminated in a flight to the hills to found or join a runaway community.[31] Though European observers occasionally thought that runaways were seeking to drive the colonists out, and even put such terms in their mouths, it is unlikely that most "rebels" had this in mind. Instead, they sought by violent means to establish themselves somewhere outside the slaveholding community.

Ultimately, founding or joining some sort of independent settlement was the real goal of most of those who ran away or rebelled. Comprehending runaways therefore requires first an understanding of the type of communities that were needed to sustain them in the conditions they desired. It seems that those who ran away hoped to find an already existing community beyond European jurisdiction that was willing to take them in. Native American settlements were an obvious potential

[28] David Barry Gaspar, "Runaways in Seventeenth Century Antigua, West Indies," *Boletin de Estudos Latinoamericanas y del Caribe*, June, 1979, pp. 3–13.

[29] The difference is obscured in Spanish documents by the fact that the term *alzado* means both "runaway" and "rebel" (i.e., someone who seeks to overthrow established order).

[30] Described in Oviedo, *Historia*, bk. 2, chap. 100.

[31] For details, see Michael Craton, *Testing the Chains*, pp. 75–81.

shelter, especially if they were hostile to the colonizers. Alternatively, runaway slaves could found new communities of their own or join those of previous runaways. Since many of these communities were under the direction of former slaves, it is not surprising that here African models and skills were employed to create the new society.

If Native Americans made it known that they welcomed runaways or if earlier runaways had established secure camps, then the remaining slaves would know that for them the task would be much simpler than it was for the pioneers. Furthermore, as we saw in the case of the Angolan domestic slave mentioned by Nicholas González in the Claver inquest, the existence of successful runaway communities made bargaining easier for those slaves who probably had no real intention of seeking to break away.

For these reasons, it was important for colonial societies to neutralize situations that favored running away, even if the number of people actually in these hideouts was few, for they had an impact on colonial society far beyond their numbers. Therefore, we should not be surprised to see how often the return of runaway slaves was a touchstone of negotiations between Native Americans and colonial societies, or how diligently colonial authorities attempted the difficult military task of wiping out runaway settlements in mountain and forest. This can also explain why the colonists, failing in military solutions, sought to enlist runaways in their own security forces by recognizing their independence in exchange for guarantees to return other runaways.

In view of the difficulty that Africans first arriving in a strange land would have in founding a community, the formation of the earliest communities probably took time or fortunate circumstances. A good number arose quite accidentally, commonly from the wrecks of slave ships in a hospitable region. Often, of course, the wreck of a ship was simply a disaster for the slaves, who, chained and kept below decks, were drowned. Alonso de Sandoval recorded the loss of a ship with no less than 900 slaves in Cartagena harbor, in spite of the relatively easy prospects of rescue of a valuable cargo.[32] Such disasters would clearly also follow ships that wrecked under even less favorable circumstances.

Nevertheless, some shipwrecks did result in enough slaves surviving to form a community. Spanish explorers in Panama in 1513 reported the existence of a community of Africans there who had come off a wrecked ship a few years earlier, at the very dawn of the transatlantic trade.[33] Likewise, in the mid-sixteenth century, a wrecked ship from Angola

[32] De Sandoval, *Instauranda*, p. 100.

[33] The primary documents are contradictory; for an interpretation see José Antonio Saco, *Historia de la esclavitud de la Raza Africana en el Nuevo Mundo* (Barcelona, 1879), pp. 75–8.

allowed the formation of the community called "Angolars" in São Tomé.[34] Other cases were reported later in the Caribbean; for example, Governor Molesworth of Jamaica noted in a report of 1686 that the island held a community that had formed after a shipwreck around 1670.[35]

Many communities seem to have formed in otherwise-uninhabited lands, but for many salvation lay in Native Americans who sheltered them. After a shipwreck on the coast of Peru around 1533, the twenty-three slaves it was carrying joined (and then led, according to the sources) the local Native American community.[36] Vázquez de Espinosa records the existence of one such shipwrecked community of five hundred slaves on the island of "Potapotura" near Grenada that formed around 1600 after a slave ship had been captured by the Caribs, who kept the slaves themselves.[37] Several mixed communities in the Caribbean were said to have originated from shipwrecks: the "Zambos Mosquitos" of Nicaragua from one about 1641[38] and the Black Caribs of Saint Vincent from a shipwreck on Bequia Island in 1675.[39]

Although accidents might allow independent communities of Africans who were no longer slaves to form, they were still relatively few. Most settlements had to be created by runaways from the plantations and estates in spite of the difficulties of building self-sustaining and defensible communities in unfamiliar areas. As with the communities that arose by accident, these can be divided into two groups: those that were created in uninhabited areas and those that formed near or among Native Americans.

For regions without native inhabitants, like São Tomé, the going must have been difficult for these pioneer runaways. But in spite of the dense virgin rain forest that covered the island, slaves did run away. Already in 1528, João Lobato, ordered to establish a sugar plantation for the king on the island, reported that some of his slaves had run away "to the woods."[40] Moreover, by at least 1535, runaways had formed a commu-

34 Their early history is recounted on the basis of early eighteenth-century local traditions and records that no longer exist by Manuel Rosário Pinto, "Rellação do descubrimento the o prezente . . ." (1734), bk. 1, chap. 12, fol. 9 (modern ed., António Ambrósio, "Manuel Rosário Pinto (a sua vida)," *Stvdia* 30/31 [1970]: 205–329).

35 Molesworth to William Blathwayte, 28 September 1686, summarized in *Calender of State Papers: America*, 44 vols. (London, 1860–1969), 12: no. 883, p. 251.

36 See the careful study of the original texts in Jacinto Jijón y Caamaño, *El Ecuador Interandiano y Ocidental antes de la conquista castellana*, 2 vols. (Quito, 1941), 1:72–7.

37 Vázquez de Espinosa, *Compendio*, nos. 198–9.

38 Documents cited in Michael D. Olien, "Black and Part-Black Populations in Colonial Costa Rica: Ethnohistorical Resources and Problems," *Ethnohistory* 27 (1980): 15–16; Floyd, *Mosquito Coast*, pp. 22–5.

39 See William Young, *An Account of the Black Charaibs in the Island of St. Vincent's* (London, 1795; reprint, 1971), p. 6. Young's account is implacably hostile to the Black Caribs but used considerable early documentation.

40 João Lobato to João III, 13 April 1529, *MMA* 1:506, 517.

nity, for that year the judges of the island petitioned the Crown to give them funds to attack the "mocambo [Kimbundu term for a runaway settlement] with many people who go off into the wilderness."[41] In Barbados, too, early slaves ran away to the wooded interior of the island, but as the planters gradually cleared and cultivated the island, runaways had to seek shelter elsewhere, often fleeing in boats to nearby islands.[42] Gaspar has argued that the same process took place in Antigua; during the early phases of settlement, the mountainous interior offered runaways an opportunity to form camps, but that in time the clearing and settlement of the island reached a point where there was not sufficient room for runaways to maintain themselves.[43]

The origins of the maroon communities of Jamaica were somewhat different. The Native American population of the island disappeared as a distinct community shortly after the Spanish conquest in the early sixteenth century, and slaves who wished to run away could not hope for help from that quarter. When the English invaded Jamaica in 1655, many slaves took advantage of the situation to flee to the mountains, where they built several independent communities in the confused period between the English attack and a final peace between two sets of runaway communities in 1662–3 and 1670.[44]

In most other parts of the Atlantic world, however, Native Americans were present and contributed either directly or indirectly to the escape of slaves and the building of free communities. In some cases, it was simply that Native American military power inhibited the ability of the colonial forces to operate freely in the wilderness areas; in other cases, slaves joined or settled near Native American communities.

Runaway communities among Native Americans formed quickly, especially if the Native Americans were unconquered or hostile to the European colonists. Nicholás de Ovando was already expressing concern about slaves running away to the Tainos of Hispaniola in 1502, when there could hardly have been more than a handful of slaves there, and his successors echoed his worries.[45] Runaway African slaves assisted the Taino ruler Enrique in his rebellion against the Spanish in 1519–32, and although his rebellion was crushed and Native Ameri-

41 Judges of São Tomé to Crown, 6 September 1535, *MMA* 2:46.

42 Ligon, *Trve History*, p. 105; Beckles, "From Land to Sea," pp. 81–9.

43 D. Barry Gaspar, *Bondsmen and Rebels: A Survey of Master–Slave Relations in Antigua: With Implications for Colonial British America* (Baltimore, 1985), pp. 172–85.

44 Mavis Campbell, *The Maroons of Jamaica, 1655–1796: A History of Resistance, Collaboration and Betrayal* (Trenton, N.J., 1990), pp. 16–24.

45 Dieve, *Esclavitud* 2:434. Although one might see Columbus's campaigns of 1495 as the conquest of Hispaniola, in fact, Spanish forces did not really conquer most of the island until about 1510, and even then, many of the Taino leaders were more like independent allies than subjects of the Spanish.

can–African cooperation effectively ended, the runaway communities that formed during that period continued to dominate the mountains of Hispaniola.[46]

Likewise, early African runaways in Mexico fled to the yet-unconquered Zapotecs, where they were reportedly "going around rebelling throughout the country" in 1523.[47] Runaway Africans and Native Americans cooperated in anti-Spanish wars in Cuba, being suppressed only in 1529.[48] When the Spanish armed their slaves in their attempt to conquer Santa Marta (Venezuela) in 1550, the slaves decided to "leave their condition of slavery" and "follow their own desires . . . and live among the Indians," resulting in a revolt/breakout that severely threatened the colony as 250 slaves rose up to join the Native Americans.[49] Elsewhere in Venezuela, a rising in the copper mines of Buria in 1552 resulted in the slaves running away to the Jirajara of the mountains. There they formed a racially mixed community that dominated the area.[50] In Panama, as early as 1546, the city fathers tried to tax the citizens to form groups to hunt down the runaways,[51] and by the 1550s the runaways had joined with Native Americans of the area and were harassing travelers between the Atlantic and the Pacific.[52]

The prospect of slaves running away and joining Native American communities was sufficiently distressing to warrant Spanish action even if the natives were not in rebellion. A court in Nicaragua sentenced Pedro Gilofo to death in 1540 simply for being in a Native American community, for the court noted that many slaves were in Native American communities, and it feared the effect on other slaves.[53] Obviously, the dangers of unsubdued Native American communities who might harbor slaves were an important concern of colonial authorities.

Even if the Native Americans did not harbor slaves, their very presence might allow runaways more freedom to develop their own communities. Such circumstances may have contributed to the formation of the great runaway state of Palmares, which grew up in the woods and mountains behind the Portuguese plantations on the coast of Alagoas in Brazil. The Portuguese had to conquer the Tupinambá to gain control of

46 Ibid., pp. 434–57.

47 Antonio de Herrera y Tordesillas, *Historia general de los hechos de los castellanos en las islas y tierra firme del Mar Océano* (modern ed., 17 vols., Madrid, 1934–57), decada 3, bk. 5, chap. 8.

48 Bartolomé Ortiz to Council of Indies, 30 March 1529 and 8 November 1529, quoted in Saco, *Historia*, p. 174.

49 Herrera y Tordesillas, *Historia general*, decada 8, bk. 6, chap. 12.

50 Acosta Saignes, *Vida*, pp. 261–3.

51 Saco, *Historia*, p. 193.

52 Alvaro de Sosa to Carlos V, 15 May 1553, cited in Saco, *Historia*, p. 206.

53 Processo de Pedro Gilofo, 1 September 1540, Andrés Vega Bolaños, ed., *Documentos para la historia de Nicaragua*, 17 vols. (Madrid, 1954–7), 6:496.

the coast and establish their plantations, but the immediate interior lay under the control of the Tapuya (Aimoré). The Tapuya were implacably hostile to the Tupinambá and proved an insurmountable barrier to Portuguese penetration any farther into the interior for the best part of the next century.[54] But they were obviously not a barrier to runaway slaves, who fled in fair numbers to the region. Already in 1602, Diogo Botelho, the first governor of the colony, was required to make a systematic attack on the runaway settlements.[55] Indeed, similar attacks continued on an average of every two or three years, but without success. The presence of hostile Ţubinambá and Tapuya groups and the absence of local allies made all these attempts futile. It was only in the 1680s, when Portuguese cattle ranchers advancing up the São Francisco River finally succeeded in recruiting Tapuya allies and in conquering the rest that a Portuguese–Tapuya force conquered Palmares and resettled the area with loyal Tapuya troops.[56]

This Brazilian case illustrates some of the dynamics of the relations between the slaves and Native Americans. Runaways seeking aid in native societies did not always find a good reception. Native American attitudes toward helping runaway slaves depended on many factors, including the structures of the Native American societies themselves, their relations with the Europeans, and the goals of their leaders. Sometimes these converged to help runaways; sometimes they contributed to the destruction of runaway communities or to runaways being returned to their masters.

In Mexico and Brazil, where early alliances between African runaways and Native Americans were significant, when Native Americans were conquered or became allied with the Europeans, they maintained good relations by returning runaways. Hence, although the documents of Sergipe do Conde in Brazil occasionally mention slaves running away "to the Indians," they also mention Native Americans returning runaways.[57] Likewise, the books of the Cortés hacienda in Mexico show the same set of relations.[58]

In the eastern Caribbean, the Caribs remained unconquered but in close contact with major slaveholding societies throughout the period before 1680. From an early time, slaves ran away to the Caribs from the

54 Hemming, *Red Gold*, pp. 93–6, 209, 346–51.

55 Vicente do Salvador, *História do Brasil, 1500–1627*, 7th ed. (São Paulo, 1982), bk. 40, chap. 40, p. 287.

56 Raymond Kent, "Palmares, an African State in Brazil," *Journal of African History* 6 (1965): 354–6. See documents on the attacks in Ernesto Eannes, *As guerras de Palmares (subsídios para a sua história)* (São Paulo, Rio de Janeiro, Recife, and Pôrto Alegre, 1938), vol. 1 (only volume published), pp. 194–213.

57 "Livro de Contas," in *Documentos* 2:87, 144, 157, 174, 222.

58 Barrett, *Sugar Hacienda*, pp. 84–5.

Spanish possessions in the Greater Antilles or joined their ranks as soldiers, for a letter from the governor of Margarita to the city council of San Juan (Puerto Rico) of 1546 warned it to be on the lookout for Caribs and "the blacks who go with them."[59]

The opportunities for Carib–African cooperation were greatly increased when English and French colonists began settling in the Lesser Antilles and the Guyanas, the home bases of the Caribs. The French chronicler du Tertre notes that many slaves ran away to the Caribs after 1640 in Martinique and Saint Christopher, being openly received by them. This hospitality continued as long as relations between France and the Caribs were strained and indeed was repaid when war broke out between the French and the Caribs in 1654, for the runaways (who had formed separate communities under Carib protection) joined the Caribs and were responsible for the most destructive depredations.[60] The English also had cause to complain of this Carib alliance with runaways, for the English governor William Stapleton complained in 1667 that the Caribs posed the biggest threat to English settlements in Antigua and that of the 1,500 Carib effectives, some 600 were African bowmen.[61]

But this congenial relationship only lasted as long as Carib hostility did. When the French ended the Franco–Carib war with a peace treaty, the Caribs agreed to return runaways and help expel the remaining ones. They were slow to do this, however, and their failure was one major cause for the French campaign to drive the Caribs from Martinique in 1658. In 1660, after another episode of war, the Caribs again agreed to return runaways, this time with more conviction.[62] However, the Caribs continued harboring runaways from the English possessions, as indeed they continued playing off the two European powers against each other.[63]

The English were able to obtain a similar treaty with the Saint Vincent Caribs, but as in the French case, it was subject to constant renegotiation – from 1670 to 1680 the Caribs returned runaways (in fact, they sold them back), but then after 1680 they began regarding them as "an addition to their nation." Ultimately, the Saint Vincent Caribs agreed to return runaways when the runaway community became so numerous and powerful that it threatened Carib security, and they even went so far as to enlist English help in attacking the runaways.[64]

59 Cabildo de San Juan, Diego Ramos, and Sebastian Rodriguez to the king, 10 and 14 May 1546, in Vincent Murga, ed., *Historia documental de Puerto Rico*, 2 vols. (Rio Pedras, n.d. [1956]), 1:227.
60 Du Tertre, *Histoire* 1:502–3, 467–8.
61 William Stapleton, in *Calender of State Papers (America)* 5: no. 1152, p. 499.
62 Du Tertre, *Histoire* 1: 468–9, 521, 544, 575–7.
63 On the general situation, see William Willoughby to Lord Arlington, 25 May 1667, *Calender of State Papers (America)* 5: no. 1488, p. 470; and Stapleton letter, p. 502.
64 Beckles, "Land to Sea," pp. 89–91.

On the mainland as in the islands, the natives played a role in assisting runaways. As on the islands, much of the attitude of the Caribs was determined by the exact state of their relations with the Europeans. This on-again–off-again attitude is clearly revealed in the police registers of Dutch Surinam, where slave revolts, flights to the Caribs, Carib–runaway cooperation, and treaties to ensure that runaways were returned can all be found.[65] Obviously this was not confined to the Carib world, for it was no doubt a similar situation that caused the "Piscattaway and other Nations" of Native Americans in Maryland to sign a treaty with the English colonists in 1666 guaranteeing the return of runaway slaves.[66]

Native American reception of runaways did not depend only on the relations between Native Americans and colonists, it also depended on the dynamics of the Native American societies themselves. Many Native American groups were slaveholding societies themselves, for like African society, they did not have the institution of private property in land. Consequently, slaves who fled to them might find themselves enslaved, sometimes under difficult conditions that made slaves decide to return to European settlements.

Once again the case of the Caribs can serve as an illustration. The Caribs were a militant people who often raided neighboring peoples or other Carib groups for slaves, especially females. The earliest description of Carib society, from 1493, was taken from testimony of a Taino woman from Hispaniola who had been captured in a raid, and noted that Carib households often built up their strength through incorporating captives.[67] Although an often repeated myth maintained that the Caribs always ate their male captives, the testimony of escaped captives taken in Puerto Rico in 1580 shows that this was clearly untrue, for many male Spaniards were held in Dominica in more or less permanent captivity (indeed, enough had run away that Dominica contained a community of European runaway slaves for a time).[68]

65 Van der Linde, *Surinaamse suikerheren*, pp. 90–6.

66 Reproduced in J. Thomas Scharf, *History of Maryland from the Earliest Period to the Present Day*, 3 vols. (Baltimore, 1879; reprint, 1970), 1:291.

67 Letter of Dr. Alvaro Chanca, undated, but probably written in late 1493, in Martin Fernandes de Navarette, ed., *Coleccion de los viages y descubrimientos que hiceron por mar los españoles desde fines del siglo XV*, 5 vols. (Buenos Aires, 1945), pp. 331–5; see also Americo Vespucci to Pedro Soderini, 4 September 1504 (describing voyage of 1498–9), Spanish translation in Joaquín Gabaldorón Márquez, ed., *Descubrimiento y conquista de Venezuela*, 2 vols. (Caracas, 1962), 1:43–54. In commenting on this text, Las Casas places the events in Paria (it might also be Trinidad) and provides slightly different structures for society; see *Historia de las Indias*, bk. 1, chap. 164.

68 Baromé, "Spain and Dominica," pp. 35–7, quoting testimony in Arquivo General de Indias (Seville), Patronato, legajo 179, no. 4, an extensive inquest into the depredations of the Caribs in Puerto Rico, 1558–80.

Thus, when the Caribs harassed Puerto Rico, as they frequently did in the sixteenth and early seventeenth centuries, they often carried off African slaves and employed them in their own society as slaves.[69] One such slave, the Afro–Puerto Rican Luiza de Navarette, who returned to the island in 1576 after four years of Carib slavery, described the conditions of her captivity (and that of many other slaves of the Caribs) in harsh terms, detailing mistreatment and degrading work.[70] This was so much a pronounced part of Carib policy toward slaves of the Spanish that one official, Sancho de Alquiza, estimated in 1612 that as many as two thousand African slaves were in captivity in the Carib islands.[71] Vázquez de Espinosa noted that as many as five hundred such slaves were kept on the island of Potapotura (near Grenada) when a slave ship fell into Carib hands around 1600.[72]

The taking or using of Africans as slaves by the Caribs was not as characteristic of the earlier period of French and English settlement in the Lesser Antilles, because the general hostility between the Caribs and the settlers often engendered Carib alliances with runaways. But even in this setting, there were instances of the Caribs' penchant for enslaving people affecting their actions. Return and treatment of runaways took a curious turn in the earlier period of French settlement in Grenada, for example. Here, the Caribs accused the French of stealing their African slaves in 1658, after a French group was accosted by a party of Africans who had run away from the Caribs, complaining of bad treatment and "barbaric customs." The upshot was a series of protracted negotiations and ultimately hostilities between French and Carib groups over the insistence of several French settlers that they would continue to harbor African slaves who had fled from the Caribs.[73]

Because of the uncertainties inherent in flight to Native American communities, many African runaways decided to build their own separate communities near the native societies. In building their own settlements, African runaways naturally enough looked to the social institutions of their homeland for reconstructing their society. Had Native Americans absorbed them completely, such institutions would have been irrelevant, but since in so many cases runaways could not trust the Native Americans, a new start was necessary. This was true of the numerous runaway

69 Ibid., pp. 31–6. For one such raid, see Cabildo de San Juan to Carlos V, 30 October 1530, in Murga, *Historia documental* 1: 6–8.

70 Ibid., 35–6.

71 Sancho de Alquiza to king, 11 February 1612, cited in Baromé, "Spain and Dominica," p. 37.

72 Vázquez de Espinosa, *Compendio*, nos. 198–9.

73 [Bénigne Bresson], *Histoire de l'isle de Grenade en Amérique*, fols. 80v–83 and passim (modern ed. Jacques Petitjean Roget, Montreal, 1975). The text is anonymous, but Petitjean Roget has determined the author by internal evidence; see pp. 26–35.

communities of Hispaniola in the early sixteenth century. Although the runaways assisted the Taino ruler Enrique in his revolt against the Spanish in 1519–32, they suffered when he signed a treaty with the Spanish that enlisted his support against African runaways. Fortunately for the Africans, their having organized in separate settlements meant that they were not immediately hurt by this development and, indeed, took revenge by massacring the Taino inhabitants of several villages.[74]

The politics of Native Americans, with their numerous small political units often hostile to each other, favored the formation of separate runaway communities. When Sir Francis Drake made his alliances with the runaways of Panama in the 1560s, they lived in settlements entirely under their own control, even though earlier observers noted their frequent alliances with the Native Americans of the area.[75] However, the runaways in Drake's day had cause to fear that the Spanish and their Native American allies might attack their camps; it is obvious that the local Native American groups varied greatly in their alliances.[76]

The runaways of Buria and the Orinoco valley (Venezuela) and the Mosquito Coast (Nicaragua) formed racially and culturally mixed communities with Native Americans, but the more common situation was for culturally distinct communities to coexist side by side, even where Native Americans were allied to the runaways, as in Panama and the runaway camps around Cartagena.[77] This was the situation in the French Caribbean during the extensive Franco–Carib wars of the mid-seventeenth century, and it ensured the survival of the runaway communities even after the Carib defection in 1658–60.[78] When the English pirate Henry Morgan was making alliances with the natives of Gracias a Dios (near Cartagena) in the 1680s, he noted that "the Negroes they have among them remain apart, in order to follow their own customes."[79]

The ultimate goal of most runaways, whether they fled to Native Americans or built their own communities, was the establishment of a secure, self-sufficient community under their own leadership. By the

74 For a detailed survey of the role of runaways in Enrique's rebellion, see Dieve, *Esclavitud* 2:442–45.

75 See the communities near Nombre de Dios and their alliance with natives, in Alvaro de Sosa to Felipe II, 15 May 1553, cited in Saco, *Historia*, p. 206. For English comments, see Philip Nichols, *Sir Francis Drake Revisited* (London, 1628), pp. 7–8, 29–30, 52–5. A modern edition of this text, with the original pagination marked, is Irene A. Wright, ed., *Documents Concerning English Voyages to the Spanish Main, 1569–80* (London, 1932), pp. 253–312.

76 Nichols, *Francis Drake*, p. 34.

77 Francisco de Murga to king, 30 December 1630, in Roberto Arrazola, *Palenque, Primer Pueblo libre de America* (Cartagena, 1970), pp. 62–3. This book is a collection of documents interspersed between narrative and commentary.

78 Du Tertre, *Histoire* 1:457–9, 502–3, 521, 544, 575–7.

79 Esquemeling, *Bucaneers*, p. 238.

middle of the seventeenth century there were probably hundreds of runaway communities scattered from one end of the American world to the other. Most were small, one-village societies of fifty to perhaps a few hundred members. In a few cases villages coalesced to form small states: The Panama marrons had built such a small, loosely coordinated organization by the end of the sixteenth century, and another like it would emerge in Jamaica by the end of the seventeenth century. Only in the Palmares region of Brazil, where by 1680 there were thousands of runaways living in a fairly centralized polity of more than a dozen separate communities, did the runaways form sizable states that threatened colonial society.

A few of these communities succeeded in obtaining formal recognition from the colonial governments that guaranteed their independence. But victories of this sort did not come without cost and had consequences for the nature of runaway society and leadership. Once they were well established, runaway communities themselves were not free from their own forms of class system or inequality, including slavery. Moreover, the independent communities often behaved in the same way that Native American communities did, especially in that they put their own survival well ahead of ending slavery or helping later runaways escape.

Runaway communities: African background and the politics of independence

Earlier writers saw these independent runaway communities as islands of liberty and imagined them as free republics. When this image was tarnished by careful study, some seemed clearly disappointed that the runaways were not more "revolutionary" in their outlook, or that those who had recently experienced slavery should so rapidly install it in their own communities. An expectation of revolutionary sentiment seems fairly clear in the search for class consciousness in the writing of radicals such as Genovese and Craton.

In fact, a fuller understanding of the African background of the slaves would help in understanding the attitudes of runaways and their leaders. The slaves came from societies where slavery was normal and widespread, and as we shall see, the leadership of many of the communities was drawn from the African upper class, who, had it not been for the misfortune of their own enslavement, would surely have owned and traded in slaves themselves. Of course, coming from a slaveholding society does not mean that one wishes to be a slave oneself or that one (especially if not specifically from a slaveholding social group) would feel compelled to institute it after regaining freedom. However, whatever the sentiments of the individual runaways may have been about freedom, military necessity often required strong leadership, and this often came with hierarchical authority and inequality.

Perhaps the most important reason that African institutions were transferred to the runaway communities instead of some sort of generalized libertarian democracy was the necessity for military defense. Not only was a military background helpful in the runaways' initial decision to escape, but it was essential in defending the new communities against both Euro-American and native hostility. We should remember that a large percentage of the slaves were captured in wars and thus had at least some experience with African military systems. Hence, runaway communities almost always were under strong, even autocratic leadership. The slaves' military background would ease their acceptance of a military government, particularly if the leaders exercised the same sort of authority and used the same symbols that characterized African armies. In areas with professional armies, such as the Gold Coast and Angola, military skills (especially in hand-to-hand fighting with lances, for example, or equestrian skills among the Senegambians) played an important role in helping the community.[80] In other instances, and after 1680 as warfare was transformed in many parts of Africa, the mass induction of Africans into armies certainly helped to make deference to military orders common on the part of the general population and hence of most of the American slaves.[81]

The possession of military skills and generalship certainly helped slaves to run away, especially if the breakout was violent, and certainly contributed to the military survival and even expansion of the runaway communities. For example, many of the early leaders of the Hispaniola runaways were Wolofs, who the Spanish poet Juan de Castellanos, a resident of Puerto Rico, thought were great fighters, "with vain presumptions to be knights":

> Destros son los Gilofos y muy guerreros,
> Con vana presunción de caballeros.[82]

These Wolofs were probably captured during the numerous wars that wracked the Jolof kingdom in the early sixteenth century,[83] and many, if not most, of the males had probably seen extensive military service in Africa, where knowledge of horses and how to stand up to cavalry

[80] On professionalism of the military in Angola, see Thornton, "Art of War"; for the Gold Coast, see Kea, *Settlements*, pp. 130–63.

[81] On this revolution in the art of war, see Kea, *Settlements*, pp. 164–6, the only systematic study. Similar changes probably took place in Angola and the Slave Coast as well at about the same time.

[82] Castellanos, *Varones illustres*, elegy 5, canto 2.

[83] These wars are detailed in Jean Boulègue, *Les ancien royaumes du Sénégal, I, Le royaume de Jolof* (Paris, 1988).

charges was critical. Not only did the Wolof slaves who revolted in 1522 show great coolness in the face of a Spanish cavalry charge, opening their ranks and allowing the Spanish horse to pass through, then wheeling to meet the countercharge,[84] but they created a cavalry of their own and used it to harass the sugar plantations of Hispaniola in the 1540s.[85]

Certainly runaways had a penchant for selecting leaders whom European authorities often called "kings" and who may have been aristocrats at home. African aristocrats were, of course, the leaders of African armies, and quite apart from whatever residual respect Africans might have had for their social betters, they would have valued those virtues that made them capable of defending their communities.[86] King Bayano, leader of the runaways in Venezuela, was reputed to have come from aristocratic stock, as did Nyanga, leader of the Vera Cruz (Mexico) runaways in the early seventeenth century.[87] Even if the leaders were not literally African aristocrats transported by the accident of slavery to America, their use of symbols and marks of authority derived from African military culture provided a reference point for their African-born followers. Africa, after all, had seen military fate place upstarts and even ex-slaves in positions of authority.

However that may be, the Europeans often accepted their claims of nobility and notions of authority. Castellanos wrote verse honoring Sebastian Lemba, leader of the Hispaniola runaways in the 1540s, calling him an "illustrious man [*varone*]." He extended his praise to other runaway leaders as well.[88]

One of the first things that runaways did was to choose a king and captains, as they did in the Santa Marta revolt/mass flight in 1550.[89] In 1604 Domingo Bioho, leader of an important runaway community near Cartagena, ruled in conjunction with a "captain general" named Lorencillo, and their settlement had a complicated system of ranks that the Spanish officer Jeronimo de Suazo believed included a "treasurer, war lieutenant [*teniente de guerra*], bailiff [*alguazil mayor*]," and others.[90] These Spanish titles may have been a sign of a certain Americanization of these

84 The encounter is described in Oviedo, *Historia*, bk. 2, chap. 100.

85 Detailed in Dieve, *Esclavitud* 2:445–54.

86 One might add that in European peasant revolts, the closest analogy to slave revolts in European history, leadership also often fell into the hands of the lesser nobility, precisely for the same reasons.

87 Simon, *Historia*, bk. 9, chaps. 9–13. Alegre, *Historia* (ed. Burrus and Zubillaga) 2:176.

88 Castellanos, *Varones ilustres*, elegy 5, canto 2. Ibid., elegy 12, canto 3, on Miguel, leader of the Buria community of 1552.

89 Herrera y Tordesillas, *Historia*, decade 8, bk. 6, chap. 2.

90 Jeronimo de Suazo to king, 25 January 1604, in Arranzola, *Palenque*, pp. 41–2. Suazo refers to this settlement as a "republic," but not in the sense of its being a democratic one.

Africans or, alternatively, like so many European descriptions of Africa, simply a translation of another social system.

Although we cannot trace its development in detail, the fairly autocratic state of Palmares consisted of over a dozen settlements, some of them numbering in the thousands.[91] People from Palmares told members of the Dutch expedition to Palmares in 1644 led by Jan Blaer that their king demanded absolute obedience.[92] Kent and others have suggested that the autocratic politics may have been an influence of the Imbangala, a military organization in Angola that created large armies from its captive slaves, making promotion available to anyone with competence regardless of their former ethnic or class background. It eventually founded states, like the kingdom of Kasanje.[93] Certainly Angolan ethnic leadership was noticeable in Palmares, for the people interviewed by Blaer noted that the "Angola negroes" especially feared the king,[94] and the titles of the officers in the 1680s were mostly drawn from Kimbundu, and there was a "captain of the Angolans."[95]

If military necessity created this centralized leadership, the status of runaway communities required its maintenance. European settlers took great pains to destroy them. The settlers were generally unwilling to ever live in peace with runaways, if for no other reason than their presence made it easier for more slaves to flee or gave bargaining power to those who might threaten to run away. Therefore, virtually no runaway community was safe. Large armies were raised to go into the hills to search for them, like the "cleanup" campaigns organized against the Hispaniola runaways by Alonso López de Cerrato in 1545–8,[96] the many attacks on the Palmares settlement,[97] and the extended Spanish campaign against the Panama communities in the 1580s.[98] Northern Europeans did this as well, for the English government in Jamaica certainly expended considerable effort to round up and control runaways from

91 For details, see Kent, "Palmares." As Kent himself noted, the idea that Palmares was a "republic" rather than a monarchy of some sort developed from eighteenth-century histories of Brazil strongly influenced by romantic and liberal ideas and not from the primary sources.

92 Jan Blaer diary, published by Alfredo de Carvalho, trans., "Diario da viagem do capitão João Blaer aos Palmares em 1645," *Revista do Instituto Archeologico e Geographico Pernambucano* 10 (1902): 92–3.

93 Kent, "Palmares"; see also Stuart Schwartz, "Le Brésil des esclaves fugatifs," *Histoire* (September, 1981). For contemporary details on the organization of the Imbangala, see Purchas, ed., "Strange Adventures," in Ravenstein, *Strange Adventures;* and MSS Araldi, Cavazzi, "Missione evangelica," vol. A, bks. 1 and 3.

94 Blaer diary (ed. Carvalho), p. 93.

95 "Relação das guerras" (ed. Drummond), pp. 304–5, 310–20.

96 Dieve, *Esclavitud*, pp. 445–53.

97 Kent, "Palmares."

98 As documented in Wright, *English Voyages*, 215–38, passim.

the 1670s onward.[99] Indeed, it is probably safe to say that the European colonists spent as much time and military energy fighting runaways and invading their territory as they spent fighting Native Americans along the unconquered frontier.

Thus, military necessity required that most camps be heavily fortified, like the camp near Mariscal Castellanos (Lake Maracaibo region of Venezuela), which was compared to a "New Troy" by its attacker, Luis de Rojas, in 1586,[100] or the palisaded fort built by runaways in Zaragosa (New Granada, modern Colombia) that resisted an extended siege in 1599.[101] Padrejan, a runaway from the French Saint Domingue in 1679, built a strongly stockaded fortress in the hills that greatly troubled the French colonists.[102]

Attacks on these camps were the scenes of desperate defense and audacious courage, as was witnessed in the campaign against the Cartagena runaways fortified in the Cienaga de Mantua. The Spanish leader, Jeronimo de Suazo, who attacked the camp in 1603, thought the runaways were "very valiant and suffered well" and were well armed with "swords and muskets [*arcabuses*] and many bows and lances." They were very skilled in the use of bows and lances and in one dramatic incident their "black lieutenant died with the standard in his hands" after sustaining multiple wounds.[103]

The necessity of maintaining military preparedness and thus autocratic leadership often led to attacks on other communities in the area. Native American communities, other settlements of runaways, or, of course, the European settlers could be attacked. Runaway communities became one more actor in the world of fragmented Native American and Euro-American colonial politics, with its shaky alliances and rivalries.

Thus, at times, runaways might seek to dominate the Native American communities in their area. Some runaways in Peru succeeded in completely dominating a Native American group in the 1530s though they themselves numbered only a dozen or so (including several women).[104] Some of the runaways established above Cartagena attacked neighboring Native American groups, for Miguel Diez Armendaria complained in 1545 that a runaway group was harassing allied natives at the village of Tafeme and had depopulated it.[105] A powerful runaway community in Castilla del Oro (Venezuela), led by Bayano, had the Native

99 Campbell, *Maroons of Jamaica*, pp. 36–43.
100 Luis de Rojas to king, 16 April 1586, in Tronchis Veracoechea, *Documentos*, pp. 79–80.
101 Vázquez de Espinosa, *Compendio*, no. 1028.
102 Charlevoix, *Histoire*, 2:123.
103 Jeronimo de Suazo to king, 16 February 1603 and 25 January 1604, in Arranzola, *Palenque*, pp. 36, 41–2.
104 Jijón y Caamaño, *Ecuador Interandino*, pp. 72–5.
105 Miguel Diez Armendaria to Crown, 24 July 1545, cited in Saco, *Historia*, p. 193.

Americans of nearby Caricuna cultivate their fields for them.[106] Likewise, when the Spanish forces under Diego de Frias Trejo occupied a runaway settlement on the Piñas River in Panama in 1578, he noted that the community had some Native American women among them whom they had seized from various Native American communities with which they were at war.[107]

The shifting attitudes of the Caribs of Saint Vincent to the runaway community established on their island, ranging from protection and alliance to suspicion and support for European attacks on it, reflects exactly the kind of situation that runaways faced in their relations with Native American communities. When weak and isolated, runaways were forced to accept whatever local politics gave them; once they gained sufficient power, they were capable of dealing with the natives from a position of equality or even strength and could became participants in the complicated politics of inter–Native American relations and Native American–European relations and even formalize their relationship to the Europeans.

The same processes were involved in interactions between neighboring runaway communities. Beginning in the late seventeenth century and culminating in the 1720s, the runaways of Jamaica formed two fairly large states on different parts of the island. On the leeward side, the maroons eventually formed a fairly centralized state whose leader, Cudjoe, was a strict autocrat, whereas on the windward side, a looser federation prevailed. Cudjoe's maroons had succeeded in building their state by conquest of neighboring maroon communities and their forced inclusion into the larger polity.[108] Other multisettlement states grew up out of the runaway communities: Palmares in Brazil, of course, and the loose federation of communities in Panama. We know little of the internal organization of such political units, although Francis Drake's visit to the Panama runaways in the 1560s provides some insights. The various settlements there recognized a "king," although from the testimony of the English visitors one does not get the idea of much centralization.[109]

Conquest or at least harassment of Native American communities and other runaway settlements may well have been an important part of the overall politics of runaways, but the best documented aspect is their own offensive warfare (rather than the defense of their settlements)

[106] Aguado, *Historia de Venezuela*, bk. 9, chap. 10.

[107] Diego de Frias Trejo to Crown, 15 May 1578, in Irene Wright, ed. and trans., *Documents Concerning English Voyages to the Spanish Main, 1569–90* (London, 1932), p. 215.

[108] Campbell, *Maroons of Jamaica*, pp. 44–53; Barbara Klamon Kopytoff, "The Early Political Development of Jamaica Maroon Societies," *William and Mary Quarterly* 35 (1978): 287–307.

[109] Nichols, *Francis Drake*, p. 53.

against their former masters. Some have seen this as an extension of class warfare, with the runaway settlements being something like the base areas of a modern revolutionary guerrilla war. But it is probably best to see it as the same sort of action as their attacks on neighboring runaway or Native American settlements, that is, as a way of increasing wealth or power. Of course, the runaways may have wished to take over the government of a colony, but they were probably realistic enough to know that this was impossible and were content with raids and looting.

This type of warfare is described in the reports of the extensive attacks made by runaways against the mills and ranches of Hispaniola in the early 1540s. These runaways, perhaps drawing on the Senegambian cavalry tradition, went about "always on horses" and "were skilled and audacious, both in the charge and in the use of the lance," and moreover were now used to travel in the mountainous terrain.[110] Much of their action was devoted to robbery; they burned estates and seized the slaves. When Spanish soldiers looted their camps during the cleanup campaign, they found considerable luxury goods in the possession of the leaders.[111]

Brigand groups of runaway slaves often dominated the highways of the Iberian-American world, such as the road from Lima to Trujillo.[112] This same sort of hit-and-run robbery characterized the Panama runaways, as numerous complaints to the Spanish Crown reveal.[113] When English visitors came to their headquarters, they found that some of the elite were wearing luxury goods of Spanish origin, and the runaways joined the English in their robbery, sharing in the spoils.[114]

Some of the raids undertaken by runaways may have had freeing slaves as the object; at other times, slaves taken on raids remained slaves in their new society. Dutch reports on Palmares specifically stated that the slaves they stole from the Portuguese estates remained in captivity in the runaway state. Only those slaves who ran away on their own from their masters to the community could be free upon joining, and the slaves in Palmares could obtain freedom only by stealing slaves to replace themselves.[115] A similar route to freedom may have been followed in the Hispaniola raids of the 1540s, or much later when the runaways around Cartagena repeatedly raided ranches and estates near their mountains, killing some slaves and carrying others off with them.[116]

110 Grajeda to king, 28 June 1546, quoted in Dieve, *Esclavitud*, p. 449.
111 Dieve, *Esclavitud*, pp. 449–52.
112 See documents cited in Jean-Pierre Tardieu, "Le marronage à Lima (1535–1650): Atermoiements et répression," *Revue Historique* 546 (1987): 294–6.
113 See the summary in Wright, *English Voyages*, introduction.
114 Nichols, *Francis Drake*, pp. 51–2, 56, 63–9.
115 G. Piso and G. Marcgrave, *Historia Naturalis Brasiliae* (Batavia, 1648), VIII, 1:261.
116 Fernando Ruiz de Contreras to Crown, 18 August 1632, in Arranzola, *Palenque*, pp. 63–4.

The Spanish who attacked the runaway settlements in Hispaniola in the 1540s believed that although most runaways wanted simply to live in peace in the mountains, there were robbers among them, who forced the Spanish retaliation. Indeed, the Spanish often found that the runaways would agree to serve the Spanish in exchange for their personal freedom, suggesting that there was some tension between leaders and the regular residents.[117] This sort of tension was evident in Panama, for when the Spanish reacted to the depredations of the runaways and the English in the 1570s and 1580s, the runaways were upset with their leadership and denounced their greed (at the same time rejecting the English alliance).[118]

Finally, as runaway communities grew into small self-governing states, they hoped to achieve more political status and participate in peace as well as war. Thus, when circumstances favored it, runaways often made alliances and peace with the political authorities of the colonial world. Normally, peace would be dependent upon their agreeing to cease raids, cease harboring runaways, and help return future runaways to their masters. Often, such communities would pledge to provide military assistance to the colonial authorities as well.

After long and damaging campaigns in the 1570s, for example, the Panama runaways agreed to peace terms that granted them freedom and municipal status in exchange for action against English privateers.[119] The plan must have been successful, for Vázquez de Espinosa mentions villages of freemen, former rebel slaves, in Panama, now assisting in protecting the colony in the early seventeenth century.[120] Spanish authorities settled with the Vera Cruz runaways in the early seventeenth century after military force failed, granting them freedom and municipal status in exchange for their future assistance against runaways.[121] The English conquerors of Jamaica found it in their interests to settle with the runaway communities that had formed during the turbulent period 1655–70 by making special charters with them guaranteeing them independence and self-government.[122] Likewise, this was the ultimate solution to the Cartagena runaway problem, first proposed in 1540 but

117 Letter of Grajeda, 16 October 1547, in Dieve, *Esclavitud*, pp. 451–2.

118 Diego de Faria Trejo to Crown, 20 October 1577; Pedro de Arana to Crown, 21 May 1578, in Wright, *Documents*, pp. 181, 217.

119 These events can be traced in contemporary documents; see Diego de Frias Trejo to king, 18 February and 15 May 1578, in Wright, *Documents*, pp. 200, 217; Diego de Villanueva to Crown, 2 October 1579, in ibid., p. 235; and *The Observations of Sir Richard Hawkins, Knight, in His Voyage to the South Seas* (London, 1593), p. 165, an edition of which is in ibid., pp. 339ff., with original pagination.

120 Vázquez de Espinosa, *Compendio*, no. 896.

121 These events are detailed in Palmer, *Slaves of White God*, pp. 173–8.

122 Campbell, *Maroons of Jamaica*, pp. 25–33.

only actually carried out in 1693, resulting in what Roberto Arranzola called (erroneously) the "first free community of America."[123]

Often colonial authorities could break the runaways by using the ultimate desire of most of these former slaves: personal freedom or a better life. Thus, there were always those who were willing to give up the runaway life if the price was right. The Spanish attacks on the runaway communities in the 1540s in Hispaniola benefited greatly by offering freedom to those who would join them to track down the others.[124] Nyanga, leader of the Vera Cruz runaways, after treating with the Spanish, agreed not only to help them track down runaways but also to pay tribute in exchange for guarantees that the Spanish would allow him to be king of the community and that succession would remain in his family.[125] The Portuguese used such offers of freedom to good effect on occasion in their operations against Palmares, buying off dissident members of the Palmares nobility in 1680.[126] Likewise, the French authorities succeeded in bringing one famous runaway of Martinique, Francisque Fabulé, to their side with offers of freedom, a commission, and a sword in 1665.[127]

Plots and rebellion: overthrowing the slave owners

Certainly, the events that most writers in colonial America called rebellions aimed at nothing more than establishing independent states away from colonial control. But there were a few rebels (or rather plotters, in most cases) who sought to build a new society in the midst of the colonial world. These plotters wished to overthrow their masters and rulers and rule themselves.

The plots have attracted considerable attention from historians, for unlike the runaways, such slaves appear to have been revolutionaries, prefiguring the great revolutions of the nineteenth-century world, and more specifically the Haitian revolution of 1791–1804. Moreover, because they came from within slave society, they reveal something about the development of the slave community and its political consciousness.

[123] Royal cedula, 7 September 1540 (first proposal), and extensive documentation on the settlement of 1693 quoted and analyzed in Arranzola, *Palenque*, pp. 12, 85ff.

[124] Dieve, *Esclavitud*, pp. 451–2.

[125] See the unpublished Inquisition documents on this affair, Archivo General de la Nación (Mexico), Inquisición, vol. 238, fols. 186–7, and vol. 285, fol. 715v, cited by Frederick Mars Rodriguez, "Cimarron Revolts and Pacification in New Spain, the Isthmus of Panama and Colonial Colombia" (Ph.D. diss., University of Chicago, 1979), p. 99.

[126] Bando of Manuel Lopes, 1680, in Edison Carneiro, *As guerras de Palmares* (Rio de Janeiro, 1947), p. 247 (the documents are found only in the 1947 edition of this book and not in the several later versions).

[127] Du Tertre, *Histoire*, 1:201. Fabulé was subsequently involved in criminal activity, which resulted in his sentencing to serve on the galleys; see Peytraud, *Esclavage*, p. 347.

One problem with the analysis of slave plots is that most of them may not have developed as the documents portray them. The colonial authorities were naturally desperately fearful that the slaves, who often outnumbered them, might decide to rise up and overthrow them. Their fears naturally caused them to exaggerate the possibilities of mass revolt, and in the process of interrogating slaves suspected of plotting (given that torture or instilling the fear of it was a part of the judicial process), they might unwittingly have forced the plotters to confess to more grandiose schemes than they really planned. But certainly there were plots, and we need not dismiss them all as simply the delusions of overcharged slave-owner minds, even if we must always be suspicious of what the documents tell us.

One of the most interesting things about the plots is the fact that the national organizations seem to have been involved. It should not be surprising that the sometimes inchoate agglomeration of secret societies (in the African sense), self-help groups, burial societies, or entertainment clubs organized on African national lines might also have engaged in more advanced political activities, including revolutionary ones. After all, they were one segment of slave society that was more or less under slave control, organized large numbers of people, had some leadership, and cut across other types of lines (family, estate, etc.). This may well explain why the slaveholders, while recognizing the social functions performed by the national organizations, and perhaps even joining in the festivities when they had dances and coronations, still feared them. It would also explain why the Church sought to control the lay brotherhoods and to promote them to ultimate control over the nations in Iberian-American countries.

This sort of paranoia clearly lay behind the fear that the Mexico City plot of 1609 was in fact to destroy Spanish rule and replace it with rule by the slaves. Witnesses believed that a secret meeting in which a king and queen were elected and offices distributed prefigured a revolt and eventual takeover of the colony. Of course, such elections were frequently conducted in national organizations, and indeed there were those who doubted the seditious intentions of the participants in the 1609 meeting for exactly those reasons. But the secrecy and perhaps other elements of this meeting certainly made the suspicious anxious to be sure by eliminating any possible threat.[128] In very much the same way, the investigators in Cartagena interviewing the free mulatto Juan Francisco de Vera concerning the possible plot in 1693 focused on the African national organizations with their elected kings and queens and other officers as

[128] The plot is discussed in detail in Palmer, *Slaves of White God*, pp. 133–44.

potentially threatening, though de Vera testified these were simply social events.[129]

Plots, whether directly linked to national organizations or not, generally sought to take control of the colonial society. If they were revolutionary in that sense, however, they were often not revolutionary in the social sense, for many did not aim either at abolishing slavery for everyone or at proclaiming a new government, unless it was an African-type government similar in structure to the colonial government.

For example, in 1537 Antonio de Mendoza reported the discovery of a plot in Mexico City. As he understood it, the plotters planned to elect a king, rise up and kill the Spanish, and take over the country. The fruits of this insurrection, should it be successful, would be that the slaves would then rule the "mines and pueblos [Aztec villages under Spanish rule]" – in other words, the basic structure of Spanish Mexico without the Spanish.[130] Likewise, as Herrera reports it, the leaders of the Santa Marta uprising of 1550 hoped to kill the Spanish or drive them out and had "assigned a white woman to each to marry" (though, failing that, they might just run away, as in fact they did).[131] The Barbados plot of 1675 probably had similar objectives. Some sort of national organization did play a role in this one, for the plotters were all Akan (Koromanti) and sought to make one of their number, named Cuffy, king over the society.[132]

Such corporate feelings and social organizations built on them might even work when African nations were not involved. The 1692 plot in Barbados reveals a slightly different twist to the nationally organized Akan plot of 1675, being organized by creole rather than African slaves, but they probably sought the same sort of goals. Creoles often formed their own organizations, in Iberian-American countries sometimes their own lay brotherhoods (though often they joined national brotherhoods, too), and generally represented the more privileged among the slave community. In the 1692 plot, the future state they envisioned was one in which only they would benefit. They hoped to kill the Europeans but to take over their "surnames and offices" and to appoint one of their own as governor. Moreover, the African-born slaves on the island would remain slaves until they chose to give them liberty.[133]

129 "Testimonio de la culpa que resulta de autos cirminales contra Francisco de Vera . . ." (6 May 1693), in Arranzola, *Palenque*, pp. 135–62.

130 Antonio de Mendoza to king, 1537, quoted in Saco, *Historia*, p. 172.

131 Herrera y Tordesillas, *Historia*, decade 8, bk. 6, chap. 12.

132 The plot is studied on the basis of original documents in Craton, *Testing the Chains*, pp. 108–14.

133 Ibid., pp. 113–16. In this book Craton revises his earlier, more dramatic hypothesis that the differences between the 1675 and 1692 plots represented a growth of consciousness, and instead distinguishes between the interests and outlook of creoles as opposed to Africans.

The advantages and pitfalls of national organizations in making plots are revealed in the Martinique plot and rebellion of 1656. The two leaders, Pedro and Jean le Blanc, according to du Tertre, were planning to kill the masters and take over their women. The main plot involved many Angolans, and the leadership of the resulting state would be under two Angolan kings. But the Cape Verdian (probably Senegambian) slaves rejected this, and as a result, the uprising was unable to achieve its main objective, although it did result in a major breakout to the hills, where the rebels joined the Caribs.[134]

The African background may have figured in these plots in two ways. First of all, insofar as the national organizations preserved African culture and political ideas, they would contribute to the leadership, organization, and goals of the future state. Second, insofar as Africans with military or political experience participated in the plots, whether through national organizations or not, a state with strong leadership and continued inequality, such as was found in the runaway communities, was likely to be perpetuated.

In the overall analysis of resistance, one can conclude that a great deal of American resistance simply arose from the exploitative nature of social and economic relations. It ought not to be seen as being any different from the reactions of any exploited group anywhere in the world. Moreover, such an analysis can be extended to the motives for revolt. But rebels were not necessarily free to choose the type of society that they would have. Here, the African background of soldiers, officers, and nobles both assisted the rebels and runaways in escaping and shaped the ultimate structure of the communities that resulted.

[134] Du Tertre, *Histoire,* 1:500.

11

Africans in the eighteenth-century Atlantic world

From 1680 to 1800, the Atlantic slave trade grew immensely. From about 36,000 persons per year at the beginning of the century, the trade had more than doubled by the 1760s, and it reached a high point of nearly 80,000 per year in the last two decades of the century.[1] Of the six trading regions identified by David Richardson in his study of the volume of the slave trade (Senegambia, Sierra Leone, Gold Coast, Bight of Benin, Bight of Biafra, and West Central Africa), West Central Africa had consistently the largest volume of exports, running between 30 and 45 percent of the overall trade. The Bight of Benin, mainly from the ports around the Kingdom of Dahomey, was the second most important, with nearly 40 percent of all exports in 1700, which declined to just over 10 percent by century's end. The Bight of Biafra, whose export trade grew rapidly during this time, supplying only 6 percent at the start of the period but peaking at nearly 30 percent in the 1780s, was close behind it. Among them, these three regions supplied nearly three-quarters of all the Africans transported across the Atlantic during the eighteenth century to labor in the Americas. Of the remaining areas, Sierra Leone provided more than one-fifth of the exports for a brief period between 1760 and 1780, at other times less than 10 percent; the Gold Coast never supplied more than 15 percent of the exports; and the exports from Senegal exceeded 10 percent only in the 1720s.[2]

The causes of the prodigious growth of the slave trade are not hard to find. There was certainly a great rise in the demand for slaves in the

[1] The best comprehensive overview of the eighteenth-century trade remains David Richardson, "Slave Exports from West and West-Central Africa, 1700–1810: New Estimates of Volume and Distribution," *Journal of African History* 30 (1989): Table 4, p. 10. More recent detailed work and modifications have changed some sections of Richardson's survey, and such modification is likely to continue as the growing data base on shipping at Harvard University's Dubois Institute Slave Trade Project is analyzed. These changes are unlikely to affect the larger picture presented in Richardson.

[2] Richardson, "New Estimates," Table 7, p. 17.

Americas, especially from the Caribbean islands, settled in the second half of the seventeenth century and transformed economically in the eighteenth, and from Brazil, constantly growing first as a sugar and tobacco producer and then as a mining colony. Sugar in the Caribbean and gold in Brazil paid the increasingly high prices for slaves demanded by those Africans in a position to sell them, and as higher prices brought larger numbers of slaves, promoted continued growth and still higher slave prices in an upward cycle that continued throughout the century.

The role this higher demand and increasing price of slaves had in raising the rate of enslavement in Africa is harder to determine. Easy answers proposing that somehow European buyers were able to extort the sales of slaves from Africans through the operation of economic domination or the gun–slave cycle are inadequate. The conditions described in Chapter 4 for earlier periods had not changed decisively in the eighteenth century, and it would not be until the Industrial Revolution had changed Europe's economy that traders could exert significant economic pressure on Africans. Similarly, it was impossible to manipulate weapon sales, even after many African armies had adopted the flintlock musket as the standard weapon, in such a way as to force the reluctant to sell slaves.

At the same time, it would be foolhardy to argue that those Africans who made the crucial decisions concerning capture, enslavement, and sale of other Africans were moved neither by the prospect of economic gains to be made in this way nor by important decisions concerning the supply of munitions. The complex dynamics of enslavement resist broad generalization, as can be seen by more specific examination of the supplying regions, focusing on those in the arc from Angola to the Gold Coast, who collectively supplied more than 85 percent of Africa's eighteenth-century slave exports.

War, politics, and protest: enslavement in eighteenth-century Africa

The tragic history of the Kongo civil wars that supplied America with so many people in the eighteenth century is an excellent example of the complexity of enslavement. The wars, which began as a succession dispute in 1665, became more or less endemic in the eighteenth century.[3] Rival candidates for the throne from different branches of the royal

[3] See John Thornton, *Kingdom of Kongo: Civil War and Transition, 1641–1718* (Madison, 1983), for an overview of the period and the early stages of the civil war. Much more detail will be available for the period 1685–1730 in John Thornton, *The Kongolese Saint Anthony: D. Beatriz Kimpa Vita, 1684–1706* (forthcoming).

family divided the country, established headquarters in mountainous and otherwise defensible regions, and fought one another frequently. The unfortunate captives of these wars were often sold to British or Dutch shippers who had come to dominate the ports along the coast north of Kongo, and to the Portuguese in Luanda.[4] Those captured were primarily soldiers and the many noncombatant men, women, and even children who provided the supply trains and attendants for the soldiers.[5] As the Italian priest Marcellino d'Atri discovered when he crossed one of the war zones in 1702, the adult, especially the male, civilian population was often stripped from whole areas – some recruited into armies, some having fled to safety, many taken up by passing forces and sold.[6] There was a constant lower level of war consisting of small border raids, spoiling attacks, and punitive expeditions between rivals or as power holders disciplined subordinates outside the major wars between these rivals, which punctuated the history of Kongo about once every five years. One such raid, denounced by another Italian priest, Luca de Caltanisetta, to one of the rival kings, Pedro IV, was launched against a subject accused of treason but netted 58 slaves from among the people in his town, including many who were there simply visiting markets. "With these captives," an indignant Father Luca wrote, "they buy hats and other merchandise, making no distinction between the innocent and the guilty."[7]

A breakdown of order and discipline that contributed to the trade accompanied civil war. In 1694, for example, Pedro Mpanzu a Mvemba, a minor noble established by one of the great families to rule a small district, had become a local raider, entrenched on a flat-topped mountain and indiscriminately raiding the merchants who passed and stripping the countryside around him.[8] As the wars stretched into the eighteenth century, despite several attempts to patch up differences, such bandits became more common. In 1785, a noble turned bandit near the capital of São Salvador created a scandal when his men shot at a priest who had come to deliver a royal order for him to break camp. Known as Mbwa Lau, or "Mad Dog," a fitting sobriquet for such a man, he had built an armed camp and raided the surrounding countryside as well as presumed rivals. The shock provoked in Kongo by his assault on a priest when there was a long tradition of according the clergy great respect set

4 For the participation of the various powers, see Richardson, "New Estimates."

5 For the techniques of organizing an army, and their result, see Thornton, *Kongolese Saint Anthony*, making use especially of d'Atri, "Giornate apostoliche," fol. 53, 519–21; da Caltanisetta, "Relatione," fol. 8v–9v; Biblioteca Nacional de Madrid, MS 3165, Andrea da Pavia, "Viaggio apostolico alle missioni" (1692), fols. 94v–95.

6 d'Atri, "Giornate apostoliche", fols. 547–53.

7 da Caltanisetta, "Relatione," fol. 99.

8 d'Atri, "Giornate apostoliche," fols. 76–90.

off a crisis of confidence that eventually unseated the king.[9] This priest, Raphael de Castello de Vide, denounced the elite of the country, arguing that it was the vanity of those in power and their desire for imported textiles that led them to abuse their subjects and sell people into slavery. "In this way," he noted, "many thousands are sent out."[10]

Yet it would be too easy simply to ascribe the slave trade from Kongo to the untrammeled greed of a handful of African leaders. After all, Pedro IV, who sold the victims of the border raid, denounced by Luca de Caltanisetta was a great compromiser, a man who ultimately did care for his people, who were, he argued, "tired of all these embarrassments, being killed, stripped naked, sold and having their wives, families, and children killed on all sides,"[11] and who was neither callous nor venal.[12] Leaders in the country where a king could mobilize thirty thousand soldiers, all "armed with power and ball," as King José I did in 1781,[13] clearly had to acquire munitions from overseas sources if they wished to prevail. They could not even survive without participating in international trade, and that in slaves was lucrative. If weapon suppliers, who had little to do with the civil wars – indeed generally did not even know of them[14] – did not cause the wars, the military and social dynamics of civil wars were certainly affected by their trade.

Although it did not involve a civil war and the breakdown of order, the situation on the eighteenth-century Gold Coast often resembled that in Kongo. Gold Coast states in the early eighteenth century were small, sufficiently small that they were not always able to control their own people, and they certainly could not single-handedly cope with regional trade disputes. At the same time their elites were commercially minded, oriented toward the trade with both the interior and the Atlantic world. A result was that a good many wars involved commercial disputes, and sometimes they were fought with and by commercial groups that hired mercenaries from various bands, even hiring other states with pay-

9 Academiadas Cienças, Lisbon, MS Vermelho 296, Raphael de Castello de Vide, "Viagem do Congo do Missionario Fr. Raphael de Castello de Vide, hoje Bispo de S. Thomé" (MS of 1800 recopying four letter reports from 1779–88), pp. 284–94. The semantic field of *lau* is broad – a translation such as "lucky dog" is also possible. In this instance, I have followed the translation supplied by Castello de Vide, who, however, chose to translate it as "mad puppy," although *mbwa* is not a diminutive and does not imply an immature animal.

10 Academia das Cienças, MS Vermelho 296, de Castello de Vide, "Viagem," p. 289.

11 Bernardo da Gallo, "Relazione dell'ultime Guerre civili del Regno di Congo . . . ," 12 December 1710, fol. 303v in Filesi (ed.), "Nazionalismo."

12 For Pedro IV and his project, see Thornton, *Kingdom of Kongo*, pp. 103–13, and *Kongolese Saint Anthony*.

13 Academia das Cienças, Lisbon, MS Vermelho 296, da Castello de Vide, "Viagem," p. 114.

14 The records of Dutch, French, and English traders on the coast of central Africa are remarkably sparse with respect to information about what went on in the interior. We know a great deal largely through ecclesiastical sources.

ments, to settle disputes and form alliances. Often such disputes took the form of "panyarring"; that is, the officials of one state seized people from another because of unpaid debts or other disputed matters. The Komenda War in the late seventeenth century, which involved many states and factions, including hired bands from various European factories who sought to participate in the war to gain trading advantages and garner favors from various African partners, was one example of this complex arrangement.[15] Such wars were frequent enough for one Dutch trader to write in 1705 that the coast "has already changed into a Slave Coast, and . . . nowadays the natives no longer occupy themselves with the search for gold, but rather make war on each other to furnish slaves, nay, go to the extent of violating the public roads."[16] Although this is exaggerated, for gold continued to be a major export of the region, the episodes of extended war often had this appearance. Europeans played an important part in these wars, often by "bribing" states to join or break alliances, supplying money and arms, sometimes even soldiers, to one side or another. The wars of this period are, therefore, often seen as linked to the growth of the Atlantic slave trade, although a careful reading of the documents does not suggest that Europeans were able to cause or change the leaders' courses of action. Many regard the end of the seventeenth century as a period of dramatic breaks in politics and warfare, with the interior states using their demographic weight to overthrow the coastal states or force them into the federation alliance with the state of Fante.[17]

The larger states that emerged in the interior, such as Denkyira and Akwamu in the late seventeenth century and then Asante and Akyem in the early eighteenth, did not alter the politics of the region much, for they were quite loosely constituted.[18] Indeed, even the king of Asante

[15] Bossman, *Description*, pp. 30–46. Many documents on the war are published in translation in Albert van Dantzig (ed. and trans.), *The Dutch and the Guinea Coast, 1674–1742* (Accra, 1978), for example, Elmina Journal, entry of 24 November 1693, pp. 55–6; van Sevenhuysen to X, 15 April 1700, p. 71; Elmina Council minutes, 10 March 1700, pp. 60–1; Sevenhuysen to X, 15 April 1700, p. 72. Secondary literature: Daaku, *Trade and Politics*, pp. 83–91; van Dantzig, *Les hollandaise sur la côte de Guinée à l'epoque de l'essor de l'Ashanti de du Dahomey: 1680–1740* (Paris, 1980), pp. 106–14.

[16] Factor de la Palma to X, 5 September 1705, van Dantzig (ed. and trans.), *Dutch on the Gold Coast*, p. 112.

[17] There is little agreement on specifics; see Kea, *Settlements*, pp. 97–168; Yann Deffontaine, *Guerre et société au royaume de Fetu: Ghana, 1471–1720* (Paris, 1993), pp. 183–210.

[18] The image of Asante as a centralized, dominant regional state is largely that of the last years of the eighteenth century and the nineteenth century; see Ivor Wilks, *Asante in the Nineteenth Century* (Cambridge, 1975), and with some differences, Thomas McCaskie, *State and Society in Pre-colonial Asante* (Cambridge, 1995). These images, well documented and subtly argued, do not fully reveal the more chaotic character of the earlier period, which is also lost, to some extent, in the literature on the eighteenth century, for

could not always harness his own troops, who raided the countryside, out of control, after their war on Aowin in 1715.[19] Two years later, some of these soldiers who had deserted were engaged by a private merchant, Jan Konny, to threaten Akyem.[20] Although Asante humbled many of its neighbors and forced some to pay tribute, its rule was not unitary,[21] as is illustrated by the case of Ntsiful (Intuffer in Dutch documents) of Wassa, who rebelled against the overlordship of Asante in 1726, then took to raiding the area around him. This set off a series of disputes and alliances that showed that Asante had no real control anywhere in the region, as Fante and other states in varying degrees of nominal alliance to Asante, and even pro- and anti-Asante factions within these states, necessitated and complicated the task of Asante bringing Ntsiful to heel.[22] Eventually he took refuge in the state of Nzim. By 1729 he was reannexing territory from Asante, and by 1732 he was described as a bandit operating over a wide area, seizing people indiscriminately on the high roads and blocking commerce.[23]

Wars and banditry resulted in the sale of floods of slaves, as the victors "ate the country," as the local expression went: When Aowin invaded Asante in 1718, the invaders brought back no fewer than twenty thousand women and children for sale, in addition to the men.[24] Indeed, Akyem was regarded as remarkable in that it did not completely pillage Akwamu after its notable victory in 1730 but, rather, kept the people on the land, so as to use them as a source from which to draw larger armies. The strategy succeeded, for within five years the former Akwamu subjects were completely integrated into Akyem.[25] But such a strategy was

example, J. K. Fynn, *Asante and Its Neighbours, 1700–1807* (Oxford, 1971), which focuses on the growth of Asante centralization and nationality.

19 Elmina Journal, entry of 25 October 1715, van Dantzig, *Dutch and the Guinea Coast*, p. 186; Algemeen Rijksarchief, Nederlands Bezittungen ter Kust Guinea 82, Elmina Journal, entry of 11 October 1715 and entry of 25 October 1715, Butler to Elmina, 20 October 1715.

20 Minutes of Elmina Council, report of W. Butler, 26 August 1717, in van Dantzig, *Dutch and the Guinea Coast*, p. 194.

21 On the general problem of creating unitary order (and peace), see Fynn, *Asante*, pp. 55–6, 81–3.

22 The details of this war are too complicated to describe in detail here, and it is not fully described in the secondary literature. My observations have come from primary sources, among them, Algemeen Rijksarchief, Nederlands Bezittungen ter Kust Guinea, 93, Elmina Journal, entries for 26 April 1726, 28 May 1726, 11 June 1726; Ockers to Valknier 30 and 31 May 1726, fols 406, 411–12; Valcknier to Elet, 5 May 1726; ibid. 94, Elmina Journal, entries for 24 July, 12 October 1727; ibid., Norre to van Leeuwen, 22 June 1727 (all published in van Dantzig), *Dutch and the Guinea Coast*, p. 223.

23 Algemeen Rijksarchief, Nederlands Bezittungen ter Kust Guinea, 95, Elmina Journal, entry of 27 June 1729; ibid. 98, Elmina Journal, entry of 7 June 1732.

24 Munnickhoven to Elmina, 21 March 1718, van Dantzig, *Dutch and the Guinea Coast*, p. 188.

25 Ludvig Ferdinand Rømer, *Le Golfe de Guinée 1700–1750: Récit de L. F. Römer, marchand d'escalves sur la côte ouest-africaine* (tr. Mette Dige-Hesse, Paris, 1989), p. 120.

considered risky in other cases, for former subjects were generally not to be trusted, and the demographic drain of enemies could help the victors. Akyem, like other states before it, sought to weaken enemies before major wars by employing bands of specially selected skirmishers to harass border villages and, by means of raiding, weaken the population, most of whom were sold both to finance the war and to remove them from the theater of operations.[26]

The Igbo country, second-largest regional supplier of slaves to the Atlantic markets in the eighteenth century, also had splintered sovereignty, with a lack of order and inadequate protection of large areas. Almost all we know about the region in the eighteenth century comes from the testimony of Olaudah Equiano, an Igbo who was enslaved as a youth around 1755.[27] Equiano provides descriptions of the small states around his native state, as well as of the numerous wars, "the irruptions of one little state or district upon the other, to obtain prisoners or booty," which led to the enslavement of many. Some of these wars were undoubtedly born of rivalries and diplomacy of which even modern-day oral tradition is ignorant; others, according to Equiano, were products of the seductions of merchants who, because they would be granted the right to purchase the captives to be enslaved, persuaded kings to make war on each other.[28] In the absence of any overarching authority, wars could not easily be arbitrated, although what is more important, the unscrupulous, whether merchants or bandits and thieves, like Equiano's own captors, who sneaked over a compound wall to steal him,[29] could not be controlled or stopped.

Of course, the enslavement did not always take place in a context of social disorder, civil war, or banditry. In the Bight of Benin area, the reason for it was not civil war, small-scale wars between tiny states, or uncontrolled banditry. Rather, the causes and effects were of war on a much larger scale, between large and orderly states. Dahomey, whose arrival as a great power in Africa was signaled for the outside world by its successful invasion of Allada in 1724, dominated the region. Dahomey has often been seen as a military pariah state that lived on the booty

[26] Rømer, *Golfe de Guinée* (trans. Digge-Hess), pp. 97, 103, 110 – all on the use of these raiders, called *sikadings*, in various situations.

[27] The original edition, entitled *The Interesting Narrative of Olaudah Equiano, or Gustavus Vasa, the African* (2 vols., London, 1789), has been frequently reedited. For our purposes, the best edition is that of the first two (African) chapters, by G. I. Jones, "Olaudah Equiano of the Niger Ibo," in Philip Curtin (ed.), *Africa Remembered: Narratives by West Africans from the Era of the Slave Trade* (Madison, 1968), pp. 60–98. Equiano was only about ten when captured, but he may well have rounded out his knowledge by talking with older Igbos in America.

[28] *Equiano* (ed. Jones), p. 77.

[29] Ibid. pp. 84–6.

from slave raids against its neighbors, its invincible army raiding its neighbors at will, while seeking to monopolize the external trade of the region.[30] But the view has always been challenged, as scholars have seen Dahomey's wars as having more conventional diplomatic, cultural, and even ideological goals.[31]

Although there is no doubt that Dahomey fought frequently – its armies advanced against its neighbors almost every year in the eighteenth century, according to careful annual enumerations by eyewitnesses[32] – its motives have been the issue in question. In any case, when one considers that many of the wars were disastrous defeats for Dahomey, for example, those against Serechi in 1775 or Mahi in 1776 and 1777, and others bloody draws that resulted in the capture of no slaves, like that against Mahi in 1778, it is hard to see Dahomey as living on income from the slave trade.[33]

Dahomey existed in a complex interstate political system.[34] Dahomey's neighbors possessed their own military forces, and the wars, far from being raids intended to achieve surprise and capture slaves, were set-piece affairs linked to diplomatic and political aims.[35] Dahomey took up a long-standing attempt to dominate the coastal states of Allada and Whydah, and many wars, such as the Badagri wars of 1783–4, were designed to protect its own rulers in those areas or to hunt down pretenders or rebels. A similar concern drove Dahomey's policy vis-à-vis the Mahi country to the northwest, where a long-standing attempt to create a unified Mahi state on behalf of a relative of the Dahomean royal family's who promised to be friendly was caught in a web of Mahi politics and Dahomean ambition.[36] Finally, Dahomey had to contend with its inland neighbor Oyo, a state so powerful that even Dahomey had to pay it tribute, and should it fail to obey was ruthlessly invaded and pillaged as it was repeatedly between 1726 and 1748. Oyo, more-

30 This view was advanced since the eighteenth century in Abolitionist circles and eloquently reinvoked in the 1960s by scholars such as Basil Davidson and Karl Polanyi. Robin Law, "Dahomey and the Slave Trade: Reflections on the Historiography of the Rise of Dahomey," *Journal of African History* 27 (1986): 237–67, contains a review of the literature.

31 I. A. Akinjogbin, *Dahomey and Its Neighbours, 1708–1818* (Cambridge, 1967), was an earlier pioneer of this approach.

32 See Werner Peukert, *Der Atlantische Skayenhandel von Dahomey, 1740–1797: Wirtschaftanthropologie und Socialgeschichte* (Wiesbaden, 1978), pp. 73–6, and in tabular form in Appendix III, pp. 300–304.

33 Ibid. p. 76, where Peukert says that Dahomean rulers were driven by desires for personal glory and for heads of opponents to glorify their ancestors and gods.

34 The best description of the system is found in Robin Law, *The Slave Coast* (Oxford, 1992).

35 For military details of the wars, see John Thornton, "African Soldiers in the Haitian Revolution," *Journal of Caribbean History* 25 (1991): 62–3, 68–70.

36 For political motives in Mahi, see Robert Norris, *Memoirs of the Reign of Bossa Ahâdee, King of Dahomey an Inland Country of Guiney* (London, 1789, reprinted London, 1968).

over, was a cavalry empire, and as such made little use of the imported firearms that dictated military logic and logistics on the coast, or even in areas like Kongo, where decisions were made by people who had no direct commercial contact with Europeans. Such was the situation until, in the nineteenth century, Oyo was enmeshed in its own civil war, a rich source of slaves for that period.[37]

The lands around Portuguese Angola fit into this Dahomean pattern. Although Portugal's direct involvement in African wars diminished greatly after its less than successful intervention in wars between Kasanje and Matamba in 1681,[38] a substantial Portuguese drive into the central highlands of Angola began with the foundation of the presidio of Caconda in 1682. Although that drive took on force when it became involved in regional politics between 1716 and 1722, it soon petered out.[39] Much of the Portuguese activity was subsequently limited to seeking fiscal control of the export trade through factories, and even its wars were directed more to that end than to fulfilling the more grandiose plans of the preceding century.[40] Smaller wars and raids, reminiscent of those on the Gold Coast, were conducted in the Dembos regions, which lay in the mountainous area between Ndongo and Kongo, where a combination of raiding and banditry was sometimes supported by rulers. These included small-scale civil wars, such as those in Mutemo a Kinjengo in 1720[41] and in Kahenda in 1768 and again in 1772,[42] and personal disputes between the petty rulers that escalated into wars, such as those between Kahenda and Gombe a Mukiama and between Gombe a Kijengo and Bango a Kaputo in the same period.[43] Occasionally, larger

[37] For Oyo and its relations with Dahomey, see Robin Law, *The Oyo Empire, c. 1600 – c. 1836: A West African Imperialism in the Era of the Slave Trade* (Oxford, 1977), pp. 150–69.

[38] Luis Lobo da Silva to King, 25 November 1684, *MMA* 13: 582–6; see also Birmingham, *Trade and Conflict*, pp. 129–30, and material based on Arquivo Histórico Ultramarino, Lisbon, Cx 12, João da Silva e Sousa, 18 March 1682.

[39] Elias Alexandre da Silva Corrêa, *História de Angola* (1798; modern ed. 2 vols., Lisbon, 1937) 2: 338–9; 348–56, based on a local chronicle, "Catalogo dos Governadores de Angola," of the late eighteenth century.

[40] Joseph C. Miller, *Way of Death: Merchant Capitalism and the Angolan Slave Trade* 1726–1826 (Madison, 1988).

[41] Archives of Cahenda (Angola), Certificate of Fernando Sanches e Sousa, 23 October 1720, summarized in António de Almeida, "Relações com os Dembos das Cartas do Dembado de Kakulu-Kahenda," *I. Congresso da História da Expansão Portuguesa no Mundo*, Section 4 (Lisbon, 1938), p. 32.

[42] Archives of Cahenda (Angola) António Anselmo Duarte de Siqueira to Dembo Paulo Sebastião, April 1768, and same to same n.d. 1768; António de Lencastro to Dembo of Mufuco and sobas of Hungo, Danla and Malundu, Mani Quissele and Bambi-ia-Sumba, 25 November 1772, summarized in Almeida, "Relações com os Dembos," pp. 38–9, 41.

[43] Archives of Cahenda (Angola), António de Lencastro to Dembo Paulo of Cahenda, 21 August 1772; Sousa Coutinho to Dembo Paulo Sebastião, 1767, and Processo of 1772, summarized in Almeida, "Relações com os Dembos," pp. 37 and 40–41; Archives of Dembo Bango a Caputo, Município de Samba Cajú, Província de Kwanza Norte (An-

regional states formed and, as on the Gold Coast, affected a larger area. One was the "Grand Empire of the Sosos," a complex alliance of Soso, Hungu, and the Kongolese province of Wandu, formed around 1760.[44] At first the alliance expanded, but after 1770 it engaged more in raiding and banditry.[45] Additional low-level violence sometimes involving the slaves and soldiers of Portuguese garrisons[46] acting on their own supplied some of the slaves. Capuchin priests complained of these activities in 1705,[47] and sometimes the troops were unofficially involved in local wars, for instance, the conflict around the post of Ambaca in 1759.[48] Some Portuguese officials used legal measures to enslave people, a practice denounced by governor Sousa Cutin in 1770.[49]

After 1750, the rise of the Lunda empire in the far interior came to be very important. According to the first written accounts of Lunda expansion,[50] it was a veritable "war of slaves" in which Lunda armies moved westward, traveling quickly from fortified outposts, and stripping the country of people, some for local use, some for sale.[51] In many respects, it seems that Lunda, even more than Dahomey, fits the model of a slave-raiding state, although it did not use firearms.

Warmaking and the capture and sale of slaves were matters for the powerful and were not necessarily supported or accepted by the majority of the population. Popular protest movements occasionally emerged, less often directed against the trade itself than against deeper social harm in which the trade was implicated. Islamic social movements in

gola), letter of sobeto Bango a Caputo. My thanks to Eva Sebastyén, who photocopied these documents in local archives in 1988 and provided me with copies.

44 Biblioteca Nacional de Lisboa, Fundo Geral Códice 8742, fol. 3, Sousa Coutinho 31 January 1766; fol. 3v, Sousa Coutinho to Joze Vieira de Araujo, 3 February 1766; fols. 10v–11v, Sousa Coutinho to Bishop of Pernambuco, 5 March 1766.

45 Archives of the Sobado of Caxinda, Município de Samba Cajú, Província de Kwanza Norte, (Angola) (photographed in 1988 by Eva Sebastyén), "Informacão . . . informante Dom Diogo Miguel," n.d. (ca. 1770); Archives of Cahenda (Angola), António de Lancastro to Dembo Paulo of Cahenda, 1773; archives of Cahenda, summarized in Almeida, "Relações com os Dembos," pp. 41–2.

46 On the office and official status of *capitães mores*, see Caros Couto, *Os capitães-mores em Angola no século XVIII (subsídios para o estudo da sua actuação)* (Luanda, 1972); see also Miller, *Way of Death*, pp. 256–62.

47 Archivio de Propaganda Fide: Scritture Originale delli Congregazioni Generale 552, fols. 62–62v, Bernardo da Firenze to Propaganda Fide, 22 June 1705.

48 Arquivo Histórico Ultramarino, Cx. 42, doc. 58, Moradores of Ambaca to Governor, 24 April 1759.

49 Arquivo Histórico Ultramarino, Cx. 55, doc. 1, Bando of Sousa Coutinho, 2 January 1771.

50 Manoel Correia Leitão, "Relação e breve summário da viagem que eu Manoel Correia Leitão, o sargento-mór, fis à remotas partes de Cassange e Olos," published in Gastão Sousa Dias, "Uma viagem a Cassange nos meados do seculo XVIII," *Boletim da Sociedade de Geografia de Lisboa* 56 (1938): 3–30.

51 For a full examination of this approach, see John Thornton, "Lunda Expansion to the West," *Zambia Journal of History* 1 (1981): 1–16.

west Africa, a good example, were in part a reaction against the slave trade,[52] and indeed, contemporary French witnesses to the first of the movements, the Toubenan (Purification) led by the reformer Nasr al-Din from 1673 to 1677, make explicit his hostility to the Atlantic slave trade. They believed his ban on the export of slaves to Christians ruined the trade temporarily and led French factors to oppose his movement and play a major role in supporting his opponents, leading to the Toubenan's defeat.[53]

Although the Toubenan opposed the export slave trade, it was also a larger social movement for Islamic justice and was caught up in the complex politics of the Senegalese states and their Arab and Moorish desert neighbors.[54] The people of the area were equally concerned about the depredations of the *ceddo*, as the soldier-administrators of the Senegal-valley kingdoms were called, which included the arbitrary exaction of taxes and the enslavement of people even within their own jurisdictions. Hence, Nasr al-Din's conquest in the Senegal valley was facilitated because many ordinary people supported the movement against their leaders. Nasr al-Din "went from village to village," the French governor Chambonneau noted, "preaching in the public square . . . that God never allowed Kings to pillage, kill, or make their people captives; instead he was to keep them and protect them from their enemies; the people were not made for the kings, but the kings for the people."[55] Although they denounced slave trade aimed at providing captives to the Christian European buyers, the Toubenan leaders were hostile neither to slavery itself nor to the sale and ownership of slaves within Senegambian society.[56]

52 Boubacar Barry, in *Le royaume de Waalo*, pp. 135–59, was a pioneer of this approach, see the general statement, "Senegambia from the Sixteenth to the Eighteenth Century: Evolution of the Wolof, Sereer, and 'Tukuloor,' " in B. A. Ogot (ed.), *UNESCO General History of Africa* (8 vols., Berkeley and Los Angeles, 1981–93) 5: 273–99. See Jean Boulèque with Jean Suret-Canale, "The Western Atlantic Coast," in J. F. A. Ajayi and Michael Crowder, (eds.), *History of West Africa* (3d ed., 1985), 1: 503–30.

53 Louis Moreau de Chambonneau, "L'histoire du Toubenan," in Carson I. A. Ritchie, "Deux textes sur le Sénégal (1673–77," *Bulletin de l'Institut Foundamental de l'Afrique Noire* ser. B, 30 (1968): 289–353.

54 Philip Curtin, "Jihad in West Africa: Early Phases and Interrelations in Mauritania and Senegal," *Journal of African History* 12 (1971): 11–24. On the historiography of the movement, with special attention to the "desert side" of the region, see James Webb, *Desert Frontier: Ecological and Economic Change along the Western Sahel, 1600–1850* (Madison, 1995), pp. 32–35. The desert politics are well revealed in a local chronicle composed around 1730, [Muhammad al-Yadali], "Amr El Oualy Nacer Eddine (Histoire du Saint Nacer Eddine)," in Ismael Hamet (ed. and trans.), *Chroniques de la Mauretanie Sénégalaise* (Paris, 1911), pp. 164–218.

55 Moreau de Chambonneau, "Histoire," in Ritchie, "Deux textes," p. 338.

56 Additional discussion of this debate can be found in Curtin, *Economic Change*, esp. p. 50, and his review of Barry's book in *International Journal of African Historical Studies* 6 (1973): 679–81; and Abdel Wedoud Ould Cheikh, "Herders, Traders and Clerics: The Impact of

The 'Abd al-Kadir and Sulayman Baal Islamic revival in the same area in 1776 mirrored the Toubenan,[57] opposing the tyrannical exactions of the *ceddo*, raids by the Arabs of the desert, and all enslavement.[58] When 'Abd al- Kadir's forces invaded Futa Tooro, they took no slaves (unlike their Arab allies), commanded as they were by "priests," whose goal was to "submit them to the cult of Mahomet." 'Abd al-Kadir said they wanted "nothing of the people; on the contrary they wanted to make them free." This message led people to flock to his banner: "They raised up the people against their legitimate sovereigns."[59] As in the case of the Toubenan, however, the leadership did not long persist in such attitudes, and the slave trade was restored.

There was more ambiguity in the Islamic reform south of Senegal. In 1727, a Muslim party overthrew the rulers of Futa Jallon in modern Guinea and moved to establish an Islamic theocracy led by Karamokho Alfa.[60] In its early stages, it aimed at the overthrow of tyranny, but it does not appear to have had the kind of anti–slave trade ideology found farther north. The movement soon became, under the leadership of Ibrahima Sory (1751–91), an aggressive force that sought to conquer neighboring areas and convert their inhabitants to its militant form of Islam.[61] The militants sold slaves in order to acquire munitions necessary for their wars, so the Sierra Leone coast supplied one out of five Africans sold as slaves into the Atlantic world in the period 1760–80. Many leaders whom James Watt, a delegate of the Abolitionist Sierra Leone Company, interviewed while in Futa Jallon in 1794 were not at all troubled by

Trade, Religion, and Warfare on the Evolution of Moorish Society," in John Galaty and Pierre Bonte (eds.), *Herders, Warriors, and Tyrants: Pastoralism in Africa* (Boulder, 1991), pp. 199–218, and H. T. Norris, *The Arab Conquest of the Western Sahara* (Harlow, Essex, 1986), pp. 510–18.

57 David Robinson, "The Islamic Revolution of Futa Toro," *International Journal of African Historical Studies* 8 (1975): 185–221; Barry, "Senegambia," pp. 295–9.

58 On the Islamic side of the movement, see S. A. Sow, *Chronique du Fouta Sénégalais* (Paris, 1913); on the forbidding of enslavement, see Pruneau de Pommegorge, *Description de la Nigritie* (Paris, 1789), p. 74.

59 M. Lamiral, *L'Affrique et le people affriquain* (Paris, 1789), p. 176. For more details on the policy of 'Abd al-Kadir and the conditions that led to the movement, see Mirabeau to Clarkson, 20–3 December 1789, in François Thesée, "Au Sénégal, en 1789: Traite des nègres et société africaine dans les royaumes de Sallum, de Sin et de Cayor," in Serge Daget (ed.), *De la traite à l'esclavage du Ve au XVIIIe siècle* (2 vols., Nantes and Paris, 1988) 1: 226–36.

60 Gordon Laing, *Voyage dans le Timmani, le Kouranko et le Soulimana* (Paris, 1826), based on oral traditions available at the time. A number of locally composed chronicles, mostly from the nineteenth century, complement this account.

61 Barry, "Senegambia," pp. 288–95; the pioneering study, suggesting a social agenda rather than a Fulbe ethnic one, is Walter Rodney, "Jihad and Social Revolution in Futa Djalon in the Eighteenth Century," *Journal of the Historical Society of Nigeria* 4 (1968): 269–84; for a more recent approach, see Roger Botte, "Les rapports nord-sud, la traite négrière et le Fuuta Jaloo à la fin du XVIIIe siècle," *Annales: Economies, Societes, Civilisations* 46 (1991): 1418–22.

the idea that the sale of slaves to Christians was contrary to Islamic law, as their northern coreligionists were. They told him that their wars were waged to capture slaves and had been commanded by religion, as they could only acquire military supplies by selling slaves.[62] On the other hand, the leaders did feel that it was wrong to sell Muslim slaves.[63] Some Muslims were enslaved when the armies of the Futa were defeated, most notable among them being Ibrahima Abd al-Rahmen, a prince captured about 1790 and sold to Louisiana, where his case became celebrated twenty years later when he was repatriated by the fledgling government of the United States.[64]

In Kongo, social movements for justice did not challenge the slave trade directly but did protest the warfare and greed of the rivals in the civil wars, from which enslavement and deportation were only two of several possible problems. In 1704, Dona Beatriz Kimpa Vita, who believed herself to be possessed by Saint Anthony, blamed the elite of the country for its problems, which she ascribed to their greed and desire to rule. In deciding to reestablish a peaceful kingdom under her own leadership, she took control of the abandoned capital of São Salvador and soon repopulated it with thousands of followers, to whom her appearance signified an end to the wars.[65]

The widespread belief among many Africans exported as slaves that they had been sold to cannibals to be cooked and eaten was not simply a bizarre way of interpreting their fate.[66] It was also a way of saying that they were the victims of a plot involving greedy and selfish people. Some central Africans such as the Imbangala, rootless raiders in Angola, literally engaged in cannibalism as a way of displaying their power and their unconcern for the larger community. In central African ideology, such people were witches, and their power was often manifested in holding political office, owning wealth in goods or people, or being able to attack others violently. The reaction against power misused in this way, expressed as opposition to cannibalism, the symbol of witchcraft, was a reaction against a whole complex of social injustices, including taking, holding, and selling slaves. In the case of the slaves in the Atlantic world,

62 "Journal of Mr. James Watt, in his Expedition to and from Teembo in the Year 1794," modern ed.: Bruce Mouser, *Journal of James Watt, Expedition to Timbo, Capital of the Fula Empire in 1794 (Madison, 1994), fols. 47v, 62v, 76v, 85, 113 (foliation of original).*

63 Thomas Winterbottom, *An Account of the Native Africans in the Neighbourhood of Sierra Leone* (London, 1803), p. 8 (based on notes of the author's brother who visited Futa Jallon in 1794).

64 Recounted, along with an excellent brief history of the history of Futa Jallon at the time, in Terry Alford, *Prince among Slaves* (New York, 1977; reprinted Oxford, 1986).

65 For a full study, see Thornton, *Kongolese Saint Anthony;* also *Kingdom of Kongo,* pp. 106–11, for this interpretation.

66 On this belief, see William Piersen, *Black Legacy: America's Hidden Heritage,* pp. 5–14.

it was an indictment of the whole system that led to their enslavement, from capture in wars waged by the power-hungry for their own aggrandizement to the sale of slaves to greedy shippers and plantation owners.[67]

Africans in the American world

More than half of all the Africans who were transported to the Americas in the eighteenth century went to the island colonies of the Caribbean, and almost another third went to Brazil. Fewer than a tenth went to Spanish America, and only about 6 percent went to North America. They came to a world in which thousands of their predecessors were already established. In many cases, however, the newcomers were so overwhelming in numbers that they remade the society of the American territories. This was true in North America, despite the relatively small number of Africans landed there. There were some 22,000 persons of African descent in 1700 residing on estates and in towns, of which no fewer than 13,000 were in the Chesapeake Bay region. In the first two decades of the eighteenth century, Africans arrived at a rate of about 1,000 per year, and the total population of African descent reached 61,000 by 1720. But then Africans started to arrive faster – 2,500 per year to bring the population of ex-Africans to 160,000 in 1740, then doubling in the next two decades to 5,000 per year, pushing up the population to 327,000 by 1760.[68] Natural increase played a role in this growth, of course, but the speed of the arrival of slaves, to work Chesapeake-country tobacco farms and then the rice and indigo plantations of South Carolina, probably contributed more.

These rates of importation were dwarfed by those to the West Indies. When 1,000 slaves were being delivered to North American ports each year in the first two decades of the eighteenth century, more than 20,000 were coming annually to the Caribbean colonies of England, France, and the Netherlands, and by the 1760s and 1770s the number was nearly 40,000 per year, eight times as many as came to their North American neighbors. High mortality rates, a product of the grinding labor and poor nutrition of the great sugar-producing areas, meant that the base of Africans or their descendants already on the islands grew much more slowly than these rates of importation suggest.[69]

67 John Thornton, "Cannibals and Slave Traders in the Atlantic World," a paper presented at the conference "Possible Pasts," Philadelphia, June 1994, gives fuller documentation.

68 Figures derived from Curtin, *Atlantic Slave Trade*, p. 216, and David Galenson, "The Settlement and Growth of the Colonies: Population, Labor and Economic Development," in Stanley Engerman and Robert Gallman (eds.), *The Cambridge Economic History of the United States* (3 vols. projected, Cambridge, 1996–) 1: 172.

69 Based on Curtin, *Atlantic Slave Trade*, p. 216.

In the Caribbean and Brazil, the newly arrived Africans were often slated to maintain labor forces on sugar estates and in mines whose owners had been unable to keep up the slave populations by natural increase. In addition to the mortality caused by problems of labor and nutrition, women on sugar-producing estates often had very low fertility rates, and their offspring often suffered very high rates of infant and child mortality. This was true even of the large estates of Peru carefully managed by the Jesuits in the last half of the century.[70]

In addition, the recently arrived were employed to open new enterprises as the economy spread to new land and put larger and larger areas under cultivation. In almost all the colonies, the eighteenth century witnessed increasing density of settlement, as well as colonization of new lands in a relentless movement to take over all the land available for crops that could be profitably grown with slave labor. In these frontier areas, a combination of the newly arrived and creoles would form the colonizing group. The cultivation of coffee, which allowed the exploitation of new areas in existing colonies, brought largely African labor forces to these frontier areas.[71] In Virginia, where the population of African descent soon became self-sustaining and even growing within a generation of the accelerated arrival of slaves, movement inland and up rivers still brought a mix of the newly imported and a minority of creoles.[72]

The flood of African arrivals often Africanized the areas to which they came. Even areas where there was a preexisting population of African descent were "re-Africanized," as Ira Berlin characterized the early eighteenth-century influx around the Chesapeake.[73] The re-Africanization was dramatic in Cuba. The colony had a well-established, even ancient Afro-creole population, but its subsequent transformation into coffee- and sugar-producing colonies in the 1770s brought thousands of Africans in, raising the population of slaves of African origin from just under 40,000 in 1774 to 212,000 by the early nineteenth century.[74]

In North America, an exceptional area, survival rates of the newly arrived were relatively good and, combined with the much higher survival rates of the creoles already there, made the African or "re-African" phase short-lived. Kulikoff's research suggests that in Virginia the Afri-

70 Nicholas Cushner, "Slave Mortality and Reproduction on Jesuit Haciendas in Colonial Peru," *Hispanic American Historial Review* 55 (1975): 190.

71 Michel-Rolph Trouillot, "Coffee Planters and Coffee Slaves in the Antilles: The Impact of a Secondary Crop," in Ira Berlin and Philip Morgan (eds.), *Cultivation and Culture: Labor and the Shaping of Slave Life in the Americas* (Charlottesville, 1993), pp. 128–30.

72 Kulikoff, *Tobacco and Slaves*, pp. 141–61.

73 Berlin, "Time, Space, and the Evolution of Afro-American Society on British Mainland North America," *American Historical Review* 85 (1980).

74 Leslie Rout, *The African Experience in Spanish America: 1502 to the Present Day* (Cambridge, 1976), p. 97.

can period lasted only about forty years, roughly from 1700 to 1740. In 1728, Slaves who had arrived within the preceding decade made up half the population, but the figure was only 15 percent in 1755; and by the time of the American Revolution, there were few African-born people in the population.[75]

The demography of the British West Indies makes a striking contrast to that of North America: In 1700, the West Indies had a population of some 115,000 persons of African descent while North America had only 22,000. Over the next seventy years, the West Indies received a total of nearly a million Africans, and yet the total population grew by only about 315,000 persons. North America received a bit more than 350,000 Africans, and yet its population grew by 434,000 persons.[76] In the West Indies, it took nearly three African arrivals to increase the population by one person, while in North America one arrival matched with a bit more than a one-person increase. In spite of the huge volume of the slave trade to the West Indies, there were more people of African descent in North America than in the West Indies by 1770, but far more of the West Indians were African-born.

In the islands, then, the period when African-born people were dominant lasted much longer than in North America. A relatively low number of creoles combined with bad rates of survival and low rates of reproduction to require the constant restocking of plantations, as was true in Brazil for virtually the entire period.[77] As a result, a higher percentage of the population were African-born, and moreover, a substantial number were quite newly arrived. Africans may have been the majority throughout the eighteenth century in Jamaica: African-born slaves formed some 60 percent of St. Domingue's population on the eve of the revolution there in 1790.[78]

The demography of the eighteenth-century Americas points to an important fact – that African-born people, socialized and bearing African culture were often the majority in American societies – among those of African descent in places like North America where there was a large European or Euro-American population, and in absolute terms in areas

75 Kulikoff, *Tobacco and Slaves*, pp. 319–40.

76 Statistics drawn from Galenson, "Settlement," p. 172, and Curtin, *Atlantic Slave Trade*, p. 216.

77 Stuart Schwartz, *Slaves, Peasants, and Rebels: Reconsidering Brazilian Slavery* (Urbana, 1992), p. 41; for a good study of the demographic regime on a Jamaican estate, see Richard S. Dunn, "Sugar Production and Slave Women in Jamaica," in Berlin and Morgan (eds.), *Cultivation and Culture*, pp. 49–72.

78 Inferred from data presented in David Geggus, "Sugar and Coffee Cultivation in Saint Domingue and the Shaping of the Slave Labor Force," in Berlin and Morgan (eds.), *Cultivation and Culture*, pp. 76–83.

like the Caribbean islands and Brazil. In cultural terms the point is vitally significant. Although many scholars discuss the possibility of the survival of African culture into the present day, an important issue to be sure, the fact is that in the eighteenth century African culture was not surviving: It was arriving. Whatever the brutalities of the Middle Passage or slave life, it was not going to cause the African-born to forget their mother language or change their ideas about beauty in design or music; nor would it cause them to abandon the ideological underpinnings of religion or ethics – not on arrival in America, not ever in their lives.

The newly arrived Africans, like those who had come before them, used this African culture to adapt to the Americas. In the New World they were subject to a restrictive regime created by slavery. Slave owners, concerned to the point of paranoia about security, were often hostile to group activities outside of labor, a factor that might restrict many cultural activities, as seen in the formal statements like the French *Code Noir* or the Spanish *Codigo Carolina.*[79] More important, these Africans came to America to work, and the slave regime often made incredibly heavy labor demands, pushing them to, and sometimes beyond, their physical capacity, shortening life spans, and reducing time for cultural life. Nevertheless, masters were not always willing or able to restrict cultural life, group meetings, or networks of friendship. Within the space that the slave regime allowed, the Africans re-created an African culture in America, although it was never identical with the one they had left in Africa.

Of course, the Africans retained their native languages, and African languages were widely spoken in eighteenth-century America. There were more first-language speakers of African languages in many parts of America than speakers of English, French, Dutch, Spanish, or Portuguese. Many of these Africans developed a certain necessary proficiency in the colonial language, the European language of their masters and other European or Euro-American settlers, after some years' residence, but it was always a second language, spoken with an accent. They were like the runaway woman, described in a late eighteenth-century Jamaican newspaper advertisement, who "speaks not altogether plain English; but from her talk she may easily be discovered to be a Coramantee."[80] She, like other African-born Americans, probably thought, dreamed, and communicated more often in her native language than in the colonial language.

79 On the Spanish areas, see Tardieu, *Destin,* p. 203; for France, and especially St. Domingue, see the lengthy discussion in Pluchon, *Vaudou,* pp. 57–69.

80 Cited in Mullin, *Africa in America,* p. 30. See note 105 below.

Around 1750, for example, some 40 percent of the people of African origin in Jamaica spoke Coromantee (or, as it is called today, Akan or Twi) as their mother tongue: It was probably the single most commonly spoken first language on the island.[81] No fewer than 60 percent of the Africans who formed the core of the surge in population in Virginia in the early eighteenth century were speakers of one or another dialect of the Igbo language.[82] At the same time, well over half the people in the surge of imports that raised South Carolina's population of African-born or their descendants from 3,000 in 1700 to 50,000 in 1740 were speakers of Kikongo.[83] On the eve of the revolution in St. Domingue, Kikongo was also, in all likelihood, the most commonly spoken first language, or was a close runner up to French.[84] In fact, the creole leaders of the revolution in 1791 complained that most of their followers could "scarcely make out two words of French."[85]

These African languages formed the basis for the nation, which along with the estate was one of the two groups that had claims on every new African's time, loyalty, and service. It was in the context of the nation that the African cultures of the Americas reemerged, albeit in a new form. Since the sixteenth century, African religious and aesthetic (music and dance especially) ideas were displayed in gatherings of people from the same nation. The nation was the locus for the maintenance of those elements of African culture that continued on American soil.

African nations in the New World were new and unique to the Americas and did not correspond well to political or social units in Africa, in that they were based on language alone.[86] The "Coromantee" nation in the English-speaking world (often called "Minas" in French, Spanish,

81 On the origins of Afro-Jamaicans, see Curtin, *Atlantic Slave Trade*, p. 160. This estimate is tentative, for it is based on shipping data only. To approach an accurate estimate, one would have to know survival rates of earlier groups by nation as well as the number imported. Whether the modern form of the "Coromantee" language is to be called Akan or Twi is debated among Ghanaians today, but neither term was in use in the eighteenth century.

82 Kulikoff, *Tobacco and Slaves*, p. 322; Douglas Chambers, " 'He Is an African, but Speaks Plain': Historical Creolization in Eighteenth Century Virginia," in Alusine Jalloh and Stephen Maizlish (eds.), *The African Diaspora* (College Station, Tex., 1996), pp. 106–7.

83 On total population, Galenson, "Settlement," p. 172; on origins, see Joseph Halloway, *Africanisms in American Life*, p. 7. Statistics normally use "Angola" as their origin, but given shipping routes and African events, the Kingdom of Kongo and its Kikongo-speaking northern neighbors probably provided the vast majority; see John Thornton, "African Dimensions of the Stono Rebellion," *American Historical Review* 96 (1991): 1101–5.

84 Geggus, "Sugar and Coffee," p. 81.

85 Archives Nationales (France) D–xxv, 1, 4, doc. 6, Jean-François and Biassou to commissioners, 12 October 1791.

86 Karen Fog Olwig, "African Cultural Principles in Caribbean Slave Societies: A View from the Danish West Indies," in Stephan Palmié (ed.), *Slave Cultures and the Cultures of Slavery* (Knoxville, 1995), pp. 23–39, is applicable much more widely than to just the Danish colonies.

Portuguese, Dutch, and Danish sources), for example, was certainly made up of Akan speakers from the Gold Coast, but by no means from the little fishing village of Koromanti from which the nation's name derived. Indeed, there was apparently no common name for the language in Africa. Jacobus Elisa Joannes Capitein, a native speaker of Akan and author of an Akan catechism in 1744, called the language "Negro language which is customary from Abrowarie to Afam" (two points defining the Gold Coast).[87] Sometimes the term "Fante" was used by eighteenth-century sources, such as the missionary Thomas Thompson, who lived on the Gold Coast from 1751 to 1756, although he was aware that only a small part of that region was actually a part of the region called Fante.[88] Christian Protten, a native speaker, and author of the first linguistic description, of the language (1764), called it "Fanté or Amina," although he argued that these were really only terms of convenience, because many who spoke it would not have used the name.[89] Indeed, loyalties in their homeland were likely to be to a village, or perhaps one of dozens of independent, often hostile states, or to a leader of wealth and status – but not to a language group.

Yet, in America these African distinctions were put aside, and linguistic loyalty formed a first order of contact and companionship. Although the linguistically formed nations often united those whose relatives in Africa might have been at war with each other, as the Coromantee nation certainly did, they were real enough entities in America. At Pinkster, a Dutch celebration observed in New York, dancers in 1737 "divided into Companies, I suppose according to their different nations."[90] The distinctions were sufficiently significant for a certain rivalry between groups to be noticeable: One South Carolina observer about 1775 noted how "Ibas" and "Gully" often chided each other.[91] A mid-eighteenth century Virginia preacher urged his flock to "not only pray for your Country-men, who are with you in America but . . . for all the inhabitants of your own Native land."[92]

[87] Jacobus Elisa Joannes Capitein, *Vertaaling van het Onze Vater, de Twaalf Geloofs-Artykelen, en det Tien Geboden des Heeren . . .* (Leiden, 1744, mod. ed. by H. M. J. Trutenau, as appendix in *Christian Protten's 1764 Introduction to the Fante and Accra (Gã) Languages* [London, 1971]), pp. 59–66. Original pagination is marked in the edition, pp. 1, 3, 5.

[88] Thomas Thompson, *An Account of Two Missionary Voyages to New Jersey and the Coast of Guiney* (London, 1758), p. 70.

[89] Christian Protten, *En nyttig Grammaticalsk Indledelse tel Tvwene hidintil gandske ubekiente Sprog, Fanteisk og Acraisk* (Copenhagen, 1764, modern corrected ed. and English translation in Trutenau, *Protten's Introduction*, pp. 2–67, with pagination of the unpaginated original introduced), pp. 2–8.

[90] "A Spy," *Zengers New-York Weekly Journal*, 7 March 1737.

[91] James Barclay, *The Voyages and Travels of James Barclay* (London, 1777), p. 21.

[92] Benjamin Fawcett, *A Compassionate Address to the Christian Negroes in Virginia* (London, 1756), p. 26, quoted in Chambers, " 'He Is an African,' " p. 107.

A nation could also form the locus of a religious community to the degree that it organized funerals, as in the seventeenth century they were likely to be associated with the cult of ancestors, which was fairly ubiquitous in Africa. In 1765, a planter named Monnereau noted that most assemblies of nations in St. Domingue were to honor the dead. Descendants of a dead person would announce the ceremony, which friends and members of the deceased's nation would attend.[93] Funeral services, conducted according to the "custom of the coast," that is, following national religious norms, were common in the Danish West Indies[94] and elsewhere.

There were also specific religious ideas particular to each nation that made them distinctive. The Anglican bishop Griffith Hughes noted that the Africans of Barbados in the mid-eighteenth century followed the "Rites, Ceremonies and Superstitions of their own Countries."[95] The Kongolese of St. Jan in the Danish West Indies in the 1750s, as Christians of many generations' standing, took it upon themselves to baptize all newly arrived slaves, serving as godparents of sorts to them.[96] Father Jean Baptiste le Pers, an early Jesuit missionary in St. Domingue, identified three different national religious groups there: the Congos, who were Christians (even if all did not properly know the faith); the Senegalese, who were Muslims; and the Ardas (Fon-speaking peoples), who were "idolatrous" snake worshipers.[97] On the eve of the revolution, Moreau de Saint-Méry grouped these various nations under the general term "Voudou."[98] People from the cultural area around Dahomey (the Jeje nation in Brazil) were indulging in religious practices from their homeland when authorities in Cachoeira, Bahia (Brazil), invaded and seized their goods in 1785.[99]

Many Brazilian slaves, as well as those of Spanish colonies, expressed

93 Monnereau, *Le parfait ingotier* (Marseilles, 1765), pp. 110–13.

94 I. C. Schmidt, "Blandede Anmaerkninger, samlede paa og over Ejlandet St. Croix i Amerika 1788," *Samleren* 2 (1788): 261; see also Richard Haagensen, *Beskrivelse over Eylandet St. Croix i America i Vestindien* (Copenhagen, 1758), pp. 65–6.

95 Griffith Hughes, *The Natural History of Barbados* (London, 1750), p. 15.

96 Georg Christian Oldendorp, *Geschichte der Mission der evangelischen Brüder auf den Caraibischen Inseln St. Tomas, St Croix und St Jan* (ed. Johann Jakob Bossart, Barby and Leipzig, 1777), p. 441. See English translation, Arnold Highfield and Vladimir Barac, *C. G. A. Oldendorp's History of the Mission of the Evangelical Brethren on the Caribbean Islands . . .* (Ann Arbor, 1987), p. 263.

97 Pierre François Xavier de Charlevoix (ed.), *Historie de l'Ile Espagnole ou de S. Domingue* (2 vols., Paris, 1730–1) 2: 501–2. The editor ascribes the original manuscript to le Pers in the introduction, 1: vii. Le Pers worked in St. Domingue for twenty-five-years in the early eighteenth century.

98 Louis Médéric Elie Moreau de Saint-Méry, *Description topographique, physique, civile, politique et historique de al partie française de l'isle de Saint-Domingue* (3 vols., Philadelphia, 1796) 1: 64–9; similar statement in M. E. Descourtilz, *Voyage d'un naturaliste et ses observations* (Paris, 1809), p. 180. Descourtilz visited the island between 1799 and 1803.

99 "1785 Devassa ex-ofício de feitiçaria," in João José Reis, "Magia Jeje na Bahia: A invasão do Calundu do Pasto de Cachoeira, 1785," *Revista Brasileira da História* 8/16 (1988): 57–81, 235–50; see, especially, pp. 68–71 to place the testimony of the witnesses in perspective.

their national identities in ethnically specific lay brotherhoods. The rules of these brotherhoods, which were intended by the clergy to promote Christian life and charitable works, often specified that members of only one or another nation could be members, and often their charitable works were directed toward the nation at large, presumably even toward those who were not official members of the brotherhood (a minority, and the richest at that). In addition to doing charitable work, brotherhoods proudly paraded on saints' days, performing dances of their nation and singing in their national language.[100]

For the newly arrived, the nation formed a surrogate for the family left behind in Africa. Within that group there were often shipmates who had traveled together to America probably, given shipping patterns, from the same nation – which facilitated communication on board ship. Advertisements in Jamaica often noted that runaways could name "their shipmates and countrymen" or might be going to where "shipmates and countrymen" live.[101] National solidarity provided moral support, cultural reinforcement, and familiarity of practices. Often slaves chose their spouses or other domestic partners from their home nation or closely related ones, as they had earlier.[102]

One gets a feeling for the nature of national support from the testimony given at the trial in 1736–7 of an Antiguan Coromantee named Court, accused of a plot to rebel when he was chosen to be king of the Coromantees. Court, a wealthy man for a slave (considered the richest slave in Antigua), used some of his money to sponsor parties and other get-togethers for his nation, sometimes serving food and offering entertainment.[103] In North America as elsewhere, the network of linguistic unity extended to running away, for people ran away in groups often paired by language, often bound for areas where other runaways had settled or for urban areas where they might know of fellow nationals who could harbor or otherwise help them.[104] An advertisement in the

[100] The most detailed study is Patricia Mulvey, "Black Brothers and Sisters: Membership in Black Brotherhoods of Colonial Brazil," *Luso-Brazilian Review* 17 (1980): 253–79.

[101] Mullin, *Africa in America*, p. 32.

[102] This was true in eighteenth-century Brazil, see Schwartz, *Sugar Plantation*, pp. 391–3, and Luna and Nero da Costa, "Vila Rica," pp. 108–9; and in Trinidad, see Barry Higman, "African and Creole Slave Family Patterns in Trinidad," *Journal of Family History* 3 (1978): 163–80. For the earlier periods, see Colin Palmer, "From Africa to the Americas: Ethnicity in the Early Black Communities of the Americas," *Journal of World History* 6 (1995): 223–36.

[103] His trial record is found in PRO, Colonial Office 9, doc. 10, "Antigua Minutes of Council, 1 November 1736–31 January 1737. Negro's Conspiracy," fols. 44–5, 60–8, 70–4, and *passim*.

[104] For a study of runaway advertisements on this point, see Gerald Mullin, *Flight and Rebellion*, pp. 35–9 (for South Carolina and Virginia), and Betty Wood, *Slavery in Colonial Georgia, 1730–1775* (Athens, Ga., 1984), pp. 173–9. For similar material with a wider reach: Mullin, *Africa in America*, pp. 36–40. See note 105 below.

South Carolina Gazette, for example, warned readers that one runaway was perhaps harbored by fellow nationals, as there is "an abundance of that Nation" in South Carolina.[105]

Leaders of nations sought to re-create as much of Africa as possible, even political forms. Of course, both the restrictions of slavery and the nationals' own modifications or idealizations of their home politics altered the resulting organization. When Court had himself crowned king in Antigua, he chose to focus on Akan political ideology, going to some length to reconstruct the ceremony of ennoblement that commoners often used in the rough and tumble world of Akan politics. On the eighteenth-century Gold Coast, status was uncertain, being contested by a variety of people including mercenaries, merchants, and even foreigners. By drawing on those elements of Akan political thought that allowed for changes in status and accorded power to former nonentities, Court and other Coromantees in America were reshaping the older political ideology in the new environment.

Court's coronation ceremony was called, according to the record of his trial, an *ikyem*, or shield ceremony, clearly related to a contemporary Gold Coast "shield" ceremony whereby the political authorities conferred nobility on people who had acquired wealth.[106] But in the Akan region the distinction was conferred by an existing authority on a subject, whereas in Antigua it was self-conferred in a context of election by the mass of Coromantees, whose support Court had sought through meetings and parties.

A similar concern to meet Akan ideals in the changed circumstances in America underlay the elaborate ceremony that the runaway Cudjoe arranged in swearing loyalty to the English government in Jamaica in 1739. This ceremony, which also had traditions on the Gold Coast, was similar to the commissioning of a successful merchant or distinguished soldier who was thus being ennobled. The prevalence of horn blowing in the treaty negotiations suggests that the second of the two Akan ceremonies (the shield and horn) described in contemporary sources was employed in Cudjoe's ennoblement.[107] Again, however, Cudjoe was more self-appointed and rebellious than accepted, although the British did in fact confer a rank upon him. In both instances, Africans of Akan heritage were taking political principles from their homeland and injecting them

105 Michael Mullin, *Africa in America: Slave Acculturation and Resistance in the American South and the British Caribbean, 1736–1831* (Urbana, 1992), p. 24, citing the *South Carolina Gazette* 13 August 1737.

106 Bosman, *Description*, pp. 135–6.

107 Ibid. The detailed evidence is contained in a letter written by a witness printed in 1798 in the *Jamaica Journal and Royal Gazette*, quoted in Mullin, *Africa in America*, pp. 50–1.

into the new environment of America.[108] Other African kings and queens, selected in a variety of ways and recognized to varying degrees by political authorities, reached for ideals from African politics but transformed them in the Americas.

Revolts and plots often reveal the complicated way in which the nation worked politically in its American environment. Political ideology in Africa often was contested between advocates of autocratic government and those who held that a more decentralized and democratic system would work better. Such ideas could be found in the Kongo civil war, for example, a conflict between the ideal of the "blacksmith king" who rules by consensus and that of the "conqueror king" who rules by decree. In the Haitian Revolution, kings and queens, often of Kongolese origin, were selected by their nation as a means of ruling areas freed by rebels. Their own understanding of the constitution that would govern these new "kingdoms" within Haiti was underpinned by the contests present in Kongolese ideology.[109] The African nations of the New World were not simply re-creating Africa; they were developing African concepts in the radically new political and cultural environment of the Americas.

While the nation as a surrogate family and society was the organizing principle of the Africans, they were subject to the parallel social organization imposed by their master, the estate. Depending on the arrangements on individual properties, slaves were often assigned a quarter for themselves, ranging from a substantial village in the sugar plantations of the West Indies to a small group of houses in areas like that near the Chesapeake.[110] These houses were often at a distance from the residence of the owner of the estate, and large or small, they formed the basic unit of residence for daily life, and were often responsible for a significant portion of daily subsistence.[111] Estates were normally not ethnically homogeneous, slaves of several nations living on each. Indeed, virtually all

[108] John Thornton, "War, the State, and Religious Norms in 'Coromantee' Thought: The Ideology of an African Nation in the Americas," in Robert St. George and Ronald Hoffman (eds.), *Possible Pasts* (Ithaca, in press).

[109] Thornton, " 'I Am the Subject of the King of Congo.' "

[110] Contrast the situation around the Chesapeake as described in Kulikoff, *Tobacco and Slaves*, pp. 339–43, with that of the great West Indian estates with their hundreds of slaves formed into a village, as described in Mullin, *Africa in America*, pp. 126–58.

[111] Ira Berlin and Philip Morgan, "Labor and the Shaping of Slave Life in the Americas," in Berlin and Morgan (eds.), *Cultivation and Culture*, pp. 1–45, and Woodville K. Marshall, "Provision Ground and Plantation Labor in Four Windward Islands: Competition for Resources during Slavery," in ibid., pp. 203–20; Neville A. T. Hall, *Slave Society in the Danish West Indies: St. Thomas, St. John and St. Croix* (ed. Barry Higman, Mona [Jamaica], 1992), pp. 72–93, *passim*; for Brazil, see B. J. Barickman, " 'A Bit of Land, Which They Call *Roça*': Slave Provision Grounds in the Bahian Recôncavo, 1780–1860," *Hispanic American Historical Review* 74 (1994): 649–87; Roderick McDonald, *The Economy and Material Culture of Slaves: Goods and Chattels on the Sugar Plantations of Jamaica and Louisiana* (Baton Rouge, 1993).

estate registers that record national data reveal this fact. In the times when most slaves were Africans, this condition undoubtedly caused substantial cultural and especially linguistic differences among the slaves in a community.

But the estate, whatever barriers there might be to communication among its members, could not help but become a community. It was the residence of all the slaves, and it was from among their members that daily work was organized. Living together, suffering under the harsh conditions of life, and laboring daily for the master and for themselves, where cultivating ground provided to them was required or permitted, forged a bond that was strong and meaningful.

The estate was a hierarchical unit, for masters and overseers (whether Africans, creoles, European, or European-descended) dominated their lives, sometimes closely. It is scarcely a wonder that Justin Girod de Chantrans, a traveler in prerevolutionary St. Domingue, likened the organization among the slaves of the estates there to the supposed despotism of the Ottoman empire, with a sultan and his servants and slaves.[112]

The hierarchy of occupational status was complemented by a hierarchy of wealth. Favored slaves, with skills and supervisory duties, typically had larger houses and more personal property than their unskilled charges. Often, in areas like the Caribbean or the South Carolina lowlands where they grew crops on their own lands and sold produce in local markets, they had much more opportunity than elsewhere to avail themselves of these avenues for material benefit. As these slaves were much more likely to be creoles than newly arrived Africans, a perception of ethnic difference between creole and African might correlate with the differences of wealth and status, as Kulikoff argues was true in Virginia.[113] In Jamaica, the distinctions of status were clear-cut in housing, and in the practice of the wealthier employing the poorer on lands they controlled.[114] In eighteenth-century Brazil, large numbers of mulatto slaves enjoyed superior status along with creoles.[115]

African slaves in America lived, then, at the intersection of the two groups to which they belonged – the estate community, where they lived and worked, and the nation, where they might find cultural and linguistic familiarity. National assemblies, like Court's parties in Antigua, might bring people from many different estates together, so nations were typically networks that stretched across areas connecting estates that might be

112 Justin Girod de Chantrans, *Voyage d'un suisse dans les colonies d'Amerique* (Neufchatel, 1785, 2d ed., ed. Pierre Pluchon, Paris, 1980), p. 124.

113 Kulikoff, *Tobacco and Slaves*, pp. 333–4.

114 Mullin, *Africa in America*, pp. 147–9.

115 Schwartz, *Slaves, Peasants, and Rebels*, p. 44.

widely separated. Slave celebrations to honor the dead in St. Domingue in the mid-eighteenth century might include people from nearby plantations of the same nation, but if masters prevented interstate visiting, the slaves would observe the ceremony among themselves. Although friends who were not of the deceased's nation might attend, the nation led the procession and provided the music.[116]

Friendship bonds that formed on estates from proximity and shared conditions tended to unite nations. For one of his parties on Antigua, Court invited the residents of his former estate, Windward, to attend. Many, like Primus and Oliver, were "Eboes" (Igbos) known to him from their association with the estate, now able to mix with Coromantees not only from their home but from elsewhere on the island.[117] In 1768, in a less dramatic way, Vine, a slave in Jamaica, spent many nights telling stories about "Nancy" (Anansi), the trickster spider of the Coromantees. Although her audience was largely Coromantee, she told the tales in English to accommodate the non-Coromantees who came to hear them, including her overseer.[118] Proximity and friendships beyond the nation on the estate made it impossible for national gatherings to be exclusive. Marinna, a Kongolese Jamaican, hosted a gathering in 1751 to celebrate a housewarming. It included many of her Kongolese shipmates, for whom she cooked eighteen pints of "fungi" (nfundi, a porridge), and then the guests "danced Congo" through most of the night. But at least one of the guests, who danced a pretty good "Congo" with the others, was Phibbah, a Coromantee.[119]

Africans clung to their nations socially because they provided a surrogate family, but there were strong forces that made second-generation Africans less likely to view the nation as a useful organization. In part this was because creoles probably did not have the commitment of a native speaker to the language of the nation.

Undoubtedly, the linguistic diversity of the estate community helped make the colonial language the lingua franca of the estate. Everyone had to learn the language anyway, at least for the rudimentary communication they needed with their masters; this position also made it a natural bridge between the various African languages. Originally, the colonial language was in a creole form, perhaps imported from Africa along with multilingual slaves, many of whom spoke creole forms of languages that

[116] Monnereau, *Parfait ingotier*, pp. 110–13.

[117] Public Record Office (henceforth PRO), Colonial Office, 9/10 Antigua Minutes, "Negro's Conspiracy," fols. 77, 90.

[118] Diary of Thomas Thistlewood, entries of 17, 20, 21, 23, 24, and 27 September 1768, in Douglas Hall (ed. and commentator), *In Miserable Slavery: Thomas Thistlewood in Jamaica, 1750–86* (London, 1989), p. 160.

[119] Ibid., entry of 6 July 1751, p. 18.

would be colonial languages in America. In other areas, especially those regions of North America where the African period was fairly brief, language might quickly approach the dialect of the colonial language spoken by the local Europeans and European creoles.[120] Consider the case of Olaudah Equiano, an Igbo who arrived in coastal Maryland in 1757 and could not find anyone who understood his language,[121] despite the fact that about half the population in the distinct was of Igbo ancestry and few were beyond the second generation in America.

Creoles were typically native speakers of the colonial language, in either a creole or European form, because being American-born they had learned it as children. They might be bilingual, of course, if their parents were of the same nation, spoke the national language at home, and made some commitment to preserving the language for their children. This was not always so, for the Antiguan creole Quashee, who regarded himself as a Coromantee and had a Coromantee mother, could not speak the Coromantee language when he attended Court's gatherings.[122] Creoles who, like Quashee, had parents of different nations were less likely to have intensive youthful contact with the national language. Although some creoles might learn a national language, in no circumstances would they fail to learn the colonial language.

Consequently, creoles often considered themselves part of a nation of their own. Certainly some of the creole visitors to one of Court's parties, who were disdainful of the Coromantees they met there, regarded themselves as separate because of their language.[123] Linguistic change made creoles a separate nation, but it was the development of biological families that provided creoles with a new social base. If the nation was a surrogate family, it was not a substitute for a real one, and creoles quickly developed loyalty and support networks through biological ties. If they married off the estate, or if children or a parent had been sold off or forced to move away, the families might form smaller networks that crossed estate boundaries as well, since such relationships were never forgotten, as runaway advertisements in North America, where a large creole community formed quickly, attest.[124]

The combination of the rapid development of a creole population with the frequently small size of the African-born population and its scatter over small and dispersed landholdings gave much of North America a

[120] Cogently argued in Chambers, " 'He is an African,' " pp. 107–24. There is little evidence of a creole language in Brazil in the eighteenth century, although such languages are found throughout the Caribbean even today.

[121] Equiano, *Interesting Narrative*

[122] PRO, Colonial Office, 9/10 Antigua Minutes, "Negro's Conspiracy," fol. 60.

[123] Ibid., fols. 70, 72.

[124] Mullin, *Africa in America*, pp. 159–73.

distinctive character. The estate would tend to take prominence over the nation if people of the same nation were scattered and were rarely visited, thus placing greater emphasis on creole culture and hastening the demise of the nation as a social principle. It surrendered to the family, which rose to prominence quickly, given the good survival rates of creole children, alone among slaves possessed by Europeans in America.

The evolution of a new set of social networks involving creoles was rapid in North America. When slaves rose in New York in 1712, it was an affair of the "Caramantee and Papa" nations, organized through the informal national network that allowed them to keep "their Conspiracy Secret that there was not the lest Suspicion of it" and strengthened by oaths.[125] Yet, when a new conspiracy was discovered in 1741, the situation had changed. Although many of the alleged plotters had Coromantee names, they were organized in gangs and other groups that were not national at all – indeed, they involved a wide variety of both slaves and free people.[126]

National identity also surrendered to the church community, more prominent in North America than elsewhere. Such communities were formed in the late eighteenth century, as the wave of arrivals was faltering and the creole population was growing. The epitome of continuous revelation, the evangelical churches of the Great Awakening were able to win both Africans and creoles to their vision and at the same time manage to build self-help networks consistent with religious exercises. In this way, they offered an alternative to the nation both for Africans and for the creoles that could reach beyond the estate to a larger world.[127] Independent churches probably also combined some national elements in their service, as Margaret Washington Creel has proposed took place among the "Gullahs" of South Carolina.[128] It is not surprising that the evangelical churches soon were subject to the same suspicions as nations were, and were held to be involved in plots to kill whites and free

[125] John Sharpe to secretary of Society for the Propagation of the Gospel, 23 June 1712, in Raswell Hoes, "The Negro Plot of 1712," *New York Genealogical and Biographical Record* 21 (1890): 162–3; see also *Boston Weekly News-Letter*, 14 April 1712. A detailed secondary account is Kenneth Scott, "The Slave Insurrection in New York in 1712," *New-York Historical Society Quarterly* 45 (1961): 43–74.

[126] See the records of the trials related to the plot in Daniel Horsmanden, *The New-York Conspiracy; or, a History of the Negro Plot . . . 1741–42* (New York, 1810; facsimile reprint, New York, 1969).

[127] See Sobel, *Travelin' On*, for a detailed and well-documented study of the growth of evangelical churches among African Americans. The Evangelical churches also had an impact in the West Indies (both English and Danish), where they probably parallelled and enriched national feeling rather than displaced it.

[128] Margaret Washington Creel, *"A Peculiar People": Slave Religion and Community Culture among the Gullahs* (New York, 1988).

slaves, such as Vesey's alleged plot in South Carolina (1822).[129] In North America, the churches helped supplant the nation in a creolizing population, while in the Danish and English West Indies, where evangelical churches also had success, the church community may well have supplemented rather than supplanted the nation. In the Danish West Indies, the Moravians did much to popularize the creole language, "Kreolsk," with its Dutch vocabulary, giving it a literature and promoting its speech in religion.[130]

The intersection of estate and nation and the role of creoles ultimately affected how slaves participated in such activities as revolts, from small plots to great undertakings like the Haitian Revolution. In the eighteenth century as in the seventeenth, slave revolts were largely national affairs such as the 1733 revolt that nearly captured Saint Jan (Coromantee),[131] the 1739 Stono Rebellion in South Carolina (Kongolese),[132] or the 1760 Jamaica revolt (Coromantee).[133] Although the alleged conspiracy in Prince George's County, Maryland, in 1739–40 was organized by a nation using "their country language," the name of the nation was not specified in the allegation,[134] although it may have been the Coromantees, since a fictional account of the country written about the same time speaks of a conspiracy and revolt led by Gold Coast people.[135] Members of a nation had a remarkable capability: By speaking a language that could be understood only by a small group, they might more easily plot undiscovered, especially as it was the newly arrived and most desperate who would be included. The networks of nationals, united for social gatherings and engaging in mutual aid, that crisscrossed large regions provided an excellent platform for plots they could turn into major revolts by coordinating uprisings on many different estates simultaneously. The Coromantee revolts in Jamaica in 1760–5 were carried out with deliberate disregard for non-Coromantees, and as a result the initial outbreak took even their fellow estate residents by surprise. By using the

129 John Oliver Killens (ed.), *The Trial Records of Denmark Vessey* (Boston, 1970), contains many references to the "African Church," a breakaway from the Methodist church.

130 Jens Vibaek, *Dansk Vestidnien 1755–1848*, vol. 2 of Johannes Brønsted, *Vore Gamle Tropekolonier* (Copenhagen, 1966), pp. 195–203.

131 P. Gardelin to Marquis de Champigny, 21 March 1734, in Aimery Caron and Arnold Highfield (ed. and trans.), *The French Intervention in the St. John Slave Revolt of 1733–34* (St. Thomas, 1981), p. 26.

132 Thornton, "African Dimensions."

133 The most detailed contemporary description is Edward Long, *History of Jamaica* (3 vols., London, 1774; facsimile reprint, London, 1970), Book III, chapter III, pp. 470–5. For a fair survey and analysis of most of the major revolts in the English-speaking West Indies, including the 1760 one, see Craton, *Testing*.

134 On the Prince George's County conspiracy, see Kulikoff, *Tobacco and Slaves*, pp. 329–30.

135 Edward Kimber, *The History of the Life and Adventures of Mr. Anderson* (Dublin, 1754), pp. 261, 273–8.

Coromantee network, the rebels were able to recruit in five parishes more or less simultaneously.[136] When this organizational advantage was added to the fact that so many of the newly arrived slaves had military experience in Africa, and hence friendship networks might unite comrades in arms from African wars, it made the nation a logical focus for revolt on a large scale.[137]

But the national feature, for all its power, also hindered revolts. In the Jamaican revolts of 1760–5, many slaves, especially non-Coromantees, remained loyal, but many Coromantees did as well. Therefore, Thomas Thistlewood, an eyewitnesses, did not hesitate to arm his own slaves and schedule them for watches against the rebels, nor did many of his neighbors. Often when plantations were raided by the rebels, the inhabitants put up resistance.[138] This same sort of mixture of revolt and resistance allowed many planters on St. Domingue to continue production in the midst of the revolution,[139] and even in its early days, estates might or might not revolt; indeed, the decision to do so was often a subject of long debates between rebel leaders and the slave leaders on the estates.[140]

National and estate loyalty coalesced in the early formation of the longer-lasting and larger maroon communities, as has been documented with regard to the runaways of Surinam and French Guiana. The earliest communities were organized both by estates – often taking their group names from the names of the estates from which they had fled – and sometimes from their nations, for there were runaway villages exclusively from one or another nation. As the maroons remained free long enough to create new generations, these distinctions dissolved among matrilinear families.[141]

Although scholars such as Eugene Genovese and Michael Craton have

[136] PRO Colonial Office, 137/32 Council Minutes of Jamaica, 1760–62, fols. 3–6, meeting minutes for 10 April 1760, fol. 7, minutes for 17 April 1760; fols. 21–23, minutes for 14 July and 20 August 1760 (these notes are primarily military dispatches); Edward Long, *The History of Jamaica* (3 vols., London, 1776; reprinted 1970) 2: 447–58.

[137] Argued in detail about the Haitian Revolution in John Thornton, "African Soldiers in the Haitian Revolution," *Journal of Caribbean History* 25 (1991): 58–80.

[138] Thistlewood Diary, entries of 26 May – 4 June 1760 in Hall (ed.), *Miserable Slavery*, pp. 98–101. A number of the loyal slaves were subsequently rewarded with freedom. PRO Colonial Office 137/32, Council Minutes, Jamaica, fol. 80v, no. 24, Act Freeing several negroe and mulattoe slaves . . . , 4 November 1761.

[139] Michel Etienne Descourtilz, *Histoire des désastres de Saint Domingue* (Paris, An V [1795]), pp. 189, 197–8; Brian Edwards, *The History Civil and Commercial of the British Colonies in the West Indies* (4 vols., Philadelphia, 1803) 4: 146 (volume 4 is *An Historical Survey of the French Colony on the Island of St. Domingo* based on an account written during the English occupation).

[140] See, especially, Archives Nationales (France) D–xxv, 78, "Tableau des evenements qui ont eu lieu dans la Paroisse du Trou depuis la Revolte des Négres, [1791]"; *Philadelphia General Advertiser* no. 347 (9 November 1791), "Journal kept at Cap Francis," extract of a letter, 4 October 1791.

[141] Wim Hoogbergen, "Aluku," *Nieuwe West Indische Gids* 63 (1989): 190.

argued that the creoles were the slaves most likely to promote large revolts, thanks to their knowledge of affairs in the wider world and contact with revolutionary ideas,[142] creoles also had visions and concerns different from those of the African-born. As a group, many had a larger share in the economy of slavery, and in some places, such as St. Domingue, they played a substantial role in promoting and developing the estate economy, even if they sought a place in it where their efforts would be better rewarded. They had a stake in the stability of the economy, in their families, in their positions of authority in the hierarchy of slavery. For many, the estate was their best organization, along with the network formed by a church. When they had become sufficiently numerous, they showed great strength in organizing work stoppages and slowdowns and in negotiating better conditions.[143]

For them, the best chance to revolt might lie, as it did in the Haitian Revolution and in Denmark Vessey's alleged slave plot of 1822, in an alliance between creoles, with their connections to munitions and networks of intelligence with the masters' community, and the African-born, organized in national units.[144]

Nowhere was the possibility of African-creole cooperation and its pitfalls more apparent than in the great Haitian Revolution. The initial slave revolt of 1791 was largely led by creoles, and succeeded in mobilizing tens of thousands of slaves, many organized into bands on national lines, because creoles were prepared to lead it and could count on the national organization of the slaves to provide skilled fighters and even military units. Using these skills, in fact, in a matter of weeks from the start of the revolt, revolutionary leaders could boast armies that numbered in the thousands and could stand their ground against the colonial militias and even reinforcements from the metropolis.[145]

On the other hand, the creole leaders wanted the revolt to serve their own interests, which were not always those of the African-born. Two months into the revolt, the two leading revolutionary leaders, Jean-

142 Eugene Genovese, *From Rebellion to Revolution: Afro-American Slave Revolts in the Making of the Modern World* (Baton Rouge, 1979); Michael Craton, *Testing the Chains: Resistance to Slavery in the British West Indies* (Ithaca, 1982).

143 Mary Turner, "Chattel Slaves into Wage Slaves: A Jamaican Case Study," pp. 35–6; Richard Sheridan, "Strategies of Slave Subsistence: A Jamaican Case Reconsidered," pp. 48–67; Michael Mullin, "Slave Economic Strategies: Food Markets and Property," pp. 68–78; Betty Wood, " 'Never on a Sunday?': Slavery and the Sabbath in Low Country Georgia 1750–1830," pp. 79–96; and Lorena S. Walsh, "Work and Resistance in the New Republic: The Case of the Chesapeake, 1770–1820," pp. 79–122 – all in Mary Turner (ed.), *From Chattel Slaves to Wage Slaves: The Dynamics of Labour Bargaining in the Americas* (Kingston, 1995). For similar cases in Brazil, see Schwartz, *Slaves, Peasants, and Rebels*, pp. 50–63.

144 Killens (ed.), *Trial Records*, esp. pp. 91, 100, 114, 116, and 120.

145 Thornton, "African Soldiers."

François and Biassou, showing haughty disdain for what they considered their African supporters' lack of culture, were prepared to deliver them back into slavery for a handful of pardons for themselves and their creole compatriots.[146] As the revolution advanced, Africans organized in bands by nation, and creoles organizing their own armies with the help of various French, Spanish, and English allies came increasingly to clash on issues that counted. When Toussaint-Louverture, who replaced Jean-François and Biassou as the main creole leader, sought to all intents and purposes to restore slavery with his creole colleagues as the masters and managers, a new revolt, African-led, broke out within the revolution. The tensions continued when Napoleon ordered his brother-in-law General Leclerc to reestablish slavery on the island with a new army in 1801. The creoles, led by Toussaint and Jean-Jacques Dessalines, agreed to terms and hoped for power within the imperial system, but the Africans refused to accept the terms.[147] Were it not for Napoleon's bad faith in refusing to compromise, the creoles might have realized their dream, but forced by treachery into resistance, they fell back on the Africans again to drive out the French once and for all.[148] The postrevolutionary period was a partially successful creole (and mulatto) counterrevolution directed at African culture as well as against the former African slaves.

The eighteenth century, then, witnessed a great surge of slave importation from Africa, both fueled by and fueling the wars and banditry that often led to enslavement. This wave of new arrivals, coming in unprecedented numbers in a short time, allowed the creation in the Americas of a host of neo-African cultures, promoted by many nations, which dominated the cultural lives of the eighteenth-century African Americans. From them and the older, African-descended creoles came the Afro-American creoles, with their own cultural ways and place in the larger system. Creole families, churches, and other organizations eventually replaced the nation as the primary slave-centered focus for community, although significant conflicts divided the African Americans from the creoles in the process.

[146] Archives Nationales (France) D–xxv, 1, 4, doc. 6, Jean-François and Biassou to Commissioners, 12 October 1791, and ibid., doc. A, same to same, 12 December 1791; a more general statement based on more correspondence, some now lost, is in Jean-Philippe Garran de Coulon, *Rapport sur les Troubles de St. Domingue* (4 vols., Paris, An IV–V [1794–5]) 2: 305; see also *Boston Independent Chronicle* no. 1251, 18 October 1792, for a later attempt.

[147] For a critical study of Toussaint as a revolutionary, see Pierre Pluchon, *Toussaint L'Ouverture: De l'esclavage au pouvoir* (Paris, 1979), pp. 151–380.

[148] For this interpretation of the Revolution, see Thornton, "African Soldiers" and "African Political Ideology."

Index

Place names found only on the maps or gazeteer to the maps are not included in the index, nor are authors whose work appears only in footnotes.

So long,

So fast.

to GBAC.

Katie, Greg, Amanda, Lindsay, Fuchs

It is impossible to even ~~be~~ begin to say goodbye and thank you here

I love all of you.